ALONG THIS WAY

ALONG THIS WAY

THE AUTOBIOGRAPHY OF

James Weldon Johnson

DA CAPO PRESS • NEW YORK • 1973

Library of Congress Cataloging in Publication Data

Johnson, James Weldon, 1871-1938.
  Along this way.

  I. Title.
E185.97.J692A3   1973   818'.5'209   72-8404
ISBN 0-306-70539-7

This Da Capo Press edition of *Along This Way*
is an unabridged republication of the 1933 edition
published in New York. It is reprinted by special
arrangement with The Viking Press.

Published by Da Capo Press, Inc.
A Subsidiary of Plenum Publishing Corporation
227 West 17th Street, New York, New York 10011

ALONG THIS WAY

JAMES WELDON JOHNSON

AUTHOR OF

SAINT PETER RELATES AN INCIDENT
NEGRO AMERICANS, WHAT NOW?
GOD'S TROMBONES
FIFTY YEARS AND OTHER POEMS
BLACK MANHATTAN
THE AUTOBIOGRAPHY OF AN EX-COLORED MAN

EDITOR OF

THE BOOK OF AMERICAN NEGRO POETRY
THE BOOK OF AMERICAN NEGRO SPIRITUALS
THE SECOND BOOK OF NEGRO SPIRITUALS

James Weldon Johnson
PHOTOGRAPH BY CARL VAN VECHTEN

ALONG THIS WAY

THE AUTOBIOGRAPHY OF

JAMES WELDON JOHNSON

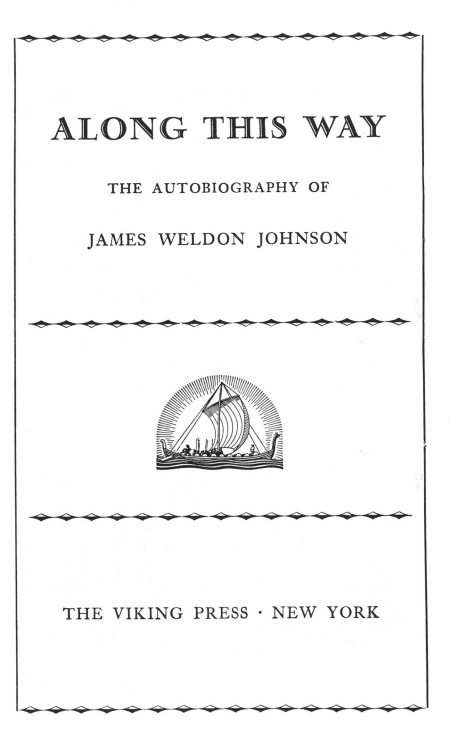

THE VIKING PRESS · NEW YORK

PUBLISHED OCTOBER 1933

To my wife,

GRACE NAIL JOHNSON,

in love and comradeship.

CONTENTS

ILLUSTRATIONS

PART ONE

I

IN 1802 Étienne Dillet, a French army officer in Haiti, placed Hester Argo, a native Haitian woman, together with her three children, aboard a schooner bound for Cuba. This was eleven years after the first insurrection of the slaves in Haiti, and during the war that resulted in the extermination of the French forces on the island and the establishment of Haitian independence. Hester Argo and her children were being sent to a place of refuge. One of these children was a boy, then about six years old, the son of the Frenchman by Hester. The boy's name became Stephen Dillet.

But the schooner never reached her destination; she was captured by a British privateer and taken into Nassau, the capital of the Bahama Islands. Some of the Haitian refugees fared very badly; but Hester Argo and her children, fortunately, were befriended by a well-to-do Spaniard (he may have been a Frenchman) named Lamotte. They had, however, been robbed of everything; and when young Stephen landed in Nassau his entire clothing consisted of the long shirt in which he was clad; and his sole possession, one to which he had somehow clung, was a silver spoon.

A silver spoon . . . Young Stephen was apprenticed to a tailor. He became the tailor of the English garrison stationed at Nassau, and later the leading tailor of the town. England had abolished the slave trade by 1808; and in 1811 she made it a felony. On August 7, 1833, slavery was abolished in her colonies; but in 1830 she had already given the vote to free Negroes in the Bahamas. By 1835 bars that prevented Negroes from holding political office were removed. While still a young man, Stephen Dillet left trade for politics. He stood for election to the Bahaman House of Assembly as a member for the city of Nassau and was elected. The House, however, rather than seat him, effected a dissolution. But in the new House he was seated and remained a member for some thirty consecutive years. Early in the forties he was appointed Chief Inspector of Police and, soon after, Postmaster of the city of Nassau. He held these two offices conjointly about twenty years; that is, until they were separated by the legislature.

when he was allowed to choose which of them he would retain. He chose to retain the postmastership, and held that position until late in the seventies. It was also in the forties that he was made Deputy Adjutant General of Militia and, so, a member of the Governor's staff. He was a vestryman of Christ Church Cathedral and a trustee of the Public Bank. He died at the age of eighty-four.

Hester Argo, the Haitian woman, was one of my maternal great-grandmothers, and this Stephen Dillet was my grandfather.

Ten or twelve years after the little schooner sailed with the refugees from Haiti, a slaver with a cargo bound for Brazil was captured by a British man-of-war and taken into Nassau. The Africans aboard were parceled out among the white inhabitants. To Captain Symonett, a former seafaring man, fell a slim, rather sharp-featured girl, who was later called Sarah. Just who Captain Symonett was, even just what his nationality was, I cannot tell. I know that he spoke English, and I know, too, that his vocabulary included all the sonorous and racy swear words of several languages. Had he been captain of a merchant vessel or had he been a buccaneer? The latter is quite possible. He did not live in the city of Nassau but across on one of the neighboring islands. There, as a sort of patriarchal head of a clan, he ruled; one of his rules being that at the sounding of a horn at daybreak all had to get up and assemble to receive the allowance of coffee and rum which he himself issued to each one: men, women, and children. I wish I knew more about this picturesque old sinner, but before I realized how much I would value the information its sources were cut off.

It was to his island domain that Captain Symonett took the slim African girl. Shortly afterwards his white wife died and he took Sarah to wife and by her reared a large family of sons and daughters, nine of them. Sarah, the African woman, was my other maternal great-grandmother, and one of her daughters, Mary Symonett, born November 16, 1823, was my grandmother.

In the later forties of the last century James Johnson, my father, was working at the old Stevens House in Bowling Green, New York City. He was born a freeman in Richmond, Virginia, August 26, 1830, and as a boy went to New York to work. And here I am again confronted with my lack of foresight; I know nothing of my father's early life and of his background, aside from the meager facts just stated. I never heard him speak of his childhood and what lay back of and beyond it; and I never questioned him. I have a hazy notion that he belonged to a fairly large family, but I never saw one of his relatives. There is among our family relics an old daguerreotype of his mother, a stern-looking woman, seated in a chair and wearing a silk skirt that ballooned about her. My only definite impression of her was one I gained as a child, derived from the fact that on my birth she wrote my father a letter telling him not to "spare the rod and spoil the child." It may be that this first impression had some bearings on my neglect in learning about my father's people. I do know, however, that this grandmother died in Richmond in 1887.

My maternal grandmother, following her eldest sister, Sarah, went to New York in the middle forties, taking with her her only child, Helen Louise Dillet, my mother, born in Nassau, August 4, 1842. My mother grew up in New York. She attended one of the public schools for colored children and secured a good English education. Special attention must have been paid to penmanship, for my mother, even in her old age, wrote a hand that was copperplate. At school she also had opportunity to cultivate her considerable talent for music. When she was between eighteen and nineteen she sang at a concert, and James Johnson, who was in the audience, fell in love with the singer. But the course of true love . . . Within a few months after the concert the Civil War was raging, and my grandmother, listening to the rumors that the colored people in the North would be put in slavery if the South won, became panic-stricken and, taking her daughter with her, boarded a ship and returned to Nassau.

Not long afterwards James Johnson sailed from New York to Nassau. He went to become headwaiter at the Royal Victoria Hotel and to continue his courtship of Helen Louise. They were married at Christ Church Cathedral on April 22, 1864. Nassau was the chief harbor for blockade runners during the War, and gold, English and American, was plentiful. James Johnson was thrifty and enterprising, and he prospered. His job at the Royal Victoria was lucrative, and he added to his income by purchasing two small schooners and engaging in sponge-fishing, then a most flourishing business in the Bahamas. He also bought a team of horses, which he used for draying. He built a nice home and became a part of the local life. Helen Louise's voice gained her a place in the choir of Christ Church. A daughter, Marie

Louise, was born to them on July 10, 1868. It looked as though James Johnson would become a British citizen and make his permanent home in Nassau.

But prosperity in Nassau had collapsed with the close of the Civil War; and the great hurricane of 1866 had blown away its remnants. James Johnson stayed on until the spring of 1869, but he had been thinking for some time of returning to New York. In the meantime some American guests at the Royal Victoria had talked to him about Florida and its possibilities, especially its possibilities as a winter hotel resort; so he resolved to look the field over. He left his family in Nassau and went to Jacksonville.

Jacksonville at that time was little more than a village. Bay Street, then the main street, turned its back, as it still does, on the St. Johns River, and from the rear of a row of five or six blocks of low wooden and brick buildings several rickety wharves jutted out into the magnificent stream. (Of course, water-fronts had not yet entered the list of civic responsibilities.) From the river the town extended back eight or ten blocks and straggled out on the three sides. North and west of the town was a forest of tall pines, and to the east, where the river makes a bend northward before taking its course to the Atlantic, thus giving the present-day city a water-front on two sides, the east as well as the south, there was a thick grove of oaks. Most of the houses were cheaply constructed wooden buildings, but there were a few fine homes. The streets, straight and laid out at right angles, were of deep, grayish sand and were flanked along the sides by narrow boardwalks. In front of the better business places and richer homes the sidewalks were of brick. The streets in the main part of the town were lined with splendid, moss-draped oaks, and so were redeemed from barren ugliness. In almost every yard there were flowers and orange trees. On a spring night there actually was perfumed air. One street, Pine, was paved, paved with crushed oyster shells. It led out to the Shell Road, a road that extended four or five miles into the country and was used as a drive.

This was the Jacksonville James Johnson saw when he arrived: small, insignificant, and, for the most part, crude and primitive. So unlike the Richmond of his boyhood or the New York of his youth; even so unlike Nassau, where there was a high standard of English life. Perhaps he exercised foresight. Perhaps he relied on the tip that Northern people and capital were already interested in Jacksonville and Florida. At any rate, he decided to stay. In the western part of the town, in a suburb known as La Villa—a very misleading name— he bought a lot one hundred and five feet square, on the corner of which stood a four- or five-room dwelling, old, rough, and unpainted, a typical "poor white" house. For this property he paid three hundred dollars cash. This was to be home. He then sent for his family.

With all their transportable goods stored aboard a small sailing vessel, his wife and child arrived safely in Jacksonville in the winter of 1869; the only loss being several missing boxes of books. There also came his wife's mother, now Mary Barton, who, probably, was as apprehensive as she had been at the outbreak of the Civil War. Her husband, John Barton, a very good carpenter, came with her; they, too, came seeking a better field. Strictly attached to Helen Louise was one, Mary Bethel, who served her as nurse for the child and as cook, and who remained a sort of faithful retainer in the household more than thirty years. She took care of me and my brother in our babyhood and childhood. We knew her as "Bar," and in talking to us our elders always referred to her as "your Bar." We learned that "Bar" had been the result of Marie Louise's efforts to say "Bethel." Mary Bethel, in turn, and in true Cockney style, absolutely ignored the "H" in "Helen" and always said "Ellen," a name that Helen Louise detested.

When Helen Louise was ushered into her new home, she broke down and wept. The contrast with the cleanliness and comfort of the home she had just left was sufficient justification for tears. The comparatively cold weather greatly increased the discomfort. The frosty winds blew through the cracks in the walls and up through the cracks in the floor. Within it was gloomy because the batten shutters to the sashless, paneless windows had to be kept closed. The family sought comfort by huddling with scorching faces and chilly backs close around the smoky fireplace in the main room. The outlook from the house was equally disheartening; instead of the clean, dazzling white streets of Nassau, here were streets or rather roads of that grayish sand six inches deep, and no place to walk except through it. The surrounding houses were poorer and more dilapidated than the Johnson house. The neighbors—we still absurdly apply "neighbor" to people merely because they live near—spoke in terms and words often utterly foreign to Helen Louise. The nearest person who could possibly be a neighbor for her was a white woman who lived a block away on a corner diagonally across the main street or road. She was

Mrs. McCleary. Her husband was the foreman at Clark's sawmill in the eastern end of the town, a large plant that employed a big force of Negroes and turned an immense quantity of Florida pine into lumber for local use, shipment North, and for export. Mrs. McCleary belonged to a family then rather prominent in Jacksonville, the Hollands. Her brother was at one time sheriff of the county.

And this was to be home! The heartsickness of Helen Louise can be understood. But it did become home. She and her husband lived together on that plot of ground forty-three years.

During this first winter little Marie Louise was taken sick, and died in June 1870.

II

I WAS born June 17, 1871, in the old house on the corner; but I have no recollection of having lived in it. Before I could be aware of such a thing my father had built a new house near the middle of his lot. In this new house was formed my first consciousness of home. My childish idea of it was that it was a great mansion. I saw nothing in the neighborhood that surpassed it in splendor. Of course, it was only a neat cottage. The house had three bedrooms, a parlor, and a kitchen. The four main rooms were situated, two on each side of a hall that ran through the center of the house. The kitchen, used also as a room in which the family ate, was at the rear of the house and opened on a porch that was an extension of the hall. On the front a broad piazza ran the width of the house. Under the roof was an attic to which a narrow set of steps in one of the back rooms gave access.

But the house was painted, and there were glass windows and green blinds. Before long there were some flowers and trees. One of the first things my father did was to plant two maple trees at the front gate and a dozen or more orange trees in the yard. The maples managed to live; the orange trees, naturally, flourished. The hallway of the house was covered with a strip of oilcloth and the floors of the rooms with matting. There were curtains at the windows and some pictures on the walls. In the parlor there were two or three dozen books and a cottage organ. When I was seven or eight years old, the organ gave way to a square piano. It was a tinkling old instrument, but a source of rapturous pleasure. It is one of the indelible impressions on my mind. I can still remember just how the name "Bacon" looked, stamped in gold letters above the keyboard. There was a center marble-top table on which rested a big, illustrated Bible and a couple of photograph albums. In a corner stood a what-not filled with bric-a-brac and knickknacks. On a small stand was a glass-domed receptacle in which was a stuffed canary perched on a diminutive tree; on this stand there was also kept a stereoscope and an assortment of views photographed in various parts of the world. For my brother and me, in our childhood (my brother, John Rosamond, was born in the new house August 11, 1873), this room was an Aladdin's cave. We used to stand before the what-not and stake out our claims to the objects on its shelves with a "that's mine" and a "that's mine." We never tired of looking at the stereoscopic scenes, examining the photographs in the album, or putting the big Bible and other books on the floor and exploring for pictures. Two large conch shells decorated the ends of the hearth. We greatly admired their pink, polished inner surface; and loved to put them to our ears to hear the "roar of the sea" from their cavernous depths. But the undiminishing thrill was derived from our experiments on the piano.

When I was born, my mother was very ill, too ill to nurse me. Then she found a friend and neighbor in an unexpected quarter. Mrs. McCleary, her white neighbor who lived a block away, had a short while before given birth to a girl baby. When this baby was christened she was named Angel. The mother of Angel, hearing of my mother's plight, took me and nursed me at her breast until my mother had recovered sufficiently to give me her own milk. So it appears that in the land of black mammies I had a white one. Between her and me there existed an affectionate relation through all my childhood; and even in after years when I had grown up and moved away I never, up to the time of her death, went back to my old home without paying her a visit and taking her some small gift.

I do not intend to boast about a white mammy, for I have perceived bad taste in those Southern white people who are continually boasting about their black mammies. I know the temptation for them to do so is very strong, because the honor point on the escutcheon of Southern aristocracy, the *sine qua non* of a background of family, of good breeding and social prestige, in the South is the Black Mammy. Of course, many of the white people who boast of having had black mammies are romancing. Naturally, Negroes had black mammies, but black mammies for white people were expensive luxuries, and comparatively few white people had them.

When I was about a year old, my father made a trip to New York, taking my mother and me with him. It was during this visit that I developed from a creeping infant into a walking child. Without doubt, my mother welcomed this trip. She was, naturally, glad to see again the city and friends of her girlhood; and it is probable that she brought some pressure on my father to make another move—back to New York. If she did, it was without effect. I say she probably made some such effort because I know what a long time it took her to become reconciled to life in the South; in fact, she never did entirely. The New York of her childhood and youth was all the United States she knew. Latterly she had lived in a British colony under conditions that rendered the weight of race comparatively light. During the earlier days of her life in Jacksonville she had no adequate conception of her "place."

And so it was that one Sunday morning she went to worship at St. John's Episcopal Church. As one who had been a member of the choir of Christ Church Cathedral she went quite innocently. She went, in fact, not knowing any better. In the chanting of the service her soprano voice rang out clear and beautiful, and necks were craned to discover the singer. On leaving the church she was politely but definitely informed that the St. John's congregation would prefer to have her worship the Lord elsewhere. Certainly she never went back to St. John's nor to any other Episcopal church; she followed her mother and joined Ebenezer, the colored Methodist Episcopal Church in Jacksonville, and became the choir leader.

Racially she continued to be a nonconformist and a rebel. A decade or so after the St. John's Church incident Lemuel W. Livingston, a student at Cookman Institute, the Negro school in Jacksonville founded and maintained by the Methodist Church (North), was appointed as a cadet to West Point. Livingston passed his written examinations, and the colored people were exultant. The members of Ebenezer Church gave a benefit that netted for him a purse of several hundred dollars. There was good reason for a show of pride; Livingston was a handsome, bronze-colored boy with a high reputation as a student, and appeared to be ideal material for a soldier and officer. But at the Academy he was turned down. The examining officials there stated that his eyesight was in some manner defective. The news that Livingston had been denied admission to West Point was given out at a Sunday service at Ebenezer Church. When at the same service the minister announced "America" as a hymn, my mother refused to sing it.

My mother was artistic and more or less impractical and in my father's opinion had absolutely no sense about money. She was a splendid singer and she had a talent for drawing. One day when I was about fifteen years old, she revealed to me that she had written verse, and showed me a thin sheaf of poems copied out in her almost perfect handwriting. She was intelligent and possessed a quick though limited sense of humor. But the limitation of her sense of humor was quite the normal one: she had no relish for a joke whose butt was herself or her children; my father had the rarer capacity for laughing even at himself. She belonged to the type of mothers whose love completely surrounds their children and is all-pervading; mothers for whom sacrifice for the child means only an extension of love. Love of this kind often haunts the child in later years. He runs back again and again through all his memories, searching for a lapse or a lack or a falling short in that love so that he might in some degree balance his own innumerable thoughtlessnesses, his petty and great selfishnesses, his failures to begin to understand or value the thing that was once his like the air he breathed; and the search is vain.

The childhood memories that cluster round my mother are still intensely vivid to me; many of them are poignantly tender. I am between five and six years old. . . . In the early evening the lamp in the little parlor is lit. . . . If the weather is chilly, pine logs are sputtering and blazing in the fireplace. . . . I and my brother, who is a tot, are seated on the floor. . . . My mother takes a book and reads. . . . The book is *David Copperfield*. . . . Night after night I follow the story, always hungry for the next installment. . . . Then the book is *Tales of a Grandfather*. . . . Then it is a story by Samuel Lover. I laugh till the tears roll down my cheeks at the mishaps of Handy Andy. And my brother laughs too, doubtless because he sees me laughing. . . . My mother's voice is beautiful; I especially enjoy it when she mimics the Irish brogue and Cockney accents. . . . My brother grows sleepy.

. . . My mother closes the book and puts us both to bed—me feverish concerning the outcome of David's affairs or thrilling over the exploits of Wallace or Robert the Bruce, or still laughing at Andy. She tucks us in and kisses us good-night. What a debt for a child to take on!

She was my first teacher and began my lessons in reading before ever I went to school. She was, in fact, the first colored woman public school teacher in Florida; and, when my school days began at Stanton, the central school in Jacksonville for colored children, she was one of the teachers there. And that, perhaps, is why I have no sharp recollection of just when I started school. I have a blurred and hazy picture in my memory of being in a large room with fifty, maybe sixty boys and girls, most of whom were several years older than I. The picture of the teacher is fainter, and would probably be fainter still had I not afterwards come to know that she was Diana Grant, the wife of the man who was for a number of years the pastor of Ebenezer Church. But I recall more clearly my sense of discomfort. The room was too crowded; some of the children I was packed in with were not clean; I rebelled at the situation.

At this point there must have been some sort of a hiatus; I remember nothing further about that class and classroom, but I do remember distinctly being in a larger, less crowded room with nicer children and with a young lady named Carrie Sampson as my teacher. At once I fell in love with Miss Sampson; and small wonder, she was so lovely. When the time came for me to leave her class, the honor of promotion seemed to be no recompense for my desolation. I wanted to continue without end my education at her feet. It took persuasion and some sterner measures to induce a change of mind, if not of heart. The episode forms a pleasant memory of childhood; and the knowing that this my earliest judgment upon living beauty disclosed such exacting standards has always been a matter of certain pride to me. I saw my teacher many times when I was no longer a child, and I know she was one of the most beautiful women I have ever seen.

The development of the ability to read opened up for me a world of wonders that I never grew tired of exploring. My father gave me my first own books, a "library" consisting of seven volumes packed in a cardboard case four and a half inches high, three inches wide, and two inches deep. I still have the books; they are intact, but show the passage of the years. Each book contains a story about good little girls and good and bad little boys. I need not add that each story pointed a wholesome lesson. I list them: *Peter and His Pony, The Tent in the Garden, Harry the Shrimper, The White Kitten, Willie Wilson the Newsboy*, and *The Water Melon*.

Peter and His Pony opens thus:

"Dear papa," said Peter one morning to his father, "you said when I was nine years old, you would give me a pony to ride on. Don't you know that I shall be nine years old in three months' time? and will you keep your promise?"

Mr. Howard smiled at Peter's eagerness, and said, "I promised to give you a present of a pony when you should be nine years of age, provided you were sufficiently careful to be trusted with the charge of it; for, though I can afford to buy you a pony, I cannot afford to keep a man to clean and look after it."

"Oh, father," cried Peter, "I will do all that. I will brush his coat every day, and feed him regularly. I shall be fond of him, and he will be fond of me. If you will be so kind as to let me have a pony, I shall be very happy."

"I do not doubt that you will be very happy if I give you a pony," replied Mr. Howard; "but before I promise to give you one, I wish to be quite sure that the pony will be happy also; and if he is not well cleaned and regularly fed, and his shoes looked carefully after, he will not be happy."

"Dear papa," said Peter, "I do assure you that I will always attend to my pony before I eat my breakfast—you may be sure he shall want for nothing."

"Very well," said Mr. Howard, "I will think upon what you have said, and will let you know at the proper time what I intend to do."

Peter got the pony on his ninth birthday, and was very faithful in attending him. But for just once Peter neglected his duties, and when he rode that day the pony lost a shoe, cut his foot, and went lame. Peter's negligence brought upon him the retribution of being deprived for a month of the pleasure of riding.

The chief effect of the story on me was a long season of importuning my father to buy me a pony—the which I never got.

I finished these little books in short order, and looked for stronger meat. In fact, my father had underestimated my stage of development; my mother's readings had already carried me far beyond books of this grade. I read for myself *Pickwick Papers*, some of the *Waverly Novels, Pilgrim's Progress*, the fairy tales of the Brothers Grimm, and took my first dip into poetry through Sir Walter Scott. I think that of these books the stories by the Brothers Grimm made the deepest effect. These stories left me haunted by the elusiveness of beauty— elusiveness, its very quintessence. Years after, when I read Keats's *Ode to a Nightingale* the thought flashed through my mind that for one whose spirit had not been thus pervaded in childhood it would be impossible even to catch at the tenuous beauty in:

The same that oft-times hath
Charm'd magic casements, opening on the foam
Of perilous seas, in faery lands forlorn.

I exhausted the little supply in our parlor and began laying hands on any book that came within my reach. I remember one day when I was absorbed in a novel I had got hold of with the title, as I remember it, *Vashti—Or Until Death Do Us Part*, my mother said to me, "You had better leave that book till you are older." How good were her grounds for censorship I cannot tell but I remember that I finished the book without, I think, doing myself any appreciable harm. Several years later I began buying regularly two magazines published for boys, *Golden Days* and *Golden Argosy*.

My mother was also my first music teacher. She had less than ordinary proficiency on the organ and piano, but she knew enough to give me and my brother a start. Before we began to learn our notes and the keys of the instrument, we used to stand, whenever we were allowed, close by on either side while she picked out hymns or other simple pieces. It was our great delight, my brother at one end of the keyboard and I at the other, to chime in with what were then wholly futuristic harmonies.

Pardonable sentiment does not make me completely forget that my mother's love was not manifested in unchanging gentleness. There were times when her love or her sense of responsibility for the kind of men her two boys would grow up to be prompted sterner treatment. Then the mental or moral lesson would be impressed upon us otherwise than through our intellectual processes or our higher emotions. Whenever I was spanked my brother always received vicariously whatever benefits there might be. When I cried he cried even more piteously or more lustily than I. These spankings were literally dark moments in my life. It was not the stinging sensation of the sole of the slipper or the back of the hairbrush that I dreaded, for the force applied was never excessive; it was the moment of darkness that terrified me. My mother's method was to put my head face down between her knees. This made the operation convenient for her, but it had on me somewhat the effect of a total eclipse of the sun on primitive peoples; the world was blotted out and, in addition, I underwent the horrors of the sensation of being smothered.

One instance stands out almost singly in my mind. Often a spanking comes to a child like a thunderclap out of a clear sky, and he doesn't fully realize why he is being punished. He suffers it like the brave man, who dies but once. But one evening after dark I and my brother, being in possession of a few pennies, conspired to run around the corner to Mrs. Handy's grocery store and buy two "prize" boxes of candy. We went without giving notice or asking permission. On starting back I became immediately aware of the gravity of the situation. With each step homeward my forebodings increased. I recognized the inevitable and had a thousand foretastes of it. When I entered the house it was with as heavy a sense of sin as any infant conscience could carry. However, summoning all the gayety we could, we exhibited the baubles we had won—these trinkets, not the candy, were the chief objects of our desires—but that did not stay the hand of fate.

Before my spanking days were entirely over, I took the matter up frankly with my mother and made a plea for open-air spanking. I conceded her right to punish me when I did wrong, but protested against having my eyes and nose and mouth buried in the dark depths of her skirts. She didn't fall back on parental prerogatives, but yielded me the point.

My Richmond grandmother's advice to my father about not sparing the rod and spoiling the child had no effect on him; not once in his life did he lay a finger in punishment on me or my brother. Nevertheless, by firmness and sometimes by sternness, he did exercise a strong control over us. But I am fogy enough to believe that the spankings my mother gave me did me good.

I cannot remember when I did not know my mother, but I can easily recall the at first hazy and then gradually more distinct notions about my father. My impressions of him began to take shape from finding under my pillow in the mornings an orange, some nuts, and raisins, and learning that he had put them there after I had gone to sleep. Shortly after my father got to Jacksonville the St. James Hotel was built and opened. When it was opened he was the headwaiter, a job he held for twelve or thirteen years. Doubtless the hotel had been planned, and may even have been under construction, before he arrived; probably this was the definite prospect before him when he set out for Jacksonville. The St. James was for many years the most famous and the most fashionable of all the Florida resort hotels. A number of summers my father was the headwaiter at some mountain or seaside hotel in the North. So in my babyhood and first days of childhood I didn't see very much of him. His work at the St. James took him from home early in the mornings to see breakfast served, and he remained at the hotel until dinner was finished, by which time I had been put away in the little bed in which I slept. It was from the hotel that he brought the fruit and sweets that he put under my pillow. I remember, too, that our Sunday dinner always came from the hotel. It was brought in a hamper by one of the waiters, and the meat was usually fricasseed chicken.

I got acquainted with my father by being taken to the hotel to see him. As soon as Rosamond was big enough, he was taken too. My mother never went; one of the waiters fetched us until we were old enough to go alone. These visiting days were great days for us: the wide steps, the crowded verandas, the music, the soft, deep carpets of the lobby; this was a world of enchantment. My first definite thought about the hotel was that it belonged to my father. True, there was always around in the office a Mr. Campbell, a rather stooped man with a short reddish beard, who habitually gave me a friendly pat on the shoulder, and who evidently had something to do with the place. But just to the right, at the entrance to the big dining-room stands my father, peerless and imposing in full-dress clothes; he opens the door and takes me in; countless waiters, it seems, are standing around in groups; my father strikes a gong and the waiters spring to their stations and stand like soldiers at attention; I am struck with wonder at the endless rows of tables now revealed, the glitter of silver, china, and glass, and the array of napkins folded so that they look like many miniature white pyramids. Another gong, and the waiters relax; but one of them tucks a napkin under my chin and serves me as though I were a princeling. Then, with desires of heart and stomach satisfied and a quantity of reserves tied in a napkin, I am tucked away in a corner. Again the gong, the doors are thrown open, the guests stream in. My father snaps his fingers, waiters jump to carry out his orders, and guests smile him their thanks. He lords it over everything that falls within my ken. He is, quite obviously, the most important man in the St. James Hotel.

This childish portrait needs, of course, some rectification. No boy can make a fair estimate of his father. I was thirty years old before I was able to do it. The average boy all along thinks highly of his mother. In manhood he is likely even to sentimentalize her faults into tender virtues. With his male parent it is not so; his opinion goes through a range of changes and tends to be critical rather than sentimental. Up to ten a boy thinks his father knows everything; at twenty he indulgently looks upon the "old man" as a back number or, maybe, something less complimentary; at thirty, if the boy himself has any sense, he recognizes all of his father's qualities pretty fairly.

My father was a quiet, unpretentious man. He was naturally conservative and cautious, and generally displayed common sense in what he said and did. He never went to school; such education as he had was self-acquired. Later in life, I appreciated the fact that his self-development was little less than remarkable. He had a knowledge of general affairs and was familiar with many of the chief events and characters in the history of the world. I have the old sheepskin bound volume of *Plutarch's Lives* which he owned before I was born. He had gained by study a working knowledge of the Spanish language; this he had done to increase his value as a hotel employee. When he was a young man in New York, he attended the theater a good deal, and, before I was aware of where the lines came from or of what they meant, I used to go around the house parroting after him certain snatches from the Shakespearean plays. I particularly recall: "To be or not to be; that is the question" and "A horse! a horse! my kingdom for a horse!"

The quality in my father that impressed me most was his high and rigid sense of honesty. I simply could not conceive of him as a party to any monetary transaction that was questionable in the least. I think he got his greatest satisfaction in life out of the reputation he had built up as a man of probity, and took his greatest pride in the consequent credit standing that he enjoyed. This element in his character was a source of gratification to my pride and also, more than once, to my needs. One instance of double gratification was when I was at home in Jacksonville in 1910, just a few weeks before I was to be married. My father and mother discussed an appropriate gift to me and, finally, to my undisguised joy, decided upon a check for a thousand dollars. My father, excusably, did not have a thousand dollars in cash; but he said to me, "My boy, we'll go down town tomorrow and see if we can get the money." We went the next morning to one of the principal banks and my father spoke with John C. L'Engle, the president. The transaction was put through without any delay; he got the money on his note, without collateral security, without even an endorser. I was as proud to see him able to do such a thing as I was glad to have the money.

In the narrow sense, he was an unsociable man. My mother liked company; and when I was a boy we frequently had company at the house; occasionally there was a party. I, too, liked the company and the extra nice things to eat that were always a concomitant—especially ice cream of which in my whole life I have never had too much. My father took practically no part in these affairs. In his opinion the entertaining of company as "company" was a waste of time and money.

Yet he was not devoid of graces. He played the guitar well as a solo instrument, a use seldom made of it now. He possessed a vein of eloquence and had a good ear for the well-turned phrase. He liked to get off pithy aphorisms. He keenly enjoyed witticisms, particularly his own. Some of the latter, through repetition, became fixed in my mind. On a hot afternoon he would say to me, "Bubs, draw a fresh bucket of water from the well, and be sure to get it from the north side." Or on a still hotter afternoon, "Son, suppose while you're resting you take the ax and chop a little wood." Not infrequently he would achieve a penetrating truth. It was not until he was in his middle forties that he became a church member; when he was past fifty he became a preacher; one day, after he had been a preacher for some years, he said to me, "My boy, do you know I was never *compelled* to associate with bad people until I joined the church?"

He was a jolly companion for a boy, and I loved to be with him and go about with him. He made my first kites. He was adept at folding paper, and he made me windmills and fashioned little boats to be sailed in a tub. He made shadow-figures on the wall at night. He took me and my brother to places along the river where we could paddle about and learn to swim. After we were big enough to trot around with him, he played with us a good deal in this way during the times between hotel seasons. Before I was able to hold the instrument on my knees he began to teach me the guitar. I had to stand up to it in the same manner in which a player stands up to a bass viol. By the time I was ten years old I was, for a child, a remarkable performer—I judge; for I remember people, sometimes guests from the hotel, coming to our house to hear me play.

My father was a man of medium size, but constitutionally strong. One of the traditions of the home was that he was never sick. His color was light bronze, and so, a number of shades darker than that of my mother. She at fifty bore more than a slight resemblance to the later portraits of Queen Victoria; so much so that the family doctor christened her "Queen," a name to which she afterwards answered among her intimate friends.

The years as they pass keep revealing how the impressions made upon me as a child by my parents are constantly strengthening controls over my forms of habit, behavior, and conduct as a man. It appeared to me, starting into manhood, that I was to grow into something different from them; into something on a so much larger plan, a so much grander scale. As life tapers off I can see that in the deep and fundamental qualities I am each day more and more like them.

III

THERE was another force that I came under in those most plastic years. My grandmother Barton was a woman of strong will and determination. These traits were manifest in her physical appearance, her manner, and her speech. She had a spare, energetic body; and, in contradistinction to the tastes of her daughter, disdained the desire for ease and luxury. She was an expert laundress, and got high prices from the hotel guests in Jacksonville for her work. In this way she must have earned considerable money, because at that time the Florida season opened at Thanksgiving and lasted about five months, and there was no competition from steam laundries. She also ran a little bake shop, and her bread and cake enjoyed a high reputation for excellency. In addition, she was an indefatigable church worker.

She was a comely woman with well-chiseled features. Her eyes were rather piercing, and she had a nose of which she was very proud, even boastful; a nose which, she said, she got from her own mother. As a child I used to feel that my grandmother's references to her aristocratic nose were frequently made as an implied comparison with the decidedly snub nose of my mother. But my mother could retort effectively by making any sort of gesture with her lovely hands or breaking into the enhancing smile that disclosed her perfectly formed teeth. My grandmother was more than plain in her speech. She often said things that brought an "Oh, mother!" from my mother and a roar of laughter from my father. (I don't know how it happened that my brother and I were not taught to address our mother as "mother," as she did hers. For a long while we used "mamma," which as a word is little beyond the "bar-bar" of infancy. When we were big boys, we changed to the somewhat slangy "mumsey." I actually regret that I never had the direct use of this word of the greatest combined beauty, nobility and tenderness in the English language.) Her speech was sharp as well as plain, and she was well able to hold her own in a battle of tongues. She was a rigid disciplinarian and also, I judge, as firm a believer in the efficacy of the rod as my Richmond grandmother. But I was very fond of her and she was, perhaps, more fond of me. For reasons that were satisfactory for her I was her favorite grandchild. At times the display of her favoritism was so flagrant that it pained my mother and embarrassed me. My brother often manifested his recognition of it by loud wails.

John Barton was very indulgent toward me. I remember him quite distinctly, though I was but seven years old when he died. He was a tall, very dark brown man with a Lincoln-like face, even to the short beard. But he was dapper; I might say elegant. He was a grand sight, I thought, in his long-tailed, black broadcloth coat on Sundays. My grandmother used to say that she fell in love with him because of the graceful way in which he would handle himself in friendly boxing bouts. I liked John Barton very much. I called him "Pa John" and never knew until I had stopped using the term that it consisted of two words instead of one. He bought me a goat one day, a pretty white and black young billy goat. When Billy was presented to me, he was tied to a tree in the yard. He was a nice, tame goat; he let me pet him, and nibbled from my hand the grass or any other kind of food that I could forage. Pa John set to work to make a wagon and harness. Never did the anticipation of driving my own automobile equal in thrills the anticipation of driving my goat cart. But Billy got loose and out into the street; and the dogs chased and killed him. Such a thing could not seem less than a tragedy to a grown-up; what it meant to a child cannot be measured. I never got another goat, and the wagon and harness were never finished. Pa John died before he could attend to either.

I was in the room when he died, standing at the foot of the bed,

How I got there I do not know. But there I stand, perhaps unnoticed because I am barely able to peep over the foot-piece. I am bewildered. I cannot understand what is taking place. I see my grandmother almost hysterical, and my mother weeping. I see my father bend over the dying man and take his hand; I hear him call his name several times without any answer. Then my grandmother's wild scream; then the strange silence. I am snatched away, and I know nothing more about what has happened until the day of the funeral. I have never been to a funeral; but I understand that I shall not see Pa John any more. The thought saddens me; but how quickly I forget! There are five or six big carriages, each drawn by two horses. The carriages are all crowded, and I am boosted and perched on the high seat of one of them beside the driver. I ask him to let me drive, and he gives me the reins and puts his two big hands over my two tiny ones. I forget everything except the pull of the reins against the palms of my hands, the motion of the two great animals under me, and the aroma that rises from their sweating flanks. Of course, I do not want anybody else whom I know to die; but I would enjoy going to funerals, if I might sit on the high seat beside the driver and help hold the reins over the horses.

I loved to go down to my grandmother's house. The going of those two blocks alone was for a long time charged with a sense of adventure, to which was often added the weight of responsibility as guardian for my brother. I would come out of our front gate, turn to the right, and go some seventy-five or eighty feet to the corner, where stood the old house that was once home. I had to get on the other side of the street I had reached, but I never crossed at this point because on the corner directly opposite lived Mr. Cole, a white man, and I was dreadfully afraid of him. I was not afraid of him because he was white—his or anybody else's being white had no special significance for me at that time—I was afraid of him because everybody said he was crazy. Perhaps he was—he was poor and did no work of any kind—and perhaps he wasn't crazy. His wife, a very good sort of a woman, took in sewing and did all the rest of the necessary work. Mr. Cole, a tall, gaunt, black-haired man, spent most of his time on his piazza seated in a chair and grinding out wheezy tunes from an old music box. He would periodically interrupt his artistic endeavors by leaping to his feet, striding up and down his piazza, and consigning the whole neighborhood to hell with the most violent profanity. Usually some children, all colored, would be gathered around to listen to the music or, probably, to tease Mr. Cole; and when the outburst came they would scream and scamper in all directions. I never dared the passage on the side of the Cole house.

I always turned to the left and crossed over to the corner where Aunt Elsie Andrews lived. Aunt Elsie lived in a little house that was almost covered with honeysuckle vines. In her yard was a marvelous fig tree. She was a very old and benign woman with a noble, black face that took on a positive beauty under the red bandanna she always wore over the white cotton of her head. Whenever figs were in season and Aunt Elsie saw me and my brother passing she would stop us and give us a handful of the syrupy fruit. In the same yard, but in a separate little house back of Aunt Elsie's, lived Aunt Venie. She was a small, light-brown woman, much younger than Aunt Elsie but, following the manner of according respect to a woman who had reached a certain age, we addressed her also as "Aunt." We were a little bit afraid of Aunt Venie, too; for she was said to have fits. (In a former age she would have been classed among those "possessed with devils.") Aunt Venie's fits were probably the results of religious excesses. At St. Paul's Church, the colored church on the corner above to the west, she was the champion of all "ring shouters." When there was a "ring shout" the weird music and the sound of thudding feet set the silences of the night vibrating and throbbing with a vague terror. Many a time I woke suddenly and lay a long while strangely troubled by these sounds, the like of which my great-grandmother Sarah had heard as a child. The shouters, formed in a ring, men and women alternating, their bodies close together, moved round and round on shuffling feet that never left the floor. With the heel of the right foot they pounded out the fundamental beat of the dance and with their hands clapped out the varying rhythmical accents of the chant; for the music was, in fact, an African chant and the shout an African dance, the whole pagan rite transplanted and adapted to Christian worship. Round and round the ring would go: one, two, three, four, five hours, the very monotony of sound and motion inducing an ecstatic frenzy. Aunt Venie, it seems, never, even after the hardest day of washing and ironing, missed a "ring shout."

From Aunt Elsie's corner I usually crossed, passing under two very largely prickly pear trees, to where the Morrisons, a noisy colored family with five children, lived. Then I would go east down the length of the block, past three other colored families and around to the right at the next corner to my grandmother's. But when I was leading my brother I often kept on Aunt Elsie's side of the street, past the next house, where a big, ferocious dog always ran the length of the fence, giving every indication that he would chew us to bits if he could get at us. Rosamond would hold my hand more tightly; and it took all my prestige as an elder to assure him that there was no real danger. Once, discounting my assurances and my ability to protect him, he did break away and run back home. The sight of his skirts (all boys of his age then wore kilts) flying in the breeze and his feet digging up the sand was very funny to me. It was an incident that I related at home with a feeling of superiority.

At the end of the fence of the barking dog I would cut diagonally across the street to the corner around which my grandmother lived. I took this cut because I was always cautioned about passing Henry Arpen's. Henry Arpen was a Dutchman, short but not fat, who with his wife, a very tall and angular woman, ran a general store. The store included a bar, and it seemed that there were never less than a dozen drunks, black and white, hanging around. There was generally lots of profane and obscene language, and not infrequently a play of pistols and knives; so I always heeded the caution. But Arpen's store was a place that pricked my curiosity, and I was always glad of the chance to be taken there when something was to be bought. It was exciting; it was a glimpse into the big world; and, besides, Mr. Arpen and his wife were always nice to me. In their broken English they inquired about my health and as to whether I was a good boy or not while one of them fished out from a tall glass jar a ball of red and white candy for me. These hard candy balls were warranted to wear any ordinary child a full day and, in addition, to give him a gumboil on the roof of his mouth.

This little journey had, in mid-summer, one other element of adventure. The streets I have been talking about were actually very wide roads of loose, deep sand dotted here and there with little oases of grass. There were neither pavements nor sidewalks, except the veranda round Arpen's store. When the sands of these streets were heated, the sands of Sahara couldn't be hotter. And at that season the thing above all others that I and my brother implored of our mother was to let us leave off our shoes and stockings. Whenever she did, and often she didn't because of the prevalence of ground itch, we felt so light-footed; we could run so much faster; and the feel of the earth and water on naked feet made us such happy little animals. We sincerely envied the children around who had no shoes and stockings. And so sometimes the expedition to our grandmother's house gave us, in proportion, all the thrills that a traveler gets in exploring the world's perilous places. Our method was to run from one patch of grass to another, waiting at each until our feet cooled off before daring to set out for the next. But even these islands of refuge were not free from hazard; the grass was filled with sand-spurs that pierced the feet like hot needles. Under these conditions the journey was one that called for agility, endurance, and courage.

But the goal was always worth the dangers run; there were sure to be small cakes and jumbles and benne candy, and at times a cool glass of limeade. But I must be fair to myself and say that it was more than a matter of the palate; to go into the little shop and catch the good, clean smell of fresh-baked bread and cake satisfied a sense related to, yet apart from hunger, and I liked the lively scene of coming and going customers. It was exciting to ramble round the comparatively strange yard; to play with a black dog named Bull, a much better playmate than our own dog, Stump, who had reached the philosophical age; to explore the recesses of the garden, help chase the chickens out, and search for blackberries that might be ripe along the edge of the fence. My grandmother's little parlor also had attractions, consisting of the few household treasures she had brought from Nassau. In the center was a table holding the photograph album, a stereoscope with views, and some trinkets. This table was of solid West Indian mahogany, with four straight, slender legs, two hinged leaves and a drawer. I use it now as a writing table in my study. On the wall hung a long, two-sectioned, gilt-framed mirror in which I could see myself from any part of the room. This mirror was flanked by two large portrait reproductions in color, one of Queen Victoria and the other of the Prince Consort in their royal robes. There was also a smaller portrait of the Prince of Wales dressed in the height of fashion. My grandmother remained a royalist. She never relinquished or forfeited her British citizenship. She took great pride in telling me about the Queen and about the Prince of Wales and his visit to New York. I admired these pictures very much, for they were larger and brighter than any we had at our house.

But the objects in this little room that held the greatest charm for me were two tall candlesticks, ornamented with lusters, that stood on the mantelpiece. My grandmother would take one down and let me look through the prismatic, cut-glass pendants; instantly all that I saw was embroidered with crimson and purple and green and gold. How I longed to possess one of those magical glasses. If one would only drop off accidentally, and I might have it to carry round in my pocket so that I could turn it on any object I chose and make it more beautiful than it actually was; in fine, that I might always have an ever-ready rainbow.

After John Barton died I spent a good deal of time at my grandmother's house to keep her company. I made myself handy, especially in the shop, where I served a part of each day as clerk. I often slept at her house. On those evenings, after the shop was closed, she usually read to me for an hour or so. She read from the Bible and from a thick, illustrated book bound in green cloth called *Home Life in the Bible*. She also read me stories from books that she drew from the library of Ebenezer Church Sunday School. These stories were better written and slightly less juvenile than those in the "library" my father had given me, but they were of the same genre. My grandmother had had very little schooling, and could not read as my mother did; that, however, did not daunt her, she read a great deal, and more and more as she grew older. When she read Bible stories aloud to me she came across many names difficult to pronounce, especially in the stories from the Old Testament, but I never knew her to be stumped by a single one; she'd call it something and pass right on. In this way she coined, I am sure, a number of wonderful words.

It was during this period that she disclosed her consuming ambition, her ambition for me to become a preacher. She lived until I was thirty years old, and I believe she never felt that I had done other than choose the lesser part. She took me to Sunday school each week and to some of the church services. I was practically living at my grandmother's when there came a revivalist to Ebenezer. She attended the meetings every night, taking me along with her, always walking the distance of about a mile each way. Sometimes that homeward mile for my short legs seemed without end. In these revival meetings the decorum of the regular Sunday services gave way to something primitive. It was hard to realize that this was the same congregation which on Sunday mornings sat quietly listening to the preacher's exegesis of his text and joining in singing conventional hymns and anthems led by a choir. Now the scene is changed. The revivalist rants and roars, he exhorts and implores, he warns and threatens. The air is charged. Overlaid emotions come to surface. A woman gives a piercing scream and begins to "shout"; then another, and another. The more hysterical ones must be held to be kept from "shouting" out of their clothes. Sinners crowd to the mourners' bench. Prayers and songs go up for the redemption of their souls. Strapping men break down in agonizing sobs, and emotionally strained women fall out in a rigid trance. A mourner "comes through" and his testimony of conversion brings a tumult of rejoicing.

I was only about nine years old but younger souls had been consecrated to God; and I was led to the mourners' bench. I knelt down at the altar. I was so wedged in that I could hardly breathe. I tried to pray. I tried to feel a conviction of sin. I, finally, fell asleep. . . . The meeting was about to close; somebody shook me by the shoulder. . . . I woke up but did not open my eyes or stir. . . . Whence sprang the whim, as cunning as could have occurred to one of the devil's own imps? The shaking continued, but I neither opened my eyes nor stirred. They gathered round me. I heard, "Glory to God, the child's gone off!" But I did not open my eyes or stir. My grandmother got a big, strong fellow who took me on his back and toted me that long mile home. Several people going our way accompanied us, and the conversation reverted to me, with some rather far-fetched allusions to the conversion of Saul of Tarsus. The situation stirred my sense of humor, and a chuckle ran round and round inside of me, because I did not dare to let it get out. The sensation was a delicious one, but it was suddenly chilled by the appalling thought that I could not postpone my awakening indefinitely. Each step homeward, I knew, brought the moment of reckoning nearer. I needed to think and think fast; and I did. I evolved a plan that I thought was good; when I reached home and "awoke" I recounted a vision. The vision was based on a remembered illustration in *Home Life in the Bible* that purported to be the artist's conception of a scene in heaven. To that conception I added some original embellishments. Apparently my plan worked out to the satisfaction of everybody concerned. Indeed, for me, it worked out almost too satisfactorily, for I was called upon to repeat the vision many times thereafter—to my inward shame.

But I had put my hand to the plow, and there was no turning back. I was taken into the church for the probationary period, after which

I would be made a full member if I proved worthy. My grandmother
went with me to my home to tell my father and mother about it. The
conference took place in our yard. My mother was hesitant, but
acquiescent—she never reached the place where she could pit her will
against her mother's. My father expressed his disapproval strongly, and
it looked as though the matter would lead to a break between him
and my grandmother. He said to my mother, "B" (his familiar name
for her), "we ought not let the child join the church at his age; he
doesn't understand what he's doing; he ought to be able to know what
joining the church means before we allow him to take such a step."
And to my grandmother, "Mrs. Barton" (he always addressed her in
this formal manner), "you're doing the boy more harm than good;
you're forcing him into something that he ought to be left to go into
of his own free will. He'll make a better church member and a better
Christian if he makes up his own mind about it." But the moral club
was in my grandmother's hand and she wielded it vigorously. "If being
a church member," she countered, "is a good thing, how can a child
start too young? . . . Train up a child in the way he should go,
because when he is old he may not choose that way." And she capped
her arguments with the sanction of the words of Jesus, "Suffer little
children to come unto me and forbid them not."

This controversy left me uneasy. Joining the church had seemed
to me a matter of course, somewhat like entering school. Now I was
impressed with its gravity and, in addition to the weight that a consideration of sin and salvation imposed upon me, I was disquieted by
the family rift. After the family conference I talked church and
religion a great deal with my grandmother. It was then she told me
about my father's conversion. He was standing in the dining room of
the St. James Hotel, looking out of a window, waiting for the doors
to be thrown open, when suddenly he cried out aloud. His waiters ran
to him, thinking he was ill. He told them that he had recognized himself as a sinner and had found God. He was then in his middle forties.

I was taken into the church as a full member on a Sunday morning.
The church was crowded in pews and aisles. The space around the
pulpit was filled with the church officers. As I stood at the altar rail
in the long line of those being received as communicants my childish
thoughts regarding religion vanished. The minister extended his hand
to each probationer and welcomed him into the bond of Christian
fellowship. When he reached me he paid special tribute to my tender

years. I was lifted up, transported. The vision I had recounted came back a reality. I felt myself, like young Samuel, the son of Hannah, dedicated to the service of God.

Naturally, I could not hold such an emotional height. My normal boyish instincts, alone, would have caused some reaction. As it happened, the inevitable ebb of that first fervor was aided by contributing factors. My grandmother, with the highest motives and in furtherance of her great ambition for me, carried me along to church with her on every possible occasion. On Sundays I went to Sunday school, stayed for the preaching service, returned to an afternoon service, and occasionally went to the night meeting. I did not have to be forced to attend these meetings. I liked to mingle with the boys and girls at Sunday school. It was gayer than day school because the work and discipline were not so hard, and being dressed in our best clothes injected a holiday spirit. And the lessons attracted me, too; illustrated, as they generally were, by highly colored charts. And such attraction as the lessons lacked was made up for in a wholly mysterious and incomprehensible way by the presence of little Mamie Gibbs in my class. Nor was attendance at the other Sunday meetings a hardship; for I did fairly realize that I was a member of the church and in a manner set apart from most of the boys and girls that I knew, and I did to the extent of my powers try to fulfill my religious obligations.

It was attendance at weekday meetings that began to surfeit me. On Tuesday nights I was taken to class meetings. Class meeting is, in a measure, the Methodist substitute for the Catholic confession. Each member of a class rises in turn and tells his class leader what his spiritual experiences have been during the week past; whether there has been a falling from or a growth in grace. The leader then gives words of comfort and counsel to each as his case may require—a very self-satisfying function. However, through the many, many weeks that I attended class meetings I heard very few who did not testify to a constant growth in grace. The chief difficulty of the leader, it seemed, was to find terms devout and at the same time sufficiently laudatory in which to make a fitting response at each of these progressive stages toward sainthood. My grandmother was my class leader, and I found this relationship exceedingly embarrassing. She knew me as intimately as did my mother; so any special emphasis on my growth in grace, probably, would not carry much conviction; on the other hand, I recoiled from exposing my little sins and failings before a group of virtual strangers. Other weekday meetings that I attended were the Friday afternoon prayer meetings for young people, the experience meetings, and the love feasts. The afternoon prayer meetings caused me some regret when I saw boys I knew playing ball or marbles or tops or shinny—at all of which I was adept—while I was on my way to church. But a greater infliction than the loss of an afternoon's play went with the prayer meetings, and the same infliction, still heavier, went with the experience meetings. In prayer meetings I was expected to lead aloud in prayer, and in experience meetings to rise before the whole congregation and give my testimony. In neither case was there any escape. At prayer meetings the leader would say, "We'll now be led in prayer by Brother James Johnson." And at experience meetings the minister, who was the leader, would say, "We haven't heard from Brother James Johnson yet. Rise, Brother, and be a witness for the Lord." In both cases I was confronted by the impossible; and not because I objected to praying or being a witness for the Lord, but simply because I was utterly incapable of making anything analogous to a public utterance.

Once Rosamond and I were both down for recitations at one of the Sunday school exhibitions—or concerts, as they were called. He got off his "Little Tommy Tucker" in fine style. I knew my recitation perfectly, but when the superintendent announced my name and I stood before the audience, I was as one struck dumb. I had no command over my vocal organs. The promptings of my mother from behind the curtained-off wings helped me not one whit. I remember that I had on a pair of short, linen pants and that I caught hold of the right leg at the knee and twisted it until I had formed a regular corkscrew. The terrible tension broke in a whimper, then tears; and I was led off in ignominy. My mother was disappointed; but my stupid showing so humiliated my grandmother that she then and there handed me a couple of resounding thwacks. My only successful appearance on the Sunday school stage was in a silent part; I recall that I made a hit as Joshua in a tableau, "Joshua Commanding the Sun to Stand Still." On my left arm I wore a cardboard shield covered with silver paper and in my right hand I carried a wooden spear, which I pointed after the manner of the illustration in our big Bible; but the words of Joshua I did not repeat. If anyone had predicted to me at that period that a good part of my life was to be spent on the platform as a public speaker, the future would have been filled with terror.

My distaste—that is the precise word—for the love feasts was a physical reaction. In this survival of a practice of the early Christians, long, narrow slices of bread with the crust cut away were distributed; then to the singing of hymns the members circulated among each other, shaking hands and exchanging pinches of bread that were to be eaten. This ceremony constituted a symbol of brotherly love. The pinch of bread came from some sweaty fingers a clammy lump of none-too-white dough, and I found that whatever impulse toward brotherly love that rose in my heart was routed by the revolt in my stomach against actual participation in the feast. I had also to overcome a reaction that was similar, though less in degree, at the communion service, that most barbarously insanitary practice—though at that time I did not know the term "insanitary" or its meaning. The sacrament raised many persons to a high emotional pitch and there was much weeping and slobbering into the cup from which all had to drink. But the taste of the wine—not grape juice in those days—afforded a recompense that the lumps of damp dough did not. I got a satisfaction from learning later that on these last two points my mother wasn't a very good Methodist either.

These combined factors at length produced reluctance, doubt, rebellion. I began to ask myself questions that frightened me. I groped within the narrow boundaries of my own knowledge and experience and between the covers of the Bible for answers, because I did not know to whom I could turn. I might, it seems, have turned to my father but I did not; and it was just as well, for a later incident showed that he would not have given me any real help. I was alone with my questionings and doubts, questionings and doubts that went deeper than mere recalcitrance; and alone I had to fight my way out. At fourteen I was skeptical. By the time I reached my Freshman year at Atlanta University I had avowed myself an agnostic. It can be imagined what an unholy distinction this position brought me in a missionary-founded school, in which playing a game of cards and smoking a cigarette were grave offenses. I now recall with some amusement how my agnostic reasonings left most of my fellow students aghast—there was only one other student in Atlanta University at that time who confessed similar views. Sometimes one or two of the more zealous ones would combat me; but I was well grounded in the arguments of Paine and Ingersoll, and was not an easy opponent. Efforts at reconverting me were futile. . . . I had been through all that. Certainly, the best retort the proselytizers might have made, but did not, was that I had never been converted. These debates usually ended with resolves to pray for God to save my soul from hell.

I examine my mind and heart to find out what has come to me from this early religious experience, this swing from almost the one extreme to almost the other. In that swing through the arc, rapidly forth and gradually back, I came to that conception of religion and that philosophy of life that are now my guide-posts, and I feel that if my experience had been otherwise I might not have come to an adjustment as nearly in emotional and intellectual balance as that which I have reached. And, too, because of that experience I became familiar with the Bible. I read it constantly; first to answer my doubts, then to confirm them, and, finally, with an increasing realization that, all in all, the King James Version is the greatest book in the world.

IV

MY RELIGIOUS experience preceded any experiences of race. Neither my father nor mother had taught me directly anything about race. Naturally, I gained some impressions and picked up some information. Many things I would have learned much sooner had I not been restricted in play. My vague, early impressions constituted what might be called an unconscious race-superiority complex. All the most interesting things that came under my observation were being done by colored men. They drove the horse and mule teams, they built the houses, they laid the bricks, they painted the buildings and fences, they loaded and unloaded the ships. When I was a child, I did not know that there existed such a thing as a white carpenter or bricklayer or painter or plasterer or tinner. The thought that white men might be able to load and unload the heavy drays or the big ships was too far removed from everyday life to enter my mind. There were yet some years for me to live before I would feel the brutal impact of race and learn how race prejudice permeated the whole American social organism.

At first, my brother was my only playmate. We had many ways of amusing ourselves, some of them our own inventions. We, of course, dug in the sand; and, according to the hygienic theories of the time, that did us lots of good. One of the first things Northern tourists were supposed to do was to strip the children and put them out in the sand. We used to sit on the floor with our legs outspread and roll a ball between us the length of the hallway of the house. On days when torrential semi-tropical showers came down, we liked to crawl under the chairs on the front piazza in which our mother or grandmother or "Bar" sat, and pull their skirts around as far as they would go—in those days they went pretty far. We sat in our "tents" very quiet, listening to the falling rain and feeling content and secure. On days when wind-pushed clouds rolled in ever-changing forms across the sky, we had exciting times watching for pictures. Like all normal children, we were not afraid to handle insects and bugs; we caught doodle-bugs; June-bugs we kept captive on pieces of thread in order to have them go humming round and round our heads; of big grasshoppers we sought to make "horses," trying to train them to pull little loads. As we grew older we learned to play tops and marbles.

The first outside playmates I can recollect were two white boys, brothers, both of them older than I. I can't recall their names or where they lived, but I know they did for a while come from somewhere over to our yard to play. One day they were playing with me on our front steps; it must have been a few days after Christmas, for I had a new drum, my first. The bigger brother persuaded me to let him cut open the head of the drum so as to see where the sound came from. After his successful operation the only sounds made came from me. My mother rushed out and drove both boys away with a strong request to stay away. Those two playmates vanished from my life completely, but the incident remained in my mind. It was a low, mean trick; however, I am glad I remembered it.

As often as I got the chance I played in the street with the children of the neighborhood. They were the Morrisons, who lived diagonally across and whose father was a carpenter and often got pretty drunk; Beck and Carrie Wright, who lived next door to Mr. Cole; and Camilla Sherman, a pretty, saucy-looking little brown girl, who lived just above the Wrights. The games we played oftenest were hide-and-seek and prisoner's base. In the house on the lot adjoining us on the north lived the two little Ross girls, who looked white but were not. They went by the lovely pet names of "Sing" and "Babe." Sometimes my brother and I went over to their yard to play and sometimes they came over to ours. But the playmates that had our mother's unqualified approval lived at a considerable distance. We used to go across town to play with Alvin and Mamie Gibbs, whose father was steward on one of the steamboats that then plied the St. Johns River; with Sam and Charlie Grant, sons of the pastor of Ebenezer Church; and with Carrie, Fred, and "Trixie" (a boy) Onley, whose father was a contractor and builder. The houses of these playmates were very much like our own; that of the Onleys was, perhaps, a bit more pretentious. Our visits were regularly returned. The visit that for a long time interested me most was the one to the Gibbses. Mrs. Gibbs often invited us to dinner, and she generally gave us gumbo. Do not for an instant think it was the watery, tasteless concoction that goes by the same name in Northern hotels and restaurants. Mrs. Gibbs was a native of Charleston, South Carolina, and knew how to cook Charlestonian gumbo. Into the big pot went not only okra and water and salt and pepper, but at the proper intervals bits of chicken; ham first fried then cut into small squares; whole shrimps; crab meat, some of it left in pieces of the shell; onions and tomatoes; thyme and other savory herbs; the whole allowed to simmer until it reached an almost viscous consistency; then served in a deep plate over rice cooked as white and dry as it is cooked by the Chinese. This gumbo, a dish for—reference to the epicure and the *vrai gourmet* are not in place—this more than a savory dish—the dish irresistible—the most soul-satisfying of all the dishes that Negro cookery has given the South. Moreover, there was the subtle attraction of Mamie, and Alvin's ownership of a velocipede. After dinner we used to take the velocipede down to the St. James, where there was the best continuous sidewalk in town, and ride round and round the block. There were other houses that we visited, but not quite so regularly. But it was at school, when I was about eight years old, that I formed my closest boyhood friendship. D—— and I were unlike each other in more ways than one, yet we instantly became chums and mutual confidants—a relationship that was to run through boyhood, youth, and early manhood, and strangely to influence, cross, and interact upon both our lives.

Among this latter set of children, made up from a dozen or so families, birthday parties and parties in celebration of nothing in particular were frequently given. They were held in the afternoons, and we always had lemonade and cake and candies, sometimes ice cream; and we always played kissing games. I liked these kissing games, and didn't like them. There were always one or two girls that I knew I would prefer to kiss, but when I got into the ring I stood shamefaced; I did not find it easy to fly to the east and the west and to the very one that I loved best. I simply could not expose my delicate desires to the crowd; so, usually, I diffidently kissed some other girl in order to get out of the ring as quickly as possible. I frequently got out of the game altogether, watching with envy and admiration those who played with assurance, I might say effrontery. My prowess as a ring player was on a par with my ability as a public speaker; as a result, I went away from many a party filled with haunting regrets.

But it was not all play; I had certain tasks to do, and when my brother grew large enough he shared them with me. I raked the yard, cleaned the steel table knives by working them up and down in the sand and giving them a very bright polish. I cleaned, filled, and trimmed the lamps. Later Rosamond and I were assigned the job of washing and drying the dishes, a job we never stopped hating. Many of the children in the neighborhood performed a task that never fell to us because a supply of matches was always kept at our house. . . . Every morning they could be seen carrying a coal of fire between two sticks, blowing on it to keep it alive as they ran home. They had been sent to "borrow a piece of fire."

At school I learned the real boys' games, and played them with some pretty rough boys. I judge that Stanton, with respect to rough boys, held its own with any school in the country. I am glad, however, that the situation was such that my mother could not with good grace take me out and send me to a softer school. I learned in those school days democracy as it is practiced in the world of boys, and there it is practiced without hypocrisy and cant. In the world of boys it is always the frank and sometimes the brutal thing that democracy needs must be. This experience I count one of the most vital in the course of my education. Stanton School, so named after Lincoln's Secretary of War, was built shortly after Emancipation by the Freedmen's Bureau, I think, and later turned over to the county as a public school. The original structure (the one now standing is the fourth) was a large, two-story, frame building, extremely well built, that occupied, with the grounds, an entire city block, and was surrounded by a high fence. A little more than half of the grounds was on the "boys' side," but a strip of the boys' playground was taken up by a garden cultivated by the janitor, and woe to those who for a lost ball invaded the demesne of this old ogre. The first principal and most of the teachers were white. When I began as a pupil there were still several white women among the teachers, but the staff, including the principal, was practically all colored. The principal was James C. Waters, a well-educated man and an eloquent speaker. He was a brown-skinned man; he wore a cropped mustache and had what I thought of as fierce eyes. He was, I judge, a youngish man, but among themselves the boys called him "Old J.C.," and "Old J.C." was a terror to the toughest boys at Stanton. At recess, like a stalking Nemesis, he walked about on the boys' side with a long cane that he brought into action with lightning rapidity. I regarded him with awe, and could not have imagined a worse stroke of fate than to be called up before him. I never presumed on any immunity because my mother was one of the teachers; in fact, I had a feeling that with J.C. this would have aggravated the seriousness of my case.

School began with chapel exercises. All the pupils marched by classes in single file into the chapel, where devotions were held for twenty or thirty minutes. The chapel was an airy room that seated five or six hundred pupils. Running entirely across the farther end was a platform on which were a desk, a row of chairs, and a fine square piano, the latter a gift from a piano manufacturer who had visited the school. I have an uncertain recollection that on the walls there were framed pictures of Lincoln and several other important figures on the Union side in the Civil War. When chapel exercises began, the gates were locked, and the tardy scholars were kept in the street until they were over. J.C. would then go down to the lower hall with a strap or ruler in his hand and greet the late comers as they passed him one by one giving excuses that were seldom accepted. At recess time we scurried out to play, and when it was over we marched back in strict order. There was a row of young oaks planted in a straight line; when the bell rang each class formed at its tree. Always there was a rush to be the first at the tree, and so head the line. The ambition to gain and hold this honor caused a good deal of pushing and scuffling and even fisticuffs that often brought J.C.'s long cane into action. It was, of course, infinitely far from my knowledge that J.C. was making a set of impressions on my mind against the time when I should stand in his place as the head of Stanton; impressions that would come back fresh and constrain me either to follow or avoid his example.

I never had any serious business with him; I was a small boy, and, before I was big enough to get into any scrapes that would bring down on me the sort of punishment then commonly meted out in public schools, there was another and milder principal at Stanton. I really look back with complacency—though that is a quality I positively dislike—upon my behavior as a boy in public school. I know I was slyly mischievous, but I stayed out of ugly, dishonorable things. I had the minimum number of fights that a boy in public school must have if he is to retain the respect of his fellows and his self-respect; but there is nothing ugly or dishonorable about that. I regret only that none of these fights can I now recollect as material for this record. I can see that I should have had at least one gallant, memorable battle, with Victory flitting from one side to the other before she finally perched upon my shoulder.

The games I learned to play at school were: marbles, tops, shinny, and baseball. Baseball was my game; the one in which I developed more than ordinary expertness. I was well adapted to the game physically, being slight of figure but muscular. And I not only practiced steadily but studied assiduously. I worked to master what is now known as "inside" baseball. I read regularly a weekly publication called *Sporting Life*, which was devoted chiefly to baseball, so I was familiar with the names and records of all the noted professional players. My favorite club was the old Detroits, and my particular heroes of the diamond were Fred Dunlap and Dan Brouthers, its famous second baseman and first baseman. Before I left Stanton to go to Atlanta University, one of the pitchers on the "Cuban Giants," the crack Negro professional team of New York, imparted to me the secrets of the art of curve pitching. (The Cuban Giants were originally organized from among the waiters at the Ponce de Leon Hotel in St. Augustine. They played professional ball in the North in the summer but for a number of seasons they worked in winter in the St. Augustine hotels and played ball, principally for the entertainment of the guests.) Under my instructor, who had taken a liking to me because he thought I showed the makings of a real player, I gained control of a wide out-curve, a sharp in-shoot, a slow and tantalizing "drop" and a deceptive "rise." I was at the time the only local colored boy who could do the trick. I practiced by the hour with my friend Sam Grant as catcher. We were the battery of our nine, "The Domestics" (why we chose this name I cannot tell), a club made up of boys ranging from fourteen to sixteen years of age. Our fame as a battery began to spread.

My first taste of athletic glory came when Sam and I were called on to serve as the battery for "The Roman Cities" (I am more puzzled by the significance of this name than by that of the club to which I belonged), the leading colored club of Jacksonville and, thereby, the best club in the whole city, in a big game with a formidable team from Savannah. The Roman Cities was a first-rate club. The chief strength of the team was Bill Broad, so nicknamed because of the abnormal breadth of his face. Bill Broad was a wonderful outfielder and, I think, the best natural batter I have ever seen. In either capacity his most strenuous exertions always appeared to be effortless. There were other good players on The Roman Cities, but the team was a little apprehensive over the impending game, and decided to take a chance on strengthening their offensive with my style of pitching, which they had watched. They tried to fit Sam and me out in the blue and red uniforms of the club, but those were all too large; so we played in the white flannel suits, white caps and black stockings of our own club.

The crowd was big and vociferous. It was made up of both whites and blacks. (A good Negro team was then as great a drawing card for whites in the South as one is now for whites in the North.) The white people of Jacksonville were ardent boosters for The Roman Cities, especially when the club played against a team from a Georgia town. For this game a good many shops were closed, and street cars and hacks went out to the grounds loaded beyond capacity. When the visiting nine took the field, I glued my eyes on the opposing pitcher. He was a tall, slender fellow and a fine exponent of the classic style of pitching. He stood holding the ball in front of him in both hands while he intently studied the batter. Then shifting his entire weight to the right foot, he slowly twirled his body round to the right until he almost faced second base, his left foot rising from the ground as his body turned; then back again he twirled with accelerating speed. At the same time his right arm swung back, under, upward, forward and under, describing an almost complete figure 8. He turned swiftly. His left foot came down and dug into the earth, holding the momentum of his body in check, while the right rose into the air, and the ball shot out, projected by every ounce of his weight and energy. The motion began in a gentle sweeping curve and culminated in a pose, held for an instant, of tense power. It was an exhibition of the perfection of masculine grace. Beautiful pitching like that is among the lost arts.

This pitcher's strategy lay in a ball of blinding speed, change of pace, and the ability to trim the corners of the plate. I guessed at once that Sam and I would make a poor showing at the bat; and I guessed right. But we counterbalanced all that. When I ran out to go into the box for the home team, there was every reason for me to feel nervous, but I didn't. No medicine man ever appeared before the tribe with more confidence in his magic than I had in mine when I faced the crowd. As I stooped and picked up a handful of dirt to rub into the cover of the ball to roughen it somewhat, and glanced at the hulking young giant who came to bat, if I had the presumption to draw an analogy between myself and little David choosing his five smooth stones from the brook, I ought, perhaps, to be pardoned. But the analogy was not so far-fetched, at that; David used long-range artillery against a short sword, and I had up my sleeve what was practically a magic power, the power to make the ball suddenly change its course and dart out of the path of the on-coming bat. The advantage, over those to whom it was new, was so great as to amount to unfairness. Yet it was not apparent enough to prevent my being greeted by a chorus of groans and yells as well as applause and cheers.

My delivery was, necessarily, quite different from that of my opponent. It was overhand, rapid, even jerky, and ended with the quick snap of the wrist required to produce the curve. I started with the use of a wide out-curve aimed at the plate, and the break timed so as to tempt the batter to fan the air; varying it by aiming straight at the batter so that the break was over the plate, my purpose being to cause the batter to duck and have a strike called. The coaches finally solved this, and cautioned the batters, "When you see it coming for the plate, don't hit at it. Wait till you see it coming at you." Of course, I immediately began working in a straight ball, an in-shoot, and the drop; and the mystery deepened. As the game went on it assumed a humorous aspect. As many spectators as could do so crowded behind the catcher to watch the vagaries of the ball, and yells of derision greeted bewildered batters, especially when they lunged at the elusive, wide-breaking out-curves. The Roman Cities won the game by a one-sided score. I struck out sixteen men and held the others down to ineffectiveness. My reward was a pretty full cup of the sensation of being a popular hero.

One of the most interested spectators at the game was a man named Haines Spearing. He was a colored sport and said to be the best-dressed man in Jacksonville. He loudly declared that the whole thing was a hoax, a physical impossibility, merely an optical illusion—or words to that effect—and offered to bet that it could not be demonstrated. I couldn't cover his bet, but offered to give him a demonstration free of any risk on his part. I did what I had often done in practice and what I was confident I could do ninety-five times out of a hundred. A group followed us to where two trees stood ten or twelve feet apart. I took my stand in line with the trees and about fifty feet away. I stepped a couple of feet to the left and threw the ball so that it passed to the right of the first tree, between the two, and out to the left of the second. Q.E.D.

V

BEFORE the happenings just related—to be more precise, when I was about five years old—I made a memorable trip—"the trip to Nassau." I say "memorable" not because it was memorable for me but because it became memorable as a family tradition. Indeed, I remember very little about it. The trip over was made in a little two-masted schooner named the *Ida Smith*. I have a dim recollection of being on the water in a boat, and very uncomfortable. Less faintly comes back a sense of being suffocated in the place where I slept and a resurgence of the sickening odor of bilge water. The stay in Nassau was only a few months, but the trip back is a good deal clearer. The ship was bigger and I was happier. The captain, a colored man, was a very nice man and devoted some attention to me. I have a pretty clear recollection, too, of strange-looking women in Nassau coming by the house where we lived with trays or baskets on their heads loaded with mangoes, guavas, pineapples, pomegranates, sapodillas, sour-sops, tamarinds, and other tropical fruits, crying out their wares in words I couldn't understand beyond knowing that they meant things very good to eat. I retain a faint picture of streets dazzlingly white under the sun and ghostly pale under the moon. Other memory films are blurred and faded. Only one incident stands out: It was a bright morning. I was all dressed up. I was cautioned dozens of times not to soil my clothes by eating sticky, staining fruit. A very high wagon pulled up at the door. I could not imagine a higher one. It had four wheels and was drawn by two horses. My mother and grandmother and, seemingly, a lot of other people got into the wagon. They had to get in by stepping up on a chair. Baskets of food were also loaded in. We were going to visit the African Village, where a remnant of former slaves lived in primitive fashion under their own chief. The ride was for me a great adventure. When we got to the village, I went around with my elders looking at curious people, peeping into their huts, seeing them dance under a large, hut-like pavilion in the center of the village to the beating of drums—drums of many sizes and sounds, drums, drums, drums.

While I was in Nassau I must have many times seen Stephen Dillet, son of my grandfather, and himself a man of prominence, but I brought away no clear image of him. When we were leaving, he made me a present of a cricket bat, but I cannot recall his presenting me with it. When I got back home I found it among my possessions, and was told that it had been given to me by my Uncle Stephen. And it was in this way that I learned most of what I know about the trip to Nassau—by being told. In later years my wife and my brother's wife heard those incidents of the trip that concerned their respective husbands so often that they reached the point where they held up both hands whenever the subject was even indirectly introduced.

My cricket bat was the only tangible and substantial evidence I had of ever having been to Nassau. It was my convincing proof to all the boys who heard my second-hand versions of the adventures of the voyage; for not in all Jacksonville was there another bat like it. True, it was also proof that my uncle knew absolutely nothing about American athletic games; so the bat never rose to the punctilious use for which it was designed. Finally, it suffered the indignity of being worn out by Big Bill Broad in batting flies in our street for a crowd of youngsters.

It was during the visit to Nassau that I became vaguely aware of having a sister. My sister, Marie Louise, died before I was born. When my brother was about to be born, my mother was hoping for a girl, and picked out for her name, Rosamond. When it turned out not to be that kind of child, she made the best of the situation by using the name, anyhow, and coupling it with a sex-indicating "John." But Rosamond is the name by which my brother was always called, and it caused him a good deal of embarrassment before he got it established, and even after.

My mother, however, was not to be outdone, so she adopted a daughter, not a baby, but a girl in her teens. Her name was Agnes Marion Edwards. This adopted daughter was one of the party that made the trip to Nassau, and she became one of the chief repositories of the lore relating to that epochal event. She was very gentle and capable of unselfish devotion to others that I have seen equaled in. no one else. As I grew up I knew her and loved her as a sister.

When I was, perhaps, ten years old a strange being came to Jacksonville, the first colored doctor. He practiced there a number of years and made a success; but he had a hard, up-hill fight. Few were the colored people at that time who had the faith to believe that one of their own number knew how to make those cabalistic marks on a piece of paper that would bring from the drugstore something to stand between them and death. Dr. Darnes made himself a big chum to Rosamond and me, and we liked him tremendously. He constantly brought us some of the odds and ends so much prized by boys. He once gave us fifty cents apiece for learning the deaf and dumb alphabet within a given time. I suppose in doing that he merely wanted us to feel that we had done something to earn the money; for I couldn't see even then what practical benefit this knowledge would be to us. We did, however, for a while get some amusement out of trying to communicate with each other in this sign language. But, best of all, Dr. Darnes was an enthusiastic fisherman, and he opened up a new world of fun and sport by teaching us how to fish.

During my first decade two events from the big outside world made an impression on me; and that outside world was still a shadowy land. The most momentous decade in the history of the nation was the one preceding my birth, but, as yet, it had no real significance for me. I had heard talk about the Civil War from men who had seen it. I remember well a remnant in Jacksonville of a Negro regiment of the Union Army, which during Reconstruction had formed a part of the Florida militia. Some of these men were friends of my father, and it was from them that I heard the talk. All the boys of my age knew something about "The War," and there was still plenty of evidence around Jacksonville that there had been a war. Any boy, by searching round a little, could make a collection of rusty bayonets, old belts, brass buttons, and the like; and nearly every boy had such a collection. The bayonets and buttons, polished bright, were highly prized. But I doubt that any of us had an idea of the meaning of the War. As for myself, my interest centered in tales about the fighting, and did not extend to what the fighting was about. But there were two names connected with the war that we knew well: Abraham Lincoln and General Grant. At that time Grant was for me the greater hero. He was President when I was born, so his name was sounded in my young ears a good many times. One of the clearest-cut of my early memories is of a very big colored man on a night of some excitement passing our house and yelling lustily, madly, truculently (he may have been drunk): "Hurrah for General Grant! Hurrah for General Grant!" In addition, through the tales of ex-soldiers I had caught some of the glamour of Grant's great military fame. And the news flashed and spread through the town that General Grant was coming to Jacksonville.

I was with my parents in the crowd that met him at the station. This visit must have taken place early in the year 1877. The crowd at the station was dense and mixed, white and black. There was no reason why the General should have been popular with the native whites; probably they were just curious to see the man. We waited, it seemed to me, for hours. Finally, the sound of the approaching train was heard; then the wood-burning locomotive, pouring a thick stream of black smoke from its wide-mouthed funnel and with a loud-clanging bell, hove into sight and drew alongside the dingy, shedless station. With hurrahs and yells the crowd swayed and bulged over the line that the police and militia were trying to maintain. Excitement and panicky fear struggled in me for the mastery; and I clutched my mother's hand more tightly.

The General with his party alighted and was standing in the open space receiving introductions of those in charge of his reception, when through the line burst an old harridan, well known to everybody in the town. She lived out our way, and there was not a child in that section who did not fear her violent tongue. Her real name was, I guess, Tucker; and I guess, too, that she was not so very old, but everybody called her "Old Dan Tucker." She was a woman brown in color, not at all bad-looking, and very active. On this day she was dressed in new clothes, but wore them in her usual manner: her long, wide calico skirt was tucked up about her waist so that it reached only a little below her knees; and a brand-new, bright red bandanna was wound round her head. In her hands she carried a big bunch of flowers. Before anyone could anticipate her intention, she darted across the open space straight for General Grant, threw her arms around his neck, gave him a resounding kiss on the cheek, then kneeling down presented him with her bunch of flowers. The crowd was too much astonished for expression. Some people, especially some of the colored people, were scandalized by "Old Dan's" action. What General Grant thought about it, no one ever found out.

Old Dan Tucker's *coup de théâtre* strengthened me in a much less daring project which I had been revolving in my own mind for several days. All the colored school and Sunday school children had been organized to pass in review before the General, and there were hundreds in line, with teachers, principals, and superintendents. He took his stand on the hotel veranda, and we were marched up the steps at one end, along and down and off at the other end. Along the veranda the crowd moved slowly. As we approached the reviewing group it took all that I could do to make my courage stick. When I reached the point where the General stood I timidly put out my hand; he took it in his for an instant, and I passed on. But it was a proud instant; I had carried out my project; I had shaken hands with General Grant.

The second of these two outside world events was the assassination of President Garfield. I was now four years older, old enough to take an interest in newspapers, and I kept up with the President's condition until he died. I thought it was a terrible thing to have shot down the President of the United States. I think this sentiment was intensified by talk that I heard among the colored people, talk consisting of dark hints about a deep plot on the part of the ex-Confederates to capture the government. On the day that Garfield was buried, funeral exercises were held in Jacksonville. Those who took part in the program and other prominent citizens were seated on the veranda of the hotel. The crowd packed the street in front and extended back into St. James Park. I think the greater part of the crowd was made up of Negroes. The eloquence of the several orations that were pronounced left little impression on me, but the prayer that opened the exercises, because of its length, I remembered for years. This prayer was delivered by the Reverend D. W. Culp. Mr. Culp was a slender young man of medium height, and was pure black. He was well educated, a graduate of Biddle University in North Carolina and of the theological seminary of Princeton. He had recently come to Jacksonville and was the pastor of the local colored Presbyterian Church, and had just been appointed as the new principal of Stanton School. The exercises were, naturally, in the hands of Federal officeholders, and Mr. Culp was chosen, representing the Negroes, to make the opening prayer, the which he did within the course of some thirty-five or forty minutes. He stammered terribly, but the length of this particular prayer could not be charged to the impediment in his speech. It was due rather, I suspect, to his realization that he had an opportunity to impress himself upon certain leading citizens of Jacksonville as well as upon the Lord. I have heard some queer prayers but never any one prayer in which so wide a range of topics was introduced. Many times I have been forced to conclude that the most absurd utterances that pass human lips are some of the prayers that are, ostensibly, addressed to God. Those officious, pompous prayers that summarize affairs on this terrestrial globe and offer Him specific directions for working out the difficulties and carrying on. If such prayers do reach God, and He can listen to them, He possesses an attribute no one ever thinks of ascribing to Him—an infinite sense of humor.

The Negro citizens of Jacksonville took great pride in the part they played in both of the ceremonies I have referred to. They were especially pleased with the brave showing they made before General Grant. I suppose, if the truth were known, the taciturn Grant was greatly bored by the performances of both whites and blacks. It occurs to me that the Negro citizens of Jacksonville would not at the present time be accorded an equivalent degree of recognition and participation in ceremonies or celebrations of this kind. And that comment would apply, I think, to Southern communities generally. Mr. Will Alexander of Atlanta holds that this shift in attitude is principally due to the rise to power of the poor whites, between whom and the Negro there is an old antagonism based on the differences in their actual economic status under the slave system, an antagonism that then bore more heavily upon the poor whites than upon the blacks. Of course, the settling down from the temporary heights of Reconstruction must be taken into account, but I feel that Mr. Alexander is, in the main, right. Long after the close of the Reconstruction period Jacksonville was known far and wide as a good town for Negroes. When I was growing up, most of the city policemen were Negroes; several members of the city council were Negroes; one or two justices of the peace were Negroes. When a paid fire department was established, one station was manned by Negroes. I was in my teens when the city government was reorganized and Joseph E. Lee, a Negro and a very able man and astute politician, was made Judge of the Municipal Court. Many of the best stalls in the city market were owned and operated by Negroes; Davis and Robinson, a firm of Negro commission merchants, were land stewards for the Clyde Steamship Company; and there was no such thing as a white-owned barber shop. I know that there was a direct relation between that state of affairs and the fact that Jacksonville was controlled by certain aristocratic families, families like the L'Engles, Hartridges, and Daniels's, who were sensitive to the code, *noblesse oblige*. The aristocratic families have lost control and the old conditions have been changed. Jacksonville is today a one hundred per cent Cracker town, and each time I have been back there I have marked greater and greater changes.

In this is epitomized one of the paradoxes of American democracy that the Negro has to wrestle with. We are told and we tell ourselves that as a race we belong to the proletariat and that our economic and political salvation lies in joining hands with our white fellow workers. Notwithstanding, it is true that the black worker finds getting into most of the white labor unions no easier than getting an invitation to a white bourgeois dinner party.

There is another fact that bears interestingly on Mr. Alexander's theory, perhaps to confirm it further, a fact that must strike every observant person who goes through the deep rural South: Among the white people of those regions, people who have not yet tasted social or political power nor yet possessed the rewards of industrialism or come within its brutal field of competition, active antagonism against the Negro is lowest; so low indeed, it would probably die out if it were not continuously and furiously stirred by the working classes and the politicians (the social factor is powerful and intransigent, but at this level is in abeyance); by the working classes, determined to hold certain grades of work for white men only, and by the politicians, bent on preserving their rotten oligarchy by keeping alive the sole political issue upon which the "Solid South" rests. An important part is played also by those intellectuals who write to uphold the present status, many of whom are, I know, conscious that the system is unjust and uncivilized but are too timid to oppose or even question it. Their timidity often sinks to pusillanimity.

VI

IN 1884, when I was between twelve and thirteen years old, my grandmother went to New York and took me with her. We made the trip by sea. She went to visit her sister, Sarah, who lived on what was then South Second Street in Williamsburg, Brooklyn. My grandaunt Sarah was older than my grandmother. She was quite stout and moved round with difficulty. She was also much lighter in complexion than my grandmother, but her features were slightly heavier. Still, when she smiled she showed that she had once been very pretty. Dimples came into her cheek and her mouth became winsome. My mother looked a great deal more like her aunt than she did like her own mother. The difference between the two sisters in temperament and disposition was even greater than it was in physical appearance. Aunt Sarah was jolly and easy-going. She was nominally a member of the Episcopal Church, but I am sure she did not contemplate the everlasting fate of her soul with any particular anxiety. She loved her mug of beer and was always willing to give me a generous taste. My grandmother, who was one of the leaders of the Band of Hope, a temperance crusading society to which I belonged, objected to this strenuously; and her objections led one day to a pretty hot row between the sisters.

Aunt Sarah's husband was named William C. H. Curtis. He was a small, rather wizened, light brown man. He had a grave face that was curiously lighted by his gray eyes. His head was absolutely bald on the whole top, but the hair grew thick and bushy low on the sides and in the back. He wore a beard of medium length but scanty. He moved about the house almost stealthily in slippers, and talked so little that everyone listened whenever he did speak. Uncle William was a journeyman jeweler, but he had long given up his trade to become a manufacturer of regalia for secret societies. He carried on his business at home, and a good part of each day he spent at a big table cutting out badges and aprons and banners from bright-colored silks. My aunt and two hired women sat and stitched on the gold and silver braid and fringe and tassels and the various emblems and insignia. It must have been a profitable business, for Aframerica did then and does now constitute a good market for these commodities. At any rate, he had been able to purchase the house in which he lived, a two-story and basement brick building with a brownstone stoop. This house seemed to me palatial, and I regarded my uncle as a very rich man. I think he was in a way fond of me, but he never deviated from the even tenor of his manner to demonstrate whatever affection he may have had. However, he did give me a gold ring which he himself had made.

Moreover, he showed that he liked to take me with him when he went over to New York to shop for materials for his business; and that trip was always a great treat to me. We would go to Broadway in Williamsburg and take the ferry to Grand Street in New York. I loved the ferryboats—the rushing crowds, the stamping teams and yelling teamsters, the tooting whistles, the rattling windlasses and clanging chains when we left and entered the slip. I loved to stand on the forward end to watch the busy-body tugs; they amused me tremendously and made me think of what, in Jacksonville, we called "biggity" boys. But above all, I enjoyed the sensation of approaching the great city.

It would not have taken a psychologist to understand that I was born to be a New Yorker. In fact, I was partly a New Yorker already. Even then I had a dual sense of home. From the time that I could distinguish the meaning of words I had been hearing about New York. My parents talked about the city much in the manner that exiles or emigrants talk about the homeland; and I had long thought of New York, as well as Jacksonville, as my home. But being born for a New

Yorker means being born, no matter where, with a love for cosmopolitanism; and one either is or is not. If, among other requirements for happiness, one needs neighbors; that is, feels that he must be on friendly terms with the people who live next door, and, in addition know all about them; if one must be able to talk across from front porches and chat over back fences; if one is possessed by a zeal to regulate the conduct of people who are neither neighbors nor friends—he is not born for a New Yorker.

When my uncle and I got off in New York we would take a horse car and go as far as Lord and Taylor's, then located in Grand Street. I had a lively time going through the big store while he bought his goods, some at one counter and some at another. When he had finished, we would go down to the Grand Street ferry and take the boat back to Williamsburg. I went to lots of other places in New York City, but my uncle never spent the time to take me. Yet, among the memories of all my goings about those of the excursions to Lord and Taylor's with him remain sharpest. I still love an old ferryboat because it is evocative of those days. I never board one and catch the smell from the deck planks redolent of horses that I do not recapture some of the sensations I experienced as a boy in crossing the East River and making the trip back and forth to Lord and Taylor's.

During my stay I learned to play all the New York sidewalk games; but, in comparison with the field games we played in Jacksonville, they seemed to me very childish. My playmates were for the greater part the white boys and girls who lived near on our side of the street and those across. The only colored playmates I had were a girl named Edith Matthews, who lived just around the corner, and two brothers by the name of Jackson, who lived on the same street four or five blocks away. When I went to the Jacksons, I frequently saw T. Thomas Fortune; he lived in the same house. I knew him well; he was a native of Florida and before he moved to New York was a frequent visitor at our house. My two playmates and I were sometimes in a room where he sat at a desk writing, covering sheet after sheet that he dropped on the floor, and all the while running his fingers through his long hair. He was writing his first book, *Black and White: Land, Labor, and Politics in the South*, an economic study of the race problem. We were usually playing parchesi on the floor, and when we annoyed him too much he made us scamper. But we stood in no awe of him; we had no conception of how great a man he was, though not yet thirty, and of course no thought of how much greater a man he was to become.

I did have another colored playmate, my aunt. She never felt that the day was properly ended unless she and I had our round of dominoes. She played a good game, and, at the same time, was not above doing a little cheating. She always crooned softly to herself when the game was going well for her. It distressed her so much to lose that I didn't very much enjoy winning. I got more fun out of her exuberant pleasure in beating me, even when she had cheated a bit. After the domino game there was one more thing to be done in which I had to join her. Every night she took one of Carter's Little Liver Pills—a product which gigantic advertising, then at its beginning in the United States, had literally injected into hundreds of thousands of American households—and every night during my stay in New York I took one too, whether I needed it or not.

My grandmother took me about with her a good deal visiting old friends she had known twenty or thirty or more years before. Most of the houses she visited were on Bleecker Street or Sullivan Street or Thompson Street or in the vicinity, then the principal Negro section of New York. None of her old friends or acquaintances interested me; and hardly ever did I meet anyone near my own age. I was bored terribly by long conversations about old times and people who had died or, perhaps, done something worse; and I disliked the generally stuffy rooms in which I had to sit while the talk went on. But I loved to go on these trips because we rode endless miles, it seemed, on the horse cars and I was constantly seeing new sights. I especially enjoyed riding on the Broadway stage coaches. Only one of these old friends of my grandmother stuck in my memory. She was a gray-haired woman and quite stout, and sat all the while in a large armchair; she may have been lame. Suddenly she produced a pair of scissors and called me over to clip her finger nails. I found this job exceedingly distasteful; and, furthermore, she was very particular about how the work should be done. If I had been a modern-reared child I should have told the old lady to her face that I didn't want to and wouldn't clip her hard old nails; but to a product of the system under which I was brought up such action was unthinkable. When I had finished, she gave me a nickel, which I considered pretty poor pay. On one trip we went to Central Park, and I had the belated joy of riding in a goat wagon. And I mixed pleasure with duty by going round with a notebook industriously taking down a long list of the monuments to great men—names, dates, and deeds. I cannot imagine that this was a self-imposed duty, for I innately rebel at cataloguing statistical details. I must have been following the admonishment of one of my teachers. Nor do I remember that the collected data were ever of any use to me. I think the time could have been better spent in the monkey house. With my grandmother I made the trip across and back over the Brooklyn Bridge. The great suspension bridges of New York are now commonplace; so the thrill of crossing Brooklyn Bridge when it was new cannot now be duplicated. But when I crossed, the echoes of the panic of the opening day, when the swaying of the great span under the tread of the crowd gave rise to the cry that the bridge was falling, had not quite died down; and I was far from feeling confident that it would not fall. Once we made a trip far up toward Harlem, a region then inhabited largely by squatters and goats.

But a good many of my happiest hours were passed in the house. In addition to watching the gorgeous paraphernalia for Masons, Odd Fellows, Good Samaritans, and various Sons and Daughters of this and that take form, partaking of surreptitious sips of beer with my aunt, and keeping up our domino playing and pill taking, I spent a lot of time reading. At home I had discovered a small bound volume of an old English periodical called *The Mirror*, which contained many things that interested me. But in my aunt's parlor I found perhaps a dozen volumes of a magazine (it may have been *The Waverly Magazine*) so large that the only way I could handle them was to lay them on the floor. These volumes were filled with illustrated serial stories, many of them Indian stories. Here was a mine of interest and excitement, and I worked it in long shifts; especially on rainy days. What a combination for contentment—a rainy day and a thirteen-year-old boy who loved to read stretched out on the floor with an inexhaustible supply of Indian stories! Sometimes I played the piano; at that age I played fairly well. One of the conditions on which I was given the trip was that I should keep up my piano lessons; so I studied once a week with a very good teacher with a French name that I cannot recall. During this stay in New York I formed a lasting affection for my grandaunt. While yet a boy I visited her twice again.

The following summer my mother visited Aunt Sarah and took my brother and my sister with her. I stayed at home with my grandmother, who had given up her cottage and moved to our house. She and I were practically alone, because my father had by this time gone into the ministry, and he spent most of his time in Fernandina, thirty miles away, where he was pastor of a large Baptist church. For a half-dozen years I had been able to boast to my brother that I had shaken hands with General Grant. When he got back home from New York, he could boast to me that he had seen General Grant's funeral. He related how they had gone up to Riverside Drive (then only one of the rocky frontiers of northern Manhattan) early in the morning with their lunch and camped there till the procession passed. He told me about the bands and the soldiers and the twenty-four colored men, each leading one of the black, black-plumed horses that drew the funeral car. I was compelled to admit that, between him and me, he had seen the best of General Grant.

But that was not the limit of our friendly rivalry. For several years I had been making a struggle, that grew more hopeless each day, to keep up with my brother in music. I played the guitar better than he; probably because he never exerted himself to learn that instrument. We considered the piano the greatest instrument, and my ambition was to maintain, at least, parity with him in piano playing. I finally gave over in the struggle and took up an instrument that did not attract him very much—the violin. But during the summer he was in New York my ambition was burning high. While he was away, I found a book entitled *Music and Some Highly Musical People*, a compilation of biographical sketches of a number of Negro musicians, including Blind Tom, The Black Swan, and others not so well known. In the back were various musical compositions by Negro composers. Among these compositions I found a piece, "Welcome to the Era," a stirring march, which I mastered after many hours of practice. At the first good opportunity I went to the piano and knocked the piece off for my brother. He at once wanted to know where I had got it; and I would not tell him. He searched through all the sheets of music and music books we had; naturally, not thinking to look in a book that appeared to be filled only with reading matter. I got keen joy out of the satisfaction that I had, at least, one piece that he couldn't beat me playing. However, my satisfaction lasted only until Rosamond let go the repertory of six or eight new pieces he had learned in New York, his star piece being *See-Saw*, a waltz song and the overwhelmingly popular hit of the year Eighteen Hundred and

Eighty-Five. I may say that *See-Saw* snuffed out any future as a pianist that I might have had.

But I had in store another surprise for my brother; one that he didn't get over so easily; nor, for that matter, did my mother and father and sister. The pastor of Ebenezer Church at the time was the Reverend Peter Swearingen. I was a regular attendant at church, more regular during this period than ever before—or since; and so I heard Mr. Swearingen preach every Sunday. I thought he was a very good preacher; but as much as his preaching I admired a pair of black broadcloth, "spring-bottom" trousers he wore. "Spring-bottom" trousers were extremely popular at that time. They were an adaptation of the style so long standard for sailors. As I think of it now, the style was not entirely in keeping with ministerial garb. Notwithstanding, these "spring-bottoms" appealed to me as the acme of elegance; so much so that I set my heart on having a pair. I was wearing short pants, but my grandmother approved the idea; pleased, no doubt, that I was at any rate following clerical example. That much settled, it became a question of money, for I had already gone to Trumpeller, the leading merchant tailor, and inquired about the cost and had been dazed to learn that to make the trousers, finished in the best style, would cost fourteen dollars. I could not think of suggesting such an amount to my grandmother for a pair of boy's pants. I had been earning fifty cents on Saturdays. My father had torn down the old house on the corner and built a shop, which he rented to a white man named Mott. This man ran a grocery store, and gave me fifty cents for helping around on his busiest day. It was a very easy problem in arithmetic for me to figure out that at this rate I should have to work more than half a year before I could earn enough to pay for the pants; so I decided to look for another job.

One very hot morning I stopped under one of the great oaks on Laura Street and watched the work on the foundation for a new house. The building was being put up by Hart and DeLyons, a firm of Negro contractors. Here was a chance for a job. Why not? I walked up to Mr. Hart, whom I knew, and asked him to give me a job. He smiled and asked, "Well, what can you do?" I answered seriously, "I'll do anything." He took it as a joke, and said to me, "All right, get a board and bring bricks to the masons." I went to work at that task. When noon came, one of the men gave me a bite to eat. and I finished up the afternoon. It was hard labor, but whenever the heat seemed about to force me to weaken, I had only to think of my "spring-bottoms" to summon renewed energy. When we knocked off, Mr. Hart said to me, "Come back tomorrow, if you want to."

When I got home I found my grandmother anxious over my long absence; I told her what I had done, and she agreed that getting a job and earning some money would be the best way in which I could spend the summer. We planned for my making time the next morning. I said I should have to carry lunch, and she offered to fix me a nice basket. I told her a basket would not do; that I had seen no workman with a basket; that they all carried pails. So the next morning I started to work with my tin pail. Mr. Hart was surprised to see me show up; of course, he knew nothing of the goad of desire that was driving me on. I carried bricks to the bricklayers until they began to work on scaffolds; then I was promoted with a raise of wages and made the driver of a horse and cart—another belated realization. As a brick carrier I was paid $2 a week, and as a driver of the cart I received $3. This seemed to me much more than a promotion; it was like being paid money for having a good time. Except for the fact that I wanted the pants, I should have been glad to drive the cart for nothing. I worked the whole summer and earned about $40.

Of course, I got my black broadcloth "spring-bottom" trousers. The fact that the only coats I had were little bobtail jackets didn't embarrass me. I had worn my pants several times before my mother returned; my grandmother said I looked nice in them. When my mother saw me, she said seriously that I looked funny; my sister smiled and said that I looked funny; my brother laughed and said that I looked funny; and my father roared. Well, four people out of one family couldn't be absolutely wrong.

My father occasionally took me and my brother over to Fernandina to stay with him for a few days at a time. Fernandina was then and still is a small town. At the time of which I am writing it had a population of a couple of thousand; and at the present time it has only about a thousand more. As a Floridian, I often wondered why Fernandina failed to become the metropolis of the State. It is one of the oldest settlements in Florida, going back to the days of the Spanish. It is situated on the Atlantic Ocean, thirty miles north and east of Jacksonville, and has a deep, commodious, natural harbor. Jacksonville, on the other hand, is eighteen or twenty miles from the mouth of the St. Johns River, and was for a long time shut off from deep-draft vessels by a shallow bar. Perhaps the railroads made Jacksonville. We liked going over to Fernandina. There was the trip on the train; and in the town the streets, nice and grassy with a hard, white center of crushed oyster shells, were fine to play in; and beyond the town, the wide, firm beach. In Fernandina we got our first salt-water fishing experience. When we talked with the Fernandina boys, we displayed that superiority that metropolitans always assume over rustics. We overwhelmed them with stories of the grandeur of Jacksonville. The business section of Fernandina comprised a scanty block; and when we told them that Bay Street in Jacksonville had eight solid blocks of stores on both sides of the street, they could hardly believe their ears. But everything in life is relative; we did the same thing to boys in Jacksonville with stories of New York.

After my mother returned from New York, my grandmother continued to make our house her home; so, with my father's absence, our number was the same. She immediately took charge of the kitchen. She was a good cook; so was my father; my mother was a good school-teacher. My father once gave my mother some lessons in cooking, and she essayed a pie for Sunday dinner. Our anticipations ran high. The interior of the pie was not bad, but getting to it was another matter. I thought I had played a clever practical joke when I went out and brought the ax in to the table. Anyhow, it was the only joke on herself, so far as I can remember, that my mother ever enjoyed. As long as she lived, I could make her laugh about it. My grandmother was especially skillful in the preparation of West Indian dishes: piquant fish dishes, chicken pilau, shrimp pilau, crab stew, crab and okra gumbo, poppin' John, and Johnny cake. She also knew how to cook the Southern delicacies. We talk a great deal about impressions made upon us in childhood that influence us through life, but we seldom recognize the importance of the tastes formed for the things we loved to eat. Whether I am eating in a humble home or an expensive restaurant, it is difficult for me to understand why there is not hominy for breakfast and rice for dinner—not the mushy, gruel-like messes some people make of these two staple foods, but hominy cooked stiff and rice cooked dry. Dry rice and a well-seasoned gravy make a satisfying dinner for me at any time.

The sensation of earning my first money was so pleasant that I was glad of the opportunity which came the next winter to get another job.

The Times-Union, the morning newspaper, sent to the principal of Stanton and asked him to recommend three or four boys to deliver papers to local subscribers. The wages were $2.50 a week. I had to leave home at four o'clock in the morning, because the papers came from the press flat, and each carrier had to fold his own before starting out on his route. I took Rosamond along with me for company and gave him the odd fifty cents. The majority of the carriers, a half-dozen or so, were white schoolboys. I formed a fast friendship with two of them, the Lund boys, that lasted a good many years. George was freckled and red-haired, and Gilbert was very handsome with his pale face and jet-black hair. Gilbert and I had a binding common interest in baseball. Their mother was one of the best musicians in Jacksonville. Later, Rosamond and I came to know her quite well. There was another one of the white boys I can't forget. His name was Bob Bailey. Bob was a cracker boy with a whimsical, pinched face. He chewed tobacco and swore like a sailor. I gradually perceived that his orbit was in many respects farther from that of the Lund boys than was mine. He was older than the rest of us and a sort of super-carrier; he taught me my route and had done the same for all the other boys. I admired Bob; he was so capable and seemed to be so wise. He was the unquestioned authority among us on newspaper work from the carriers' end of it. He could fold papers at lightning speed, and was always willing to help out the slower boys.

This work was new and enjoyable. The camaraderie at the office was different from the companionship at school. It involved a common purpose and a definite object; school could be closed a day or a week for a holiday or four months for vacation, but what sort of a morning would it be in Jacksonville if the *Times-Union* failed to appear! All of us caught a share of the spirit of being a part of "the greatest newspaper in Florida." The work did me good physically; the breakfasts I ate were sufficient for a longshoreman. On my route I used to meet a certain milkman regularly and give him a paper for a pint of milk that I drank from his measure. I used to make another "exchange," one with a hobo-looking individual that drove a street car on the newly built line which passed within a half-block of our house, whom I dubbed "Old Grizzly." The Jacksonville street cars of that period were tiny one-man affairs with a coin box at the front end; they ran on a narrow-gauge track, each car pulled by a pair of small mules. As I write these lines I grow curious about this man

I had half forgotten. It is strange that I have never before thought of him as a person. I try to recall him—a tall, broad-shouldered man with unkempt, reddish hair and beard, but a large, well-shaped head and a grave, intelligent face. When it was cold he wore a big, shabby, fuzzy overcoat; whence my nickname for him. His manner was taciturn, but he generally exchanged a pleasant word or two with me. He was always eager to get his copy of the paper, and whenever I missed him he was keenly disappointed. I rode with him many, many times; and only now it occurs to me to wonder who he had been and how he came to be what he was. To me he was only "Old Grizzly." Probably, to everybody else in Jacksonville he was a good deal less.

I worked at the *Times-Union* until I went away to school. I worked in several capacities. For a while I was office boy to the editor, Charles H. Jones, whom we all called "C.H." Later, Mr. Jones became editor of *The (New York) World*. Occasionally I held copy for proofreaders in the job office. When I left I was assistant in the mailing room, where the paper was wrapped and addressed to out-of-town subscribers and dealers. The world of the newspaper fascinated me, and I formed a new ambition.

My grandmother cherished the ambition for me to become a preacher. My father and mother never expressed a fixed ambition for me. The question of the child's future is a serious dilemma for Negro parents. Awaiting each colored boy and girl are cramping limitations and buttressed obstacles, in addition to those that must be met by youth in general; and this dilemma approaches suffering in proportion to the parents' knowledge of and the child's innocence of those conditions. Some parents up to the last moment strive to spare the child the bitter knowledge; the child of less sensitive parents is likely to have this knowledge driven in upon him from infancy. And no Negro parent can definitely say which is the wiser course, for either of them may lead to spiritual disaster for the child.

As I look back it appears that my parents must have followed a medium course. It seems to me that I acquired quite gradually the knowledge of the peculiar difficulties I should have to face; and it seems to me, too, that while I was acquiring that knowledge I never received from my parents a dash of cold water on any of my dreams. Once, I remember, a visiting preacher, Presiding Elder Robinson, put his hand on my head and pompously inquired, "Well, my boy, what are you going to be when you grow up?" And I replied in much the same tone, "I am going to be Governor of Florida." I was talking by the copybook. I was using the language of the high-minded young hero of the Sunday school romance, in whom it is set forth that the practice of the common virtues may lead to the Presidency of the United States; and, though I was not yet ten years old, I knew exactly that that was what I was doing. It is possible that my father and mother saw through me, but my pretentious proclamation met with no squelching.

Recollections of our fast-changing childhood ambitions ought to furnish amusement though they reveal nothing significant. The very earliest ambition that I can recall having was wanting to be the driver of a dray or any kind of a vehicle drawn by a horse or a mule. Holding the reins over these big beasts possessed a fascination for me that many of my later ambitions lacked. My next ambition was to be a drummer in a band. When I was quite small, the crack brass band of Jacksonville was the Union Cornet Band, a Negro band; in fact every good brass band in Florida at that time was a Negro band. I remember going to the state fair at Jacksonville and seeing a review of the state militia, all white. Every contingent in the review marched behind a black band, for the reason that there were no good white ones. The companies even from far-away Pensacola brought their own colored band. The Union Cornet Band had a wonderful drummer. He was Martin Dixon, a slim, good-looking black dandy, who had been a drummer boy in the Civil War. The boys in Jacksonville, black and white, boasted that when the band played for a funeral Martin could beat a continuous and unbroken roll on his muffled drum all the way from the church to the cemetery. I did not see how life could offer anything happier than marching behind the blaring brass beating a drum as Martin Dixon did and enjoying the admiration and envy of all the boys in town. I lost my ambition to be a drummer, but drums have never lost their tumultuous effect on me. Ambition then took me by the hand and pointed to the path that led to glory. I determined to be a soldier. But not a soldier like the men I knew who had been in the Civil War; I set my heart on going to West Point, and I talked the matter over seriously with my father. I was familiar with the case of Lemuel Livingston, who had been turned down when he reported at the Academy, and understood that there would be special difficulties in my way, but I did not know the magnitude of those difficulties and was not discouraged. I also knew about Henry O. Flipper, the first of the three Negro graduates from West Point. But I was directly influenced by the case of Thomas Van Rensselaer Gibbs. He was a slender, indeed delicate-looking, light brown young man, who was a frequent visitor at our house. His father was a well-educated Northern Negro, who, during Reconstruction, had been State Superintendent of Public Instruction of Florida and was, in fact, the man who organized and established the Florida public school system. Tom Gibbs had spent a year at West Point. He used to talk about his cadet days, and assigned his physical condition rather than race prejudice as the reason for having to leave the Academy. This young man, despite his quiet, reserved, soft-spoken manner, always carried himself like a soldier. He impressed me as an exemplar more than anyone else that I used to see at our house; and I saw many men prominent at that time in the Negro world. Some of these I have mentioned; among the others, I have a very clear recollection of J. H. Menard, looking a good deal like the pictures of Alexandre Dumas; he was the first Negro elected to Congress, and, when I knew him, was running a weekly newspaper in Jacksonville; of Bishop Daniel A. Payne, a small shriveled figure, deep-lined face and sunken cheeks, the intellectual leader of the African Methodist Church; and of Joseph C. Price, broad-shouldered, vigorous, radiating vitality, jet-black and handsome, renowned as an orator and educator and who, had he not died young, might have rivaled Booker T. Washington for the leadership of the Negro race. Before I left my job at the *Times-Union* all dreams about leading my company or my regiment to fight for my country's glory—and my own—had vanished. I gradually became possessed with the idea that I should like to run a newspaper—to edit it—to write. From this idea I have swerved, but back to it again and again I have come.

In the year following my mother's visit to New York we found ourselves really a big family. My father had become pastor of a little church in Jacksonville, and so was at home again. Then one day Señor Echemendia, who was one of the heads of El Modelo cigar factory, came to our house and brought with him a very distinguished and aristocratic-looking gentleman, Señor Ricardo Ponce of Havana. The elegance and courtliness—such as I had never seen before—of this gentleman was emphasized by Señor Echemendia's dumpiness and untidy appearance. Señor Ponce had come to Jacksonville to find a

family with which a Cuban boy in whom he was much interested
might live and learn English. Señor Echemendia knew us—he lived
in the same neighborhood—and brought the stranger in the hope that
we might take the boy. He acted as spokesman because Señor Ponce
spoke no English. My parents talked the matter over with Señor
Echemendia, my father exchanging a few words in Spanish with
Señor Ponce, and it was settled that the boy would come. The boy
was Ricardo Rodriguez—later he added the name Ponce. He was
about my age, very good-looking, with the light bronze complexion
that so many colored Cubans have, and also with the proverbial
Latin temperament. When he came, he knew but one English expression, "All right." He picked up English from Rosamond and me
quite rapidly, but not more rapidly than we picked up Spanish from
him. I think the early advantage lay with us. One of the things our
father had made a great effort to do was to teach us the Spanish
language. We used to sit for an hour at a time while he drilled us
in exercises from *Olendorf's Method*. We committed to memory a
great many useless sentences, like, "Have you seen the tame antelope
of the blacksmith's niece?" but at the same time learned a large
number of Spanish words. He also gave us a pretty thorough drill
in the principal Spanish verbs. It was natural then that Ricardo,
when he found himself alone amidst strangers speaking an alien tongue,
followed the line of least resistance and took refuge in the fragmentary
Spanish that we knew. It was, of course, also natural that in the end
his knowledge and use of English exceeded ours of Spanish. When
he came, my father was adding a second story to our house. We made
a dining room out of the room back of the parlor, for the size to
which the family had increased would have made eating in the
kitchen, as we formerly did, a question of double shifts. And now
with three boys at the table carrying on a bi-lingual conversation,
meals were little less than exciting.

In addition to learning to speak Spanish, I learned to smoke. Ricardo,
though only fourteen, smoked incessantly. He smoked cigarettes made
of Havana clippings wrapped in a dark brown, sweetish paper. He
had dozens of packages, and periodically he received from home a
box in which was packed a fresh supply. There also came in those
boxes packages of Cuban sweets and preserves, and fresh supplies of
fine linen handkerchiefs, hand-made shirts, initialed underwear, French
neckties, French lisle socks, high-heeled Cuban shoes. Rosamond and

I had always thought of ourselves as well-dressed boys—our mother spent a good part of her salary on clothes for us—but such finery as this, for a boy, we had not even imagined. Opening Ricardo's box was always an event. I smoked surreptitiously; at least, I thought I was doing so, but the aroma of Havana tobacco does not lend itself to deception. When I was found out, my father had hardly anything to say about it; he was a smoker himself and, perhaps, remembering when and how he learned, did not indulge in any cant. My mother was taken aback. The first time she saw me smoking she snatched the cigarette out of my mouth. I think she and my father must have talked the matter over and decided that it was best not to use any coercive measures. But my grandmother disapproved openly and vigorously. I think this was due in part to the fact that, like a true Britisher, she never fully approved of the foreigner in our midst. It was not until I was about twenty that I smoked freely in the presence of my parents.

Of course, in a city like Jacksonville smoking by boys was not the cardinal sin that it was in most communities and sections. Jacksonville was a cigar manufacturing center. It had a Cuban population of several thousand. Many boys learned the cigarmaker's trade; that was the trade my brother and my friend D—— learned. Every workman in a factory is allowed to make up for his own use a certain number of "smokers" each day. When I began to smoke cigars I started with the strong, "green smokers" given me by my many cigarmaker friends. After these "green smokers" the seasoned cigars bought from the dealer are pretty flat.

During this period there came to Jacksonville another distinguished man whose visit greatly stirred me. The Sub-Tropical Exposition was being held in the city, and Frederick Douglass was brought down to make a speech. I knew his story, for I had not only heard a great deal of talk about him, but a book I had won as a prize at Stanton was *The Life and Times of Frederick Douglass*, an autobiography, and I had read it with the same sort of feverish intensity with which I had read about my earlier heroes, Samson, and David, and Robert the Bruce. I looked forward to his coming with more than the glamorous curiosity with which I had looked forward to the coming of General Grant. I was now mature enough to experience an intellectual interest. I wanted to see him but, more, I wanted to hear him speak and catch his words. No one could ever forget a first sight of Frederick Douglass. A tall, straight, magnificent man with a lion-like head covered with a glistening white mane, who instantly called forth in one form or another Napoleon's exclamation when he first saw Goethe, "Behold a man!" As I watched and listened to him, agitator, editor, organizer, counselor, eloquent advocate, co-worker with the great abolitionists, friend and adviser of Lincoln, for a half century the unafraid champion of freedom and equality for his race, I was filled with a feeling of worshipful awe. Douglass spoke, and moved a large audience of white and colored people by his supreme eloquence. The scene, though on a less important scale, was similar to the one in which Booker T. Washington appeared nine years later at the Atlanta Exposition. Douglass was speaking in the far South, but he spoke without fear or reservation. One statement in particular that he made, I now wonder if any Negro speaker today, under the same circumstances, would dare to make, and, if he did, what the public reaction would be; Douglass, in reply to the current criticisms regarding his second marriage, said, "In my first marriage I paid my compliments to my mother's race; in my second marriage I paid my compliments to the race of my father."

Both my mother and my father had been worrying about my progress in school; contrary, however, to traditions, it was not the boy's fault. I started at Stanton advanced beyond my years, and should have finished before I was thirteen; I was almost sixteen when I did finish. Mr. Culp, who succeeded Mr. Waters as principal, was a well-educated man and may have been a good preacher, but he was a poor teacher. As an administrator he had no success. The school got to be a sort of go-as-you-please institution, and many parents took their children out and sent them elsewhere. D——, to our mutual sadness, was taken out by his father and sent to Cookman Institute, a school in Jacksonville founded and operated by the Northern Methodist Church. My father was all for doing the same, but my mother was now assistant principal of Stanton, and she felt it was hardly proper for her to take her own child out of the school. I and other pupils dawdled away our time in Mr. Culp's class; he seemed to have no definite plans about graduating us. Things came to such a pass that parents demanded that a change be made, and the school board acted on their demand. The new principal was William Artrell. Mr. Artrell had not had a college education, but he was thoroughly grounded in all the English branches. He was a native of

Nassau, and had been trained under the English public school system; so, despite the fact that his education was not extensive, he actually knew what he was supposed to know and teach. He was an administrator, a good teacher, and a strict disciplinarian. Like all educated West Indians, his handwriting was beautiful. Under him Stanton became a better school than it had ever been. Pleasantly for my mother, she found herself associated with a friend of her young womanhood. I finished at Stanton toward the end of May 1887. In the same month D—— was graduated from Cookman Institute, where he had covered the general high school subjects.

VII

NOW I entered a period which, for excitement, surpassed anything in my experience. For months my father and mother had been forming plans for sending me off to school, and the time for carrying out those plans was drawing nearer day by day. My parents had reviewed information about several schools: Howard University, Fisk University, Atlanta University, Biddle (now Johnson C. Smith) University, and Hampton Institute. My father at first favored Hampton. He had practical ideas about life, one of them being that every boy should learn a trade. I think, too, he had a sentimental leaning toward Hampton because of the fact that he was by birth a Virginian. We, for I was taken into conference, finally decided on Atlanta University. Just what was the determining factor in this choice I do not remember. Perhaps my mother and I merely outvoted my father. Most likely it was the fact that Atlanta was nearest.

I was on the eve of an adventure, and its lure was powerful, but I had my moments of misgivings. I was leaving the familiar sights and objects and associations that had so far made up life for me. I was stepping off a well-known path upon a strange road. I watched my mother preparing me for the journey, but I could not know the anxious love she put into the task. Yet I am now sure that she knew she was packing my kit for me to take a road that would ultimately lead very far from the place where she stood.

Ricardo had been urging his people to let him go to Atlanta University with me. He argued that it would help him to achieve more quickly the object for which he had been sent to the United States; namely, to learn English and study dentistry. He was sincere, but I think he had also caught some of my enthusiasm and wanted to try the new experience. I think, too, he was loath to have me go and leave him in Jacksonville. There had grown between us a strong bond of companionship; and what was, perhaps, more binding, the bond of language. Up to that time my proficiency in Spanish was much greater than his in English; so he never exerted himself to speak to me except in his own language. Anyone who has undergone the agony of having to express himself inadequately in a foreign language knows what a sweet relief it is to find somebody who understands his mother tongue. Ricardo found that relief in me. There were things he could say to me which, if expressed in English, would have made him feel embarrassed. Among these were the confidences regarding his love affairs. These affairs were numerous but always intense. I had gone through phases of love common to a boy's lot; I had felt the pull and tug of that mysterious force; indeed, involved in my misgivings about leaving Jacksonville was Jennie, a golden-hued, fifteen-year-old bit of femininity, and my heart's desire; but the idea that love could be the frenzied, frantic thing it was with Ricardo was not yet within my comprehension. One night after we had gone to bed he actually frightened me. He complained emphatically of violent pains in and round his heart; the indications were that that organ was about to break or explode. I called my mother and she came in and gave him a dose of tincture of lavender. My sympathy cooled when he divulged to me that the attack was caused by a sudden passion he had conceived for Jennie, my own heart's desire.

The letter and the money came from Havana. Ricardo was to go with me to Atlanta University. I was glad that I would have a friend and companion from the start. D—— and I had long expected that we should go off to school together, but early in the summer he confided to me that he was going to run away from home. His mother, whom he loved very dearly, had died when he was small. His father married a second wife, who died shortly afterwards. He then took a third wife. D——'s second stepmother was very kind to him, but his father, always harsh, grew harsher. I tried to dissuade my friend from his plan to leave home. I begged him to stick it out until he got off to school. However, he did run away and go to New York. And so I was doubly glad that Ricardo was going with me. On the night my mother was putting the final touches on my packing there was a rumbling sound; the house trembled and swayed; we rushed downstairs and out, and became aware that there was an earthquake. This was a part of the tremor that came to be known as the Charleston Earthquake, and bore no relation whatever to the fact that I was leaving Jacksonville.

Ricardo and I boarded the train that left Jacksonville at night and arrived in Atlanta the next morning. We had first-class tickets, and my father put us in the first-class car. (This was the year in which Florida passed its law separating the races in railroad cars, and it was just being put into operation; a matter that I, at least, was then ignorant of.) We had a good send-off; many of our friends, boys and girls, came to bid us good-by. My heart's desire, looking very pretty, was there, and kept quite close to my mother. I wonder if keeping close to my mother was one of those feminine traits that a girl of fifteen knows intuitively. At any rate, the effect on me was full, and I clearly remember how strangely I was stirred by this simple, perhaps incidental, matter of juxtaposition. We got aboard midst a lot of noisy chatter that enabled me to cover up my choked condition when I kissed my mother good-by.

The train pulled out and we settled down comfortably in one seat after having arranged our packages, among which was a box of lunch. In those days no one would think of boarding a train without a lunch, not even for a trip of two or three hours; and no lunch was a real lunch that did not consist of fried chicken, slices of buttered bread, hard-boiled eggs, a little paper of salt and pepper, an orange or two, and a piece of cake. We had a real lunch and were waiting only for the train to get fully under way before opening it. A number of colored people had got on the train but we were the only ones in the first-class car. Before we could open our lunch the conductor came round. I gave him the tickets, and he looked at them and looked at us. Then he said to me gruffly, "You had better get out of this car and into the one ahead." "But," I answered, "we have first-class tickets; and this is the first-class car, isn't it?" It is probable that the new law was very new to him, and he said not unkindly,

"You'll be likely to have trouble if you try to stay in this car." Ricardo knew there was something wrong but didn't fully understand the conversation or the situation, and asked me, "*¿Que dice?*" (What is he saying?) I explained to him what the conductor was trying to make us do; we decided to stay where we were. But we did not have to enforce the decision. As soon as the conductor heard us speaking a foreign language, his attitude changed; he punched our tickets and gave them back, and treated us just as he did the other passengers in the car. We ate our lunch, lay back in our seats, and went to sleep. We didn't wake up until it was broad daylight and the engine was puffing its way up through the gullies of the red clay hills on which Atlanta sits.

This was my first impact against race prejudice as a concrete fact. Fifteen years later, an incident similar to the experience with this conductor drove home to me the conclusion that in such situations any kind of a Negro will do; provided he is not one who is an American citizen.

Atlanta disappointed me. It was a larger city than Jacksonville, but did not seem to me to be nearly so attractive. Many of the thoroughfares were still red clay roads. It was a long time before I grew accustomed to the bloody aspect of Atlanta's highways. Trees were rare and there was no city park or square within walking distance. The city was neither picturesque nor smart; it was merely drab. Atlanta University was a pleasant relief. The Confederate ramparts on the hill where the school was built had been leveled, the ground terraced, and grass and avenues of trees planted. The three main buildings were ivy-covered. Here was a spot fresh and beautiful, a rest for the eyes from what surrounded it, a green island in a dull, red sea. The University, as I was soon to learn, was a little world in itself, with ideas of social conduct and of the approach to life distinct from those of the city within which it was situated. When students or teachers stepped off the campus into West Mitchell Street, they underwent as great a transition as would have resulted from being instantaneously shot from a Boston drawing room into the wilds of Borneo. They had to make an immediate readjustment of many of their fundamental notions about life. When I was at the University, there were twenty-odd teachers, of whom all, except four, were white. These white teachers by eating at table with the students rendered themselves "unclean," not fit to sit at table with any Atlanta white family. The president was Horace Bumstead, a cultured gentleman, educated at Yale and in Germany, yet there was only one white door in all Atlanta thrown open to him socially, the door of a German family. No observance of caste in India was more cruelly rigid. The year before I entered, the state of Georgia had cut off its annual appropriation of $8000 because the school stood by its principles and refused to exclude the children of the white teachers from the regular classes.

I was at the University only a short time before I began to get an insight into the ramifications of race prejudice and an understanding of the American race problem. Indeed, it was in this early period that I received my initiation into the arcana of "race." I perceived that education for me meant, fundamentally: preparation to meet the tasks and exigencies of life as a Negro, a realization of the peculiar responsibilities due to my own racial group, and a comprehension of the application of American democracy to Negro citizens. Of course, I had not been entirely ignorant of these conditions and requirements, but now they rose before me in such sudden magnitude as to seem absolutely new knowledge. This knowledge was no part of classroom instruction—the college course at Atlanta University was practically the old academic course at Yale; the founder of the school was Edmund Asa Ware, a Yale man, and the two following presidents were graduates of Yale—it was simply in the spirit of the institution; the atmosphere of the place was charged with it. Students talked "race." It was the subject of essays, orations, and debates. Nearly all that was acquired, mental and moral, was destined to be fitted into a particular system of which "race" was the center.

On the day of my arrival, the opening day, I took an examination and was assigned to the Junior Preparatory class. Ricardo was not examined. He was something of a puzzle. He had a good elementary education in Spanish, but no equivalent of it in English; so he was made a special student in one of the grammar school classes—the University then had such a department. For weeks he stuck to me as closely as he could; for he felt his status as a stranger more keenly than ever. His embarrassment seemed greatest in the dining hall, where he had to sit facing a whole row of girls. The dining hall was a large, bright room that took up the main part of the basement of North Hall, the girls' dormitory building. It was filled with long tables, at each of which ten or twelve girls sat on one side and about an equal number of boys on the other. Two teachers at a table acted as hosts; but there were not enough male teachers to go round, so at a number of tables an advanced student did the carving. And the position of carver was no sinecure. The various dishes of food were placed between the hosts. The carver asked each student, "What will you have?" The girls were served first. They were generally dainty and made certain choices. But from the boys' side there rolled out a monotonous repetition of "Some of each." Three-fourths of the boys would send back for a second helping with the request for "Some of each."

Ricardo and I talked Spanish at the table and this gave us pleasant notoriety; we could not have excited more curiosity and admiration had we been talking Attic Greek. Following strictly in the Yale tradition, the students at Atlanta University thought of a foreign language as something to be studied, not spoken. We were, naturally, assigned to the same room. It was a good-sized, clean, and comfortable room with a closet. In it were a table with a lamp, two chairs, a washstand with pitcher and basin, and a wooden slop-bucket. The floor was uncovered, except for a strip of carpet in front of the bed and an oilcloth mat in front of the washstand. The walls were white and absolutely bare. There was not the slightest hint of decoration. The mattress on the bed was filled with fresh, sweet-smelling straw, and was fully two feet high before we started sleeping on it. When I first dived into it I felt as though I was plunging into the surf at Pablo Beach. We saw very little of each other during the day, except at meals; for on school days there were only about two hours, in the afternoons, that were not filled with duties of one kind or another. This proved to be the very thing that Ricardo needed, and he began mastering English with astonishing rapidity.

At some time during the day each student was required to put in one hour, at least, at work. It was the job of a group of a half-dozen boys to fill the wood bin in the kitchen every afternoon. We carried the wood in our arms, and I ruined a couple of good jackets keeping the kitchen fires burning. There was, however, an intangible recompense connected with this task that made us forget some of its irksomeness: the wood pile was located in the angle of the two wings of the girls' dormitory, and each boy could make a show of how much wood he could carry, while the unapproachable creatures looked down on him from their windows. I say "unapproachable,"

I ought to italicize the word; for there was no offense in the Atlanta University calendar that more perturbed the authorities than approaching a girl. A boy could see a girl upon a written application with the girl's name filled in, signed by himself and, if granted, countersigned by the president or dean. The caller was limited to twenty minutes in the parlor in North Hall; and he would find out that the matron was as particular about overtime as a long-distance telephone operator. He was also likely to overhear sundry remarks—in this day known as wisecracks—made by various girls as they passed to and fro in the halls and up and down the main staircase. For the "caller" could be spotted as soon as he struck the bridge on his way to North Hall, and word would be flashed from window to window and from room to room. If he was one of the constant sort, his visit did not arouse much interest, but, if he was of the other sort, it caused great speculation. Had the girls known how to gamble, they might have had exciting times betting on who the particular girl would be.

I found this whole procedure humiliating, and I made it a point of honor not to make out an application to call on a girl—a resolution I broke only twice during my six years, and for reasons that appeared to be sufficiently exigent. It might seem that these repressive regulations would have incited "sexy" talk among the boys, but they did not. The boys did talk a great deal about the girls across the bridge, but the talk was always on an expurgated, I might say, emasculated level. This was not prudery; it was idealism, and there was in it, too, something of an innate racial trait. There was an amazing absence of realistic discussion of sex; and no boy would have dared to bring the girls of North Hall into such a discussion. North Hall girls, love, and sex formed one of the spiritual mysteries. I remember that one day I was corrected by an older student in a group when I spoke of one of the teachers as "Miss." "We call her 'Miss' but she is really Mrs.," he said. This teacher was badly deformed, and, when I expressed mild surprise that she had found a husband, the whole group came down on my head. They pointed out to me that *true love* and physical passion were entirely distinct and unrelated—a doctrine that I found fully and forcibly set forth in the textbook on moral philosophy that I took up later in my course. This Sir Galahad attitude of the Atlanta University boys of that time appears to me in the present age in the light of a phenomenon.

The longest stretch of free time we had on school days was the two-hour period between the work hour and supper. The time on Sundays was pretty well filled; preaching in the morning, Sunday school in the afternoon, and prayer meeting at night. The couple of hours before the morning service we often whiled away walking about the campus, a sixty-five acre tract, part of it wooded. Saturday was our big day. We had to work two hours in the morning, but dinner was served at 1 o'clock and we had the whole afternoon up to supper time at 6. On Saturday afternoons during the fall there was usually a baseball game on. The baseball season closed with a big game on Thanksgiving Day. (We knew nothing about football until four or five years later, when it was encouraged by Professor Adams, who had been a player at Dartmouth.) These games were attended by the girls as well as the boys, and by crowds of townspeople. During the winter months Saturday afternoons were devoted to calling on friends in the city by those fortunate enough to know any Atlanta families. The girls also had the privilege, by permission, of visiting friends in town on this half-holiday. We would put on our best clothes—for Saturday not Sunday was the day we dressed up—and sally forth immediately after dinner. These afternoons formed one of the pleasantest parts of our student life; we met nice people, we would likely be offered something good to eat, and we ran a chance of meeting by accident, perhaps not wholly by accident, certain of the North Hall girls who might be visiting mutual friends.

I had been at the University a couple of weeks when, without notice, D—— appeared with his father. He had returned home from his runaway trip, and his father had agreed to let him come to Atlanta. I was glad and he was glad, for it meant that the thing we had dreamed about had come to pass. I took him to the matron, where we arranged to have a cot for him put in the room occupied by Ricardo and me. Three in a room made it a bit crowded, but the slight inconvenience didn't bother us because he was so anxious to tell me about his adventure in running away, and I wanted to talk to him about things at the University, most of them things that Ricardo would not be interested in or even understand. A good many nights, after lights were out and Ricardo had fallen asleep, D—— and I talked in subdued tones. In these talks we began to lay plans for the future: we would finish at Atlanta University, then we would study law and form a partnership.

D—— was assigned to the Freshman class; and I thought with vexation of the time I had lost with Mr. Culp as my teacher. He had some conditions to make up because Cookman Institute standards were not on a par with those of the preparatory school at the University, but this was no serious handicap for his quick mind, in fact, so quick that it often sped lightly over what should have been laboriously explored.

A few days after D——'s arrival I saw in the papers that the St. Louis Browns and another big league team were to play an exhibition game in Atlanta. I became feverish with desire to see them play. I especially wanted to see Arlie Latham, the famous third baseman of the Browns. Neither D—— nor Ricardo was much of a player, but they were both fans and caught my enthusiasm to see this game; in addition, it meant a half-day out of school for the three of us. I wrote out the application to be excused and took it to the proper authority. That authority, for the time, was Professor Francis. He read the application, looked up at me with his sharp, dark eyes, then read the application again, presumably, to be sure he had read it aright the first time. Meanwhile, there ran through my mind some of the things I had already picked up about him from the older boys. He was disliked by the majority because he was regarded as a snooper. It was said that he walked about the halls of the boys' dormitory at night with rubbers on; that he was not above listening at keyholes; that nothing delighted him more than to "find out something," and that he had tracked down numberless plots and acts against the established order of the institution. It was felt that he had no understanding of or sympathy with boyhood, and known that he made no allowances for the deeds done by those still in that semi-savage state. He was the university pastor and was not far from fanaticism in his religious zeal. The unpopularity of Professor Francis was offset by the popularity of Professor Chase, our teacher of Greek. Mr. Chase was a stocky man with a head like the pictured one of the poet Aristophanes. His ruddy face held two merry eyes and was fringed by a cropped, reddish beard. On cold days he wore a shawl in the manner of Abraham Lincoln. He spoke haltingly, but was always eloquent in his defense of the boys. It may have been more than a coincidence that the two most understanding men—from a boy's point of view—at Atlanta during my time were both from Dartmouth, Professor Chase and Professor Adams. It was the latter who gave us our first lessons in the finer points of football. Mr. Francis was from

Yale, and was the embodiment of all the stern virtues then traditional of that great school.

This was my first personal contact with Mr. Francis, and the contact made it hard to believe him to be as bad as he was painted. While he pondered my application, I shyly studied him. I was a little awe-struck. He, like Mr. Chase, was stocky and had a Greek philosopher's head, but his complexion was pallid, his eyes piercing, and his short beard—all the men teachers, except two, wore beards of varying hues—was dark and tinged with gray. He was gentle and soft-spoken; in fact, he almost purred when he spoke. I noted a furtiveness in his glance and manner that I afterwards recognized as a marked characteristic. While I waited he squirmed round in his swivel chair, frowned, plucked at his beard, and, picking up a ruler from his desk, gave his skull several resounding whacks. Then he turned and informed me in a kindly way that he had been connected with the University from its founding and that never before in its history had such a request been made—a request to be absent from classes to attend a ball game. Also he gave me to understand that had I been longer steeped in the spirit of the institution I would not have dreamed of making it. Perhaps my innocence or my ignorance appealed to him or it may have been that he was, after all, a humorist in disguise; at any rate, he turned suddenly to his desk and countersigned the application. I left his office hurriedly with the precious scrap of paper tucked away in my pocket. Among the three of us there was sufficient worldly wisdom to make us keep our holiday a secret.

There was a large crowd at the ball grounds, but we were there early and got good seats. On the way Ricardo bought a package of cigarettes and, as soon as we were seated, he and D—— lit up and began smoking. They, of course, offered me a smoke, but I declined. Furthermore, I tried to dissuade them, and once or twice snatched the lighted cigarettes from their mouths and threw them away. This last resort roused considerable anger in Ricardo, and he rolled at me a string of sonorous and untranslatable Spanish oaths. Now, I was not being actuated by any goody-goody motive. It was true that each of us on entering the University had signed the compulsory pledge to abstain from alcoholic drinks, tobacco, and profanity; and I did have some regard for my pledge; but of, at least, equal weight was my knowledge that smoking was considered an offense meriting suspension or even expulsion, and, as my knowledge on this point was, I knew, fuller than theirs, I was trying my best to give my two friends the benefit of it.

We were delighted with the game. Arlie Latham fulfilled all our expectations of him, both as a baseball player and comedian. We returned to the University happy and after supper got great satisfaction out of relating to our envious fellow students the story of the game.

The next day I was called to the president's office. I stood waiting while Mr. Francis fumbled over the papers on his desk as though he was searching anxiously for an important misplaced document. While still fumbling and not looking up he said to me very quietly, "Johnson, what about the smoking at the ball grounds yesterday?" I was astounded. If I had been given an instant in which to collect myself I should have responded with a straightforward, honest lie, in full keeping with the code of honor of normal boys, but he continued talking and rehearsed the whole scene as it had taken place, and even the conversation, almost word for word. I was stupefied. The three of us had looked around quite carefully when the smoking began, and had seen no one that we knew. I felt that I was witnessing a feat of black magic. Mr. Francis dismissed me without further questioning, and I went out wondering if he was going to press the matter or was merely giving me a confirming demonstration of his reputed powers as a detective. I am sure now that he did get a great kick out of the interview; and I suspect that all of his similar exploits were a source of great pleasure. When I left him I also knew that I had, undeservedly, gone up to the top notch in his estimation.

As soon as I could get to D—— and Ricardo I told them that the cat was out of the bag and jumping; and I gave them the best tip I could as to the direction she was taking. Their mystification was as great as mine. That night we talked of nothing else. Ricardo was indifferent about the outcome; Atlanta University didn't mean more to him than the privilege of smoking meant. What stirred him most was curiosity as to how Mr. Francis knew. But D—— was much concerned; he had just patched things up with his father, who not unreluctantly had agreed to send him to college; and he knew that his future and our joint plans for the future were at stake. He and I hoped that the incident was closed. Our hope rested on the fact that neither he nor Ricardo had been sent for. However, we decided that there was no use in going up against the indubitable powers possessed by Mr. Francis, and if they were sent for the only thing to do would be to make a clean breast of it. The summons came the following afternoon. Ricardo went in the strength of his indifference and D—— in the weakness of his concern. Mr. Francis rehearsed the scene and conversation over for them; and, as with me, gave not the slightest hint as to how the matter had become manifest to him. D—— was repentant, but Ricardo stated as plainly as possible that education or no education, he couldn't get along without smoking. He clinched his statement by saying, "Meester Francis, I wass born weet de cigarette in de mout." They were both admonished and reprieved. I think it was Ricardo's indifference rather than D——'s penitence that saved them. I am sure that Mr. Francis anticipated with pride that in the next catalogue of Atlanta University would be listed, "Ricardo Rodriguez Ponce, Havana, Cuba." And there was no way of punishing the compliant D—— while sparing the recalcitrant Ricardo.

I began my course in manual training in the carpenter shop. I enjoyed going to the industrial building as much as to any of my classes, except my Latin class. I had no exceptional difficulty with mathematics and I was interested in the subject, but I found that I had a love for language, and Latin meant more for me than mere class work. It was the same when I came to Greek, and French and German. Besides, I had found Latin to be my "snap" course. The similarity to Spanish, especially in the principal verbs, made it relatively easy for me; and through Cæsar and Cicero and Vergil and Horace and Tacitus and Livy I read at sight many lines that cost my classmates much thumbing of dictionary and grammar. Work at the shops was fascinating. I liked the bright, sharp tools, the peculiar fragrance that clings to a carpenter's chest, the good smell of the wood as the saw cut into it or as the shavings came curling up through the plane, and the experience of making things. I caught glimpses of boys working at the forges, at the turning lathes and at the draughting tables. I was intensely interested in it all, and more than once wished that my father, who believed in a trade for every boy, could see me at work.

I had been going to the shops for quite a while before I saw the engineer; that is, the man who had charge of the engine room. He was a colored man, light yellow, with a mass of black hair, and a melancholy expression of the face that was deepened by a long, dark, drooping mustache. He looked like a reformed pirate, or as a pirate ought to look if he reformed. At first glance I wondered where I had seen the face before; I racked my brain, but, to my great irritation, could not tell. The rest of the day and somewhat through the night that face puzzled and haunted me. The next day at the shops I saw the man and looked at him long and hard. What happened? Did he for an instant give off a flicker that had already been caught on the film of my memory? I cannot say, but in a flash I knew him. He was the man who sat directly behind the three of us at the baseball game. In a following flash the workings of the occult powers of Mr. Francis were revealed in broad daylight, and they looked pretty mean.

On the ground floor of Stone Hall, the main building, was the general study room. It accommodated, perhaps, three hundred students, and was furnished with modern individual desks and chairs. In this room the boys and girls of the Preparatory and Normal departments sat and studied during school hours; from it they filed out on bells to the various classrooms for recitation. The daily devotional exercises were held there. The general study room was in charge of John Young, a graduate of the University and an instructor in Latin. Mr. Young was one of the handsomest men I have ever known—and he was one of the two men teachers who did not wear short beards. He had made a reputation as an excellent scholar and a fine athlete. All the boys were proud of him, and half the girls were in love with him. During my Middle Prep year he was preparing himself to go to Harvard for his Master's degree—the degree of Doctor of Philosophy was not then the *sine qua non* of the teaching profession. He expected to return to Atlanta as a full professor of Latin. He did enter Harvard, but died before he had finished the year—of a broken heart, they said; but that is another story. Students in the College department studied in their rooms and went over to Stone Hall for recitations. The study room and recitation rooms of the Grammar department were located in South Hall, the boys' dormitory building.

The big room in Stone Hall was a pleasant place for study. The greatest distraction for a boy was the presence of so many pretty girls. Certainly, I had seen girls before, but their place in the scheme of things had been extrinsic, casual, subsidiary. Now, all at once, they assumed a vital position. They kept up a constant assault on the center of my thoughts. I could relegate them to their old place when I was on the baseball field or with a group of boys on the campus or at work in the shops, even when reciting with them in class; but sitting silent in the study room I fell, whether I would or not, under their pervasive and disquieting allure. Of course, there was the natural explanation; but more than biology was involved; there was also an element of æsthetics. The majority of these girls came from the best-to-do colored families of Georgia and the surrounding states. They really made up a selected group. Atlanta University was widely known as a school that attracted this type. As a result, the proportion of tastefully dressed, good-mannered, good-looking girls was very high. I had never seen their like in such numbers. To look at them evoked a satisfying pleasure. They ranged in color from ebony black to milk white. At one end of the scale eyes were dark and hair crisp, and at the other, eyes were blue or gray and the hair light and like fine spun silk. The bulk of them ran the full gamut of all the shades and nuances of brown, with wavy hair and the liquid velvet eyes so characteristic of women of Negro blood. There was a warmth of beauty in this variety and blend of color and shade that no group of white girls could kindle. I have been in far places and lived in strange lands since I sat in that study room in Stone Hall but the idea has grown stronger and stronger that, perhaps, the perfection of the human female is reached in the golden-hued and ivory-toned colored women of the United States, in whom there is a fusion of the fierceness in love of blond women with the responsiveness of black.

The thing of essential value that I got out of sitting through two years in this big room did not come from what I studied, but from the increasing power I gained to apply my mind to what I was studying, the power to shut out from it what I willed. This, of course, is the known power without which there can be but small achievement of intellectual or spiritual growth. And I have since found in it a boon; the ability to withdraw from the crowd while within its midst has never failed to yield me the subtlest and serenest of pleasures.

I was not long in finding my rank as a fellow student; and that is a rank not less important than the one in scholarship. It is, at any rate, a surer indicator of how the future man or woman is going to be met by the world. I found that I possessed a prestige entirely out of proportion to my age and class. Among the factors to which this could be attributed were: my prowess as a baseball pitcher, my ability to speak a foreign language, and the presumable superiority in worldly wisdom that having lived in New York gave me. I think, at the time,

D—— and I were the only students who could boast of first-hand knowledge of the great city. I could boast of having traveled even to a foreign country. Another factor was my having a college student as my chum and roommate. D—— was only three months older than I, but he was more mature and far more sophisticated. Indeed, in his youth his face began to wear a jaded appearance; and, as a young man, he had a very low droop to the corners of his mouth. He had an unlimited self-assurance, while I was almost diffident; and he had inherited or acquired a good share of his father's roughness and coarseness. He had a racy style of speech, which I envied; but many of his choicest expressions I was unable to form in my own mouth. D—— was a *rara avis* at Atlanta University; nothing like him had ever before been seen in that cage. Yet he was popular with the boys and the girls, and, strange to say, even with the teachers. His very rakishness had a definite charm. And underneath his somewhat ribald manner he was tender-hearted and generous. Moreover, he was extremely good-looking, having, in fact, a sort of Byronic beauty. He was short and inclined to stoutness. When he was a small boy, he was fat. His head, large out of proportion to his height, was covered with thick, dark brown hair that set off his pale face and fine hazel eyes. The only thing that marred his looks was the frequent raising of the drooping corners of his mouth in a cynical curl. But speaking of his face as pale does not convey the full truth; for neither in color, features, nor hair could one detect that he had a single drop of Negro blood.

D—— was entirely at ease with the older boys and the young men of the College department; and in his take-it-for-granted way he made an opening with them for me. So almost from the start my closest associates were not among the boys of the Prep school but among the students of the College classes. I became the acknowledged fifth member of a combination made up of two Juniors, a Sophomore, and D——, calling themselves the "Big Four." We grouped ourselves whenever and wherever possible. We exchanged stories, information, and confidences; and we borrowed each other's money, generally for the purpose of paying for a late supper. Why a boy in boarding school can never get enough to eat will, I suppose, always remain a question. The meals in the dining room were never stinted, but we were always ready for a late, clandestine supper. There was an old man named Watson, whose job it was to tend the fine herd of cows owned by the school. He and his wife lived in a little house on the campus. We called this house "Little Delmonico" because the good woman, who was also a good cook, furnished on short notice a supper of fried chicken, hot biscuits, and all the milk we could drink for fifteen cents. Whenever we had the money, we were ready to run the gantlet after lights were out for one of these suppers. Terms were cash, but we paid willingly; and without seeking to know whence came the milk—or the chickens either. We also passed many hours in the room of one or the other of us playing whist or seven-up, with shades drawn, hat over keyhole, crack under door chinked, and muffled voices; for playing cards was listed among the cardinal sins. But the greater part of our time together was spent seriously. We talked the eternal race question over and over, yet always found something else to say on the subject. We discussed our ambitions, and speculated upon our chances of success; each one reassuring the others that they could not fail. There was established a bond of comradeship —among men, a nobler and more enduring bond than friendship.

It is not difficult for me to blot out forty-five years and sit again with these comrades of my youth. There is A——, tall, fair, slender, and elegant . . . peering near-sightedly through his heavy, gold-rimmed spectacles, but with his agile mind always balancing the possibilities and discovering the vantage. And H——, tall, too, but bronze-colored, broad-shouldered, heavy-jowled . . . in comparison with the ready, fluent A——, cumbrous of speech, using an almost Johnsonian vocabulary, and, when roused, vehemently eloquent. T——, brown, short, and jolly, with gray eyes looking out quizzically from his moon-round face . . . speaking in anecdotes as wiser men had spoken in parables . . . always fresh stories, stories of black and white in the South, stories which, although we roared at them, we knew to have their points buried deep in the heart of the race question. And D——, worldly-wise, dare-devilish, self-confident, and combative . . . invincible on his own ground, but in danger when he exposed a superficial knowledge of other things to the adroitness of A——, to the honest logic and common sense of H——, to the humor of T——, before which what any one of the rest of us posited might be blown away like dust before a strong puff of breath. We talked, we argued, we nursed ambitions and dreams; but none of us could foretell. There is no way of getting a peep behind that dark curtain, which simply recedes with each step we take toward it; leaving in front all that we can ever know. In truth, if some mysterious being had appeared in our midst and announced to A—— that he would rise to the highest office in the church; to H—— that he was to become the most influential and powerful Negro of his time in our national politics; to T—— that he was to have his heart's desire granted in being widely recognized as a typically brilliant Georgia country lawyer; and to D—— that he was to be one of the most prosperous colored lawyers in the country, a member of the Jacksonville city council, and an important factor in Florida politics, we should all, probably, have been incredulous—but that is exactly what was behind the dark curtain. And it was also behind the dark curtain that before these lines would be written each of the four would have passed beyond the boundary of past, present, and future.

I now began to get my bearings with regard to the world and particularly with regard to my own country. I began to get the full understanding of my relationship to America, and to take on my share of the peculiar responsibilities and burdens additional to those of the common lot, which every Negro in the United States is compelled to carry. I began my mental and spiritual training to meet and cope not only with the hardships that are common, but with planned wrong, concerted injustice, and applied prejudice. Here was a deepening, but narrowing experience; an experience so narrowing that the inner problem of a Negro in America becomes that of not allowing it to choke and suffocate him. I am glad that this fuller impact of the situation came to me as late as it did, when my apprehension of it could be more or less objective. As an American Negro, I consider the most fortunate thing in my whole life to be the fact that through childhood I was reared free from undue fear of or esteem for white people as a race; otherwise, the deeper implications of American race prejudice might have become a part of my subconscious as well as of my conscious self.

I began also in this period to find myself, to think of life not only as it touched me from without but also as it moved me from within. I went in for reading, and spent many of the winter afternoons that settle down so drearily on the bleak hills of North Georgia absorbed in a book. The university library was then the Graves Memorial Library. It contained ten thousand or so volumes, an array of books that seemed infinite to me. Many of the titles snared me, but I was often disappointed to find that the books were written from the point of view of divine revelation and Christian dogma or with a bald moral purpose. Among all the books in the Graves Library it was from books of fiction that I gained the greatest satisfaction. I read more Dickens; I read George Eliot; I read *Vanity Fair*, and that jewel among novels, *Lorna Doone*. It was during this period that I also read with burning interest Alphonse Daudet's *Sapho*, a book which was not in the library but was owned by one of the boys and circulated until it was all but worn out. The episode in which Sapho is carried up the flight of stairs left a disquieting impression on my mind that lingered long.

Before I left Stanton I had begun to scribble. I had written a story about my first plug (derby) hat. Mr. Artrell thought it was fine, and it made a hit when I read it before the school. Now an impulse set me at writing poetry, and I filled several notebooks with verses. I looked over these juvenilia recently and noted that the first of my poems opened with these three lines:

> Miserable, miserable, weary of life,
> Worn with its turmoil, its din and its strife,
> And with its burden of grief.

I did not follow this vein. Perhaps even then I sensed that there was already an over-supply of poetry by people who mistake a torpid liver for a broken heart, and frustrated sex desires for yearnings of the soul. I wrote a lot of verses lampooning certain students and teachers and conditions on the campus. However, the greater part of my output consisted of rather ardent love poems. A number of these latter circulated with success in North Hall, and brought me considerable prestige as a gallant. It has struck me that the potency possessed by a few, fairly well written lines of passionate poetry is truly astounding, and altogether disproportionate to what really goes into the process of producing them. It is probable that the innate hostility of the average man toward the poet has its basis in this fact.

My chief shortcoming as an Atlanta University student I quickly recognized. It was my inaptitude as a public speaker. I was astonished to see boys no older than I rise and without fear or hesitation discourse upon weighty subjects; the weightier the subject, the more fluent the discourse. All the outstanding university orators were personages. They thrilled the large audiences that filled the chapel on special occasions; and the applause they received was without question a higher kind of approbation than the cheers given the players on the baseball field. The renown of several of the best speakers had spread beyond Atlanta. I determined to make as much of an orator out of myself as possible. I joined the Ware Lyceum, the debating society of the Preps, and looked forward to the time when I might shine in the Phi Kappa, the College society. I do not brag when I say that I achieved a measure of success. The first time I took part in a debate in the Ware Lyceum I was almost as terror-stricken as I was when I attempted my first Sunday school recitation. In my Sophomore year I won first prize in the principal oratorical contest; and in the following year I gained a tie with another speaker for that honor. Before I left Atlanta I had learned what every orator must know: that the deep secret of eloquence is rhythm—rhythm, set in motion by the speaker, that sets up a responsive rhythm in his audience. For the purpose of sheer persuasion, it is far more important than logic. There is now doubt as to whether or not oratory is an art—curiously, it is the only art in which the South as a section has gained and held pre-eminence—if it may still be classed among the arts, it is surely the least of them all. Oratory, it cannot be denied, has its uses; it has been of tremendous use to me. But the older I grow, the more I am inclined to get away from it. For rhetorical oratory I have absolute distrust. My faith in the soundness of judgment in a man addicted to opium could not be less than that in a man addicted to rhetorical oratory. Rhetorical oratory is the foundation upon which all the humbug in our political system rests.

These new activities crowded out music, and I hardly ever touched the piano during all my student days. I did, however, keep my guitar with me, and played it often. In my last two or three years I sang bass on the college quartet. I gave only the time required by the rules to religious observance. I attended all the Sunday services, because they were compulsory; but the Wednesday night prayer meetings, group prayer meetings in the reception room of the matron, and other voluntary activities I renounced. I did this at some cost. The school was founded in the missionary spirit and, although the original zeal had subsided, it was still quite high. Students who were religiously observant still enjoyed certain preferences. I am sure that I lowered Mr. Francis's first estimate of me very much; and he was, at the time, the administrative head of the institution. The preaching service on Sunday mornings was sometimes interesting. Not so much could I say for Sunday school in the afternoons. I already knew by heart the Bible stories and the lessons for the young to be drawn from them. The Sunday evening prayer meetings bored me terribly. They were conducted by Mr. Francis, and included the singing of hymns (in which he always joined loudly, and also always in a different key), a religious talk by him on student conduct, and brief admonitions by certain of the students to the others. Some students fulfilled their obligations by repeating Bible verses. These quotations were most often apropos of no subject under consideration.

I doubt not that there were students who enjoyed these prayer meetings and were spiritually benefited, but I believe the main effect was to put a premium on hypocrisy or, almost as bad, to substitute for religion a lazy and stupid conformity. I remember that in my Middle Prep year, being, for reasons that I shall presently relate, without a roommate, the matron assigned to me a new student, a loutish young fellow, in order that he might come under my refining influence; that is, by example or otherwise, I was to be the inculcator of proper ideas about bathing, changing clothes, keeping teeth brushed and shoes shined, and about other niceties that would bring him up to Atlanta University standards. A good many new boys stood in need of this kind of tutorship. A few of the boys from the back country, who all their lives had been passing in and out of their houses over one or two steps at most, had to learn even how to go up and down stairs. I have seen such boys, generally free and easy in their movements, clinging desperately to the handrail while they painfully made their way up or down; and I realized that people who trip lightly up and down long flights of stairs are really performing a difficult acrobatic stunt, mastered by long years of practice. There was not much in common between me and my new roommate, but I did my best to be faithful to my trust. Each night during study hour he would sit gloomily pondering his books for a while, then would undress and kneel down to say his prayers. And each night after I had finished studying I would wake him up and make him get into bed. One night I didn't feel very well, and went to bed first leaving him to finish studying and say his prayers. When the rising bell woke me the next morning he was still on his knees. The time it took to get him awake and limbered up enough to dress himself made me late for breakfast.

One day late in the spring, not far from commencement time, I received another summons to see Mr. Francis in his office. I was curious but not worried. When I appeared before him, he was more direct and accusatory than he was on the former similar occasion. He at once put to me a series of questions that sounded like an echo of that famous list once propounded by Cicero to Catiline.

"Where were you yesterday afternoon?"

"Well, I was called to practice with the team, and I spent most of the afternoon on the ball field."

"Didn't you go out on West Hunter Street sometime during the afternoon?"

"No, sir."

"Didn't you go with some other boys to a place where you bought a bottle of wine and drank it, and smoked cigarettes?"

"No, sir."

The interview ended with Mr. Francis somewhat nonplussed. I was ignorant of what may have happened, but I saw D—— right away and told him about the inquisition I had been put through. His face blanched. He had not breathed a word to me; and now he did not need to. The "Big Four" got together at night, and I met with them. The facts were: the four had the afternoon before walked far out on West Hunter Street—this section of it only a clay road leading into the country—to a place where an old German (he may have been an Italian) cultivated a small vineyard and manufactured home-made wine; they had bought a bottle of his wine, drunk it, and smoked cigarettes. The meeting resolved itself into a board of strategy. We discussed the matter from every angle. I ventured the opinion that Mr. Francis, judging from the questions he had asked me, had first-hand knowledge of the whole affair. It was decided that one of the number be sent out to the old vintner to find out just what the situation was. T—— was selected to go. The night was stormy. We waited anxiously with lights out for him to return. It would have been better if any one of the others had gone and left T—— to keep our spirits up. He came back wet, spattered and stained with red clay. His report confirmed our worst fears. Mr. Francis had been out and seen the old man, and wheedled and wrung from him all that had taken place. The old man had given descriptions of persons, not names, because he didn't know the names. And that explained why I had been called; he had described one of the boys as having gray eyes, and my gray eyes being the most pronounced feature of my face had led Mr. Francis to send for me. How he overlooked the fact that T——'s eyes were gray we could not say. Probably, too, the old man repeated to Mr. Francis the first names, as well as he could remember them, that he heard the boys address each other by.

The evidence appeared to be overwhelming. How Mr. Francis got his first clue we never found out. Maybe he saw the four boys leave the campus together, and shadowed them. It is possible that some neighbor or some passerby saw the boys go into the old vintner's place, and reported the fact. Professor Chase pleaded for the boys in the faculty meeting that tried the case with tears streaming down his cheeks. But Mr. Francis with a majority could not be moved; and each of the four received a sentence of indefinite suspension. That night all of them showed wretchedness. T—— did attempt a story or two, but for the first time his efforts failed to provoke even a smile. D——, despite his superb self-confidence, was terribly broken up. He thought with dread of the effect of the news on his relations with his father. Through a part of the night he wept quietly, and I wept with him. The verdict cast a gloom over the whole school. Four such boys could not be sent away from a very small college without making a mighty hole in it. None of the four ever went back to Atlanta University.

I sometimes speculate on what might have happened had I not been called for baseball practice that spring afternoon. Would I have gone with the "Big Four"? If I had, would I have stood out? Would I have tried to dissuade them, and if so, could I have succeeded? Or would I have followed along and been sent away too? Of course, I cannot answer any one of these questions. But I do know that I have always been glad that I did not make myself liable for such punishment. For, in spite of petty regulations and a puritanical zeal, Atlanta University was an excellent school. In spite of the fact that its code of moral conduct was as narrow as it was high, it was an excellent school. Its reputation for thorough work and scholarship was unsurpassed by any similar institution in the country; and the breadth of the social ideas that it carried out practically was, perhaps, unequaled. I have at times thought that, in some degree, its training might have cramped and inhibited me. But generally I have felt that for me there was probably no better school in the United States.

There is now and has been for some time a cry going up against the inadequacy of our school methods and their results. Without doubt, there is ground for complaint. But, at the same time, it is too easy to lose sight of the fact that not the school nor the teachers, but the student is the preponderant factor in education. The student who claims that he is handicapped or miscast for life through the mere inadequacy of the methods used for his instruction would not have profited discernibly more from the most superior methods in vogue or, as yet, only on paper. A good share of the complaint against the elementary schools rises out of the disappointment of fond and overambitious parents who look for a miracle. No kind of school can do the impossible; and any school that turns out the bulk of its students with a fair degree of developed mental and physical control may feel well satisfied with its work. In the higher institutions, teaching increases in importance as a factor; there must be both great teachers and capable students for the achievement of real education; but great teachers are almost as rare as great philosophers.

VIII

ON THE morning after commencement I left Atlanta for Jacksonville. There were four in our party; besides Ricardo and me, there was a boy younger than either of us and a very pretty girl named Rosa DeVoe, whose father was collector of customs at the port of Savannah. The train carried a car for Negro passengers, but Georgia had not yet passed its "Jim Crow Car" law, and, as we had first-class tickets, we got into the first-class car. When the conductor took up our tickets, he suggested very strongly that we go into the car ahead. Our little party looked to me; and I, remembering how things had worked out on the trip from Jacksonville to Atlanta, told him that we were comfortable and preferred to stay where we were. The conductor said no more; but, when it was seen that we were not going to move, a murmur started in the car, and grew until it became a hubbub. The conductor was called upon to put us out; but doubtless his instructions were to stay on the safe side of the law in such cases and he took no action. The remarks in the car now became open and loud. Threats began to reach our ears. I affected nonchalance by scanning and turning the leaves of a book I held in my hand; I might just as well have held it upside-down. Soon a white man came to me and said in tones of one who had only a deep, friendly interest in us, "I advise you people to get into the next car; they have sent a telegram down to Baxley to have a mob come on and put you out when the train gets there." "Baxley, Baxley," when had I heard that name before? It came back. I remembered that one morning in the boys' reading room at the University I had seen in the *Atlanta Constitution* that a party of Negro preachers going to a convention somewhere in Georgia, and traveling in the first-class car, had been met by a mob at one of the stations along the line and forcibly ejected. Out on the station platform one of the mob, it was reported, said, "Niggers, dance us a jig." When the preachers protested that that would not be in keeping with their Christian practices and their dignity, this member of the mob started firing into the floor close to the preachers' feet, and they, naturally, began picking their feet up. The whole mob followed this lead, and kept the party of preachers doing a sort of Hopi Indian dance until some of them were exhausted. I remembered that the name of the station was Baxley; and we were now nearing Baxley and, to all appearances, nearing a mob with guns to put three boys and a girl out of a car in which they had a legal right to be. I was frightened, but I did not suggest to my companions that we move. Soon I saw the colored porter of the car forward beckoning to me. I went out on the platform to see what he wanted. He begged me to come out of the first-class car; he knew that a mob was going to meet the train at Baxley, and he was sure we should be hurt, perhaps killed. His warnings raised my fright to the point where it broke my determination to hold my ground; I went back to my friends and told them what the porter had said, and on my decision we gathered up our luggage and packages and went into the car ahead. This was my first experience with the "Jim Crow Car." While we were getting out of our car many of the passengers expressed their satisfaction. If their satisfaction rose from any idea that I was having a sense of my inferiority impressed upon me, they were sadly in error; indeed, my sensation was the direct opposite; I felt that I was being humiliated. When we passed through Baxley I saw a crowd but no indications of a mob; and I wondered if the colored porter had merely been made a tool of by the white passengers. The more I thought of this, the more I regretted that we had moved.

I have since been through a number of experiences with "Jim Crow." These experiences have always stirred bitter resentment and even darker passions in my heart. In two instances, however, the ridiculous aspect of the whole business was shown up so glaringly that, notwithstanding the underlying injustice, all sense of indignation was lost in the absurdity of the situation. In 1896 I was returning from New York to Jacksonville. I went by steamer to Charleston, and from there to Jacksonville by train. When I boarded the train at Charleston I got into the first-class car. (South Carolina had not yet enacted its separate car law; and all my life I have made it a principle never to "Jim Crow" myself voluntarily.) The car was almost full, but I found a seat to myself, arranged my luggage, and settled down comfortably. The conductor took my ticket quietly, and made no reference whatever to the fact that the train carried a special car for me. A while later, however, he came to me and said that I would have to go into the car forward. His manner was not objectionable; in fact, it was rather apologetic. I asked him why. He replied that we had just crossed the Georgia line, and that it was against the law in Georgia for white and colored people to ride in the same railroad car. I then asked him what he proposed to do if I did not move. We were discussing the question without heat, and he answered in a matter-of-fact manner that he would call the first available officer of the law and have me arrested. I realized that my opposition to the law and all the forces of the state of Georgia would have hardly any other effect in this instance than to land me in some small-town jail; but I said to the conductor that I would first take a look at the car designated for me.

I went forward and looked at the car. It was the usual "Jim Crow" arrangement: one-half of a baggage coach, unkempt, unclean, and ill smelling, with one toilet for both sexes. Two of the seats were taken up by the pile of books and magazines and the baskets of fruit and chewing gum of the "news-butcher." There were a half-dozen or more Negroes in the car and two white men. White men in a "Jim Crow" car were not an unusual sight. It was—and in many parts still is—the custom for white men to go into that car whenever they felt like doing things that would not be allowed in the "white" car. They went there to smoke, to drink, and often to gamble. At times the object was to pick an acquaintance with some likely-looking Negro girl. After my inspection I went back and told the conductor that I couldn't ride in the forward car either. When he asked why, I gave as a reason the fact that there were white passengers in that car, too. He looked at me astonished, and hastily explained that the two men were a deputy sheriff and a dangerously insane man, who was being taken to the asylum. I listened to his explanation, but pointed out that it didn't change the race of either of the men. He pleaded, "But I can't bring that crazy man into the 'white' car." "Maybe you can't," I said, "but if I've got to break this law I prefer breaking it in the first-class car." The conductor was, after all, a reasonable fellow; and he decided to stand squarely by the law, and bring the two white men into the "white" car.

While this colloquy between the conductor and me was going on the passengers were fully aware of what it was about. There had been no open talk or threats regarding my being in the car. Probably they felt that the matter was in capable hands or it may be that there was no individual among them to take the initiative in stirring up protest or action. However, when I began to get my belongings together there were smiles and nudges and *sotto voce* comments all through the car. The sheriff and his insane charge were brought in, and I began to move out. The first thing the insane man did after sitting down was to thrust his manacled hands through the glass of the window, cutting himself horribly. Then he not only let out a stream of oaths and ordinary obscenity, but made use of all the unprintable (perhaps no longer so) four-letter words of Anglo-Saxon origin. As I left the car, there were protests from men and women against the change. The maniac continued his ravings; but both I and the conductor stood squarely by the law.

Several years later I was going from Jacksonville to New York. I had a Pullman ticket. Negroes who are interstate passengers on a Pullman car are not subject to the "Jim Crow" laws of the various states. Of course, they are not exempt from violence. There are still parts of the country where a Negro puts his life in jeopardy when-

ever he travels in a Pullman car. When I entered, the main body of
the car was empty, except for two or three women passengers. The
train left about seven-thirty in the evening, and as soon as it pulled
out I asked the porter to make down my berth. When he began, I
started for the men's room to smoke a cigar in the meantime. When
I reached the door, from which the curtain had been drawn aside,
a hurried glance showed me that there were five men in the compartment, sprawled out over practically all of the seating space. In an
instant, as Negroes must often do, I was rapidly balancing the vital
chances in a suddenly presented situation that involved "race." That
instant took me past the open door to the extreme end of the car.
There I came to a physical and a mental stop. I pulled myself together, and I said to me, "Jim Johnson, what's the matter with you?"
I turned and walked quietly into the compartment. The three men
on the long seat moved up. I sat down in the corner, and proceeded
to light my cigar. Under the cover of that most handy of all masculine
makeshifts I took in the scene. As I sat down, the conversation ceased,
and I could feel myself being scrutinized more carefully than politely.
My own quickened powers of observation were at work. A stout,
ruddy, successful-looking man sat in the armchair, the dominating
figure of the group, he had been talking animatedly when I entered.
I learned later that he was an official of the railroad on which we
were riding, with headquarters in Savannah. A clean-cut young man
sat on the side seat, directly in front of me. He was regarding me
in a not unfriendly way. I was to learn that he was the son of the
stout man, had gone into the army as an officer during the Spanish-
American War, and was just returning from Cuba. I was right in
surmising that one of the men on the long seat was a preacher. He
was pastor of a church in Tampa. The two others were nondescript.
The silence was broken by the young man just back from Cuba, who
said, "Dad, there's a genuine Panama hat." The elder man looked over
intently at the hat I was wearing. Without saying anything, I took
it off and passed it to him for closer inspection. Panama hats were then
rare in the United States. The hat was passed round and examined
with expressions of admiration; it was a very good one. When it
reached the young man he noticed the Havana-stamped lining and
said to me, "¿Habla Vd. español?" "Sí, señor," I answered. Thereupon
he and I exchanged several commonplace phrases in Spanish; but in a
short while his knowledge of that language was exhausted, and general

conversation in English was resumed. I said little except in answer to some questions the preacher asked me about conditions in Cuba, where I had not yet been but concerning which I had a good deal of information. The preacher pressed an invitation on me to come and talk about Cuba at his church the next time I happened to be in Tampa. The run from Jacksonville to Savannah takes a little over three hours, but before we got out of Florida our train came to a standstill because of engine trouble, and we were a couple of hours late. The whole party spent the time in the smoking compartment, talking, joking, laughing. The railroad official went into his bag and brought out his private flask of whisky, from which each of us, including the preacher, took several samples, all drinking out of the same glass. Before we reached Savannah a bond of mellow friendship had been established. My newly made friends got off at Savannah, and I went to bed repeating to myself: In such situations any kind of a Negro will do; provided he is not one who is an American citizen.

IX

I WAS happy to get back home and see my parents, my brother and sister, and my heart's desire. Atlanta suddenly receded into something distant and unimportant. It was good to be again with the boys I had grown up with. I was burning to tell them my experiences and to show them how I had improved as a baseball player. In the single year I had grown much bigger and stronger, and practicing and playing almost daily during the season had developed my game remarkably. For a while I was kept busy noting changes. My parents and sister seemed the same, but my brother seemed almost like a different boy. I was surprised to see how much bigger and stronger he was. When I went away he was wearing short pants; now he was wearing long trousers and talking in a changed voice. When I saw my heart's desire I looked at her with some trepidation; I was anxious to see if she was going to stand the inevitable comparison with the girls of the

University; and, too, I was anxious because I had rashly written a letter to one of the Jacksonville boys which contained a panegyric on the "Georgia peaches" and which he had with all possible speed shown to her. She stood the comparison easily. She was, indeed, pretty; so golden-hued, so soft-mannered, and yet so life-loving and gay. She played the piano better than any other colored girl in Jacksonville; and before jazz had become known, she knew the trick of transforming a piece of staid music into the most tantalizing rhythms.

It didn't take me long to discover that some connection that had existed between me and the boys I had known all my life had slipped its place. I found that the things that mutually interested them and me had abruptly shrunk. And I have noticed that this shrinkage has kept pace with the years. A good deal of sentiment is spilled over the subject of the friends of our childhood and youth, but except in the few cases where for mutually strong reasons the friendship is kept up and developed through the years, the idea is largely a myth. Rare is the situation that is more awkward than the one in which you are thrown for any length of time with the average friend of your childhood or youth. When "Do you remember this?" and "Do you remember that?" and "How is old Blank?" and "Where is old Blink?" are exhausted, the situation is likely to become painful, and the most absolute stranger would be a welcome relief.

Rosamond and I had much to say to each other. One of the first things he told me about was the new literary society. Two of the white teachers at Cookman Institute had organized a Browning Society among the young people. Rosamond took me to a meeting. It was held in the Presbyterian Church and was well attended. There were essays, orations, and a debate. There were also instrumental and vocal solos and music by the choir or chorus—of which Rosamond was, it appeared, a prominent member. I was astonished by the volume of his voice when he sang. Quite naturally, I was called on to "make a few remarks." My experience in the Ware Lyceum gave me a feeling of confidence, and I expressed great satisfaction in seeing such an organization as the Browning Society in my home city. It is more than probable that my "remarks" were a bit patronizing in tone. One of the members of the society in talking with me after the meeting revealed that he had not the slightest idea why it was called the Browning Society. He had a hazy notion that the name had some relation to colored people; that the organization was in some special sense a society for more or less brown-skinned people. This was during the great vogue of Browning Societies, and I hazard the opinion that there were throughout the country many, many members who knew nothing or very little about Robert Browning; but I am sure that the notion held by this particular member was absolutely unique.

D—— and I also had a great deal to talk over. I found that his father had declared emphatically that he would not spend another cent on his education. He had decided, instead, to put his son to work. D——'s father was operating a small cigar factory in partnership with another colored man, who bore the wholly non-Aframerican name of Eichelberger. When I went to the factory I saw D—— working as a stripper, the first step in learning the cigarmaker's trade. He stripped the stems from the leaves of tobacco, smoothed out the "rights" and "lefts" and put them in separate piles over the edge of a barrel before which he was seated. He made no effort to disguise the fact that the job was distasteful to him. He was a diminutive Prometheus chained to a tobacco barrel.

The summer promised to bring happy days; there were picnics and rides on the river and excursions to Pablo Beach to look forward to—but there were other things in store. One day I found my mother lying across her bed groaning with pain. The doctor was called. She went to bed and remained there four months. When she got up she found herself crippled by rheumatism, crippled for life. This was a great blow to everyone in the house. Ever since she had been in Jacksonville she had taken a leading part in the educational and cultural activities of the colored people; and to be thus handicapped in the prime of her life, at the age of forty-six, was a great misfortune for her and not a small loss to the community. I was sent to buy a pair of crutches for her, and Rosamond and I undertook to help her learn to use them. We both had a difficult time choking back our emotions. She had been so active that to see her struggling like an infant again was almost more than we could stand. What made it all the more heart-breaking was her brave attempt to be cheerful; if she had complained and bemoaned her fate, we should not have been so keenly pierced.

In mid-summer, while my mother was lying ill, the great yellow fever epidemic broke out. Some people fled at the first notice; but a rigid quarantine quickly made prisoners of the rest, prisoners in a charnel. There were efforts at escape, most of them futile, some of them fatal. Business was paralyzed; the churches were closed, and all forms of assembly were restricted. Deaths reached a peak of more than a hundred a day. The county pest-house was enlarged by the addition of several temporary buildings, and patients were hurriedly taken there, unless they had behind them the advantage of strong influence. The people dreaded the pest-house as much as they did the disease; and every house upon which the yellow flag was nailed became, too, a pest-house. Many of the dead were buried in common graves; and that increased the terror. The cause of yellow fever had not yet been established; and I doubt that there were in Jacksonville in 1888 facilities for applying even the little that was then known about combating the plague. A few years later, the sure method of abolishing this disease was discovered.

But the possible was done. Money, supplies, and provisions were poured into Jacksonville from all over the country. The major part of the population was fed from commissariats. Some of the money contributed was expended in giving men work. I was given a job as time-keeper for a gang of men that was put at road building. For this I received two dollars a day. The fear, the suffering, the overhanging cloud of death, and my mother lying helpless, made this a memorable period of sadness for us. I watched my father grow more anxious and haggard as the days dragged slowly along. I went to bed for a couple of days with a temperature, and it looked as though the specter had entered our door. But we were among the fortunate; he passed us by. Expectations that medical skill and effort would stay the stalking pestilence were given up, and hearts finally clung to hope for an early frost.

The fall was ended before the fever had run its course and the quarantine was lifted. Reluctantly I resigned myself to the necessity of missing the year at school. I talked with my father and told him I wanted to keep it from being a lost year; that I wanted to go on with as many of my studies as possible—if I could find a tutor. He said that he knew a West Indian who was reputed to be a fine scholar. We went to see this man and found him in a small, dingy, cobbler's shop that he ran, pegging away at old shoes. He was a little man, very black, partially bald, with a scraggly beard, and but for bright, intelligent eyes an insignificant presence. At the sight of the surroundings my heart misgave me, and I was embarrassed both for my father and myself. I wondered if he misunderstood so much as to think that I wanted to be coached in spelling and arithmetic and geography. I was reassured when the little cobbler began to talk. He spoke English as no professor at the University could speak it. My father made arrangements, and I began to study with him every night. By a lamp that was often smoky and in an atmosphere filled with the odor of smelly old shoes I read Cæsar's *Gallic War* and Cicero's orations against Catiline. I also began the study of elementary geometry. My teacher did more than correct, when necessary, the way in which I translated or construed Latin sentences; he had a considerable store of collateral knowledge, and gave me the benefit of it. He talked to me about Julius Cæsar and Cicero, and about Roman power and Roman politics in their time. So I got more than a language out of what I read; this collateral information not only made it interesting, but gave it sense and connected it up with life. Perhaps, the most common fault among teachers is the lack of collateral knowledge or the failure to make use of it. I remember that when I came to read the Greek dramatists I was plunged directly into the texts. There was no enlightenment as to how and why the plays were written or how and where they were performed. In fact, for me they were not plays at all; they were exercises in Greek grammar.

I cannot recall the name of my West Indian teacher or which of the islands he came from. Nor can I say how he was able to use this method of instruction without, apparently, any books to which to refer. I have the impression that he was a Jamaican and was educated at one of the excellent colleges there. At any rate, in the whole course of my school work the only other teacher who made a subject as interesting to me as did this little cobbler was Brander Matthews at Columbia. I wonder just what it was that kept him down on a cobbler's bench?

One day early in the winter a young man stopped at our gate. I knew him; his name was Robert Goode; he had worked for my father at the St. James; he was now cook for the family of Dr. T. O. Summers. Dr. Summers was regarded as the outstanding surgeon in Florida. He had been, I think, a professor of surgery at Vanderbilt University. Robert Goode told my father that the doctor was in need of someone to take charge of his reception room for patients; that the place had been held by a young white woman; that he had spoken to the doctor about me, and that I could get the job. He also said that the work would allow me time for my studies.

I went to see Dr. Summers. His office consisted of a suite of three rooms in one of the business blocks. He was then the only physician in Jacksonville who did not have his office in his residence. I found a man of thirty-eight or forty, very handsome, and well dressed. His features were what we term "classic," his hair and his well-trained mustache were dark, and his eyes were brooding. When I entered he was seated in a large chair, holding in one hand a small tin containing something that he languidly sniffed, first up one nostril, then up the other. He asked me to have a seat, then said, "I suppose you can read and write." I gave him the answer, and he asked, "What else have you studied?" I named the regular grammar school studies, then went on proudly with "Latin, algebra—" I got no further. He straightened up and questioned, "Can you read Latin?" I grew dismayed, and answered with sincerely felt modesty, "I can read a little." He rose quickly from his chair, went to a bookcase, took out a volume bound in black, limp leather, with gilt lettering and edges, and handing it to me said, "Read me something from that." A glance at the title showed me that the book was one unknown to me—the *Roman Missal*. I was not sure whether he wanted me to read or translate, but I proceeded as I had been taught; that is, to read the passage over first. I didn't think I should have made out so badly at translating, for the Latin did not strike me as difficult; but before I had finished reading the passage he said, "That will do," took the book from my hand and began telling me about my duties. These were the general duties of an attendant in a physician's reception room. But I had not been with him long before I took over entirely the matter of collecting his bills.

Since I have reached the point in life where the glance is more and more frequently backward, I look searching to discover the Key. I try to isolate and trace to their origins the forces that have determined the direction I have followed. This is a fascinating but inconclusive pursuit. The Key I do not find. I cannot separate the many forces that have been at work. I cannot unravel the myriad threads of influence that have drawn me here or there. The life, however simple, of every individual is far too complex for that sort of analysis. The number of forces, within and without, at work upon each one of us is infinite. Many of these forces are so subtle, so tangential that they are not even perceived. So when we set forth the manner in which we have definitely shaped the course of life, the precise steps by which certain ends have been reached, we are doing little more than rationalizing results. It is not possible to go back through the progression of causes. What more can any of us do than struggle to converge the forces at work toward some desired focus? We find some of them pliant and others stubborn. I have found many of them utterly unyielding. No intelligence or will power or industry that I possessed was able to bend or deflect them any fraction of a degree from their fixed and untoward direction. The forces at work on each individual are so manifold, so potent, so arbitrary, and often so veiled as to make fatalism a plausible philosophy.

Nevertheless, I know that in the moment in which Dr. Summers took his *Roman Missal* out of my hand and said, "That will do," I had made contact with one of those mysterious forces that play close around us or flash to us across the void from another orbit. Dr. Summers was an extraordinary man. Of course, he was educated; but I had by now known a number of educated people. What was unprecedented for me was that in him I came into close touch with a man of great culture. He was, moreover, a cosmopolite. He had traveled a good part of the world over, through Europe, to North Africa, to Greece and Turkey. He spoke French and German, the latter, because of his student days in Germany, as fluently as he did English. He had wide knowledge of literature, and was himself a poet. His local literary reputation was very high because of the poems he sometimes contributed to the *Times-Union*. He was an accomplished and brilliant talker. When alone, however, he was generally melancholy. He would sit for a long period inhaling from a small can of ether, seemingly lost in dreams. After I had learned something about ether, this habit caused me such anxiety that I spoke to him regarding it. He merely smiled sadly. I dared to speak to him about so personal a matter because from the beginning the relation between us was on a high level. It was not that of employer to employee. Less still was it that of white employer to Negro employee. Between the two of us, as individuals, "race" never showed its head. He neither condescended nor patronized; in fact, he treated me as an intellectual equal. We talked about things that only people in the same sphere may talk about. More than once, in conversation with others, he remarked that I had more sense than any of the Jacksonville doctors he knew anything about. This need not, however, be taken as extremely high praise; for his opinion with respect to the intellectuality of Jacksonville doctors in general was pretty low. In matters of money he was careless and, moreover, had the grand air. It was easy to believe what I vaguely gathered—that he had spent two fortunes, his own and his wife's. Mrs. Summers was pretty, petite, and rather demure. There were two beautiful children, "Bob" and Tom. "Bob," the elder, was about five years old, and a girl. She and I became great friends; and she never considered that I was at any time too busy to furnish her with information or entertainment.

My duties were light and gave me a good deal of time to do things that appealed to me. I explored the books the doctor kept at his office. The number was not large but the range was wide; wider than that covered by the ten thousand books at the University library, many of those being, undoubtedly, donations from the libraries of defunct clergymen. A corner of the doctor's shelves was devoted to *erotica*; there I found the *Decameron* of Boccaccio and the *Droll Stories* of Balzac. It would be interesting, at least to me, if I could now determine what effect on me these forbidden books had. I can somewhat recall the glow that pervaded my body and my mind as I read some of these stories. Others of the stories struck me as very funny. I was stirred and entertained; was I damaged? The whole case for censorship is in that question. I cannot see that these books had the slightest deleterious effect. And I do not believe that any normal person is in any manner damaged by such reading. I grant that on persons of abnormal instincts or weaknesses there may not be this lack of bad effects, but those persons are anyhow bound to get at certain facts about life, and probably from sources far more contaminating than the wit and delicacy of Boccaccio and Balzac and the other masters of erotic literature. Did these books do me any good? That is a question the advocates of censorship might follow up with, but it raises a point not involved; a book may be 100 per cent "pure" and do nobody any good.

From the doctor's library I read some of Montaigne's essays, Thomas Paine's *Age of Reason*, and Robert Ingersoll's *Some Mistakes of Moses* and *The Gods and other Lectures*. I was so much impressed with *The Age of Reason* that I carried it along with me so that I could read and reread it. One day my father summarily commanded me to "take that book out of the house and never bring it here again." I don't believe he was familiar with the book. Whether this stern action was prompted by having scanned it at the time or by "Tom" Paine's popular reputation, I do not know. Indeed, I was too much astounded by the sudden show of intolerance on my father's part to question the reason for his order. I simply obeyed it. I spent some of the time at my desk copying the text from the Greek Testament that I discovered among the doctor's books. I found this fascinating, although I did not understand a single word that I copied. My pages of Greek text drew enthusiastic praise from Dr. Summers, and he declared that I should have lived when the copying of manuscripts by hand was a fine art.

In the course of collecting the doctor's bills I made several futile efforts to get some money long due him by a Mr. Short. One day, I left a memorandum on the doctor's table about the collections I had made; reporting on Mr. Short, I scribbled this bit of doggerel:

Mr. Short—
As I "thort"—
Gave me not a single quarter;
And every time
I go to him
He seems to turn up shorter.

He thought this rather clever. Certainly the verses could not be as funny to anyone else as they were to him. At any rate, they led to my showing Dr. Summers all the verses I had written, and to his giving to me the first worthwhile literary criticism and encouragement I had yet received.

Dr. Summers had worked very hard during the yellow fever epidemic and had recorded his observations on the disease. He had prepared a large number of slides for microscopic study. In the spring he was asked to come to Washington to confer with Army medical officials as to his findings. He said to me at once, "Jimmie, I'm going to Washington, would you like to go?" He decided to go to New York by sea, and from there down to Washington. We left Jacksonville aboard a sailing vessel with auxiliary steam power, belonging to Louis K. Bucky, a Jacksonville lumber-mill owner. The ship did not carry passengers, but the exception was made because of Mr. Bucky's friendship for the doctor. I have traveled many thousands of miles by sea, and I love ships; but I am a bad sailor. This trip is memorable because it was so pleasant. The vessel lazed along through tranquil seas and perfect weather. We did not have to be dressed up; we did not have to make acquaintances; there were no shuffleboard players to obstruct the decks; and there were no romping, shouting children to break the sense of peace and quiet. For once I had no sensation of seasickness. I went to meals with a ravenous appetite. I ate at table with the captain and Dr. Summers—just the three of us, ordinarily the captain ate alone. The food was excellent; this captain, as do most sea captains, lived aboard like a nabob. I remember he had brought for his table a barrel of oysters which we depleted in the seven or eight days of the trip. At meals the doctor was more talkative and gay than I had ever seen him. He matched the captain with stories of travels to far, strange places. He gave a thrilling recital of his experiences during the bombardment of Alexandria, seven years before. At other times he walked the small deck space alone, pausing frequently to look out broodingly on the sea, as though waiting for it to give him the answer to some question burning in his brain. Or he sat for long periods, a book in one hand, in the other his *vade mecum*, a tin of ether.

I am sure it was at Dr. Summers's suggestion, perhaps on his insistence, that I ate at the captain's table. He followed the same course at the hotels in New York and Washington. In each of these cities he engaged a double room in which both of us slept. We merely passed through New York, but our stay in Washington lasted a couple of weeks. I had practically nothing to do. The doctor sent me twice with communications to an official in the State, Army, and Navy Building; that is all I can remember having to do for him. He did not concern himself as to how I spent the time. I had much curiosity about Washington, which I went around satisfying. Naturally, the first sight was Pennsylvania Avenue. I was disappointed by its shabbiness, but amazed at its width. I went up and looked at the White House; I saw the Washington Monument; I visited various government buildings; but the major portion of my time I spent in the galleries of the Senate and the House of Representatives. The experience of looking at and for hours at a time listening to the leading figures on the floors of both houses did not tire me then. It was exciting, even when they discussed matters of which I had no comprehension. Of course I had no preknowledge that thirty-odd years later I should spend weeks and months between these same galleries, and in the offices of the leading figures on both floors, whom I should come to know well, in an effort to get them to do one particular thing.

When I returned to Atlanta University in the fall I was filled with regret at parting from Dr. Summers. The regret was mutual. He had formed a strong affection for me which he did not hide. I had made him my model of all that a man and a gentleman should be. The question rose in my mind whether I was not gaining more through contact

with him than I would gain in going on in school. My father's estimate
of this influence was not so high as mine. From my boastings at home
he had formed the opinion that the doctor was a very smart man, but
visionary and impractical; in a word, without hard, common sense.
My father was partially right. I myself could see that many of the
things that Dr. Summers did and said were not governed by hard,
common sense. But what my father did not appreciate, nor I, fully,
was that that was the very point. I think he was glad that the time
had come for me to return to Atlanta. The doctor did not intimate
that I should do other than continue my schooling, but he urged upon
me to choose medicine as a profession, and had a while before set me
to the preliminary reading of a textbook on anatomy. Already, I had
assisted him in several operations by administering the anæsthetic.
When I left him I had thrown over the idea of becoming a lawyer for
that of becoming a physician and surgeon, with the emphasis on the
surgeon. I left him also with an older ambition clarified, strengthened,
and brought into some shape—the ambition to write. We exchanged
letters, and I sent him regularly whatever new things I wrote. He
moved to a western city, and we continued the correspondence for
several years. Then one day I was shocked to learn that Dr. Summers
had committed suicide. I was deeply grieved, for I had lost an understanding friend, one who was, in many ways, a kindred spirit.

X

AT THE University I found myself in the Middle Prep class, a
year behind the class I had started with. I at once asked for
permission to do the two years' work in one. It was reluctantly granted
after I gave evidence of the ground I had covered during the year
that I was out. When I went home for the summer vacation, I looked
for my cobbler, but he had disappeared; so I had to find another tutor.
He was a former principal of the Duval High School, the white high
school of Jacksonville. He had become partially paralyzed and, so,

incapacitated for the position, and was living on the generosity of a friend. He was quite a pathetic figure; he had lost his health and his position; his wife had left him; and he was now glad to tutor a Negro boy for the small fee that was in it. He lived in a little two-room cabin—it could hardly be called a cottage—that sat far back in the yard to his patron's house. I went there three times a week. I read Vergil's *Æneid* and continued the study of algebra and geometry. My teacher was good enough, as teachers go, and I got along; but he did not stir my curiosity and interest in what I studied as my little cobbler had. It was a matter of hard study and routine recitation. Not that he didn't talk to me; on the contrary, he talked a great deal, but always about his misfortunes, his fair-weather friends, his ingrate of a wife, and the general hard-heartedness of the world. At the time, I knew the complete history of this bitter period of his life. He roused my sympathies, for he was a broken and forsaken man. So, I often lingered after lessons listening to him only because I felt that it did him good to have someone to talk to, someone to whom he could rail at fate.

I earned a little money during this vacation also. In my Middle Prep year I had taken wood-turning in the industrial shops. I have said how much I liked the work in carpentry; I liked the work in turning still more. Turning is considered a trade, but it approaches very close to being an art. A rough block of wood, dead-centered on the lathe; revolving slowly; gradually assuming cylindrical form under the tools in the hands of the turner; then the lathe speeded up higher and higher; and the piece of wood, under the deft touches of the workman, becoming magically transformed into a thing of geometric beauty. There is something in this akin to sculpture. Mr. Onley, a colored contractor, ran a small mill. I presented myself as a wood-turner, and got a job. I worked during the whole summer and turned out quantities of banisters, corner blocks, and other pieces used for ornamentation in a building. One day I was assigned the job of turning a newel post. The material given me was a piece of eight by eight timber about five feet long. I had never before handled such a big piece. With the help of a man I got it dead-centered on the lathe, and began my work. But I had failed to estimate the amount of air resistance that a piece of square timber of its weight and size would generate, and started my lathe at too high a speed. In an instant there was a commotion that shook the mill like an earthquake. The piece of timber hummed like

an airplane, but with a rapid crescendo. In the next instant it had
crashed up against and almost through the ceiling. I was lucky not to
be hurt; luckier not to be killed. The piece was put back on the lathe,
and I kept it at the lowest speed until I had taken off all the rough
corners and surfaces. Finally, the finished newel post was turned out.
There was a deep satisfaction in seeing how sweetly that recalcitrant
log spun at the highest speed after it began to take on beauty.

In the fall I returned to school. Rosamond had made up his mind
that he preferred a musical to an academic education. He decided that
he would go to Boston and study at the New England Conservatory;
helping himself by working at his trade in the meantime. Ricardo
decided that going through Atlanta University would be, for him, not
a matter of time but eternity. He chose now to cast his lot with my
brother. By this time he spoke English quite well. His plan was to go
to Boston and work in the mechanical laboratory of some dentist, and
continue his studies privately. He was still receiving his liberal allowance from Havana, and his plan looked like an easy one. It was easy;
in fact, too easy. He found the opening in the mechanical laboratory,
but Boston life took up all the time he thought he was going to devote
to study. A month or so after I left, Rosamond and Ricardo sailed.
D—— was left working in his father's cigar factory. When I reached
the University I took the necessary examinations, skipped the Senior
Prep class, and entered the Freshman year with my original class.

In this year the scarcity of the sense of humor in the faculty was
reduced by the addition of a new member. Dean Hincks was a Yale
graduate and had been the editor of a newspaper in Vermont. He
was a man in his forties, tall, stoop-shouldered, with very blue eyes,
that were shaded to a deeper color under his overhanging brow. He
talked with a drawl, and his eyes twinkled when he was amused. He
had a straightforward, rather blunt manner, but his heart was an
understanding one. He was a good man for a boy in school to know.
I was fortunate, and was brought into close contact with him. In my
Freshman year I began work in the University printing office, and
continued there through my Senior year, and Dean Hincks supervised the University publications. It was while I was one day working
at a press that Dean Hincks brought a visitor into the printing office.
The visitor was a brown-skinned man, forty-odd years of age, with
shrewd gray eyes, and deep lines at the corners of his mouth. He was
quite alert and asked many questions about what he was being shown.

He came over to the press where I was working and watched me closely for a while. Dean Hincks introduced me to him. That was my first sight of Booker T. Washington, not at that time nationally known. As a writing man himself, the Dean took special interest in my literary efforts, and our personal relations became still closer.

I liked Dean Hincks. Perhaps, the thing I liked him for most was his freedom from cant. He would not indulge in cant even if it was good form to do so. One afternoon there was a general assembly of the students to listen to an address by President Hickman, the new head of Clark University, a neighboring Negro college. President Hickman was a white Methodist preacher. After a year or two he gave up his work at Clark with the parting statement that he could not be expected to do for the Negro what God Almighty hadn't been able to do. On this particular afternoon the chapel was packed to the doors. That year the University had an enrollment of more than six hundred. The classes were overcrowded and rooming accommodations in some of the nearby homes had to be secured for many of the out-of-town students, the dormitories being taxed to capacity. President Hickman rose and made the kind of speech we had often heard before. He waxed sanctimoniously eloquent in commenting on the great number of students at Atlanta; and, turning to Dean Hincks on the platform, he exclaimed with fervor, "And we want more of them, don't we, brother?" And the Dean responded with equal fervor, "Hey, no; we've got enough." This response took the balance of the wind out of Brother Hickman's speech.

Dean Hincks had a section of the college students as his Sunday school class. We had one lesson on the "gift of tongues" as set down in the second chapter of *The Acts of the Apostles*, where it is recorded how the apostles, after the Pentecostal baptism of fire, addressed the multitude in all the known languages of the world, and how Peter met the charges of certain mockers that the apostles were drunk by declaring, "For these are not drunken, as ye suppose, seeing it is but the third hour of the day." In the course of the lesson I ventured the comment: that while I disagreed with the opinion of the mockers, I felt that Peter's defense was not entirely sound; for it seemed quite possible that a group of men could be drunk by the third hour of the day, even on new wine, through the simple expedient of sitting up drinking all night. Either at the truth or the ignorance displayed in my comment, the Dean laughed; the point of the incident being that he laughed.

Professor Chase, too, had a sense of humor, without fear of letting others know that he had it. This quality made pretense or pose impossible for him. When the University decided to send out a quartet in the summers to interest people in school and raise funds, Mr. Chase was chosen to take charge of the boys. I sang with the original quartet; the other members were George Towns, my classmate—in our Senior year we were roommates—and two younger students, Robert Gadsden and Joseph Porter. In the course of time we sang, I should say, in ninety-five per cent of all the inhabited spots in New England. We sang in churches, hotel parlors, private drawing-rooms; in fact, wherever there was a promising opening. Our program consisted mainly of spirituals. George Towns and I made short talks about the school, and Mr. Chase made the appeal for funds. I filled two other spots on the program: I used to play a couple of solo pieces on the guitar—the instrument was almost unknown in many of the smaller places—and recite a story I had written about my experiences with a Georgia mule. This latter feature proved to be a very popular one.

One other feature on the program, always a sure-fire hit, was a popular song of the day entitled "He Never Came Back." The first verse told the story of a soldier kissing his wife good-by, going to the war, leaving "the one he did adore." The chorus went on to relate that he never came back—and "how happy she'll be, his sweet face to see, when they meet on that beautiful shore." The second verse told the story of a man going into a restaurant, calling the waiter, and ordering a steak; of how the man waited and waited for the waiter; but—in the chorus—he never came back, and "his face I will break, if I don't get that steak, when we meet on that beautiful shore." The remaining verses and choruses were equally incongruous with the first; however, we thought the song gave our program a harmless touch of lightness. Mr. Chase chuckled over it night after night. One day he received a letter from President Bumstead telling him to have the song cut from our program "at once." An elderly lady, who was a good friend of the University and the widow of a man who had lost his life in the Civil War, attended one of our concerts and wept over the singing of the first verse. She was shocked and pained by the second and remaining verses, and wrote to Dr. Bumstead about the song. Perhaps, the song didn't have a proper place in the serious business that was ours. I know it raised us many a laugh; I cannot say that it raised us any dollars. However, there was one instance in which it appealed to the most sober-minded in our audience. In a little town where we were to sing, George Towns went into the barber shop to get a shave, and was refused. A number of persons who heard of the incident expressed their indignation. Just before the concert Towns and I got together and turned out an extra verse and chorus that were sung to tumultuous applause:

> A certain little barber
> In a certain little town,
> Refused to shave another man
> Because his face was brown.
> That barber's face,
> Although it's white—
> His heart is very black;
> And when he goes to regions warm
> He never will come back.
>
> He'll never come back, he'll never come back,
> His face here we'll see never more;
> O, but how he will crave for a brown face to shave,
> When we meet on that beautiful shore.

I believe Professor Chase got as much fun out of these quartet tours as the boys did. He even got the amusing side of a concert we gave in one city for the entertainment of the inmates of the insane asylum—by the way, one of the most decorous and, apparently, one of the most thoughtful audiences I have ever appeared before.

These two grains of salt, Dean Hincks and Professor Chase, were wholesome ingredients in the Atlanta University faculty pot.

XI

I DID not spend the vacation after my Freshman year at home. Many of the students taught rural schools in the summer, and made enough money to cover their yearly expenses at the University.

These expenses did not call for a large sum; at that time, the cost of room, board, and lodging was about one hundred dollars. The stories I had heard from these student-teachers made me want to try the summer in the backwoods of Georgia. This was going to be a new experience for me. True, I was born in a very small city, but it was one, nevertheless, that had quite a metropolitan air; and I knew nothing at all of rural life. So I looked forward to this venture. I wrote to my parents enthusiastically about it.

My roommate was Henry M. Porter, a Sophomore and a student with a shining record for scholarship. I had moved up from back rooms, and the training of young rustics, to a room looking over the front campus, and a congenial companion with whom to share it. Henry Porter and I roomed together three years. He was about a year older than I, and a youth with an earnest brown face, quite regular features, and very good dark eyes. He wore his hair in a tall pompadour; from which he was familiarly known as "Pompadour Porter." He had his hair cut in this style in order to add to his height, which was barely over five feet. He was an insatiable reader. He told me that during his first year he went off the campus but once, using all his spare time for reading, and so spent only five cents above his necessary expenses. He planned to be a lawyer, and cultivated the Websterian style of oratory. He was considered one of the best speakers at the University. He carried out his plan; he finished in law at the University of Michigan, and is now practicing his profession in Chicago. Porter and I bore the unpopular distinction of being the only self-acknowledged agnostics in the school. Perhaps, the distinction was not wholly unpopular; I am sure that by some of the students we were regarded with awe if not with admiration. His agnosticism went farther than mine and was based upon a more extensive reading. His renunciation of religious conformity went farther than mine. The aloofness of his attitude at the Sunday night prayer meetings was one of the features of those gatherings. He always occupied a chair in the front row, directly in front of the platform. He sat rigidly erect and as immovable as a statue, his eyes fixed forward and his expression unchanging. He held this position until he rose to leave. This sitter in the seat of the scornful was, without doubt, a cause of great solicitude or of great irritation to Mr. Francis.

Porter knew all the steps to be taken in getting a country school to teach. I kept thinking of the possibility of not getting a place. He kept assuring me that there was no chance of such an outcome. His positiveness left no room for doubt; and I simply let him assume the entire responsibility. After commencement I went with him to a little town called Hampton, about thirty miles south of Atlanta. Here Porter's school was situated; it was the school he had taught the summer before. His position was a very choice one, because his school was in a town that had a railroad station. The station was the town's nucleus. It was a small, dingy frame building; the most conspicuous thing about it being two bold signs, one lettered "WHITE" and the other lettered "COLORED." The main portion of the station was divided into two rooms; over the door to the larger room the "white" sign was placed, and the "colored" sign over the door to the smaller. The ticket office was on the dividing line, so that one ticket seller could serve both sides. However, it was not expected that he would turn to the colored side as long as there was a white ticket purchaser in sight. Back of the station and along the street on that side of the railroad track was a short row of one-story brick and wooden stores. This row was lengthened out on either side by a line of residences, constantly dwindling in pretentiousness, the Negro cabins at the extremities. Nowhere was there evidence of a sense of order, of beauty, or of community pride. Hampton was not much of a town, but before the summer was past it was for me a metropolitan center. Out from the town, in all directions, lay the farms, the cotton plantations, and the backwoods.

I went with Porter to his stopping place. It was the nicest house in town occupied by a colored family. The owner of the house was an intelligent, light-complexioned man, who had a job with the railroad; the wife was a comely light-brown woman; and there was a pretty little girl named Alma. I wondered how her parents came to choose that name, a word that in Spanish means soul. I waited a day or two while Porter made some preliminary arrangements about opening his school, then the two of us started out in quest of a school for me. He secured the use of a sleek, fast-trotting mule and a buggy; and we radiated out from Hampton into the surrounding back country. We did not go to the school officials of the county; we went directly to the patrons. The first two or three of our excursions were fruitless; the people already had a teacher or they didn't expect to have school that summer or some other equally good reason made my services dispensable. These disappointments did not spoil the fun of the trips.

We were having a good time and many a good laugh. I was amazed and amused at hearing my friend dilate upon my qualifications as a teacher to the various local Negro school trustees with whom we conferred. The way in which he impressed them was wondrous, for his style of diction was elevated and his tone of voice stentorian even in ordinary conversation, and in putting forward my claims as a guide and teacher for youth he surpassed himself. In addition, we generally got a supper of fried chicken and biscuits. The swift drives back to Hampton through the mild night, the silences broken only by the steady tattoo of the mule's hoofs on the hard clay road, produced a pleasurable sort of hypnosis.

These disappointments brought back my doubts, but Porter remained supremely confident. Before the end of a week he got wind of a locality where they were looking for a teacher. We hitched up our mule and drove out seven or eight miles to the place; we were merely in the midst of a group of small and large cotton farms. It was a locality without a center, without a store, without even a name. We called on a man who, we had been informed, was the head of the local board of trustees—a farmer during the week and an "exhorter" on Sundays. He summoned several other members of the board, and we talked over the matter in hand. My advocate was more eloquent and impressive than ever, and I was engaged as teacher. If my memory is correct, I was to receive five cents a day for each day of attendance of each pupil. Out of my wages I was to pay an assistant, if one should be needed. These may not be the exact figures, but this was the plan. And it was the plan, at that time, by which all the Negro children in the rural districts of the state of Georgia received their sixty to one hundred and twenty days a year of public school instruction, a plan with but one thing to recommend it—the economic incentive it gave the teacher to get and keep as many pupils as possible in school.

My stopping place was with a woman whose name I cannot recall. She was a dark, wiry woman of, perhaps, thirty-eight, who kept her house clean and cooked fairly well. She had been a widow for some time, but was now again a bride. Her husband was a hulking, dull, hard-working fellow, several years younger than she. A boy, Lem, about fourteen years old was her son by her former husband. With this family of three I made my home. The house was an old, unpainted, wooden structure consisting of two main rooms. The windows were without sash, and were closed by the use of wooden shutters. There was a shed addition on the back, in which there was space for cooking, eating, and washing up. There may also have been another small room under this shed roof. On the front of the house was a short shed-covered porch. The partition dividing the two main rooms was only about six feet high. This partition, for the purpose of increasing the scant privacy, and, perhaps, to carry out ideas of decoration, was papered on both sides with sheets taken from illustrated publications. The walls of the rooms were in part covered in the same way. Each of the rooms contained a bed, a rough table, and a shelf or two. In the room that opened to the outside my landlady and her husband slept. At first it was proposed that Lem share the other room with me, and I was put in the awkward position of declining this arrangement with slightly more firmness than politeness. It was not that I objected to Lem personally, but to any further loss of the narrow margin of my privacy. Indeed, I liked Lem very much. He was a slim boy, tall for his age, with a lively, intelligent face. He had an inquiring mind, and I liked the unabashed way in which he would ask for information. I admired the long forelock that he carefully cultivated by wrapping it in twine, and on which he tied a gay ribbon for Sundays and all festive occasions. I enjoyed hearing his slow, musical laughter pitched in the middle tones of the flute. It was pleasant to watch him move; for already he walked with that easy swing from the hips, which is characteristic of Negro men and women. Lem was my daily companion to and fro on the two-mile walk between the house and the school. In fact, he was the most interesting companion I had. In our talks I learned a great deal from him about the country, about trees and crops and animals and woodcraft in general; and I tried to satisfy his curiosity about books and the outside world.

And Lem liked me. He openly avowed that he had made me his pattern. One day he looked at me with his dancing eyes and his ingratiating smile, and asked, "Professor, that little bresh you use, is that what keeps your teeth so white?" Now, in truth, Lem's teeth were whiter than mine; kept so with a homemade toothbrush consisting of a piece of twig chewed at one end until it became a soft, fibrous miniature mop. But Lem had an inquiring mind; and I explained to him the hygienic and social reasons for the toothbrush. Several days later I surprised him working industriously on his teeth with my "little bresh." I promptly made him a present of it and he was delighted. But, for some days, I couldn't get rid of the question as to how long he had been using it before it became his own. I wonder what became of that boy. He deserved a better opportunity than his locality could ever give him.

Speaking comparatively, I was comfortable. The house was situated back from the road on a rise; there were some fine trees round it, and the yard, front and back, was kept scrupulously clean by daily sweeping. I was gratefully surprised by the fare my landlady set before me; the main course being fried chicken twice a day, for breakfast and supper. However, at the end of two or three weeks it appeared that I had eaten every chewable chicken on the place. At first, this was something of a relief, for I had made the astounding discovery that man cannot live by fried chicken alone. But the table steadily degenerated until my diet was chiefly fat pork and greens and an unpalatable variety of corn bread. For a while I lived almost exclusively on buttermilk, because I could no longer stomach this coarse fare. Then it was that I looked longingly at every chicken I passed, and would have given a week's wages for a beefsteak. I was incommoded mainly by the lack of conveniences for taking a bath, and the lack of a suitable light by which to read or study at night. For my bath, I had to have a washtub brought into my room and filled. There were a couple of lamps in the house but they were used like lanterns—carried wherever they might be needed. In fact, they were hardly more than torches, because neither one of them had more than a fragment of a chimney. So I was obliged to spend my evenings before going to bed talking with Lem and his mother and step-father, and sometimes with their neighbors who came in. I got used to the washtub—it is not difficult for any normal person in normal health to adapt himself to mere inconveniences. As for light: well, I was no worse off than the philosophers and poets of Greece in her age of highest culture. I was actually being forced to gather some valuable information not to be found in books.

School was held in a shanty of a church, a rough, unpainted, board structure that had, probably, been built by the volunteer labor of the farmers round about. It was a rectangular building with sashless windows and without any attempt at architectural effect, except for a small belfry that straddled the roof at the front end, and in which there was no bell. There was, however, one pleasant outside feature; the church stood in the midst of a fine grove. Within, it was as crude as without. A shed at the back formed a niche for the pulpit. In front of the pulpit was a table used principally when collections were taken, for it was the custom—general in Negro churches—to have the members of the congregation march up the aisle and put their offerings on the table. The seats were benches, originally of rough boards, but now worn smooth and shiny by long rubbing. There was no organ or place for a choir. Nor was there a choir; the singing was all congregational. The sole hymn book was used by the preacher, and from it he lined out the hymns two lines at a time, so that they could be carried in mind by the congregation. Listening to this hymn-book singing was not a cheerful experience. The hymns were sung in a long-drawn-out and doleful manner, and with so many turns and quavers that the original melody was hardly recognizable. A prime favorite was Isaac Watts's immortal but lugubrious:

> Hark! from the tomb a doleful sound,
> Mine ears attend the cry—
> Ye living men, come view the ground,
> Where ye must shortly lie.

The congregation was natural, spontaneous, and musical only when they sang spirituals.

The only equipment I had was a table, which I used as a desk. There was not a single desk for a pupil, nor was there a blackboard. Nevertheless, I went at my work with enthusiasm. On the opening day I had two dozen or so pupils, most of them bright and eager to learn, and all of them, I guess, curious about the new teacher. I immediately started grading and classifying them. As soon as I got my school organized, I began canvassing the district for more pupils. They were slow coming in because so many children were still busy "choppin' cotton"; but when the crop was "laid by" they piled in. By the middle of the summer the number was more than doubled, and I had to have an assistant. These half-hundred children, who had so much to do with my education, who taught me so many things, who revealed to me some of my powers and more of my weaknesses; these children who were individuals to me, each one registering himself upon my mind by his appearance, his speech, his abilities, are now only a sort of composite picture in my memory. I try to recall them, and I get only a scene of blurred faces and forms. Only five of them can I separate from this blurred group image: Lem, of course, my prize scholar. The three Laster children; and just why I am able to remember them I cannot tell. They were not particularly bright; perhaps, it was their names. The eldest was a boy, known as "Pig" Laster, the middle was a girl named "Tempe," and the youngest a boy called "Tunk." "Tunk" is more than a memory with me; he remains a personality. I became interested in him the first day of school, when I found out that although it was his third term he had failed to master the alphabet. I wondered how he had managed to perform such a feat and I determined to make him break the series. (I never learned whether I succeeded or not.) I devoted my best personal effort to "Tunk" throughout the whole term, and I made the easy discovery that by the time he got slightly familiar with X, Y, Z, he had forgotten all about A, B, C. So it was not surprising that in his nine months' vacation his mind grew absolutely blank regarding everything from A to Z. "Tunk" was not stupid; he had consciously or unconsciously made up his mind that he wasn't going to study. Neither old-fashioned nor modern methods made any impression on him. I used to watch the little rascal, his book held up in front of his face, his brow wrinkled as though he was grappling with some Einsteinian problem, peeping at intervals around the corner of the book to see if I was watching. It was very amusing. "Tunk" so impressed his personality on me that a few years later I did my best to immortalize him in a poem that bears his unique name. The other pupil that I remember was a little mulatto girl of eight or nine whose surpassing beauty made me uneasy about her lot in the coming years.

I arranged my program so that school opened at eight o'clock in the morning and closed at three-thirty in the afternoon, with a forty-five-minute recess at eleven, and a fifteen-minute intermission in the middle of the afternoon. I was pretty well satisfied with my program and the way in which it worked. The children were willing and teachable, and I was proud of the progress they were making. I was also proud of the order and discipline I had established. "Self-expression" methods for primary schools had not yet, so far as I knew, been discovered. Just when I thought everything was going finely, I received a visit from my local board of trustees. They filed in quite solemnly a little before the time for dismissal, so I correctly surmised that they hadn't come to witness an exhibition of what the pupils and the teacher had accomplished. Indeed, they had come for an opposite reason; they had come to lodge a complaint against at least one of my ideas about conducting a school. When the pupils were let out, my

board went into business session, and officially notified me that the
hours per day I was devoting to teaching were too few. They informed me that all the teachers they had had prior to me had taught
from "sun to sun"—meaning, from the rising thereof to the going
down of the same. Euphemistically they expressed the opinion that
since a farmhand had to work twelve hours a day, there was no sound
reason why a schoolteacher should work only six. I listened to them
respectfully, but with difficulty because of the temptation to yield to
the humor of the situation; the difficulty being greater because of
their earnest solemnity. When they had finished, I proceeded to give
them all the pedagogical and other kinds of arguments I could muster
to convince them that the children would learn more through being
kept in school six hours a day than they could through being kept
double that time. I pointed to the hard, backless benches and asked if
any of them could stand being made to sit on them all day long. They
went away acquiescent, but, I fear, unconvinced. This scene remained
in my mind and some ten years afterwards I utilized it in a skit. I now
ask myself, why? Was it really laughable? It takes little analysis to
find that one of the mainsprings of laughter is a situation which has a
fundamental element of pathos, often of cruelty, in it.

A few days after the call from my board of trustees I had another
visitor. The pupils were out at recess and I was sitting at my table
reading a book. The book was a copy of *Don Quijote* in the original.
I became conscious that someone was standing in front of me, and
looking up I saw a very tall, white man, who I knew at once, did not
belong in the locality. He introduced himself as the County Superintendent of Schools. He was making his official visit. I asked him to
take my chair. As he sat down he glanced with curiosity at my book;
being, perhaps, puzzled by the Spanish spelling, "Quijote." In answer
to his question I told him that the book was a copy in Spanish of *Don
Quixote*; and I noted the occurrence, in some degree, of the phenomenon to which I have referred in previous pages. I rang the "bell"
by striking with one piece of iron on another piece suspended from a
wire, and the children came scampering to the door with loud cries
and laughter; but they formed their lines in good order and marched
in quietly. The Superintendent heard me conduct a class, and asked
a few questions, then addressed the scholars, speaking well of their
behavior and progress, not omitting to say some complimentary things

about their teacher. We had received a clean bill from the County Superintendent.

I enjoyed this rustic life. It was new, in some ways exciting, and I was interested in my school. I was getting a taste of the never-failing satisfaction in telling others important things they do not know. I had carried a baseball to the country and even tried to teach Lem how to pitch curves; but that was labor lost, for the boys thereabout didn't play baseball. The only standard game they played was marbles. The easy explanation was they had no suitable grounds on which to play baseball.

But not many weeks had passed before I realized a great loss, the loss of letters, letters from home, letters from friends, letters from a University girl who had promised to write me, letters with news from the world I had left. To get mail I had to go to Hampton; and the most convenient and dependable way I found of getting there was by walking. I used to set out on Friday afternoons after I had closed school and walk the seven or eight miles to town, keeping up a steady medium gait. Sometimes I would be late in starting, and would not reach Hampton before nightfall; then, after the lonely dark of the road how welcome a sight were the lights of the town. How good it was to see Porter and have him hand me the small but precious package of mail that had come addressed to me in his care. And the appetizing smell of a specially prepared supper gave a youngster who had just finished trudging miles of dusty roads a full measure of the zest of life.

I always tried to reach Hampton before night, because I knew enough to know that a strange Negro on a backcountry road in Georgia was not entirely secure, not even in daylight. But I was never in any way molested. One day I found myself passing over a section of road that was being repaired in accordance with the "road laws" of Georgia; that is, it was being "worked" by the abutting landowners— all white men. The afternoon was hot, and I passed along between the two rows of men, holding my umbrella over my head. The men stood stock-still, spades in hand, looking at me as I passed, in an amazement sprung from a sight of the incredible. I suppose that no such thing had ever happened before in the whole history of Henry County. I turned my eyes neither right nor left, but I could feel their gaze, burning me more fiercely than the sun. I had nearly covered the ground before one of the crowd found voice enough to yell, "Hey, Nigger! don't you know better'n to walk over a road whar white men's workin'?—and with a umbrella up?" I kept on walking, with, I confess, a slight acceleration.

There is nothing more effective as a thirst producer than walking over a hot clay road; and several times I had to stop and ask for a drink of water at a white farmhouse. This, too, is an act not without hazard for a strange Negro in the backwoods of Georgia. My requests each time brought the water, and no unpleasant consequences. These people, despite my youth, perhaps on account of my clothes, addressed me as though I were a preacher. The usual greeting was, "Well, Elder, whar you preachin' this Sunday?" The most alarming happenings on these journeys were not caused by men but by dogs. One very dark night when I was passing a place where the house stood far back from the road, I heard two or three dogs rushing down toward me with loud barking and baying—dangerous dogs. I was in terror, and cried out at the top of my voice, "Call your dogs off! Call your dogs off!" A man at the house called to them in a command they obeyed; and he added a sort of apology to me. My friend, William Pickens, who is black and also sometime star student at Yale, laughingly tells that he frequently and involuntarily passes for white. He says that in the deepest South he often finds it is most convenient to transact certain small matters of business with white people over the telephone; and in no instance does he fail to receive a "Yes, sir. Yes, sir." I judge that it was my speech coming out of the darkness that brought me at least the apology.

I always stayed with Porter until Sunday afternoon. The time passed quickly; we had so much to talk about. I would tell him about my school and community, and get his advice on the things that bothered me. We always went to the railroad station on Saturdays to see the four trains come in and go out, two in the morning and two in the afternoon. I never saw anybody that I knew getting off, but there was a faint excitement in watching the traffic. At any rate, I got an understanding of why country people love to meet passing trains. Occasionally we would take a Saturday to drive to some other community to attend a picnic or a fish-fry, confident that we should meet some other student-teachers. One Saturday we went to the county seat of an adjoining county. "Big Court" was in session, and court and Saturday combined had brought crowds of people to town. The main street was lined with hundreds of horse teams, mule teams, and ox teams packed in as automobiles are now parked on Main Street everywhere. We had an exciting day. We met some old friends and made some new ones. H— and T— of the old "Big Four" were there; they were teaching in that county. We found them standing near the courthouse. I had not seen either of them since they left the University, so the day wasn't long enough for us to talk ourselves out. They said that they had no intention of ever returning to Atlanta. In fact, they were going in the fall for their last year in law at the University of Michigan. Porter was anxious to see the court in action, so he and I joined H— and T— and listened to the trial of a black man charged with stealing a hog. We did not have to listen very long; the defense was perfunctory; the prosecutor made no pretense of extending himself in either effort or time; his speech in substance was, "Gentlemen of the jury, I don't have to tell you this nigger is guilty; you know it as well as I do. All you've got to do is to bring in a verdict of guilty." The verdict of "guilty" was promptly brought in. What I was witnessing was not actually the processes of a court of justice, but a circus, a Roman holiday; and the whites in the courtroom, at least those who had trekked into town in search of excitement, enjoyed it as such. They packed the hot, ill-smelling room, watching and laughing at the men, women, and children, too, caught and held and strangled in the meshes of the law, much in the same spirit as the Roman crowd howled its enjoyment at the sight of the victims thrown to the lions.

I do not recall how Porter and I went to this town, but I clearly remember how we got back. He rode a little horse, and I drove in a buggy with a fellow named Wilkins. We started late in the night, but the moon was radiant. As we drove through the fields of corn and cotton on either side of the road it seemed to me that I was experiencing something that I had dreamed or read in a poem or a story. I had never seen cotton growing until I went to Georgia; and driving through far-spreading miles of it in full bloom under the moon evoked a sense of enchantment. Porter was anything but a good horseman and he had continual and arduous ups and downs in trying to keep up with our fast-trotting mule. More than once we had to stop and wait for him. When we were passing where the road ran through a large cornfield Wilkins remarked to me, "Do you know, this mule hasn't had anything to eat since morning." "Well," I asked, "where are you going to get anything for him at this time of night?" He halted the mule, paused for a moment while he looked at me, then stated with an interrogating tone in his voice, "Here's lots of corn handy; I don't see why we shouldn't get some of that." Porter rode up and disapproved very strongly of Wilkins's plan. The latter, however, insisted that he simply could not drive the mule all day, and put him up at night with nothing to eat. Porter would have no part in the business, and rode along. I got out with Wilkins and helped him gather some corn. Breaking off the ears made a startling noise in the stillness of the night. We got what we thought was sufficient and drove on and overtook Porter. I did not become actually frightened about this episode until later, when I learned that for such an act we might have been "justifiably" shot down or sent to the penitentiary for something like life.

About the middle of the summer I changed stopping places. In visiting round among the school patrons and the Negro families of the locality I became acquainted with a man named Woodward. He was a keen, intelligent, enterprising farmer, who had just finished building a new house for himself. The house was weatherboarded and had windowpanes. On the inside it was ceiled and partitioned. I inspected a room that I was told I could have; it contained a comfortable bed, some other necessary furniture, and, above all, a real lamp. There was another inducement to change; Mr. Woodward owned two mules, and he told me that I could use one of them whenever I needed to do so. This, it struck me, would make the trip to Hampton to get my mail and see Porter feasible even in the middle of the week. My new stopping place necessitated a longer walk to school, but this, I felt, was overbalanced by the advantages. Moreover, Mr. Woodward interested me and I liked to talk with him. He was an uneducated man, but one with a good share of native intelligence—a cottonfield philosopher. He frequently delighted me with his original phraseology. I remember asking one morning for his forecast of the weather. He looked up, and pointing to a mass of cirro-cumulus clouds, said, "Fessar, see them rain eggs up there; hatch out 'fore noon." And they hatched out. Another day, in commenting to me on a piece of folly committed by one of his neighbors, he said in disgust, "I didn't believe the man knowed so much ignunce." In talking with him I learned that he was an elder brother of Sidney Woodward, the celebrated Boston Negro tenor, and that Sidney had been reared in the locality.

But with the good must be taken what is not so good; and, in my case, that was Mrs. Woodward. She was an unprepossessing woman of Amazonian proportions, addicted on weekdays to a snuff-stick, and on Sundays to cologne, a starched white dress, and vari-colored ribbons; of the latter she wore yards enough to fit out an ordinary Maypole. She was an atrocious cook, and her biscuits were marvels of size and weight. Her love of perfumery extended to her cooking. Once, she asked me if I had any cologne. I informed her that I didn't use it. She wanted it to flavor a cake. Mr. Woodward missed going to church whenever he had or could invent a fair excuse. One Sunday morning, when his wife had arrayed herself in an extra yard or two of ribbon, Mr. Woodward came up with an excuse, and asked me if I would not drive her to the meeting. I suspected that Mrs. Woodward was his real excuse. But I had no way out; I had already announced that I wanted to go and hear the man who was to preach; his fame was great throughout the region; so I responded with as much of a show of gallantry as I could put on, and served as the lady's escort. But my embarrassment rose till it reached the point of pain, and I determined that I should not again let this honor be thrust upon me.

In making the next trip to Hampton I became acquainted with Gypsy. Gypsy was the elder of Mr. Woodward's two mules. She was a venerable animal that, long before I met her, had earned the right to have nothing more to do than rest in green pastures. Her many years had added to her original endowment of mule sense; and mule sense, I think, involves a greater amount of intelligence than the so highly esteemed horse sense. An aristocratic horse, especially when caparisoned, will use up an incalculable amount of energy in merely capering round for show. The average horse, under the lash, will work himself to exhaustion. But no mule can be made, either through cajolery or by lambasting, to lose his dignified and balanced attitude toward life or labor. I at once found out that Gypsy had no intention of overtaxing her waning forces simply because of my impetuous desire to get to Hampton to read some letters or to talk to somebody. In riding this mule to town, the only advantage over going on foot was my safety from dogs. I must have made a comic figure astride this prehistoric-looking beast. Porter, at his first sight of me, threw off his air of a Roman senator and gave vent to a burst of laughter that would not have sounded strange coming from the throat of a Mississippi roustabout.

I made one never-to-be-forgotten trip with Gypsy. My school had grown so large that I had to have an assistant. I wrote to the principal of one of the Atlanta public schools, and he sent me down a boy who had just finished the eighth grade. Before my assistant could begin work he had to pass an examination. Why I was not examined I cannot remember; probably, an examination was not required of accredited Atlanta University students. For reasons of appearances, as well as of speed and certainty, I wanted to use the other mule for the trip to the county seat, where the examination was to be held, but Mr. Woodward couldn't spare him; so Gypsy was hitched to the buggy. Outward bound, we had little or no trouble. While waiting for my assistant to pass his test, I talked a bit with the County Superintendent, then walked round for a look at the town. I had not visited the place before, but it was typical, and I saw nothing to excite special attention. Before leaving I bought a fine watermelon. On the way home Gypsy performed very well until we had covered about half the distance; then she stopped. I used all the terms for addressing mules that I had picked up, but Gypsy responded to none of them. I thought the mule might, perhaps, be sick, and I got down and examined her as carefully as I knew how. She didn't look sick; merely meditative. Then I thought she might be hungry; and I took the watermelon and burst it on the ground before her. She ate it with relish, but still didn't move. I then tried to coax her along by pulling on the bridle. When I did this she began to back; and the harder I pulled, the more she backed. This convinced me that, at least, the animal was not incapable of motion; so I got up in the buggy again and employed all known devices for urging a mule forward, including the application of a hickory, but to no effect. I rested a while then tried pulling on the bridle again, and Gypsy started backing again. We should have been home in time for supper; and it was now nearing midnight. I sat dejected on the side of the road.

I worked this incident into a short story, the ending to the story being that I was seized with the idea of hitching the mule in upside down or wrongside out or stern end fore; that I then got back into the buggy and pulled on the bridle while the mule backed all the way home. Now, the reader may accept or reject that sequel, as he chooses. Recalling all I went through with that mule, it makes very little difference.

In all of my experience there has been no period so brief that has meant so much in my education for life as the three months I spent in the backwoods of Georgia. I was thrown for the first time on my own resources and abilities. I had my first lesson in dealing with men and conditions in the outside world. I underwent my first tryout with social forces. Certainly, the field was limited, the men and conditions simple, and the results not particularly vital; nevertheless, taken together they constituted the complex world in microcosm. It was this period that marked the beginning of my psychological change from boyhood to manhood. It was this period which marked also the beginning of my knowledge of my own people as a "race." That statement may not be entirely clear; I mean: I had in the main known my own people as individuals or as groups; and now I began to perceive them clearly as a classified division, a defined section of American society. I had learned something about the Negro as a problem, but now I was where I could touch the crude bulk of the problem itself with my own hands, where the relations between Black and White in the gross were pressed in upon me. Here there were no gradations, no nuances, no tentative approaches; what Black and White meant stood out starkly.

As I worked with my children in school and met with their parents in the homes, on the farms, and in church, I found myself studying them all with a sympathetic objectivity, as though they were something apart; but in an instant's reflection I could realize that they were me, and I was they; that a force stronger than blood made us one. In this study it was impossible to eliminate the element of hopelessness. I lived in this community three months without ever being on speaking terms with a single white person in it, yet knowing each one fairly well, knowing fairly well his family history, his habits, his reputation, his worth; and not being able among them all to find one, however ignorant or depraved, who was not superior to any and every Negro—superior in the eyes of the law, in opportunities, and in all the awards that the public decencies may assure to the individual. But the "race problem" is paradoxical; and, with all my inexperience, I could not fail to see that this superior status was not always real, but often imaginary and artificial, bolstered up by bigotry and buttressed by the forces of injustice. Nor could I fail to see that what is imaginary, artificial, and false cannot eternally withstand actuality and truth.

But had I been totally blind to any crack or weak spot in the thick wall standing on the line of race and color, I should not have come through this phase of my education a victim of utter hopelessness; intellectual curiosity would have saved me. I was anxious to learn to know the masses of my people, to know what they thought, what they felt, and the things of which they dreamed; and in trying to find out, I laid the first stones in the foundation of faith in them on which I have stood ever since. I gained a realization of their best qualities that has made any temptation for me to stand on a little, individual peak of snobbish pride seem absurd. I saw them hedged for centuries by prejudice, intolerance, and brutality; hobbled by their own ignorance, poverty, and helplessness; yet, notwithstanding, still brave and unvanquished. I discerned that the forces behind the slow but persistent movement forward of the race lie, ultimately, in them; that when the vanguard of that movement must fall back, it must fall back on them. The situation in which they were might have seemed hopeless, but they themselves were not without hope. The patent proof of this was their ability to sing and to laugh. I know something about the philosophy of song; I wish I knew as much about the philosophy of laughter. Their deep, genuine laughter often puzzled and irritated me. Why *did* they laugh so? How *could* they laugh so? Was this rolling, pealing laughter merely echoes from a mental vacuity or did it spring from an innate power to rise above the ironies of life? Or were they, in the language of a line from one of the blues, "Laughing to keep from crying"? Were they laughing because they were only thoughtless? Were they laughing at themselves? Were they laughing at the white man? I found no complete answer to these questions. Probably, some of all the elements suggested entered in. But I did discover that a part of this laughter, when among themselves, was laughter at the white man. It seems to me that for the grim white man in the backwoods of the South this deep laughter of the Negro should be the most ominous sound that reaches his ears.

We of the vanguard often look with despair at these very characteristics of the masses. We feel that these easy-going traits constitute our chief racial weaknesses and the chief hindrance to faster progress. This impatience on our part is understandable, but I believe it involves an underestimation. It takes no account of the technique for survival that the masses have evolved through the experience of generations. It does not give them credit for the fact that in their ignorance and defenselessness, with the weight of outnumbering millions on their shoulders, they persisted, they straightened up their bent backs by degrees, and from the travail of their agony buried in laughter brought us forth as tokens of their potentialities. They used the methods available; and those methods were not always aimlessness and dumb servility. For one thing, they learned the white man with whom they had to deal. They learned him through and through; and without ever completely revealing themselves. Their knowledge of that white man's weaknesses as well as his strength came to be almost intuitive. And when they felt it futile to depend upon their own strength, they took advantage of his weaknesses—the blind side of arrogance and the gullibility that always goes with overbearing pride. It is possible that these masses might have done much better—I am not unmindful of their numerous shortcomings—yet, it is certain that they might have done much worse.

The most vital factor in the future of a race is the power to survive; and the masses have an instinctive knowledge of their possession of that power. Firm confidence is theirs through having survived every degree of hardship and oppression to which any race may be subjected. I saw strong men, capable of sustained labor, hour for hour, day for day, year for year, alongside the men of any race. I saw handsome, deep-bosomed, fertile women. Here, without question, was the basic material for race building. I use the word "handsome" without reservations. To Negroes themselves, before whom "white" ideals have so long been held up, the recognition of the beauty of Negro women is often a remote idea. Being shut up in the backwoods of Georgia forced a comparison upon me, and a realization that there, at least, the Negro woman, with her rich coloring, her gayety, her laughter and song, her alluring, undulating movements—a heritage from the African jungle—was a more beautiful creature than her sallow, songless, lipless, hipless, tired-looking, tired-moving white sister.

I was graduated in 1894. The Atlanta University commencement program indicated no distinctions, but it was unwritten opinion that the first and last places on the program were the honor points; I was given last place. On this occasion I made the attempt to break through the narrow and narrowing limitations of "race," if only for the hour. I went as far beyond the boundaries as I could go, farther, certainly, than my capabilities warranted me in going, and made the subject of my oration, "The Destiny of the Human Race." At graduation I had two choices before me: through President Bumstead I had a chance for a scholarship in medicine at Harvard; in Jacksonville Mr. Artrell was retiring, and I had a call to take charge of Stanton School. I was weary of going to school; I wanted to get out and do something. I became principal of Stanton.

I frequently live again my days at Atlanta; and, now, the hardships that once appeared so huge have, naturally, dwindled to infinitesimal proportions. Indeed, I have to brush away a glamorous haze, in order to see things as they appeared to me then. Grown older, I occasionally meditate upon the kind of education Atlanta University gave me. The conception of education then held there and at other Negro colleges belonged to an age that, probably, is passing never to return. The central idea embraced a term that is now almost a butt for laughter—"service." We were never allowed to entertain any thought of being educated as "go-getters." Most of us knew that we were being educated for life work as underpaid teachers. The ideal constantly held up to us was of education as a means of living, not of making a living. It was impressed upon us that taking a classical course would have an effect of making us better and nobler, and of higher value to those we should have to serve. An odd, old-fashioned, naïve conception? Rather.

PART TWO

XII

THE time of the psychological passing over from boyhood to manhood is a movable feast. The legal date fixed on the twenty-first birthday has little or no connection with it. There are men in their teens, and there are boys in their forties. This passing over is really not across a line, but across a zone. There are some who are driven across early in life by the steady pressure of responsibility. A few, projected by some sudden stroke of fate, take the zone in a single leap. But most of us wander across somewhat as the Israelites wandered across the Arabian Desert; and a good many of us grow old without ever getting completely over.

This train of thought ran through my mind as I sat in front of the Stanton teachers, whom I had called together a day or two before the opening of school. I looked at them—some had been teachers when I was a pupil at Stanton, among these, my sister—and they looked at me. I talked to them a while; then we discussed school matters. But what I wanted most to know was their unexpressed thoughts about me; doubtless, they had a corresponding curiosity. I found myself talking almost mechanically about things not at the center of my thoughts. I am three months past my twenty-third birthday. . . . I have in my hands the administration of a public school with a thousand pupils and twenty-five teachers. . . . This is not a job for a boy; it's a man's job. . . . Can I actually do it? . . . Of course, I can; it's essentially the same job as my school in the backwoods of Georgia. . . . Yes, it's that, but it's more. It is so much more complex that it is practically a different job. Here, first of all, are twenty-five assistants, whose respect for my ability I've got to get. Some of these assistants will have to be convinced. They would laugh if I failed. . . . My position is an important one. Relatively, it is far more important than the principalship of the white grammar school. Its disproportionate importance makes me a mark. I shall be scrutinized. I shall meet with envy and antagonism on the outside; and, perhaps, with disloyalty on the inside. . . . What sort of a start am I making? . . . The first impression these teachers get of me will be far-reaching; of what sort is it?—Through all these thoughts run alternating currents of confidence and doubt.

I had an academic education, but had had no special training as a teacher. But I had already discovered for myself that three-fourths of the art of teaching consists in the ability to rouse the pupil's interest— at least, his curiosity—in the thing he is to learn; and that that ability is not imparted by a course in pedagogy. My work at Stanton, however, was not that of teaching, but of organization and administration; in fact, it was the business of conducting a large institution. Here was something concerning which I knew nothing; but it was on the technical side and could easily be learned; in the main it entailed a knowledge of methods of systematization; and I determined to learn as much about it as I could and as quickly as possible.

It seemed that the first practical step for me to take would be to see how they did things at the white central grammar school and make a comparison with the way we did things at Stanton. I talked with Mr. Glenn, the superintendent of schools, and my plan seemed to strike him favorably. He said to me, "You know McBeath; go up and see him, and tell him what you want." Mr. McBeath was the principal of the white school. I had met him a number of times in the superintendent's office, and we were on rather friendly terms. Early one morning I presented myself at his office in the Jacksonville Grammar School, and at once gave him the reason for my visit. He was pleased, perhaps flattered. He answered my questions and offered me information on methods of administration he had found to be effective. I thanked him; but there was one other thing I wanted to accomplish on my visit; I wanted to make a direct comparison between the class-room work of the teachers in his school and those in mine. I expressed my desire to go into the classes. He took me to the primary department and introduced me to one of the teachers. He saw that I had a chair, then left me, saying that I was free to visit any of the classes. I spent the entire forenoon going from class to class observing and making mental notes. As I entered each room I introduced myself to the teacher as the principal of Stanton School; at the same time stating that Mr. McBeath had extended me the privilege of visiting the class-rooms. My self-introductions were met with varying degrees of graciousness, politeness, embarrassment, and stiffness. Most of the pupils exhibited undisguised curiosity. I went away feeling that I had gained a good deal.

Several days later I was astounded to learn that my visit to the white grammar school had raised a hullabaloo. It appeared that a number of parents, hearing of it through teachers and pupils, were outraged and alarmed over my unprecedented behavior. The affair was fomented to such an extent that the board of education felt it necessary to hold a meeting to inquire into the matter and fix the responsibility for my action. This explosion from what I had thought of as merely a natural and reasonable act was not only an overwhelming surprise to me, it was a manifestation of the limits of utter asininity to which race prejudice can go. This manifestation was so clear that, in talking the matter over with members of the board, I could not but feel the superiority of my position. I knew the majority of the men on the board quite well; they were men of intelligence; and I wanted to feel for their sakes that they were ashamed of the silly exhibition they had been called to take part in. Mr. Glenn stood his ground; so did Mr. McBeath, and the affair blew over. The incident was the beginning of a close acquaintance between Mr. McBeath and me.

I did not have to teach at Stanton, but I liked to go into a teacher's room and take her class for a while. I particularly liked to take a class in arithmetic. After I left Stanton I spent six years studying branches of higher mathematics. When I returned as principal, I found that I did not know arithmetic; so I started in to remedy that defect in my educational foundation. It was pleasant work; arithmetic is not only an interesting study, it is also a most fascinating pastime. With excusable vanity, I sometimes amazed a class by performing an arithmetical stunt for them. I mastered a formula for extracting the cube root of numbers at sight. I would set the pupils to work cubing numbers, and calling off the cube—which often ran up into the hundreds of thousands—to me while I stood at the blackboard and wrote it down; then, without pausing, I would write down the cube root. This stunt never failed to rouse the interest of a class in arithmetic. It had some analogy to the inspiring of faith by the working of a miracle. I tried to discover and prove the principles that underlay the "rules of arithmetic." I saw that the "rules of arithmetic" were accepted as axiomatic and so used. For example, the rule for the division of fractions used to read: Invert the terms of the divisor, and proceed as in multiplication. I found no pupils and few teachers who understood and could explain the reason for this process. Getting at simpler and more understandable methods of solution became an absorbing game. I made frequent use of a very simple problem to illustrate the rational method of reduction to unity. The problem was: One pumping engine can fill a boiler in a minute; another can fill it in a half-minute; how long will it take both of them pumping together to fill it? I have seen pupils and teachers stumped by this problem. I have seen college graduates resort to algebra to solve it. The direct solution, of course, is: The two engines can fill the boiler *three* times in *one* minute; therefore they can fill it once in one-third of a minute, or twenty seconds.

I was astonished and amused to find myself using mannerisms when I taught a class. I found myself walking up and down, gesticulating with a ruler, and occasionally giving myself a resounding thwack on the skull with it. These were the mannerisms of Mr. Francis. At recess I walked round the grounds on the boys' side; I tried to avoid giving the impression that I was watching and seeing things; I carried a slender rattan cane, which I sometimes used to flick the legs of unruly boys; I couldn't resist a chuckle over the boyhood memories of "Old J.C." that came back to me; I discovered with a very pleasurable satisfaction that the boys spoke of me as "Old Man Johnson"; I observed that play was not so rough as it was in my boyhood at Stanton; shinny had been abandoned, baseball was the predominant game; I enjoyed giving the boys pointers on play and explanations on the workings of "inside baseball."

The matter of patrol, rattan cane, and all that sounds rather old-fashioned. The question at the bottom of the matter caused me much anxiety at the time. The attitude of the teacher toward his pupils and the response to it that he draws from them constitute a delicate problem. Shall he act the tyrant, and be feared as one? Or shall he be just one of the fellows, and loved as one? It seemed to me that efforts from either end of the scale would be about equally inefficient, so far as the business of teaching was concerned; that no fixed policy could be laid down; that it was a matter of adjustment to varying conditions. I am glad that my principalship of Stanton was in a period before the time when a director of play—or whatever is the exact title for the new profession—might have been annexed to my teaching force. That sounds more than old-fashioned, I know. It sounds archaic. We speak of carrying coals to Newcastle; the language is not capable of a metaphor to convey the idea of superfluity in an adult teaching children how to play. I know that large groups of children at play require oversight, especially is this true in the case of boys, in order that the smaller and weaker may not be molested or imposed upon by the bigger and stronger fellows, and that the spirit of rowdyism likely to crop out in any crowd of healthy boys be held in check. Aside from that, they ought to be let alone. When children play to themselves they are natural, naïve, and spontaneous. Furthermore, they are inventive, imaginative, ingenious, and resourceful; capable not only of devising games but the things needed for playing them. One of the greatest delights an adult can experience is to obliterate himself and watch them. It is an experience through which he may, perhaps, recapture some of the joy of being a happy child. But as soon as an adult pokes his nose into the business, children become unnatural, self-conscious, imitative, embarrassed, insincere, even priggish. Against this breaking into and spoiling the Child's World I should be willing to see a law passed.

At the close of my first year, twenty-six were ready to be graduated from the eighth grade. This was all the education the city of Jacksonville gave me, and it was all it was giving them. I had been thinking about them for some time. . . . They are entitled to as much as others. . . . Why shouldn't they get it? . . . But how? . . . Well, that sounds like a feasible plan. . . . Can I carry it through? . . . I think I can. . . . I'll try it. . . . I'll do it. I did do it; I made Stanton a high school.

In these latter years, since I have witnessed and participated in so many hard fights by Negroes, through petitions, legal proceedings, and by political action, to secure high schools, I look back with almost unbelief at the simplicity, the assurance and ease with which I accomplished what I set out to do. Scarcely did the school board, to say nothing of the white people in general of Jacksonville, know it was being done. This is all there was to the plan in its beginning: I first got the members of the class interested in the project; then I persuaded their parents to let them come back the following year. I laid out a course for them that was practically the Junior Prep course at Atlanta University. I myself taught the class. The next year I followed the same procedure; told the superintendent what I had done, and asked for an assistant. I discontinued the use of the general assembly room for devotions and converted it, by using curtains for partitions, into extra classrooms. The next year I obtained another assistant. I introduced Spanish as the modern language in the course, and taught it myself. That, in short, is the plan by which Stanton Grade School was developed into Stanton High School. Of course, the plan could not have succeeded if the superintendent had not supported me after that first year, and if the board of education had not accepted a *fait accompli*.

Seven years had wrought changes. I noted that Jacksonville was for me, in many ways, a different place. There were changes in the life at home—Rosamond was away; Ricardo was away; my mother was permanently lame; my grandmother was fast aging, and her terrific energies slowing down; and my father, for the first time, struck me as an elderly man. A house that had been lively, gay, and, because of the activities of three growing boys, sometimes noisy, had become quiet and subdued. So my father and I were thrown together a good deal, and in a new relationship: not only as father and son, but as two men. It was at this point that I began to distinguish between my love for him as a good father and my admiration for him as a good man. I gauged the respect he had won from the community through the simple virtues of industry and integrity. I saw the evidences of it wherever I went with him. And I saw the regard in which he was held for the work to which he had given himself. He was the pastor of a very small church made up of very poor people. He showed no ambition to have charge of a larger and richer congregation. He said to me a number of times, "I am not a preacher by trade." By which he meant that he was not influenced by the emoluments of the office. His spirit of self-sacrifice might be somewhat minimized by the fact that he had acquired a competence, but not wholly discounted. In addition to the work in his little church, he did a sort of general missionary work. He was the only colored minister—I do not know if there was any white one—who was willing or not afraid to go and pray for a dying woman in the quarter for prostitutes in Jacksonville. The women of the quarter called him "Father Johnson" and they knew whenever they sent for him in such cases that he would come. He was very simple and unostentatious in all this. He did not even affect a noticeable clerical appearance. Indeed, he was at that time one of the only two preachers I knew who did not seem to believe that a long-tailed black coat was one of the evidences of Christianity; Joseph Twitchell of Hartford was the other. This adaptation by my father of Christianity to life in good measure made a deeper impression on me than all the formal religious training I had been given.

My mother, on account of her lameness, had stopped teaching, but she was still the choir leader of her church. She asked me to join the choir, and I did. My voice had developed into a fairly good baritone, and I enjoyed the singing. My mother frequently assigned me a solo part in an anthem. My choir duties took me to church mornings and evenings each Sunday, so I was a regular attendant. An effort was made to have me take the superintendency of the Sunday school; but this, in spite of the pleas of my grandmother and my mother, I absolutely refused to do.

My mother talked to me a good deal about a matter she had mentioned in letters written to me while I was still at the University, but concerning which she could not be as free in writing as in talking. It was much in her mind; one of her best friends, Alonzo Jones, was involved. He was one of a number of colored men who, because of the steady change from the old and rather favorable attitude towards Negroes in Jacksonville, resolved to prepare to meet the worst. They ordered a rifle and a quantity of ammunition for each man in the group. Alonzo Jones made the great error of having the whole shipment consigned to him. This action was indicative of the man. He was impulsive and incautious. It is probable that some of the men were timid, and he rashly assumed the entire responsibility. But he had real courage, and would never humbly or quietly tolerate any infringement upon what he believed to be his rights. At this time he was a man of about fifty, stoutish, very dark, and rather morose in disposition. His father had been a bricklayer and a successful man, who had bought several pieces of property on a street that became one of the principal thoroughfares of the city. The son followed the father's trade and worked industriously to improve the property that had been left to him. When the incidents I am relating took place he was worth, perhaps, fifty or sixty thousand dollars. Events followed fast after the arrival of the rifles. A Negro walking along the street eating a banana throws the peel on the sidewalk. A white policeman orders him to pick it up. He refuses. The policeman draws his club, and a struggle ensues. The Negro is down and is being severely clubbed by the policeman. He somehow gets hold of the policeman's pistol and shoots him through the heart. The Negro is rushed to the Duval County jail. Excitement runs high and increases hourly. "Crackers" from the surrounding country pour into town. Lynching is in the air. The county jail is bounded on three sides by the houses of Negroes, and several hundred colored men with rifles, shotguns, and revolvers man the windows and roofs of these houses. Women supply them with food and hot coffee. Some of the more daring of the women parade cans of kerosene, vowing that if the prisoner is lynched, they will lay the town in ashes. Two or three local companies of militia are called out and thrown round the jail. They make no attempt to dislodge or disperse the armed Negroes on guard. Some of the Negro leaders confer with the militia officers and declare that, together with the troops or without them, they will defend the prisoner against any mob. The prisoner is not lynched.

My mother is stopping at a boarding house at Pablo Beach. Alonzo Jones has run down for a few days. The boarders are all friends and acquaintances. In the night the sheriff and his deputies come and demand entrance in the name of the law. They arrest Alonzo Jones, charging him with conspiracy to incite a riot. They take him away handcuffed, amidst the tears and cries of the women, who believe he is being dragged to his death. The whole affair, especially the arrest in the middle of the night, makes an impression of terror on my mother's mind that she cannot rid herself of. I am deeply moved by her recital of these happenings, and I feel an exultant pride in the men who manned the windows and housetops to safeguard the prisoner, and in the women who brought them food and coffee.

Alonzo Jones was not the only one involved; several others, all prominent Negroes, were arrested. But the chief onus was fixed on him because of the record in the office of the express company which proved it was to him that a large number of rifles had been consigned and delivered. Two or three influential white men used their good offices in behalf of the Negro leaders charged with conspiracy. Mr. Jones was released under heavy bond; another, Dan Tresvan, chef in one of the hotels, was paroled for a number of months as cook for a young millionaire; D——'s father and several others were saved from imprisonment. The affair blew over. The whites recovered from the jolt they had received, tranquilized, no doubt, by the feeling that the spirited figures among the blacks had been taught an unforgettable lesson. Alonzo Jones was financially ruined. He heeded what was probably the best advice, and jumped his bail. He went to Port Chester, New York, to live and work at his trade. His wife remained in Jacksonville to look after the property, but all of this was eventually swallowed up by the bond. He died in Port Chester, a broken man.

There were changes outside of home. D—— was away—working in a cigar factory in Tampa. Some of the boys and girls I had known best were scattered. Heart's Desire, even if she had not forgotten me, had married and gone to live in another town. More marked was the change in social life. During my boyhood the social affairs among colored people in Jacksonville were for the most part public or semi-public. There were church festivals and bazaars; there were picnics and excursions, up the river to Green Cove Springs or down to the sea at Pablo Beach; there were concerts and entertainments in National Hall, Jones' Hall, Redwood, and other halls. At secular affairs there was a band for dancers, but dancing was strictly under the ban for people who belonged to the church. Now, I found that there was a social life which had a degree of exclusiveness. There were many more homes that were comfortable and commodious; and entertainment among those who went in for society had become largely a private matter. The women who were leaders in affairs social were sharply divided into two groups: a Chautauqua group that took up culture and serious thinking, and gave mild entertainments; and a group which put more stress on the mere frivolities, gave whist parties and house dances, and served a punch of more than one-half of one per cent strength. Certainly, in my boyhood the well-to-do colored people gave entertainments of one sort or another in their homes, to which they invited those with whom they associated, but I don't think there was such a thing as "society." "Society" was one of the new things I found. I also found that the men had gone in for it. There had been organized a social club called *The Oceolas*, which gave two or three dances each winter. I was, quite naturally, invited to join this club, and I did join; thereby unwittingly starting some trouble for myself.

This social life was, in its proportionate degree, a replica of all the pettinesses of "society" in general. There were present the same snobbishness, the same envies and jealousies, the same strivings and heartburns, the same expenditure of time and energy upon futilities. And, as in "society" in general, it was the women who were the chief sticklers and arbiters; among the men there was a certain democracy. In the Oceola Club a man's occupation had little or nothing to do with his eligibility. Among the members were lawyers, doctors, teachers, bricklayers, carpenters, barbers, waiters, Pullman porters. This democracy, however, was not exactly laxness; I knew of one or two cases in which, for one reason or another, the possession of money failed to force entrance. On one point, this black "society" was precisely like Southern white "society"—anyone belonging to an "old family," regardless of his pecuniary condition or, in fact, his reputation, was eligible. Knowledge of this fact would have struck Southern white people as funny, probably, without their being able to tell just why. In Charleston, South Carolina, colored "society" was quite old, having its beginnings among the free Negroes of that city before the Civil War. And a member of the Charleston set was as proud of his social standing as any member of the *St. Cecilia*. There were then similar social groupings in all the Southern cities, in fact, in all the cities of the country where there was a considerable Negro population; and there was an interchange of privileges like those accorded to a member of an order in good standing in going from one lodge to another. At the present time, just as with white people, this punctilious phase of "society" is fast becoming obsolete among Negroes in the larger cities.

One of the first things I did with the money I was earning as a teacher was to gratify a wish that had long been denied fulfillment. When I was a small boy I longed for two playthings, above all others: a real snare drum—not of the toy kind, but of the kind used in bands—and a velocipede. But, although around Christmas time, for a number of years, I used to lie stretched out in front of the hearth and write dozens of cajoling letters to Santa Claus, I never got either of the gifts. Once, the drum seemed to be within my grasp. Some white young men had organized a brass band, and my father had in some way stood good for the purchase of the instruments. The band failed and the instruments reverted to him. I pleaded with my father to give me the drum, but in vain. The whole outfit was displayed in the window of Campbell's music store and sold piecemeal to members of the various Negro bands. The velocipede I did not get, perhaps, because there was no place within a half mile of our house where it could be ridden. On one of my childhood journeys to the St. James Hotel I saw a boy riding a bicycle, one of the old-fashioned, high-wheeled affairs, round and round in the bandstand that stood in the center of St. James Park. I watched him as long as I could, entranced. The rider was Ralph D. Paine, whose father was then pastor of the white Methodist church that stood on the side of the park opposite the hotel. My wish was then transferred from a velocipede to a bicycle.

The time had now come when I could gratify that wish. I bought a second-hand machine of the old safety type, a Victor that weighed sixty or seventy pounds, and was almost as difficult to mount as the old high-wheeled variety. Shortly afterwards, I discarded the Victor and bought a low, light model, quite like the machines used today. It was a good investment; it afforded me exercise, fresh air, and a lot of enjoyment. I rode to and from school. On many nights a crowd of bicycle owners would meet and we would ride the ten miles of shell road that ran out from Main Street and circled back along the river into the city. Also, I got lots of fun out of the then current gallantry of teaching the art of riding to young ladies, many of whom, at the first wobbling of the machine, would with nice little screams turn loose the handle-bar and throw both arms around your neck.

I bought my bicycle from a man named Gilbert; and I stopped in at his shop whenever I needed repairs. He was a pleasant sort of man, and we grew rather friendly; so friendly that I formed the habit of stopping in occasionally when I didn't need repairs, merely for a chat. In those days the bicycle shop rivaled the barber shop as a place for the exchange of masculine talk and gossip. I used to talk freely about race and racial injustices with white men in town that I knew; perhaps more freely than cautious judgment would have warranted. I got away with it, probably, because most of the men I talked with knew my father well, and had known me since my boyhood. Once, however, I did get a mild warning. One afternoon I stopped in at Gilbert's and found a half-dozen or so white men gathered there, none of whom I knew particularly well. I joined in the talk, which, through me, I suppose, finally shifted to the race question. I was expressing some of my opinions when I was interrupted by a nondescript fellow, who remarked with a superb sneer, "What wouldn't you give to be a white man?" The remark hit me between the eyes. The sheer insolence of it rocked me. The crowd tittered. The hot retort surged up for utterance. With great effort I collected and held myself and replied in as measured and level a tone as I could command, "Let me see. I don't know just how much I would give. I'd have to think it over. But, at any rate, I am sure that I wouldn't give anything to be the kind of white man you are. No, I am sure I wouldn't; I'd lose too much by the change." He went livid, then purple. The titter died. For an instant it looked as though a physical clash would break from the dark cloud of silence. But the young fellow himself seemed to realize that to beat me up would not improve his position in the eyes of the witnesses to the incident. He was spiritually licked. I rode away satisfied. I, at least, felt free from that regret which comes from thinking later of something that might have been said. Yet, I was disturbed; and I thought: I must go over this question frankly with myself; I must go down to its roots; drag it up out of my subconsciousness, if possible, and give myself the absolutely true answer. I made a sincere effort to do this. I watched myself closely and tried to analyze motives, words, actions, and reactions. The conviction I always arrived at was that the answer I gave the young man in the bicycle shop was the true one; and true not only so far as it went, but farther.

That same remark, implied if not expressed, has many times since been thrown at me. I judge that every intelligent Negro in the United States has met it in one form or another. And it is most likely that all of us have at some time toyed with the Arabian Nights-like thought of the magical change of race. As for myself, I find that I do not wish to be anyone but myself. To conceive of myself as someone else is impossible, and the effort is repugnant. If the jinnee should suddenly appear before me and, by way of introduction, say, "Name the amount of wealth you would like to have, and it shall be given you," I, gauging my personal needs and a sum sufficient to enable me to do freely the things I like to do, should reply, "Give me three hundred thousand dollars in (if such there still be) sound securities." If I thought of the sum in terms of some other things I might do with money, I should test the limits of the jinnee's generosity and power. If he should say, "Name some boon you desire, and it shall be granted," I think I should reply, "Grant me equal opportunity with other men, and the assurance of corresponding rewards for my efforts and what I may accomplish." If, coming to the principal matter, he should say, "Name any person into whom you would like to be changed, and it shall be done," I should be absolutely at a loss. If, continuing, he should say, "Name any race of which you would like to be made a member, and it shall be done," I should likewise be at a loss. If the jinnee should say, "I have come to carry out an inexorable command to change you into a member of another race; make your choice!" I should answer, probably, "Make me a Jew."

Among my youthful ambitions, teaching had never had a place. Not until I was about to finish at Atlanta University had I given it any thought as a vocation. But I liked the work, and I was intensely interested in my plan to develop Stanton into a high school. Toward the end of my first year of principalship, however, my thoughts began to rotate around one of my early ambitions; I thought again about publishing and editing a newspaper. I finally decided to undertake it. I took the few hundred dollars I had saved from my salary, borrowed from my father more than I had saved, and formed a partnership with a young man named M. J. Christopher. We planned to publish an afternoon paper to be called *The Daily American*, believing—and, so far as I can learn, we were right—that it would be the first Negro daily ever published. I was to be the editor and he the business manager; I estimated that my duties on the paper would not interfere with my school work. Two of my former classmates at Atlanta, George A. Towns and N. W. Collier, also put some money into the enterprise. We bought on time a flat-bed cylinder press that was run by a gas engine, and the necessary composing room equipment. We arranged with a concern in Atlanta to furnish us an electrotyped dispatch service. When *The Daily American* appeared, it met with the enthusiastic acclaim of the colored people.

Immediately after the closing of this first school year I went to Tampa to attend the annual meeting of the state association of colored teachers. There I saw D—— again. He was working in a cigar factory and was in a discouraged state of mind. Much had happened in his venturesome life since I had last seen him, several years before, sitting in front of a barrel stripping tobacco in his father's little factory. Between two and three thousand dollars had been realized from the sale of a piece of property that had been left to him by his mother. He had had a stiff row with his father over this money, but, by legal action, had got possession of the cash. For this, it seems, his father never forgave him. With the money in his possession he immediately left Jacksonville. This time, as Ricardo had done, he followed Rosamond's trail and went to Boston. He went with some undefined plans of continuing his education, and studying law at Harvard. Before getting down to work, he yielded to an impulse to take a little fling at life. He procured an expensive wardrobe—clothes by a fashionable tailor and haberdashery and shoes by custom makers. He ate only in the smartest places, and never took a street car if a cab was obtainable. He moved in the quite exclusive social set of Negro Boston, doubtlessly dazing those staid, more or less dark New Englanders with his opulent display. In Negro sporting circles he was an even greater favorite, a "Little Napoleon."

Before he got round to his plans, the money was gone. His jewelry and the best of his clothes found their way to the pawnshop. He steadily settled to that low level which we politely call reduced circumstances. Finally, eating regularly became a problem involving the unknown. He then made his way back to Jacksonville, and from there to Tampa.

These experiences of D——, which I have condensed into three hundred words, filled the major part of his talk with me during the six days I was in Tampa. I sat late into the night listening to his adventures. He related incident after incident in his racy, half-cynical manner, giving a punch to the whole recital by his not meager command of profanity. He caused me to laugh heartily over some of his most dire situations. I knew that he had acted recklessly, but I admired, perhaps envied, the way in which he could challenge life. I asked him if he would come to Jacksonville and take a place on *The Daily American.* He was happy to do it. When we left Tampa it was together; and he started work as a reporter at fifteen dollars a week.

The meeting of the teachers' association was not an exceptionally brilliant affair. The majority of the papers were dull or immature. The discussions that followed were often more interesting and enlightening than the papers; occasionally they were exciting. The social features were more satisfying, and, perhaps, more important than the intellectual features. It was a great pleasure to meet and know teachers from all parts of the state; and, at any rate, I gained more valuable information about the work of educating Negro youth in Florida from conversations with individuals and groups than I did from the laboriously written papers. The large number of visitors added to the social success of the gathering. Of one of these visitors I carried away a haunting recollection. I remembered her only because of her extraordinary beauty; in fact, I spoke scarcely a score of words to her, but I could hardly take away my eyes from her face. The color of her face was that delicate brown, light enough to glow rosily, which is so commonly found among women of mixed black and white blood. But under her raven hair, parted simply in the middle, her low, lovely brow took on the tint of mellow ivory. The curve of her cheek and the line of her throat were faultless. The nose was slightly fleshy, but perfectly molded. Her eyes, dark, liquid, and deeply shaded, produced in me a sensation akin to the fascinating dread of looking into unknown depths. Her red, ripe, sensuous mouth was in disquieting contrast to the Madonna-like upper portion of the face and head. That provocative mouth, with its vivid splash of color, its hint of wantonness, quickened the whole countenance out of the cold placidity of saintly beauty. What a face, I kept thinking, for a painter!

The initial success of *The Daily American* astonished its founders. Subscriptions poured in. There were, perhaps because of curiosity to know what was going on among Negroes, quite a number of white subscribers. Congratulatory letters were written by patrons and encomiastic sermons delivered by preachers. Applications from persons wishing to be agents came in from many towns in Florida and south Georgia. The plant and offices became a Mecca for visitors. I was elated. I felt that the undertaking transcended any personal ambition; that an instrument had been created that would be a strong weapon in the Negro's defense against racial inequalities and injustices; that the colored people of the community had come into possession of an adequate medium through which they could express themselves, of a voice by which they could make themselves heard across the race boundaries.

I was over-sanguine. We kept the paper going for eight months, then were forced to suspend. As I watched the press turn for the last time I was a sadly discouraged young man. It was my first disappointment at the failure of the masses to respond to what I myself felt to be an important effort towards racial advancement. Had I known how many similar experiences were in store for me, I should have taken this one more philosophically. And yet, I had used myself up so fully between my school duties and the struggle to keep the paper afloat that the definite silence of the press brought me a sense of relief. The failure of *The Daily American* was my first taste of defeat in public life, and for quite a while was bitter in my mouth; so bitter, that at a meeting held shortly thereafter in which the need of Negro business enterprises was being discussed I made the statement that the only sound investment I could at the moment think of was a Negro cemetery, because Negroes had to die, had to be buried, and, with few exceptions, had to be buried in Negro graveyards.

My disappointment at failure was natural, but I have now for a long time known that I was by no means blameless. I had allowed enthusiasm to overshoot good judgment. I ought to have discovered by other than empiric methods that the colored people of Jacksonville, regardless of what their will might be, were not able to support the kind of newspaper I sought to provide for them. There were two contributing reasons for the failure. One was the mistake of tying up all our cash capital in a plant. The other was the competition of the "colored columns" carried in the two white afternoon papers, which reported religious, fraternal, and social activities among the colored people of the city. The reader is, of course, at liberty to add another reason: the possibility that the paper was not as well run as it might have been. All in all, I now look back on this experience with satisfaction. I even reason, perhaps consolingly, that defeat was better for me then than easy success. But my biggest satisfaction has come from looking over the files of the paper. I have reread my editorials and seen that I would not feel called upon to make any apology for them today.

The closing down of the paper left D—— high and dry; and for six months or so the going for him was pretty hard. His father grudgingly gave him food and shelter, but would do nothing beyond that. He evidently got a sweet satisfaction out of proclaiming that his prediction that the boy would never amount to anything had come true. In the summer of 1896 D—— got a break. The local Democrats had split. The younger element in the party had grown recalcitrant, and was making an effort to wrest control of the machine from the old wing. This younger element, known as the Straightouts, was led by John N. C. Stockton, a banker. Mr. Stockton, as I remember, was ambitious to go to Congress. The fight was fierce and close; and while it was being waged there happened the thing that is bound to happen whenever there is a split in the Democratic Party in the South: both sides made bids for the Negro vote. The fear that such a thing might happen generally is the nightmare of the Southern political oligarchy. The determination to keep it from happening is the single foundation stone on which the political solidarity of the South rests; it is also the chief reason why white men in the South have very little if any more political independence than black men.

In some way D—— came to the attention of Mr. Stockton and was engaged by him to campaign for the Straightout ticket. He addressed colored meetings in various sections of the town and throughout Duval County. He was well fitted for this work; his rough and tumble style made him a very effective stump speaker. I wondered then and many times afterwards at the things he could say to Negroes about themselves. They took from him with indulgent laughter statements for which from me they would have demanded my head. D—— was again affluent, and life was once more a game to be played gayly. But in the election in the fall the machine won—which, except for a miracle, it always does. Within several months D——'s prosperity had dwindled, and within several months more he was back in his former condition. All that remained to him from his political activity was Mr. Stockton's promise to "do something for him"; a promise which probably meant when it was made that D—— would get some sort of political job, if the Straightouts won.

While D—— was getting his first lessons in practical politics, my thoughts were rotating around another of my earlier ambitions; I began planning to study law. Early in the fall I made arrangements and started. I didn't go to law school, but studied by the then most approved method in the Old South; that is, by reading law in a lawyer's office. The man who made it possible for me to do this was Thomas A. Ledwith, a young and, as the term is used, brilliant member of the Jacksonville bar. Mr. Ledwith's father had been a prominent man in Florida. He was a Republican of the Reconstruction era and had held several high federal offices. He was also wealthy; he had owned the building used as the city market, the Ledwith block on the principal street, and other properties. But when he died it was discovered that his wealth had shrunk to almost nothing; and young Ledwith, reared as a rich man's son, was faced with the struggle of making his own way and a living. In this struggle he did not follow the political path of his father, but, recognizing the changes, joined the Democratic Party. His office was in the Law Exchange Building, and there I spent a part of each day; when there was no school, I spent the whole day. After I had been studying about six months Mr. Ledwith turned over to me the duty of drawing most of the necessary papers. This lightened his work and was very advantageous for me. He had a good practice in divorce matters, and I gained proficiency in drawing bills in these cases. He gave me a good deal of his time in discussing knotty questions and in quizzing me in various legal subjects.

At the end of eighteen months my friend—we had become friends—said he thought I ought to try the examination for admission to the bar. I didn't feel so sure about it as he; however, my application was filed and the day for my examination set. The nearer the day approached, the more anxious I grew. I think Mr. Ledwith passed through a similar experience. This was the first time in Duval County and, for all I could learn, in the state of Florida, that a Negro had sought admission to the bar through open examination in a state court. There were two or three Negro lawyers in Jacksonville, but each of these, I believe, had been admitted in the Federal Courts during or shortly after the Reconstruction period, and were admitted to practice in the state courts through comity.

The day came. I went over to the courthouse in a state of high tension. I had spent the greater part of the night before in a last effort at preparation. There was one fact that was reassuring to me as I entered the building: I was to be examined before Judge R. M. Call, a very fair man. Negroes in the South have a simple and direct manner of estimating the moral worth of a white man. He is good or bad according to his attitude toward colored people. This test is not only a practical and logical one for Negroes to use, but the absolute truth of its results average pretty high. The results on the positive side are, I think, invariably correct; I myself have yet to know a Southern white man who is liberal in his attitude toward the Negro and on the race question and is not a man of moral worth. Judge Call, in the estimation of the colored people of Jacksonville, was a "good man," and he was a good man. My bit of reassurance was quickly lost in the realization that my examination had taken on the aspect of a spectacle. The main courtroom was full. Probably half the lawyers in Jacksonville were present. More people were present than I had many times seen at a murder trial in the same room. I judged that some were there out of curiosity, some out of mild interest, and others to see the fun. I did not look at the crowd. I felt that there was only one face in it that would reflect true sympathy; and my eyes did occasionally seek the face of my friend, Ledwith; there I could read at a glance the barometric rise and fall of my chances. But Ledwith was a highly nervous man and he freely exhibited his deep concern. He constantly fidgeted and ran his fingers through his very red hair. His undisguised anxiety was far from being a source of confidence for me. I determined to let nothing interfere with the working of my mind. I concluded that I would need to know all that I knew, and know it on the instant. So I kept my attention focused as steadily as I could on my examining committee, before whom I was seated six or eight feet away.

The judge had appointed a committee of three. One was E. J. L'Engle, a son of one of Florida's ruling families, who had been admitted to the bar several months before. Another member was Major W. B. Young. I do not know whether his military rank was derived from membership in the militia or whether he had been a very young major in the Civil War or had merely been breveted because of the legal battles he had fought. He was a medium-sized, bantam-like man; a man who, in the Negro idiom, "strutted his stuff." He had reddish hair, fierce gray eyes, a beak of a nose, and wore a mustache and imperial after the pictured tradition of the Southern aristocrat. His presence on the committee disturbed me, because by the "Negro test" and in the general estimation of the colored people of Jacksonville he was a "bad" white man. The third member was Duncan U. Fletcher, one of the outstanding members of the Jacksonville bar. In my mind, his presence on the committee balanced that of Major Young; for I knew of his reputation as a fair and just man. Mr. Fletcher is now the senior United States Senator from Florida.

The examination started. The questions were fired at me rapidly; little time being allowed for consideration. Sometimes the same question would be camouflaged and fired a second time. As the examination proceeded I gained confidence. Before it was over Major Young took up a copy of The Statutes of Florida and began examining me therefrom. It was my impression that the unfairness of this unprecedented procedure was regarded with disapproval by the other members of the committee and by Judge Call. After two hours there was a lull in the questioning. A lawyer named W. T. Walker, sitting near the committee, leaned over and asked, "Well, what are you going to do about it?" Mr. Fletcher answered, "He's passed a good examination; we've got to admit him." Major Young commented—I quote him precisely; for his words blurted out in my face, made their sizzling imprint on my brain: "Well, I can't forget he's a nigger; and I'll be damned if I'll stay here to see him admitted." With that he stalked from the courtroom. Mr. Fletcher conferred for a moment with Judge Call. The judge then asked me a few questions in equity and international law. Mr. Fletcher conferred with him a moment more, then stood before the bench and made the motion for my admission. Judge Call bade me rise and swore me in as a counselor, attorney-at-law, and solicitor in the courts of the State of Florida. Mr. Fletcher and Mr. L'Engle both congratulated me. Two or three other lawyers offered me a good word. My friend, Ledwith, was nowhere in sight; he explained to me later that when the committee began to confer he could stand the strain no longer. I found him in the office. He had already heard the news, and was beaming with satisfaction. But his first words of congratulation were: "That was the damnedest examination I ever heard or heard of."

One day, almost a year before my admission to the bar, D—— came to me and said, "Mr. Stockton wants to carry out the promise he made to do something for me. He doesn't know what he can do, and I don't know just what to ask him to do." I suggested, "Why don't you ask him to send you to law school? Ask him to send you to Ann Arbor; it's one of the best in the country." D—— jumped at the suggestion. His enthusiasm, always either very high or very low, bubbled over. He was jubilant at the prospect, and at once wanted to know, "If Mr. Stockton sends me to Ann Arbor, why can't you go too?" My answer was, "I'd certainly like to go, but I can't do it. There are two reasons: I haven't got the money; I went broke and in debt on *The Daily American*; and even if I had the money, I wouldn't want to break off my plans to develop Stanton into a high school." Mr. Stockton did carry out his pre-election promise, despite the fact that he had been defeated—which, perhaps, was evidence that he had no real aptitude for practical politics—and in the fall D—— left for the University of Michigan. At the end of his first year he returned to Jacksonville, just a few days after my admission to the bar. While we were talking about my examination it is probable that D——'s quick mind was working something like this: If Jim can pass without having gone to any kind of a law school, why can't I after a year at the University of Michigan? At any rate, he revealed his intention of trying the examination. I knew what his reasoning had been, and I told him that I had had the advantage of a year of practical legal work and of familiarity with the rules and forms of practice in Florida; that, however, with some hard work I believed he could prepare himself to pass. We worked together the whole summer and late into the fall, using the quiz method and studying the forms used in the Florida courts. D—— took the examination and was admitted. His examination was not so well attended as mine; I judge the first novelty had worn off. Immediately he and I formed a partnership. We did what I doubt would now be possible—we secured rooms in one of the principal office buildings of the town. We planned a division of work: he was to give the main attention to the office and the work in court, while I was to give as much time at the office as my school duties would allow, and draw the papers. The new firm began to pick up business from the start. We got cases of many kinds. It took me a while to rid myself of the state of depression resulting from the fact that our client in our first murder case was hanged. I gained some relief, however, from the reflection that he, being a Negro, would have been hanged anyhow, had his lawyer been Duncan U. Fletcher or even the redoubtable Major Young.

In the following spring the state teachers' association met at Tallahassee. I was bound by duty to go, and D—— thought that it would be a good thing for both of us to be there and look for the opportunity to be admitted to the State Supreme Court. In quest of that opportunity, we climbed the central red hill of the town, up to the capitol. In one of the corridors we met a man who shouted, "Hey, what are you two fellows doing here?" The man was Frank T. Clark, a Jacksonville lawyer. We told him that our main reason for visiting the capitol was to find someone, if we could, who would help us in being admitted to the Supreme Court. Mr. Clark said at once, "Why, come along with me; I'll do it myself." We followed him into the Supreme Courtroom, and in less time than it takes to tell about it he had made the motion and we had been admitted. A short while afterwards Mr. Clark was elected to Congress. For a number of years he justified his presence there by introducing at each session a bill to provide for "Jim Crow" street cars in the District of Columbia.

Years later, while I was secretary of the National Association for the Advancement of Colored People, I appeared at a hearing before the Census Committee of the House of Representatives. The Association was laying before the Committee facts concerning the prevention of Negroes from voting in Southern states, especially Florida, at the preceding general elections, and demanding the reduction of the Congressional representation of Southern states in accordance with the Fourteenth Amendment. Mr. Clark rose and made a perfect demagogic speech, which undoubtedly was mailed to his whole constituency. After the hearing adjourned, he complimented me on my presentation of our case.

XIII

ROSAMOND came back home in the spring of 1897. He had been away seven years, six of which he had spent studying music and working in Boston, and one in traveling with a theatrical company. John W. Isham had been the advance agent for the *Creole Show*, the forerunner of all the modern Negro musical comedies. Later, Mr. Isham produced *The Octoroons*. In 1896 he planned a more ambitious production, and for it secured the best trained Negro singers and musicians then available. From Boston he secured Sidney Woodward, the tenor, and my brother. The show was called *Oriental America*. Rosamond came back eager about the theater. Also, he had had two popular instrumental pieces published and was full of ideas and plans about songs and plays and operas that he and I should write together. He was impatient at finding me immersed in the study of law. His enthusiasm roused my curiosity about this new world into which he had had a peep, and I became, as I had at times before and have many times since, keenly aware of the love of venture that runs in me, a deep, strong current. But I have from my father a something—which I have often thought limits me as an artist—that generally keeps that deep, strong current from bursting out and spreading over the surface. This something hinted to me: You had better finish the business you have in hand before you jump into another that you know absolutely nothing about. So I told my brother that I should have to get through with my studies and take my examination before I could begin work with him. I have often rebelled against these cautious admonitions; but, generally, I have followed them, saying to myself in justification: One need not be an irresponsible fool in order to be a good artist. Three times in my

life, however, with a vital decision before me, I have thrown caution
to the winds, and in each instance the results have somehow worked
out better than I had dreamed.

While I went on with my study of law, Rosamond began establishing himself as a teacher of music. In starting he showed more
than a mere knowledge of music; first, he took one of the front rooms
of our house and converted it into a studio; then, following the
formulas of exclusive teachers of music in big cities, formulas that
are based on sound principles of psychology, he announced that "Mr.
Johnson, etc., etc., etc., will accept a limited number of pupils in
piano and voice on terms of twenty half-hour lessons for fifteen dollars or twenty forty-five-minute lessons for twenty dollars." This
was revolutionary. Most of the colored people in Jacksonville who had
studied music had been taught by peripatetic teachers who were glad
to collect twenty-five cents a lesson. The result of this bold stroke
together with his ability as a teacher was the rapid accumulation
of a waiting list of pupils. Several of the older local music teachers
came to study under him. In addition, he became choirmaster and
organist for one of the large Baptist churches, and taught music once
a week at the Baptist Academy. After he had been teaching seven
or eight months he "presented" his pupils in a recital. Public performance of music by children and young people was nothing new
to the colored people of Jacksonville. They had long been hearing
and applauding the extremely *adagio* playing of *Maiden's Prayers*
and the dashing off of familiar *gavottes* with steady acceleration,
but they were not prepared to hear little girls play worthwhile
music with such a show of virtuosity. This recital set a new standard for musical entertainments in Jacksonville. And it did another
new thing; it started local white music lovers coming to concerts
given by colored people.

In the meantime, Rosamond had thumbed through my notebooks
and found several lyrics which he liked and to which he composed
music. One of these was a poem on Easter. He made an anthem of
it, and had it sung by his choir. This anthem increased his local reputation more than was warranted, I think. Indeed, my personal feeling
is that it would not be gross injustice to give the composers of
most of the anthems written for church choirs a light jail sentence
for each offense. Of course, if my brother ever writes a book, I

shall not object to his saying that something of the sort ought to be done with the poets who write most of the poems on Easter.

The closing exercises of Stanton constituted an important social as well as educational event. They were held in the local theater because of the large crowd that had to be accommodated. They had been of the conventional kind—songs, solos, vocal and instrumental, original essays and declamations by the graduates, and the presentation of diplomas by the Superintendent of Schools. For the closing in the year after my brother's return, he and I decided to try an innovation. We planned the program in two parts; the first to be an operetta performed by the pupils, and the second to consist of the graduation exercises and the presentation of diplomas. We concocted a juvenile libretto with a plot adapted to music taken from *The Geisha* and *The Runaway Girl*. The operetta was a grand success. The audience was enthusiastic over it; but the joy of the children who took part in it was what pleased us most. I can remember with what verve, what sheer delight they sang "O, Listen to the Band" from *The Runaway Girl*. They had never sung such music before. But, for the finale we had arranged a simple dance movement that was performed by the whole company, and thereby was brought down on my head the wrath of several of the colored clergy; the special wrath and condemnation of the pastor of one of the large Baptist churches, who declared I was "leading the children to the ballroom." This same pastor ran a weekly newspaper which carried one of those "We Know" columns in which responsibility for slander was avoided by not using names. However, he came out openly in his paper and lambasted me on what he asserted was my reputation as one of the best dancers at the affairs given by the Oceola Club; he harshly criticized me for being the club's president and for being a smoker. These attacks caused some talk, but did not produce the effect that the reverend gentleman unquestionably expected. They nevertheless annoyed me more than I cared to confess. On the board of education they made no impression at all. The members took the matter as something to be smiled at, knowing that each year, following the custom in colleges, the white high school gave a "Junior Prom" at which students, teachers, parents, and friends danced together; and also that most of the men teachers in the white public schools smoked. This dancing finale to the operetta brought on my first skirmish with a group of colored preachers in Jacksonville over matters which I considered innocent, and which they professed to consider sinful.

My bar examination was over, school was closed, and, aside from coaching D——, I had nothing pressing to do; so I was ready to begin with Rosamond on one of his big ideas. The idea he picked for a start was big enough; it was that he and I should write a comic opera. Rosamond felt pretty confident about the music, but I felt rather shaky about a libretto. We cast around for a story; and, as unlikely as it might seem that two such amateurs could do it, we found a capital one. The United States had, the year before, annexed Hawaii, and was at the time engaged in the Spanish-American War. We decided to write a comic opera satirizing the new American imperialism. The setting was an island kingdom in the Pacific. The story was concerned with Tolsa, the beautiful princess; her prime minister, a crafty old politician; the entrance of an American man-of-war; the handsome, heroic American lieutenant; and finally annexation. Old stuff now, but not so then. In fact, nothing of the sort had yet been produced on the American stage. We worked earnestly, and at the end of about a year had the opera finished. While we were working on it Rosamond frequently played completed parts over for the leading musical people of the town: Mr. Kerrison, the director of the Jacksonville Conservatory of Music; Mr. Kahn, the manager of the principal music store; Mrs. Lund, a musician and a beautiful and aristocratic woman, and the mother of the Lund boys mentioned in an early chapter of this account; and one or two others. One night Mr. Benedict, a partner of the firm of Furchgott and Benedict, the largest dry goods store in Jacksonville, "threw a party" for us. Mr. Benedict was a business man who was at heart an artist. He had two boys still in their teens for whom, it seemed, his highest ambition was that they should become accomplished musicians. There were a dozen or so people present, and they spoke enthusiastically of our work when Rosamond played and sang parts of the opera. The host served a supper of sandwiches, potato salad, more kinds of cold meats than I knew that there were, and beer. This was the first interracial-artistic party in our experience.

The attention and praise we received from the people in Jacksonville who knew most about music, naturally, increased our confidence in our work. We decided to try our fate in New York, and early in the summer of 1899 we set out for the metropolis. We left Jackson-ville with the good wishes of friends, white and colored. Mr. Kahn gave us a letter to Mr. Freund, editor of one of the New York music trade journals. Mr. Kerrison gave us a word of warning. He cautioned us that we had a valuable piece of work which was not copyrighted, and to be very careful, because New York was full of pirates just waiting for the chance to plunder. We set out sanguine of success.

This was one of the determinative incidents in my life. As I look back on it now I can see that it was almost quixotic; that in the under-taking there was none of my father's practical sense. Two young Negroes away down in Florida, unknown and inexperienced, starting for New York thirty-three years ago to try for a place in the world of light opera. I can now recognize all the absurdities and count up all the improbabilities in it.

As soon as we had settled in a couple of rooms in West 53rd Street we presented our letter of introduction to Mr. Freund. He, in turn, gave us a letter to M. Witmark and Sons, music publishers, who had published a number of light opera scores. We got an appointment and played the opera for Isadore Witmark. We were with him a couple of hours, and he appeared to be favorably impressed by the songs and choruses. Just as we finished, Harry B. Smith and Reginald DeKoven, then the two greatest American writers of light opera, entered. Mr. Witmark introduced us as two young men who had written an opera. "Well," said Mr. Smith, "let's hear it; we might be able to steal something from it." Mr. DeKoven and Mr. Witmark laughed. We didn't quite see the joke—if it was a joke—and, remem-bering Mr. Kerrison's warning, gathered up our precious manuscript and made a quick exit. Later we did laugh about it; and later we did collaborate with both Mr. Smith and Mr. DeKoven, realizing that had it not been for our caution and the extremely high value we placed on our work we might have collaborated with them imme-diately following that first introduction.

The opera, *Toloso*, was never, as such, produced, but it served to introduce us to practically all of the important stars and producers of comic opera and musical plays in New York. The great Oscar Hammerstein climbed to our modest rooms in West 53rd Street to hear it played. It seemed to open doors by magic. Of course, the temerity of youth, our utter innocence with respect to the impas-sability of any doors—I hesitate to add, our invincible faith in ourselves—had something to do with this. We ultimately adapted most of the single numbers, and they were produced in one or another Broadway musical show. I have often looked over the score of our opera and seen that a practiced hand could have whipped it into shape for production. It is possible that the managers were a bit afraid of it; the Spanish-American War had just closed, and they may have thought that audiences would consider a burlesque of American imperialism as unpatriotic. Not long afterwards, however, George Ade, in *The Sultan of Zulu*, used the same theme successfully.

In the fall Rosamond and I went back to our teaching in Jacksonville and to do more writing. Before we left New York we met Bob Cole. Bob was one of the most talented and versatile Negroes ever connected with the stage. He could write a play, stage it, and play a part. Although he was not a trained musician, he was the originator of a long list of catchy songs. We also met Williams and Walker and Ernest Hogan, the comedians; Will Marion Cook, the Negro composer; Harry T. Burleigh, the musician and singer; and a number of others, doing pioneer work in Negro theatricals. I attended rehearsals of two Negro companies that were preparing for the coming season, and I took in something of night life in Negro Bohemia, then flourishing in the old Tenderloin District. Into one of the rehearsals I was attending walked Paul Laurence Dunbar, the Negro poet. The year before he had written in collaboration with Cook an operetta called, *Clorindy—The Origin of the Cakewalk*, which had been produced with an all-Negro cast and Ernest Hogan as star by George Lederer at the Casino Theater Roof Garden, and had run with great success the entire summer. Mr. Lederer was the principal and most skillful musical play producer of the period. His production, *The Belle of New York*, with Dan Daly and Edna May, was one of the greatest successes the American stage had seen. But he learned some new things from *Clorindy*. He judged correctly that the practice of the Negro chorus, to dance strenuously and sing at the same time, if adapted to the white stage would be a profitable novelty; so he departed considerably from the model of the easy, leisurely movements of the English light opera chorus. He also judged that some injection of Negro syncopated music would produce a like result. Mr. Lederer was, at least, the grandfather of the modern American musical play. Ironically, these adaptations from the Negro stage, first made years ago, give many present-day critics reason for condemning Negro musical comedy on the ground that it is too slavish an imitation of the white product. I had met Dunbar five years before, when he was almost unknown; now he was at the height of his fame. When he walked into the hall, those who knew him rushed to welcome him; among those who did not know him personally there were awed whispers. But it did not appear that celebrity had puffed him up; he did not meet the homage that was being shown him with anything but friendly and hearty response. There was no hint of vainglory in his bearing. He sat quiet and unassuming while the rehearsal proceeded. He was then twenty-seven years old, of medium height and slight of figure. His black, intelligent face was grave, almost sad, except when he smiled or laughed. But notwithstanding this lack of ostentation, there was on him the hallmark of distinction. He had an innate courtliness of manner, his speech was unaffectedly polished and brilliant, and he carried himself with that dignity of humility which never fails to produce a sense of the presence of greatness. Paul and I were together a great deal during those last few weeks. I was drawn to him and he to me; and a friendship was begun that grew closer and lasted until his death. A day or two before I left he took me into Dutton's on 23rd Street, where he bought a copy of his *Lyrics of Lowly Life* and inscribed it for me. It is one of my most treasured books.

These glimpses of life that I caught during our last two or three weeks in New York were not wholly unfamiliar to Rosamond, but they showed me a new world—an alluring world, a tempting world, a world of greatly lessened restraints, a world of fascinating perils; but, above all, a world of tremendous artistic potentialities. Up to this time, outside of polemical essays on the race question, I had not written a single line that had any relation to the Negro. I now began to grope toward a realization of the importance of the American Negro's cultural background and his creative folk-art, and to speculate on the superstructure of conscious art that might be reared upon them. My first step in this general direction was taken in a song that Bob Cole, my brother, and I wrote in conjunction during the last days in New York. It was an attempt to bring a higher degree of artistry to Negro songs, especially with regard to the text. The Negro songs then the rage were known as "coon songs" and were concerned with jamborees of various sorts and the play of razors, with the gastronomical delights of chicken, pork chops and watermelon, and with the experiences of red-hot "mammas" and their never too faithful "papas." These songs were for the most part crude, raucous, bawdy, often obscene. Such elements frequently are excellencies in folk-songs, but rarely so in conscious imitations. The song we did was a little love song called *Louisiana Lize* and was forerunner of a style that displaced the old "coon songs." We sold the singing rights to May Irwin for fifty dollars—our first money earned. With the check the three of us proceeded joyfully to the Garfield National Bank, then at Sixth Avenue and 23rd Street, where Bob was slightly known. The paying teller looked at the check and suggested we take it over on the next corner to the Fifth Avenue Bank, on which it was drawn and have it O.K.'d. It is always disconcerting to have a bank teller shove a check back to you, whatever his reasons may be, so we went over to the other bank not without some misgivings. The teller there looked at it and said, "Tell them over at the Garfield Bank that the check would be good if it was for fifty thousand dollars." Bob delivered the message. Next, we took the manuscript to Jos. W. Stern and Co., who published the song.

When I got back to Jacksonville I found that my artistic ideas and plans were undergoing a revolution. Frankly, I was floundering badly: the things I had been trying to do seemed vapid and non-essential, and the thing I felt a yearning to do was so nebulous that I couldn't take hold of it or even quite make it out. In this state, satisfactory expression first came through writing a short dialect poem. One night, just after I had finished the poem, I was at Mr. McBeath's house talking about school matters; then about books and literature. He read me a long poem he had written on Lincoln—a Lincoln poem, the expression of a Southern white man. I thought it was good and told him so. I also thought but did not say that there was yet to be written a great poem on Lincoln, the expression of a Negro. Aloud, I repeated for him my dialect poem, *Sence You Went Away*. He thought it was good enough for me to try it on one of the important magazines. I sent it to *Century*, and it was promptly accepted and printed. Outside of what had appeared in Atlanta University periodicals and in the local newspapers, this was my first published poem. Some years later my brother set this little poem to music. It has proved to be one of the most worthwhile and lasting songs he has written. It was first sung by Amato, the Metropolitan Opera baritone; it was afterwards recorded for the phonograph by John McCormack, with a violin obbligato played by Kreisler; and was again recorded by Louis Graveure and still again by Paul Robeson. It continues to find a place on concert programs.

During the winter I wrote more dialect poems, some of them very trite, written with an eye on Broadway. Rosamond made some pretty songs out of these trivialities and put them aside for our next migration to New York. In the same winter Rosamond planned a concert such as had not before been given by or for colored people in Jacksonville. He brought Sidney Woodward down from Boston. The affair was successful, artistically and financially, beyond our expectations. The concert sent the level of musical entertainment among the colored people many degrees higher. Nor were its effects limited to the colored people; it was a treat for the hundred or so local white music lovers who were present, for, indeed, not all of them had before heard a tenor with Woodward's voice and technical finish.

A group of young men decided to hold on February 12 a celebration of Lincoln's birthday. I was put down for an address, which I began preparing; but I wanted to do something else also. My thoughts began buzzing round a central idea of writing a poem on Lincoln, but I couldn't net them. So I gave up the project as beyond me; at any rate, beyond me to carry out in so short a time; and my poem on Lincoln is still to be written. My central idea, however, took on another form. I talked over with my brother the thought I had in mind, and we planned to write a song to be sung as a part of the exercises. We planned, better still, to have it sung by schoolchildren— a chorus of five hundred voices.

I got my first line:—Lift ev'ry voice and sing. Not a startling line; but I worked along grinding out the next five. When, near the end of the first stanza, there came to me the lines:

> Sing a song full of the faith that the dark past has taught us.
> Sing a song full of the hope that the present has brought us.

the spirit of the poem had taken hold of me. I finished the stanza and turned it over to Rosamond.

In composing the two other stanzas I did not use pen and paper. While my brother worked at his musical setting I paced back and forth on the front porch, repeating the lines over and over to myself, going through all of the agony and ecstasy of creating. As I worked through the opening and middle lines of the last stanza:

God of our weary years,
God of our silent tears,
Thou who hast brought us thus far on our way,
Thou who hast by Thy might
Let us into the light,
Keep us forever in the path, we pray;
Lest our feet stray from the places, our God, where we met Thee,
Lest, our hearts drunk with the wine of the world, we forget Thee . . .

I could not keep back the tears, and made no effort to do so. I was experiencing the transports of the poet's ecstasy. Feverish ecstasy was followed by that contentment—that sense of serene joy—which makes artistic creation the most complete of all human experiences.

When I had put the last stanza down on paper I at once recognized the Kiplingesque touch in the two longer lines quoted above; but I knew that in the stanza the American Negro was, historically and spiritually, immanent; and I decided to let it stand as it was written.

As soon as Rosamond had finished his noble setting of the poem he sent a copy of the manuscript to our publishers in New York, requesting them to have a sufficient number of mimeographed copies made for the use of the chorus. The song was taught to the children and sung very effectively at the celebration; and my brother and I went on with other work. After we had permanently moved away from Jacksonville, both the song and the occasion passed out of our minds. But the schoolchildren of Jacksonville kept singing the song; some of them went off to other schools and kept singing it; some of them became schoolteachers and taught it to their pupils. Within twenty years the song was being sung in schools and churches and on special occasions throughout the South and in some other parts of the country. Within that time the publishers had recopyrighted it and issued it in several arrangements. Later it was adopted by the National Association for the Advancement of Colored People, and is now quite generally used throughout the country as the "Negro National Hymn." The publishers consider it a valuable piece of property; however, in traveling round I have commonly found printed or typewritten copies of the words pasted in the backs of hymnals and the songbooks used in Sunday schools, Y.M.C.A.'s, and similar institutions; and I think that is the method by which it gets its widest circulation. Recently I spoke for the summer labor school at Bryn Mawr College and was surprised to hear it fervently sung by the white students there and to see it in their mimeographed folio of songs.

Nothing that I have done has paid me back so fully in satisfaction as being the part creator of this song. I am always thrilled deeply when I hear it sung by Negro children. I am lifted up on their voices, and I am also carried back and enabled to live through again the exquisite emotions I felt at the birth of the song. My brother and I, in talking, have often marveled at the results that have followed what we considered an incidental effort, an effort made under stress and with no intention other than to meet the needs of a particular moment. The only comment we can make is that we wrote better than we knew.

XIV

SCHOOLS were again closed, and Rosamond and I left Jacksonville on our second trip to Broadway. We did not carry much new work, for his teaching was taking up more and more of his time, and I had given most of my spare hours to my law practice. D—— was not exactly pleased when I announced that I was going to New York again, and I saw that our partnership could not last much longer on such a basis. A short while after we reached New York I went into another partnership, a curious partnership. My brother, Bob Cole, and I formed a partnership to produce songs and plays. I have not known of just such another combination as was ours. The three of us sometimes worked as one man. At such times it was difficult to point out specifically the part done by any one of us. But, generally, we worked in a pair, with the odd man as a sort of critic and adviser. Without regard to who or how many did the work, each of us received a third of the earnings. There was an almost complete absence of pride of authorship; and that made the partnership still more curious. At first, we printed the three names at the top of the sheet, but three names on little songs looked top-heavy; so we began printing only two; sometimes we printed but one. Our first firm name for the title page was, "Johnson, Cole, and Johnson." After Bob and Rosamond became noted in vaudeville under the name of Cole and Johnson, we changed our title-page signature to "Cole and Johnson Brothers." Furthermore, the agreement was actually a rather loose one; Rosamond collaborated with Harry B. Smith and other librettists, and I did some songs with other composers. I also worked with Will Marion Cook on a comic opera called *The Cannibal King*. The partnership lasted seven years, in which time we wrote some two hundred songs that were sung in various musical shows on Broadway and on "the road." We gained our start as a firm in the early part of the summer by writing several songs for May Irwin's new play.

On the night of August 15, 1900, we were at our rooms in West 53rd Street. Bob Cole's company had begun rehearsals for the coming season, but he had been sick for several days and unable to attend them. For that reason, Billy Johnson, his theatrical partner, had come up to 53rd Street to rehearse some of their numbers. Rosamond played the songs, but the rehearsal took longer than he expected and he had to break an engagement to go with a friend, Barry Carter, and two young women to an entertainment of some sort. He was very much disappointed over this. He worked until about ten-thirty, then he and I walked to the corner of Eighth Avenue with Billy, who would there take a street car to go down where he lived, somewhere around Thirtieth Street. We waited fifteen minutes, a half-hour, an hour; no car passed going in either direction. We thought it strange. Billy finally hailed a hansom. We had just gone off to sleep when our door bell rang. There was a young white man at the door, who asked if we knew Barry Carter. He went on to tell us that Carter had been beaten up and was in the Jefferson Market jail. When we expressed the determination of going down to see what we could do, the young man impressed on us that we shouldn't even try to go; that a mob was raging up and down Eighth Avenue and the adjacent side blocks from 27th to 42nd Streets attacking Negroes wherever they were found, and that it was not safe for any colored person to go through that section. We followed his advice. The next morning the newspapers told the story of a great race riot. We found Carter in a sad condition. He had kept the appointment, and was walking along one of the side streets with both the young women, ignorant of what was going on, when a crowd of young hoodlums ran up from behind and began beating him over the head with pieces of lead pipe. He struggled away and ran to a squad of policemen on the Avenue, but they met him with more clubbing. His scalp was cut open in several places, and his arms were terribly bruised and swollen to twice their natural size from the blows received in trying to protect his head. It was a beating from which he never fully recovered.

This was the fourth great clash in New York involving the Negro. The first the so-called "Negro Insurrection" in 1712; the second was the so-called "Conspiracy (of the Negro slaves) to burn New York and murder its inhabitants" in 1741; the third was the draft riots in 1863. The riot of 1900 grew out of an altercation between a white policeman in plain clothes and a Negro, in which the former was killed. The outbreak was, beyond doubt, fomented by New York police, but it had more than local significance; it was, in fact, only a single indication of the national spirit of the times toward the Negro. By 1900 the Negro's civil status had fallen until it was lower than it had been at any time since the Civil War; and, without noticeable protest from any part of the country, the race had been surrendered to Disfranchisement and Jim-Crowism, to outrage and violence, to the fury of the mob. In the decade ending in 1899, according to the records printed in the daily press, 1665 Negroes were lynched, numbers of them with a savagery that was satiated with nothing short of torture, mutilation, and burning alive at the stake.

At the end of the summer my brother and I were fully satisfied with the advancement we had made in gaining recognition, but the financial returns had been small; so small that we had to borrow money to get back to Jacksonville. The outlook, except from the point of view of art for art's sake, did not appear very encouraging. At home again in Jacksonville, Rosamond found that his pupils and classes and recitals took more of his time than ever before. And now that Stanton was a high school, it allowed me very little time for anything else, even for my law practice. Nevertheless, I continued writing poems, most of them in dialect, and after the style of Dunbar.

But just at this time I came across Whitman's *Leaves of Grass*. I was engulfed and submerged by the book, and set floundering again. I felt that nothing I had written, with the exception of the hymn for the Lincoln celebration, rose above puerility. I got a sudden realization of the artificiality of conventionalized Negro dialect poetry; of its exaggerated geniality, childish optimism, forced comicality, and mawkish sentiment; of its limitation as an instrument of expression to but two emotions, pathos and humor, thereby making every poem either only sad or only funny. I saw that not even Dunbar had been able to break the mold in which dialect poetry had, long before him, been set by representations made of the Negro on the minstrel stage. I saw that he had cut away much of what was coarse and "niggerish," and added a deeper tenderness, a higher polish, a more delicate finish; but also I saw that, nevertheless, practically all of his work in dialect fitted into the traditional mold. Not even he had been able to discard those stereotyped properties of minstrel-stage dialect: the watermelon and the possum. He did, however, disdain to use that other ancient "prop," the razor.

I could see that the poet writing in the conventionalized dialect, no matter how sincere he might be, was dominated by his audience; that his audience was a section of the white American reading public; that when he wrote he was expressing what often bore little relation, sometimes no relation at all, to actual Negro life; that he was really expressing only certain conceptions about Negro life that his audience was willing to accept and ready to enjoy; that, in fact, he wrote mainly for the delectation of an audience that was an outside group. And I could discern that it was on this line that the psychological attitude of the poets writing in the dialect and that of the folk artists faced in different directions: because the latter, although working in the dialect, sought only to express themselves for themselves, and to their *own group*. I have frequently speculated upon what Dunbar might have done with Negro dialect if it had come to him fresh and plastic.

In my muddled state of mind I tried to gain orientation through a number of attempts in the formless forms of Whitman.

In the early part of the spring I had the opportunity of talking these questions through with Dunbar. Following the example of Rosamond's successful venture of the winter before with Sidney Woodward, I arranged to have Paul come to Jacksonville for a public reading. This affair was equally as successful as the Woodward concert, and, likewise, it was attended by a large number of local white people. Dunbar's success on the platform, and it was great, was due not only to his fame as a poet, but also to his skill as a reader. His voice was a perfect musical instrument, and he knew how to use it with extreme effect. I furthermore arranged with Mr. Campbell, the manager of the St. James, for a reading in the hotel parlors.

But Paul's visit to Jacksonville was more than professional; in arranging for him to come down, my brother and I had asked him to stay with us as long as he liked. He visited with us about six weeks. In that time I grew to know him intimately. He was the Dunbar of the courtly manners, polished speech, and modest behavior that I had marked; but, as lovable as he was with people he liked, I learned that under this polite tongue there was a sac of bitter sarcasm that he spat out on people he did not like, and often used in his own defense. He formed a decided dislike for D——'s roughness, his aggressive and cock-sure manner. He could not tolerate what he termed D——'s "vulgar streak." So the two never met but that Paul kept his tongue moistened from that little sac and ready always to strike out at his instinctive foe. It was astonishing that D——, so glib of speech, was never able or never wanted to get back at him.

Paul and I did not clash. I recognized his genius, and in a measure regarded myself as his disciple. He was often as headstrong, as impulsive, and as irresponsible as a boy of six, but none of his whims seemed unreasonable to me. I got pleasure out of humoring him. I remember how scrupulous I was in seeing that he was provided with the bedtime snack that he wanted every night, a raw onion with salt and a bottle of beer. He had great faith in this smelly combination as an antidote for tuberculosis—the disease that he knew would some day set at naught all antidotes. During his visit he wrote a half dozen or so poems. As quickly as he finished them he sent them off; two of them, I remember, to the *Saturday Evening Post*; and I was amazed at seeing how promptly he received checks in return. Whatever he wrote was in demand.

We talked again and again about poetry. I told him my doubts regarding the further possibilities of stereotyped dialect. He was hardly less dubious than I. He said, "You know, of course, that I didn't start as a dialect poet. I simply came to the conclusion that I could write it as well, if not better, than anybody else I knew of, and that by doing so I should gain a hearing. I gained the hearing, and now they don't want me to write anything but dialect." There was a tone of self-reproach in what he said; and five years later, in his fatal illness, he sounded that same tone more deeply when he said to me, "I've kept on doing the same things, and doing them no better. I have never gotten to the things I really wanted to do." In the evenings when we did not go visiting or have visitors at the house we sat and smoked and continued our discussions. Sometimes we would break the discussion and listen to Rosamond play. Paul never told me definitely what the things were that he really wanted to do. I surmised that it was not that he desired merely to write more poems in literary English, such as he had already done, but that it was his ambition to write one or two long, perhaps epical, poems in straight English that would relate to the Negro. I could not tell him what the things were that I wanted to do, because I myself didn't know. The thing that I was sure of and kept repeating to him was that he had carried traditional dialect poetry as far as and as high as it could go; that he had brought it to the fullest measure of charm, tenderness, and beauty it could hold. We agreed that the public still demanded dialect poetry, but that as a medium, especially for the Negro poet, it was narrow and limited.

Some years later these ideas were so thoroughly clarified in my mind and I was so certain of their truth, I made a precise statement of them. No Negro poets are today writing the poetry that twenty-five years ago was considered their natural medium of expression. They realize that the essential of traditional dialect poetry—the painting of humorous, contented, or forlorn "darkies" in standardized colors against a conventional Arcadian background of log cabins and cotton-fields—is itself a smooth-worn stereotype.

In the course of our talks I showed Paul the things I had done under the sudden influence of Whitman. He read them through and, looking at me with a queer smile, said, "I don't like them, and I don't see what you are driving at." He may have been justified, but I was taken aback. I got out my copy of *Leaves of Grass* and read him some of the things I admired most. There was, at least, some personal consolation in the fact that his verdict was the same on Whitman himself.

While he was in Jacksonville Rosamond set two of his poems to music: *When the Colored Band Comes Marchin' down the Street* and *Li'l Gal*. The second of these is a classic in its field, and is still popular with concert singers who like to include a dialect song on their programs. But it was the first one that particularly delighted Paul. While Rosamond played the spirited music and sang the gay words, he liked to give a one-man impersonation of the marching band. This impersonation was, in the main, some pretty cleverly executed cakewalk steps.

Paul returned to his home in Washington early in the spring. He always spoke of his stay in Jacksonville in high terms. Before he left, the Negro Masons decided to organize a lodge of young men, and in honor of Paul, name it the Paul Laurence Dunbar Lodge. The lodge was organized, and Paul and twenty-five or thirty more of us were one night initiated and carried through the first three degrees of Masonry. The Negro Masons of that day in Jacksonville were a horny-handed set. The Odd Fellows lodges were made up of white collar workers, but the Masonic lodges were recruited largely from the stevedores, hod carriers, lumber mill and brickyard hands, and the like. The initiation was rough, and lasted all night. One of our young friends was lame for a number of weeks on account of a fall to the floor while being tossed in a blanket. I was made Worthy Master of the lodge, but it did not take me long to see that being a good Mason demanded more time than I should be willing to devote to it. The first time that I had to "turn out" with the lodge, arrayed in regalia, settled the question definitely.

XV

WE WERE in the last days of May. Stanton was closed. Rosamond was conducting the final rehearsals for the closing exercises of the Baptist Academy, and asked me to go over and give him a hand. We mounted our bicycles one morning and rode the three or four miles through the city to the Academy, situated in the eastern part. At the beginning of the afternoon the rehearsal was over and we started home. We had been riding only a few minutes when we noticed a curling volume of smoke that appeared to be rising from a point in the western end of the town. The point seemed to us to be in a line not far away from our house. We pedaled faster and faster. The cloud of smoke spread wider and grew darker. Now, under and through its mass we could see the lurid glow, and now, the vivid, darting tongues of the flames. We rode harder, and now we could see that Stanton was on the line running to the center. When we reached the school, the fire was still two or three blocks to the west. We met many people fleeing. From them we gathered excitedly related snatches:—the fiber factory catches afire—the fire department comes—fanned by a light breeze, the fire is traveling directly east and spreading out to the north, over the district where the bulk of Negroes in the western end of the city live—the firemen spend all their efforts saving a long row of frame houses just across the street on the south side of the factory, belonging to a white man named Steve Melton—when complaints about this reach the chief he exclaims, "It will be a good thing for some of these damned niggers to get burnt out."—The breeze increases to a high wind—the fire is now beyond control—Jacksonville is doomed.

Rosamond and I realize at once that if Stanton escapes it can be made a temporary lodging place for the homeless. We think there is a chance. The school consists of three buildings, but the main building is of brick and stands in the center of a block, with wide playgrounds on either side. We rush into the main building to see that the windows are all shut tight. Already people are seeking refuge. The grounds are being quickly transformed into a refugee camp. People are rushing in with household utensils hardly worth the effort to save. It is almost laughable to watch a woman running into the yard with a mattress on her head, ignorant of the fact that sparks have lit upon it and that it is already aflame. When we reach the second story we look out to the west. There we see an immense, onrolling cloud of dense black smoke, and under it a roaring, crouching and leaping pack of ravenous flames. We realize that Stanton must go unless the firemen get to work on it at once. Where are the firemen? We haven't yet seen a single stream of water. We run down into the street, where we find a half-dozen firemen pulling on a line of hose. We appeal to them—if the school building is saved it can shelter hundreds of people. They look at us listlessly and make no answer, but continue to drag the hose along, the flames almost on their heels. We hear excited rumors:—all the fire apparatus has been burned up—the fire chief has committed suicide. On top of it all, these half-dozen dazed firemen, in automatic response to some reflex, are struggling to save a few feet of hose.

I know that Stanton is to go. I rush, my brother with me, into my office on the ground floor and take out the principal records of the school. We jump on our bicycles and start for home. But we must pass, on the corner above, the fine home of S. H. Hart, the man who gave me my first job. We go in to see if we can lend a hand. The house is open, but deserted; the family has walked out and left it as it was. We ride to the south, skirting around the burning sea, and reach home. My father is silent; my mother and sister excited; my grandmother, who is in bed with what was her last illness, is worried about Ebenezer Church. But there stands our house. Due either to the reported race prejudice of the fire chief or to the direction of the wind, it is unharmed; at any rate, we are fortunate, for the house is only three blocks from the fiber factory, but due south. It isn't just our house for long. Before night, it is the refuge of more than twenty of our friends who have no other roof.

Without thought of food, Rosamond and I rush out again. We learn that all of the nearby towns in Florida and south Georgia have been telegraphed to for aid, and that special trains are rolling in from them with firemen and apparatus, even from so far away as Savannah. But all efforts are vain. The breeze has turned into a gale that hurtles a section of a burning roof through the air and sets it down on a building blocks away—a breath-taking pyrotechnical show. The speed and spread of the flames are constantly increased by the many hundreds of pitch pine houses. The fire travels east, all the while spreading to the north. Then it shifts to the south, burning to the river's edge and destroying the business section of the town. It follows the water to the eastern end of the city, and widens its zone on the north to Hogan's Creek. By nightfall more than one hundred and fifty blocks are smoldering ashes. But the row of frame houses belonging to Steve Melton, across the street from the fiber factory, is still standing.

A catastrophe! But, among the strangest paradoxes is the fact that people can take a catastrophe philosophically, good-naturedly, almost cheerfully. If a man's home burns down, he will curse his fate or lament his misfortune. But here were thousands who had lost their homes and all their household goods, and the general comment was, "Lucky it didn't happen at night."

Immediately, as in the yellow fever epidemic, relief began pouring in—money, provisions, and clothing from all parts of the country. Commissary depots were at once established. I was asked to take charge of one. For days I was kept busy issuing packages of assorted food to destitute families. Work to supply temporary housing started within a day or two, and unsightly board buildings with corrugated iron roofs sprang up as if by magic. Our "family" remained at about twenty-five for a couple of weeks; eating in camp style and sleeping on sofas, in chairs, and even on the floor. D—— had become one of the "family." In the meantime, civil law had been suspended and martial law established. Companies of state militia from central and western counties had been mustered to form a provost guard. These troops from the backwoods district of the state had many unnecessary clashes with the colored people of Jacksonville, Negroes of a kind they were not accustomed to dealing with. They interfered with me and made me move on when I tried to persuade a group of Negro men and boys not to pose for some photographers, who were taking fake pictures of "looting." I knew that the pictures were being taken for use in periodicals throughout the country.

There was a lady from New York who was an occasional contributor to various papers and magazines visiting in Jacksonville at the time of the fire. A very handsome woman she was, with eyes and hair so dark that they blanched the whiteness of her face. One afternoon she came to the commissary depot where I was engaged and told me that she had written an article on the fire, dealing especially with its effects on the Negro population, which she would like to have me read over before she sent it off. I readily consented to read the article, but told her I couldn't possibly do so until after four o'clock, when the depot closed. It was a sweltering afternoon, and I was hot and tired; so I suggested that after closing time we might take a street car and ride out to Riverside Park, where we could sit and go over the article leisurely and in comfort. She decided that instead of waiting around for me to close she would go out to the park and wait there.

At four o'clock I washed up and boarded a car. I had not yet been to this new Riverside Park; in fact, it was not yet quite a park. There was an old Riverside Park that I knew very well; but the city had recently acquired a large oak and pine covered tract on the bank of the river, a few miles farther out, which it was converting into a new park. I was, perhaps, more interested in seeing how this work had progressed than I was in reading the lady's article. When I reached the end of the car-line, I noticed a rustic waiting-pavilion near the edge of the river. I made my way to it, expecting to find the lady there. She was not there, and I looked about but saw no sign of her. I judged that she had grown tired of waiting and had returned to the city. I walked back to the car-line. The car I had come out on was still there. The conductor and motorman were standing on the ground near the rear end. I waited until they were about ready to start, then got aboard. The car was empty, except for me, and I took a seat near the center—there were then no "Jim Crow" street car laws in Jacksonville. As I settled in my seat and glanced out of the window I saw a woman approaching across a little rustic bridge a hundred or so feet away whom I at once recognized by her dress and the black and white parasol she carried to be the lady I was to meet. I jumped off the car and walked over to join her. We went back across the bridge, then along some newly laid out paths until we came to a little clearing on the other side of which was a barbed wire fence. I helped her through the fence and followed. We then walked through the trees until we came to the bank of the river, where we found a bench and sat down. She read the article to me, and I offered one or two suggestions.

We sat talking. The sun was still bright, but was preparing for his plunge under the horizon, which he makes more precipitantly in the far south than he does in the north. At the point where we were sitting the St. Johns River is several miles wide. Across the water the sun began cutting a brilliant swath that constantly changed and deepened in color until it became a flaming road between us and the dark line of trees on the opposite bank. The scene was one of perfect semi-tropical beauty. Watching it, I became conscious of an uneasiness, an uneasiness that, no doubt, had been struggling the while to get up and through from my subconscious. I became aware of noises, of growing, alarming noises; of men hallooing back and forth, and of dogs responding with the bay of bloodhounds. One thought, that they might be hunters, flashed through my mind; but even so, there was danger of a stray shot. And yet, what men would hunt with such noises, unless they were beating the bush to trap a wild, ferocious beast? I rose to go, and my companion followed. We threaded our

way back. The noises grew more ominous. They seemed to be closing in. My pulse beat faster and my senses became more alert. I glanced
at my companion; she showed no outward sign of alarm. Suddenly
we reached the barbed wire fence. There we stopped. On the other
side of the fence death was standing. Death turned and looked at
me and I looked at death. In the instant I knew that the lowering of
an eyelash meant the end.

Just across the fence in the little clearing were eight or ten militia-
men in khaki with rifles and bayonets. The abrupt appearance of me
and my companion seemed to have transfixed them. They stood as
under a spell. Quick as a flash of light the series of occurrences that
had taken place ran through my mind: The conductor and motorman
saw me leave the street car and join the woman; they saw us go back
into the park; they rushed to the city with a maddening tale of a
Negro and white woman meeting in the woods; there is no civil
authority; the military have sent out a detachment of troops with
guns and dogs to get me.

I lose self-control. But a deeper self springs up and takes command;
I follow orders. I take my companion's parasol from her hand; I
raise the loose strand of fence wire and gently pass her through; I
follow and step into the group. The spell is instantly broken. They
surge round me. They seize me. They tear my clothes and bruise my
body; all the while calling to their comrades, "Come on, we've got
'im! Come on, we've got 'im!" And from all directions these comrades rush, shouting, "Kill the damned nigger! Kill the black son
of a bitch!" I catch a glimpse of my companion; it seems that the
blood, the life is gone out of her. There is the truth; but there is no
chance to state it; nor would it be believed. As the rushing crowd
comes yelling and cursing, I feel that death is bearing in upon me.
Not death of the empty sockets, but death with the blazing eyes of a
frenzied brute. And still, I am not terror-stricken, I am carrying out
the chief command that has been given me, "Show no sign of fear;
if you do you are lost." Among the men rushing to reach me is a
slender young man clad in a white uniform. He breaks through the
men who have hold of me. We look at each other; and I feel that a
quivering message from intelligence to intelligence has been inter-
changed. He claps his hand on my shoulder and says, "You are my
prisoner." I ask him, "What is the charge?" He answers, "Being out

here with a white woman." I question once more, "Before whom do I answer this charge?" "Before Major B——, the provost marshal," he replies. At that, I answer nothing beyond "I am your prisoner."

The eternity between stepping through the barbed wire fence and the officer's words putting me under arrest passed, I judge, in less than sixty seconds. As soon as the lieutenant put his hand on me and declared me his prisoner, the howling mob of men became soldiers under discipline. Two lines were formed, with my companion and me between them, and marched to the street car. The soldiers filled the seats, jammed the aisle, and packed the platforms, and still some of them, with two men in civilian clothes holding the dogs in leash, were left over for the next car. As we began nearing the city my companion had the reactions natural to a sensitive woman. Both of us were now fairly confident that the danger of physical violence was passed, but it was easy to see that she was anxious; perhaps, about the probable notoriety; perhaps, about the opportunity for malicious tongues. I assured her as best I could that everything would come out all right. I said to her, "I know Major B——, the provost marshal, very well; he is a member of the Jacksonville bar." On the way in, the car stopped at the electric power house. It was met by a crowd of conductors, motormen, and other employees, who hailed our car with cries of, "Have you got 'em?" "Yes, we've got 'em," the soldiers cried back.

Before the car left the power house, the young lieutenant, whom I had hardly been able to see after we left the park, made his way to our seat. Again I felt the waves of mental affinity. In the midst of the brutishness that surrounded us I felt that between him and me there was somewhere a meeting place for reason. He leaned over and said, "I'm going to put these men off the car here and take you in myself." He ordered the men off. Of course, they obeyed, but they were openly a disappointed and disgruntled lot. The car moved across the aqueduct and into the heart of the city. I was thankful for the lieutenant's action; because, for reason or no reason, I did not want to be paraded through the streets of Jacksonville as a prisoner under guard of a company of soldiers. In my gratitude I was tempted to tell him what I did not have a chance to tell before I was put under arrest. But I was now comparatively light-hearted. I was already anticipating the burlesque finale to this melodrama—melodrama that might have been tragedy—and I disliked spoiling any of the effects.

However, I did say to him, "The lady with me *is* white, but not legally so." He looked at her curiously, but made no comment; instead he said to me, "You know where the provost headquarters are, don't you?" I answered that I did. He continued, "When you get off the car you walk on ahead; I'll follow behind, and nobody will know you are under arrest." I thanked him again. We got off and walked to the provost headquarters, passing numbers of people, colored and white, who knew me. We went into the provost marshal's tent, followed by the lieutenant, who turned his prisoners over.

Major B—— showed astonishment and some embarrassment when he recognized me. I said to him, "Major, here I am. What is the charge?" He repeated the charge the lieutenant had made. "Major," I went on, "I know there is no use in discussing law or my rights on any such basis as, 'Suppose the lady *is* white?' so I tell you at once that according to the customs and, possibly, the laws of Florida, she *is not* white." In spite of appearances, he, of course, knew that I spoke the truth. He was apologetic and anxious to dismiss us and the matter. He spoke of the report that had been brought in, of his duty as commanding officer of the provost guard, of how he never even dreamed what the actual facts were. In answering, I told him that I appreciated how he felt about it personally but that that did not balance the jeopardy in which my life had been put. I added, "You know as well as I do, if I had turned my back once on that crowd or taken a single step in retreat, I'd now be a dead man." He agreed with me and said he was as glad as I that nothing of the kind had happened. At this point my companion began to speak. She spoke slowly and deliberately at first; then the words came in torrents. She laid on the Major's head the sins of his fathers and his fathers' fathers. She charged him that they were the ones responsible for what had happened. As we left, the Major was flushed and flustered. I felt relieved and satisfied, especially over the actually minor outcome of the avoidance of any notoriety for my companion. It was now dark, and I took her to her stopping place, The Boyland Home, a school for colored girls supported by Northern philanthropy.

I did not get the nervous reaction from my experience until I reached home. The quick turn taken by fate had buoyed me up. When I went into the provost marshal's tent my sense of relief had mounted almost to gayety. Now, the weight of all the circumstances in the event came down and carried me under. My brother was the only one of the family to whom I confided what had taken place. He was terrified over what might have happened; I never mentioned it to my parents. For weeks and months the episode with all of its implications preyed on my mind and disturbed me in my sleep. I would wake often in the night-time, after living through again those few frightful seconds, exhausted by the nightmare of a struggle with a band of murderous, bloodthirsty men in khaki, with loaded rifles and fixed bayonets. It was not until twenty years after, through work I was then engaged in, that I was able to liberate myself completely from this horror complex.

Through it all I discerned one clear and certain truth: in the core of the heart of the American race problem the sex factor is rooted; rooted so deeply that it is not always recognized when it shows at the surface. Other factors are obvious and are the ones we dare to deal with; but, regardless of how we deal with these, the race situation will continue to be acute as long as the sex factor persists. Taken alone, it furnishes a sufficient mainspring for the rationalization of all the complexes of white racial superiority. It may be innate; I do not know. But I do know that it is strong and bitter; and that its strength and bitterness are magnified and intensified by the white man's perception, more or less, of the Negro complex of sexual superiority.

XVI

SHORTLY after the happenings just related, Rosamond and I decided to get away from Jacksonville as quickly as possible and go to New York. I went to see the mayor, a man I had known nearly all my life, and told him we were going to New York and that we should try to arrange a benefit there for the relief of fire sufferers. We stopped in Washington to see Paul Dunbar, but he was away on a reading tour. His young and beautiful wife, Alice Ruth, informed us that he would be back in a couple of days, and pressed us to stay. But we had written to Bob Cole regarding the benefit, and he was enthusiastic about starting to put it on; so we did not wait over. We had no difficulty in getting Negro theatrical performers and other artists in New York to give their services. The benefit was well attended and netted nearly a thousand dollars. The amount was sent to the mayor of Jacksonville. After we left Jacksonville, D—— set up office temporarily in Rosamond's studio.

We found that some marked changes had taken place in West 53rd Street. Two hotels that had been opened by Negro proprietors the previous fall were now running in full blast. It is true they were hotels more in name than in fact—in each case the building was an adapted private house—but they fulfilled their main purpose, providing good food, quite adequately. The Marshall, located between Sixth and Seventh Avenues, occupied a brownstone, four-story and basement house which in the years before had been a fashionable dwelling. Both hotels served very good meals. On Sunday nights there was a special dinner with music. The Sunday night dinners had become so popular that tables were booked days in advance. The music was good also. At the Marshall there was a four-piece orchestra that was excellent. The leader, a man named Wiggins, was, to me, a most remarkable man. After he had been earning his living for a number of years as a violinist, he suffered an injury to the fingers of his left hand that completely incapacitated him. What did he do? He set out at once to learn to play by bowing with his left hand and fingering with his right. There may be those who cannot appreciate the difficulty of this feat; but one who has any knowledge of the long and arduous drill in the co-ordination of brain and hands necessary to learn to play the violin can understand what it meant to make the change involved in stringing and playing the instrument backwards. It entailed the direct reversal of reflexes that had become second nature.

These hotels brought about a sudden social change. They introduced or made possible a fashionable sort of life that hitherto had not existed. Prior to their opening there was scarcely a decent restaurant in New York in which Negroes could eat; I knew of only one place with excellent food and a social air where they were welcome. The sight offered at these hotels, of crowds of well-dressed colored men and women lounging and chatting in the parlors, loitering over their coffee and cigarettes while they talked or listened to the music, was unprecedented. The sight had an immediate effect on me and my brother; we decided to give up our lodgings with our old landlady at No. 260, and move to the Marshall. We took the large backroom on the second floor, put in a piano, and started to work. This move had consequences we did not dream of.

Bob Cole lived two doors from the Marshall, and that made it convenient for the trio to work together. We worked according to a schedule. We rose between nine and ten o'clock, breakfasted at about eleven, and began work not later than twelve. When we didn't go to the theater, our working period approximated ten hours a day. We spent the time in actual writing or in planning future work. In our room and without stopping work, we snatched a bite to eat at the fag-end of the afternoon. Always, we went downstairs for a midnight supper. And this was by no means a light supper; it was our main and most enjoyed meal. Sometimes it consisted of planked steak or broiled lobster. This supper generally cost us more than we were justified in spending; but, if we had done a good day's work, the money spent seemed a minor matter; if we hadn't made much progress, the gay air of the dining room, gayer around midnight than at any other hour, stimulated us. Looking back at those days, the elation and zest with which we usually worked seem prodigious. We laid down a strict rule against interruptions; but there were several intimates who were not included under the rule: Harry T. Burleigh who sometimes brought along the manuscript of an "art song" he had just finished and played it over; Will Marion Cook, despite his animosity against Bob Cole; Theodore Drury, who had begun his productions of grand opera at the Lexington Opera House; and Paul Dunbar, who, however, had lost his interest in things theatrical. Another intimate whom we were always glad to see was young Jack Nail, then the most popular young colored man in New York, an exceedingly handsome boy. He belonged because of his real appreciation of the things the members of this group were trying to do. He came in frequently of evenings. If we were busy, he took a chair and sat quietly smoking his pipe while we, after a grunt of greeting, went on working. There was in him a quality that made his presence more helpful than distracting.

Our room, particularly of nights, was the scene of many discussions; the main question talked and wrangled over being always that of the manner and means of raising the status of the Negro as a writer, composer, and performer in the New York theater and world

of music. The opinions advanced and maintained, often with more
force than considerateness, were as diversified as the personalities in
the group. However, the only really bitter clashes were those occur-
ring between Cole and Cook. Seldom did they meet and part without
a clash. Cole was the most versatile man in the group and a true
artist. In everything he did he strove for the fine artistic effect, regardless of whether it had any direct relation to the Negro or not. Nevertheless, there was an element of pro-Negro propaganda in all his
efforts; and it showed, I think, most plainly when he was engaged
in matching the white artist on the latter's own field. Cook was the
most original genius among all the Negro musicians—probably that
statement is still true. He had received excellent training in music, both
in this country and in Berlin at the Hochschule; he had studied the
violin under Joachim. But he had thrown all these standards over; he
believed that the Negro in music and on the stage ought to be a
Negro, a genuine Negro; he declared that the Negro should eschew
"white" patterns, and not employ his efforts in doing what "the white
artist could always do as well, generally better." Both these men
tended toward eccentricity, both were hot-tempered, and the argument did not always oscillate between their divergent points of view;
it did not always keep itself above personalities. Cook never hesitated
to make belittling comments on Cole's limitations in musical and general education; he would even sneer at him on a fault in pronuncia-
tion. Cole was particularly sensitive on this side, and Cook's taunts
both humiliated and maddened him.

Burleigh's position was unique. He had been a student at the National Conservatory while Dvorák was the director. He had studied
harmony with Rubin Goldmark and counterpoint with Max Spicker.
Not only had he studied with Dvorák but he had spent considerable
time with him at his home. It was he who called the attention of
the great Bohemian composer to the Negro spirituals. He had been
the baritone soloist at St. George's Church for seven years—a position
he still holds. His reputation as a composer was already well in the
making, based on a number of "art songs" written in the best modern
manner. Among us, however, it was as a master that he was held.
On all questions in the theory and science of music he was the final
authority. In this acceptance, both Cook and my brother, with their
own very good musical training, always joined. Some years later Kurt
Schindler said to me that on a question in the theory of music he

would accept Mr. Burleigh's decision as quickly as that of any other musician in New York. Drury was the picturesque one. He was light bronze in color and quite good-looking, especially when he flashed his teeth in a smile. He cultivated a foreign air, in fact, a foreign appearance; he might easily have been taken for a member of one of the African nationalities of the Mediterranean border. He was a singer, and had forced his voice up to enable him to sing certain grand opera rôles; the result being the making of a straining tenor out of an excellent baritone. He was at the beginning of his enterprise which annually, for four or five years, gave Negro New York a one-night season of grand opera. Whatever may have been said of these productions artistically, they were, as popular social events, huge successes. They were for the first two or three seasons huge successes financially. Drury was naturally shy, and talked very little; but both these traits in him were more than offset by his personal representative and business manager, Theodore Pankey. Pankey was a small, very light-colored young man who at one time had been a jockey. He had rubbed against the world, and possessed aplomb to that degree which is irritating. Nothing short of a locked door could keep him out, if he took a notion to come in. Talk from him was always sufficient for two; and besides, no topics of conversation or discussion imposed silence upon him. Notwithstanding, all of us liked Pankey. All of us conceded that in one field we did not know his peer. No one else could have sold so many tickets and packed so many people in the Lexington Opera House for Drury's productions of Verdi, Wagner, Gounod, and Bizet. Moreover, he did qualify as an "artist" through a good tenor voice that he used very well. As for the operas, none of us, with the exception of Pankey, took them too seriously—that statement possibly includes Drury himself.

In all of our discussions and wrangles we were unanimous on one point; namely, that the managers, none of whom at that time could conceive of a Negro company playing anything but second and third-class theaters, had to be convinced. It is true that Cook's operetta, *Clorindy*, had been produced at the Casino Theater Roof Garden, and the following summer, his operetta, *Jes Lak White Folks*, had been produced at the New York Theater Roof Garden, also that many top-notch Negro performers had appeared in the best vaudeville houses; but as yet, no professional Negro company had played a regular engagement on the stage proper of any first-class, legitimate "Broadway" house.

About this time Cook persuaded me to use my good offices to have Dunbar collaborate with him on another piece, a full-length opera to be called *The Cannibal King*. *Clorindy*, for which Dunbar was the librettist, had been a big success. For *Jes Lak White Folks* Cook was his own librettist, and the piece did not go over so well as its predecessor; so Cook wanted Dunbar's touch and, still more, his name again. But the great success of the first piece was not due alone to Dunbar, nor was the partial failure of the second piece due alone to Cook. In *Clorindy*, New York had been given its first demonstration of the possibilities of Negro syncopated music, of what could be done with it in the hands of a competent and original composer. Cook's music, especially his choruses and finales, made Broadway catch its breath. In *Jes Lak White Folks*, the book and lyrics were not so good, nor was the cast; and, naturally, the music was not such a startling novelty. I did my best to persuade Paul to do the book and lyrics for *The Cannibal King*, but he was obdurate. He told me with emphasis, "No, I won't do it. I just can't work with Cook; he irritates me beyond endurance." Finally, I undertook the work of writing the lyrics, and actually got Cook to agree to have Bob Cole do the book. We began work on neutral ground, four or five blocks over, at Harry Burleigh's apartment on Park Avenue. We celebrated the end of the first day's work with a beefsteak dinner, deliciously cooked by Harry's brother, Reginald. But despite the inaugural love feast, discord entered and prevailed, and *The Cannibal King* was never wholly completed. Enough was finished, however, to enable Cook to negotiate a sale to a producer for a flat cash price that gave us several hundred dollars apiece. This was my first work with Cook; later, through the years, we wrote a number of songs in collaboration.

The Marshall gradually became New York's center for Negro artists. For a generation that center had been in Negro Bohemia, down in the Tenderloin. There, in various clubs, Negro theatrical and musical talent foregathered. The clubs of Negro Bohemia were of diverse sorts. There were gambling clubs and poker clubs—a fine distinction between the two being involved; there were clubs frequented particularly by the followers of the ring and turf, where one got a close-up of the noted Negro prize fighters and jockeys; there were "professional" clubs, that served as meeting places and exchanges for Negro theatrical performers. Among the clubs of Negro Bohemia were some that bore a social aspect corresponding to that of the modern night club. These had their regular habitués, but they also enjoyed a large patronage of white sightseers and slummers and of white theatrical performers on the lookout for "Negro stuff," and, moreover, a considerable clientele of white women who had or sought to have colored lovers. The most popular of the "professional" clubs was Ike Hine's. It was principally a club for Negroes connected with the theater, but it drew the best elements from the various circles of Bohemia—except the gamblers. No gambling was allowed, and the conduct of the place was in every respect surprisingly orderly. This club occupied what formerly was a three-story and basement dwelling. In the basement was a chop suey restaurant. The parlor, on the main floor, was carpeted and furnished with chairs and tables. The walls of this room were entirely covered with photographs and lithographs of Negro "celebrities." The back parlor contained a few chairs and tables, a piano, and also a buffet. The floor of the room was bare and provided space for the entertainers and for dancing. On the floor above one or two of the rooms were given over to "acts" for rehearsals. The top floor was used as living quarters by the proprietor and his wife.

As the Marshall gained in popularity, the more noted theatrical stars and the better-paid vaudevillians deserted the down-town clubs and made the hotel their professional and social rendezvous. Up to 53rd Street came Bert Williams; tall and broad-shouldered; on the whole, a rather handsome figure, and entirely unrecognizable as the shambling, shuffling "darky" he impersonated on the stage; luxury-loving and indolent, but highly intelligent and with a certain reserve which at times exhibited itself as downright snobbishness; talking with a very slow drawl and getting more satisfaction, it seemed, out of being considered a great raconteur than out of being a great comedian; extremely funny in his imitations in the West Indian dialect. (He was himself a West Indian; born in Nassau.) Bert was a good story teller, but not a better one, we thought, than his very pretty wife, Lottie. All of Lottie's stories centered around one character, and that character was Bert. She recited very comically—the comicality heightened by her prettiness—her trials and tribulations with Bert on the "road," the chief of them being the many devices to which she had to resort to get him out of bed in time to catch early trains, Bert the while listening meekly and grinning good-naturedly. Up, too, came George Walker, very black, very vigorous, and very dapper, being dressed always a point or two above the height of fashion. George, the hail-fellow-well-met, the mixer, the diplomat; frequently flashing that celebrated row of gleaming teeth in making his way to his objective; but serious withal and the driving force of the famous team; working tirelessly to convince New York managers that Negro companies should be booked in first-class houses, and, finally, succeeding. And Aida Overton, George Walker's wife; not as good-looking as Lottie Williams, but more than making up for what she lacked in looks by her remarkable talent; a wonderful dancer, and the possessor of a low-pitched voice with a natural sob to it, which she knew how to use with telling effect in "putting over" a song; beyond comparison, the brightest star among women on the Negro stage of the period, and hardly a lesser attraction of the Williams and Walker company than the two comedians. And up came Ernest Hogan, not an Irishman, but a natural-black-face comedian; ranked by some critics, erroneously, I think, as a greater comedian than Bert Williams; expansive, jolly, radiating infectious good humor; provoking laughter merely by the changing expressions of his mobile face—a face that never, even on the stage, required cork or paint to produce comical effects. Behind these well-known performers came others less noted, and also a crowd of those who love to follow the clouds of glory trailed by the great. In time, the Marshall came to be one of the sights of New York. But it was more than a "sight"; its importance as the radiant point of the forces that cleared the way for the Negro on the New York stage cannot be over-estimated.

Soon after our trio got settled down to work, we went to see Miss Irwin; the result of our visit was a commission to do the feature songs for her new play, *The Belle of Bridgeport*. This stroke of good fortune filled us with enthusiasm and confidence such as to make the conquest of New York seem a very easy matter. We also did the music for Peter Dailey's play, *Champagne Charlie*, and collaborated in writing a two-act musical comedy, *The Supper Club*, produced by the Sire Brothers at the Winter Garden. There were forty-odd people in the cast of *The Supper Club*, and among them were some of the best-known stars of the day: Virginia Earle, Ada Lewis, Josie Sadler, Toby Claude, Thomas Q. Seabrooke, Alexander Clarke, Junie

McCree, and—not known at all then, but later of *Merry Widow* fame —Donald Brine (as his name appeared on the program). Bob Cole helped to stage the show, and taught Donald Brian his dance steps.

One day Bob came in breathless with excitement. He had just met Ben Teal on Broadway. Teal was then stage director for the Klaw and Erlanger productions, and Klaw and Erlanger were already the most powerful factors in the whole theatrical business. Many a time we had passed their offices on Broadway and looked longingly at those awe-inspiring names in gold on the windows across the whole front of the building. Teal had asked Bob, "Do you know where I can find two brothers named Johnson, who wrote a song called *Run, Brudder Possum, Run* for the Rogers Brothers show last season?" And Bob had answered, "I know just where I can put my hands on them for you."

Klaw and Erlanger had arranged to bring over from London the Drury Lane Pantomimes, and produce them in an Americanized version in New York. They were at the time engaged in preparations for the first of these productions, *The Sleeping Beauty and the Beast*. Mr. Teal had been much impressed by the little song we had done for the Rogers Brothers, and wanted us to collaborate on *The Sleeping Beauty*. We wrote three specialty numbers for that piece: *Tell Me, Dusky Maiden; Come Out, Dinah, on the Green*, and *Nobody's Lookin' but the Owl and the Moon*, and suddenly found ourselves programmed with "top-notchers" among the writers of musical comedy. *The Sleeping Beauty and the Beast* was produced at the old Broadway Theater, the only stage in New York that was adequate in size and facilities. The success of the pantomime was instantaneous and overwhelming. New York had some years before seen *The Black Crook* but never had it seen anything to compare with *The Sleeping Beauty*. Never before had it seen such massing of performers, such lavishness of scenery and costumes, and such marvels in stage effects. New York gazed wide-eyed at the fairy parliament, the witch's cave, the palace of crystal, the prismatic fountains and, above all, the flying ballet. I myself, even after seeing at rehearsals and backstage the mechanics of the ballet, never outgrew the wonder of watching those lovely ladies rise and float through the air and alight always with such consummate ease and grace on the pointed toes of one foot. The critics and reviewers found it necessary to go to the circus advertisements (the pre-view advertisements of the movies were not yet born) and appropriate such adjectives as "stupendous," "dazzling," "gorgeous," "amazing." Among the principals in *The Sleeping Beauty and the Beast* were Joseph Cawthorne, Harry Bulger, Charles J. Ross, Ella Snyder, Viola Gillette, and the Hengler Sisters; but all the individual performers were dwarfed by the production itself. These adaptations of the Drury Lane Pantomimes continued to be the grandest spectacle on the American stage until the opening of the New York Hippodrome in 1905.

Just as the spectacular effects of *The Sleeping Beauty* dwarfed the individual performers, it dwarfed the individual musical numbers. Our songs were well applauded but their sales did not begin to reach what we thought they ought to be. But during this summer of 1901 we wrote a song that was to send our reputation to the top and make us some money. The song was *The Maiden with the Dreamy Eyes*; it was sung by Anna Held in her play, *The Little Duchess*. *The Maiden with the Dreamy Eyes* fitted Miss Held perfectly, and was one of her greatest song successes. The popularity which the song achieved was due principally to her, but not wholly; a good share of it was due to Elsie Janis. Miss Janis was then about twelve years old, extraordinarily clever and very pretty. I remember that her mother brought her to our studio several times, when Rosamond played the song over and over while she committed it to memory and perfected her imitation of Anna Held singing it.

We had a theory that great popularity in the case of any song was based upon a definite and sufficient reason; that it was not merely accidental. A song might be popular because it was silly; but silliness sufficient to give a song popularity would have to be the result of a certain cleverness. In those days a song was popular and profitable only when it reached the point where people bought it to play and sing at home. Today, a popular song is just another dance tune. In those days the royalties of a writer depended largely upon the young fellow who would buy a copy of the song and take it along with him when he went to call on his girl, so that she would play it while the two of them gave vocal vent to the sentiments. Alas, the piano in the parlor and the girl who played it are about passed. In writing *The Maiden with the Dreamy Eyes* we gave particular consideration to these fundamentals. It needed little analysis to see that a song written in exclusive praise of blue eyes was cut off at once from about three-fourths of the possible chances for universal success; that it could make but faint appeal to the heart or pocketbook of a young man going to call on a girl with brown eyes or black eyes or gray eyes. So we worked on the chorus of our song until, without making it a catalogue, it was inclusive enough to enable any girl who sang it or to whom it was sung to fancy herself the maiden with the dreamy eyes. It ran:

> There are eyes of blue,
> There are brown eyes too,
> There are eyes of every size
> And eyes of every hue;
> But I surmise
> That if you are wise
> You'll be careful of the maiden
> With the dreamy eyes.

Anna Held's singing of *The Maiden with the Dreamy Eyes* naturally introduced us to her husband and manager, Florenz Ziegfeld, and led to our doing further work for her. Indeed, the next year Mr. Ziegfeld invited us to come for a week up to Thousand Islands, where he and Miss Held were summering, and try over some songs that we thought would be suitable for her. I recall how explosively voluble Miss Held was about a song, whether in praise or condemnation of it, and how undemonstrative was her husband. But if he finally drawled out, "It's a good song, I think," it was enough to make us know that he intended to use the piece and give it every possible chance.

Mr. Ziegfeld was then on the threshold of his career as the greatest of all American producers of musical plays, but I doubt that there were many who recognized the master in him; he was so utterly different from the dictatorial, obstreperous musical producers of the period. He was always quiet and unobtrusive. He was at that time so thin and meek-looking that he struck me as a sort of semi-invalid. However, some years later than the time of which I am writing he astonished me by the amount of force and anger he could display. Rosamond and I had an appointment with him at his apartment in the Ansonia, which occupied an entire section of one of the floors of the hotel. We stepped into a waiting elevator and told the operator that we wished to go up to Mr. Ziegfeld's apartment; and he informed us that he couldn't take us up; that we should have to take the service elevator. We went over to the desk and said to the man in charge that we had a business appointment with Mr. Ziegfeld, and that the elevator boy refused to take us up. The man at the desk coldly informed us that the elevator boy was carrying out the rules of the hotel. We then called Mr. Ziegfeld on the telephone and told him we were downstairs but would not be able to come up because we were denied the use of the elevators, except one designated "service." Mr. Ziegfeld asked us to wait. He came down at once and for some minutes had the stormiest kind of scene at the desk. He protested and threatened. In protesting he said, "These gentlemen have business with me; they are my guests; they are my friends." The man at the desk pleaded that the rule was not of his making and that it was not in his power to change it. Thereupon, Mr. Ziegfeld escorted us to the elevator, ushered us in, stepped in himself and ordered the boy to take him up to his apartment. Up we went. At the end of a couple of hours, when our visit was over, he came out with us, rang for the elevator, went through a like procedure; and down we came.

This incident was indicative of Mr. Ziegfeld's attitude on race. As a producer, he not only recognized that there was Negro talent, but he dared to give that talent an opportunity. He did a brave and unprecedented thing when back in 1910 he made Bert Williams one of the principals of *The Follies*. Mutterings about quitting were made by some of the white principals, but when they learned that it was Mr. Ziegfeld's intention that Mr. Williams was to stay, whether they did or not, they stayed. Without exaggeration it may be said that when Ziegfeld put on *Show Boat*, the greatest of all his shows, he also put on the greatest colored musical show ever staged.

All in all, the summer of 1901 promised much. In August we gathered together the manuscripts of fifteen songs and took them to Jos. W. Stern and Co., our publishers. We talked the list over with the two partners, Mr. Stern and Mr. Marks, and pointed out to them that most of the songs were slated to be used in productions of the 1901-2 season. The result of our conference was the signing of a three-year contract to write for publication exclusively by Jos. W. Stern and Co., with a cash guarantee to be paid to us monthly and to be deducted from our semi-annual royalty accounts. There were, of course, other Negro song writers in New York. One of them, Gusse L. Davis, was at the height of his popularity and more widely known than we. The whole country and a good part of the world were singing his famous ballads: *In A Lighthouse by The Sea, Down in Poverty Row, The Fatal Wedding, The Baggage Coach Ahead*. But we had achieved a certain uniqueness due to the entrée we had gained to the Broadway musical stage; and our contract with Jos. W. Stern and Co. increased our uniqueness, for it was, I believe, the first contract of its kind ever executed.

During these months that we were in New York the rebuilding of Jacksonville was going ahead feverishly. Stanton was being rebuilt, but I learned that the new building would not be ready in October; then that it would not be ready in November or even in December. Finally, I received word from the board of education that the first week in February was set for the opening. This postponement was no disappointment to me; I was too eager to see the shows in which we had music. *The Sleeping Beauty* was to open in November and *The Supper Club* in December. The others opened on the road. I was also anxious, for reasons that are plain, to get my royalty statement, due in January, before going South.

We spent these early winter months pleasantly enough; our only handicap being a shortage of cash. Our main revenue was from our publishers. Bob Cole's circumstances were far more precarious than Rosamond's and mine, for he had a mother and four sisters to support. Furthermore, he had dissolved his theatrical partnership with Billy Johnson, and was not going out with a show for the first time in ten years or more. Rosamond had also cast the die. He had decided, win or lose, that he was going to try his fortune in New York. I hesitated. I argued that the decisions reached by Bob and Rosamond did not demand as much courage as the one confronting me; that they had put down work which they could freely take up again; while I should be giving up a definite position that I could not expect to get back. I decided to return to Jacksonville. I arranged with Rosamond that while I was drawing salary in Jacksonville he could draw and use my share of the monthly stipend from our publishers.

About the middle of January we went down to our publishers to get our royalty statement. We received the statement, but no royalties. We had not broken even; we found that we were in debt to the firm for nearly $1300. We went back to our studio in the Marshall a discouraged and disheartened trio. We discussed the situation until late at night—"The songs had not yet begun to sell." That was evident. "They were good songs, well placed, and would sell during the height of the season." That was problematical. We were worried. But there is nothing like youth. The gloom was lifted and we began to laugh when I suggested that, perhaps, Stern and Co. were more worried than we.

A few days before I left for Jacksonville, Bob and Rosamond received a call to entertain for a party at Sherry's, then at Fifth Avenue and 44th Street. They were to get one hundred dollars for the job. Of course, they were jubilant. They decided to sing and play only original compositions, and spent several hours rehearsing certain of our songs. While they were rehearsing, in walked Theodore Pankey. Pankey waxed so enthusiastic over what was going on that Bob and Rosamond concluded to take him along for good measure; and mighty good measure he proved to be. The three of them arrayed in evening clothes started for Sherry's, and I went to bed. About four o'clock in the morning the three of them roused me out of bed. They were excited and hilarious. Each one had with him a quart of champagne brought from the party. They roused Jimmie Marshall, our genial proprietor, and made him bring up sandwiches; then the five of us, while the "entertainers" talked about the party, sat and drank champagne till the bottles were empty.—It was a grand party—Lillian Russell was there in all her beauty—the vivacious Edna Wallace Hopper was there—a dozen other stars and a dozen influential producers and managers. But the high spot in the recital related to Pankey. He had sung *Li'l Gal* to a lady who was seated on a gentleman's knee. The lady begged him to sing it over and over. At the finish the gentleman peeled off a hundred-dollar bill and handed it to him—an action, without doubt, prompted more by interest in the lady than by interest in the song.

We were all elated and voted the party a momentous affair. For Bob and Rosamond it proved so to be.

XVII

I REACHED Jacksonville a few days before the date scheduled for the opening of Stanton. The first thing I did was to inspect the new building. I don't think I ever saw a more hideous structure. It was a huge, crude, three-story frame building that looked more like a mill or a granary than like a schoolhouse. I came in for some criticism from colored citizens who felt that it would have been different had I been on the ground when it was being planned and built. I was forced to admit to myself that this criticism was well founded. I talked with members of the board of education and learned that their plans contemplated doing away with Stanton as a central school, and for that reason they had erected a purely temporary building. The Stanton plot was an entire block in one of the best sections of the city. The blocks to the north were occupied by the residences of some of the wealthiest white citizens in Jacksonville, who, undoubtedly, had for years looked upon the school as a nuisance and considered it a factor that held back the more rapid increase in value of their neighboring property. The necessity of rebuilding the city gave an opportunity to have the school moved, and they brought pressure on the board of education to have this done. Similar situations have risen in, probably, every southern community. The town grows and a certain site becomes "too good" or "too valuable" for the use of Negroes; then by one means or another the Negroes are evicted and shoved farther out and back. The school board planned to sell the Stanton plot as soon as it could do so profitably or, failing in that, to use it as the site for a white school and to build in each of the Negro districts a schoolhouse that would be "more accessible." These plans meant the destruction of a traditional and important element in the life of Jacksonville Negro citizens and the sweeping away of one of its main centers of pride and affection. Furthermore, they probably meant the end of a Negro high school.

There was, however, a fact athwart the course that had been laid out; a fact of which no member of the school board seemed to be aware. I presented it as promptly as I could, and it was no less important a fact than that the Stanton plot did not belong to the board of education or the city or the county or the state. It had been deeded to a board of trustees made up of white and colored men as a site for a

Negro school by Governor Hart, a Reconstruction governor of Florida. I had from childhood been familiar with this beginning of Stanton's history. When I was a small boy, the old and deserted Hart mansion stood in the center of the adjoining block south of the school. I remember that frequently we used to run the risk of punishment by going over to the Hart place to hunt for berries and chinquapins during recess. And I knew it was the man who had lived in the old house who had given us the land for our school. This deed, furthermore, stated that, if the property ceased to be used for the purpose of a Negro school, it would revert to the heirs of the Hart estate. In the years, the board of education had changed so many times that sight had been lost of the original conditions under which it held the Stanton property. A search of the records verified these conditions. Indeed, the whole matter worked out for the best: the property rights of the colored people in the property were clarified and settled once and for all; and even the temporariness of the building the board had erected proved a blessing in disguise, for it was not long before the structure was condemned as unsafe and the school board erected the modern and beautiful Stanton High School which stands in its stead, such a building as it would not have built at an earlier time.

I settled down to hard work with the school. I gave almost no time to the practice of law; I no longer had sufficient interest in it. Indeed, D—— and I had about reached the mutual understanding that he would go it alone. I wrote nothing, that is, for Broadway; perhaps, my brother's absence was responsible for my lack of incentive. I had the year before been elected president of the State Teachers' Association, and I did my best to make the meeting that was to be held in Fernandina the latter part of May a success. I was actually and rapidly resigning myself to the idea that teaching was to be my main vocation, and any other pursuit secondary. Those certain qualities inherited from my father were shaping my ideas and behavior. Moreover, the girl with the forehead of a Madonna and the mouth of a Thais, whom I had seen at the meeting of the teachers' association in Tampa several years before, had come to Jacksonville on a visit. In Tampa I had adored her rather at a distance; in Jacksonville I was with her almost daily. Her disturbing beauty shook my ambitions for a New York career, and more and more made the odds against winning seem longer and less worth taking. I wrote to the State Superintendent of Education and made arrangements to take an examination at Tallahassee in the coming summer for a life certificate, so that I might continue teaching, with exemption from all further examinations.

I had been back in Jacksonville a couple of months when I received a letter from Rosamond saying that one of the managers who had been present at the party at Sherry's had engaged him and Bob to appear in vaudeville, singing and playing their original compositions. This meant an end of their immediate money worries, for they started at a salary of three hundred dollars a week. But it seemed to me that this stroke of fortune for them so altered our partnership plans that my individual chances were greatly reduced; so, amidst suffusing thoughts of love in a cottage, I applied myself as doggedly as I could to preparation for my examination.

Stanton closed after a short term of four months, but I did not leave for New York. I spent the greater part of each day studying; and I have never set a tougher task for myself. Despite the state of my heart, my mind kept running off to Broadway and the group at the Marshall. I was disturbed by the thought that my caution amounted to cowardice. Why not play the game, win or lose? One very hot afternoon I was stretched in a hammock boning Vergil's *Æneid*, one of the subjects I was to be examined in, when the postman's whistle blew, and my sister, a moment later, brought me up two letters. They were both from my brother. I studied the postmarks to learn which one had been mailed at the earlier hour, and found that the two had been mailed at the same time. I fingered them a moment, and decided to open the lighter letter first. It contained a brief note and a money order for eighty-odd dollars royalty. I then opened the second. It contained a long communication and a money order for four hundred dollars, more of the same royalty money. The cost of an extra money order was Rosamond's method of perpetrating a practical joke; I don't know why he surmised that I should open the right envelope first, and not spoil the joke. The letter was written in high spirits:—*The Maiden with the Dreamy Eyes* was selling—the other songs were beginning to move—in the January to June period we had earned enough to pay off all our indebtedness to our publishers and net nearly fifteen hundred dollars—the vaudeville act was a hit, and was now a headline attraction—why in the world was I hanging on down in Jacksonville?

"Why in the world was I hanging on in Jacksonville?" I threw Vergil the length of the porch, sprang out of the hammock, and rushed downstairs. I emptied several dollars in silver from my pockets into my mother's lap; then did a dance round her chair. The more curious my mother and sister became about the cause of my behavior, the wilder became my antics. I finally sobered down enough to ask them to help me pack for New York. I hurried down to the Post Office and cashed my two money orders. What sweet money it was! It was sweeter than money merely worked for. This was money gained for materializing the intangible. I had actually minted some rather inconsequential dreams, and the process seemed to possess an element of magic. This, for me, considerable sum gave me a larger measure of satisfaction than any money I had hitherto earned.

When I reached New York I met several surprises. I was, first of all, surprised at the opulence of Bob and Rosamond; at their clothes, modest in pattern and design but nevertheless expensive; at their dozen pairs of shoes each; at the abundance of their shirts and ties and socks. I felt like a country cousin. They were quick to assure me that this outlay was part of their stock in trade. I was also surprised to see that they had taken the front and middle rooms connecting with the back room in which Rosamond and I had lived, and that Bob himself had moved over to the Marshall. The whole floor provided ample sleeping quarters for the three of us, after reserving the back room exclusively as a workshop. My biggest surprise was Bob and Rosamond's act. They were at the time playing an engagement as headliners of the bill at Keith's 14th Street Theater, then one of the principal vaudeville houses of the country. Of course, I went at once to see them.

The act was unlike anything ever done by Negro performers; it was quiet, finished, and artistic to the minutest details. The two entered dressed in evening clothes—they did make a handsome appearance—and talking casually about the program they had best give in entertaining a party to which they were on their way. Rosamond seating himself at the piano, suggested that they open with an instrumental number, and proceeded to play Paderewski's *Minuet*, which went over well. Rosamond then suggested further that they ought to follow with a little classic song. Bob demurred slightly, but Rosamond went ahead and sang *Still wie die Nacht* in German. The singing of this song never failed to gain applause; perhaps, somewhat for the reason that Dr. Johnson assigned for admiration at seeing a dog walk on his hind legs. Bob then expressed the fear that classic music might be what the people at the party (in fact, the audience) would least like to hear, and suggested the singing of their own little song, *Mandy*. From this point on the program consisted of original songs, sung one after another, Rosamond playing the accompaniments. And novel accompaniments they were, for he was among the first musicians in America to go beyond the one-two-three and one-two-three-four styles of arrangements and to adapt counterpoint to the accompaniments of popular songs. A comparison of the arrangements of *The Maiden with the Dreamy Eyes, Under the Bamboo Tree*, and *The Congo Love Song* with those of other songs of that period will substantiate this statement. The interludes were furnished by Bob's graceful soft shoe dancing to the choruses played almost pianissimo. Those who remember their performance, certainly, do not forget the pleasing manner in which Bob Cole handled a white silk handkerchief, both in singing and dancing. This was the framework of an act that these two men played for seven or eight years with tremendous success in the United States and Europe. No small part of the success of the act was due to the fact that its planned simplicity and studied naïveté gave it the spontaneous air of an impromptu. This was the act that started a vogue of acts consisting of two men in dress suits and a piano.

Bob and Rosamond were now regularly playing two shows a day; nevertheless, we began again at once on our work of composition. Much of the time I worked alone, but the three of us worked together, sometimes in the mornings and sometimes late at nights. We worked the harder because the team was booked to play the Orpheum Circuit in the winter, and that meant playing to the Pacific Coast and back. One of the first songs we wrote in this period was *Under the Bamboo Tree*. We saw George Lederer, and he introduced us to Marie Cahill, who was playing in his *Sally in Our Alley*. Miss Cahill was delighted with the song and began using it as soon as an orchestration could be made. Before *Sally in Our Alley* was closed, Miss Cahill had set the world singing *Under the Bamboo Tree*. This song led to more work for her, and a warm relationship that has continued up to the present time.

Before I realized it, the fall of the year was on me and I was confronted with the necessity of deciding whether or not I was going back to Jacksonville as the principal of Stanton. Making the decision was by no means a simple matter. I weighed the question up and down: the prospects looked bright; I was making headway along a line that seemed to lead straight to the center of the American light opera world; *The Maiden with the Dreamy Eyes* was selling; several other songs had begun to move; and *Under the Bamboo Tree* was very promising. But, as yet, our compositions had not brought in sufficient money to live on. True, Bob and Rosamond were earning a dependable wage, but I could not and would not put myself in a position where I might become their pensioner; perhaps it would be wisest to continue my school work and come to New York in the summers as I had been doing. This last consideration was strengthened by my realization of the fact that our combination was no longer a trio working as one man, but a majority and a minority. While I was debating these questions, I wrote a letter to my father telling him that I was thinking of giving up my position in Jacksonville and remaining in New York. I wrote a somewhat similar letter to D——. My father wrote a very fatherly letter in reply, advising me to be careful, to think well before I gave up my position; but he left it for me to use my own best judgment. D—— advised strongly against the step; that if I wanted to give up schoolteaching—and he had small reverence for that occupation—I ought to devote myself entirely to law; that Jacksonville was one of the best fields in the country for a colored lawyer. I also received letters from several friends who had somehow become privy to the plans I was contemplating, giving me additional advice. One of these blankly asked, "What's the matter with you, thinking of giving up a life position to take a chance, and a Negro's chance, at writing music in New York? Have you gone crazy?"

No, I had not quite gone crazy, but my mind for a while was whirling in a void of indecision. But time put an end to that, and the day arrived when I had to act. I sat down and wrote out my resignation. I carried it in my pocket through the following day; then, at night while walking up Broadway with Bob and Rosamond I stopped suddenly at a mail box, dropped it in, and burned my bridges. As the letter dropped into the box, a load dropped from my shoulders. I at once became aware of an expanse of freedom I had not felt before. Immediately it seemed that the goal of my efforts was no longer marked by a limit just a little way in front of my eyes but reached out somewhere toward infinity. From the thought that the things I had already done, I had done, perhaps, fairly well, I got a solid satisfaction; but stepping off my beaten road on to a path that led I knew not just where gave me a thrill.

In January, a few days before Bob and Rosamond started on their western tour, we went down to our publishers for an accounting. We went with high expectations. *The Maiden with the Dreamy Eyes* and *Under the Bamboo Tree* were popular hits, and some of our other songs appeared to be selling well. With my expectations were mingled fervent hopes; for, although Rosamond had now in turn allowed me to draw his share of the monthly royalty advance, I was finding it hard to make both ends meet. We were handed our statement with the sales of the songs itemized and advances deducted, and a check for the balance due. Bob took the check and statement, and the three of us glanced quickly at the one then studied the other. We were disappointed. We felt that the songs should have made a better showing, and so expressed ourselves. Bob spoke strongly. There were words, some of them hot. Bob threw the check on the table, and the three of us walked out. We walked the half-block to Broadway, turned in at the old Continental Hotel, went into the bar, and ordered a drink. We needed it, for by the time we got that far we realized that we had actually scorned a check for close to six thousand dollars. The drink made me philosophically detached, and I mused over the matter. I made a nimble computation which showed that I had contemptuously tossed aside a sum of money accruing in six months that it would have taken me two years and six months to earn as principal of Stanton—and I marveled that such a thing could really be.

We remained away from our publishers a couple of days, but the matter was patched up and Bob and Rosamond started for the Coast. But the rumor spread that Cole and Johnson Brothers had had a serious breach with their publishers, and offers came to us from several other houses. One of the leading publishing firms in the city sent an urgent request for me to come and see them. I went, and the head of the firm kept me in conference a long time. He emphasized to me the advantage of being on the staff of their older, larger, and richer concern. He spread in front of me a contract—a very liberal one—and offered me a pen, together with a certified check for ten thousand dollars against future royalties, drawn to my order. I could not resist studying the check curiously; and, without the aid of a drink, I was again forced to marvel that such things could really be. But I declined to take the pen. I parried with the remark that my partners were out of the city and that sole action on my part would not bind them. The publisher said he knew my partners were away, but that he would be satisfied to have me sign the contract and turn over the manuscripts of such new songs as were in my possession and to wait for their signatures. I called to his attention the fact that we were still under contract. He smilingly observed that grounds were sometimes found on which contracts could be broken. But the breaking of a contract did not appear to me to be so simple or advantageous a matter as it seemed to appear to him, and I came out leaving the unsigned document and the ten-thousand-dollar check. I wrote to Rob and Rosamond about the offer; they fully agreed with my view.

One of the first things I did after we cashed our royalty check was to send my father a thousand dollars with the request that he invest it in Jacksonville property for me. I was proud to do this, and I gloated over the effect it would have on the friend who had written to ask if I had gone crazy. This was a precedent, however, that I did not follow regularly enough.

We never regretted not making the attempt to break our contract. Our relations with our publishers became entirely cordial again. At the end of another six months they gave us a check for an amount more than double that of the previous check, and we were at a height of popularity and success equal, at least, to that of any other writers of popular songs in America. We had a clean business record and a list of hits that included: *The Maiden with the Dreamy Eyes; Mandy, Won't You Let Me Be Your Beau; Nobody's Lookin' but the Owl and the Moon; Tell Me, Dusky Maiden; The Old Flag Never Touched the Ground; My Castle on the Nile; Under the Bamboo Tree;* and *Oh, Didn't He Ramble.* We had written a new song for Miss Cahill, *The Congo Love Song,* that she was to sing and to make as famous as *Under the Bamboo Tree;* and there were others still to follow. In the fullness of our vogue there were times when songs of ours were being sung in three or four current musical productions on Broadway. We managed to break in even upon the rather exclusive Weber and Fields stage with a song for Lillian Russell. The reviewers built up for us a sort of reputation as physicians for ailing musical plays. We got used to seeing notices and paragraphs and articles about ourselves in the press of New York and other cities; but the appearance of a four-column-wide cartoon of the three of us in *The Evening World* did shake us up a bit. In truth, we became, in a measure, Broadway personalities. I remember D——'s utter amazement when one night during a visit of his to the city, as he and I were walking up the famous street, a little newsboy ran up to me shouting, "Mr. Johnson, you want the latest edition?" I didn't want it, but I bought it. All of this seems to me now to belong to a distant and distinct existence.

With Bob and Rosamond away so much of the time, even New York frequently seemed lonely. I wrote and jotted down ideas for new work; I read a great deal; I went to the theater as a part of my job; nearly every Saturday night, because it was popular price night, I went to the opera, and in that way heard the whole Metropolitan repertory, but, even so, I found time on my hands. It was then that I discovered an explanation as good as any of whatever success that has come my way: I discovered my abhorrence of "spare time." I thereupon cast about to find a means of using up all I had of it in some worthwhile manner. I lit upon doing some studying at Columbia University. I secured a catalogue, and determined to take up courses in English and the history and development of the drama. I decided to go up to the University and talk the matter over with Professor Brander Matthews, whom I knew by his writings. I was flattered to find that Professor Matthews knew of my work in musical comedy, a phase of the theater that he followed and studied closely. My reception was extremely cordial. As soon as the greetings were over and I had taken a seat, he produced his cigarette case and offered me a smoke. For the life of me, I could not prevent the inculcated inhibitions of my years at Atlanta University from rushing out in full force upon me. I accepted the cigarette and smoked it, but it was difficult for me not to feel that I was breaking school rules. Of course, I had smoked constantly since my graduation from Atlanta, but to be smoking with a professor in his office on the university grounds struck me for the time as being not only incongruous but slightly unholy.

This meeting was the beginning of a warm and lasting friendship between Brander Matthews and me. He talked to me a great deal about the musical comedy stage and the important people connected with it. In his lectures he frequently set me in an enviable light before the class. When we reached the classic drama of Spain, he often called on my knowledge of the language in dealing with the plays in the original. When we came to the contemporary American stage he cited me a good many times as a journeyman in the theater. I was fascinated with my work under him. I was especially impressed with his catholicity, his freedom from pedantry, and his common sense in talking about the theater. I believe that he shocked most of us in his class when he declared that the best plays of Weber and Fields were the same sort of thing as the theater of Aristophanes; that, except for the fact that no Weber and Fields playwright ever attempted to imitate the occasional lofty lyrical flights of the Greek comedian, the two theaters were comparable.

I continued my work at Columbia for three years, not allowing for an interruption of several months in the spring of 1905. Before I left I talked with Professor Matthews about my more serious work, and showed him the draft of the first two chapters of a book which, I said to him, I proposed to call *The Autobiography of an Ex-Colored Man*. He read the manuscript and told me he liked the idea and the proposed title, and that I was wise in writing about the thing I knew best. I also showed him some of my poems. After he had looked them through, he gave me a note to Professor Harry Thurston Peck, who was then editing *The Bookman*. Professor Peck took two poems for the magazine, and appeared to be much interested in the things I was planning to do; and talked with me quite a while in his precise, punctilious manner.

I saw Professor Peck only once after that interview, about ten years later. I was on 43rd Street, just east of Fifth Avenue, and about to enter the offices of G. Ricordi and Co., the music publishers, when I saw a man approaching, walking in a dazed sort of way. As he came nearer I recognized him to be Harry Thurston Peck. He was dressed, as was his custom, in a frock coat and silk hat, but both were extremely shabby. He passed, looking neither right nor left; he seemed entirely oblivious to his surroundings. I felt a strong impulse to go after him and speak to him. I knew something of the difficulties he had had at Columbia, and which had led to his severance from the University, and it appeared as though he was in great need. The thought flashed through my mind that I might offer him some little help. But I hesitated, something held me back, and some intangible apprehensions intervened; it may have been the shadow of race; and he passed on. A day or two later I read that he had committed suicide in his room in a cheap lodging-house at Stamford, Connecticut. I never recall this incident without a pang of regret that I did not speak the words that were in my mind to say to him.

XVIII

S UCCESS is a heady beverage. It can be as deleterious as any alcoholic drink. It seems to me that a man drunk with success is more of a fool than the maudlin inebriate; and, certainly, he is more dangerous to himself and to others. Success is safe only when it comes slowly, and even then is not entirely so. We had been struggling for four years; yet, when success did come, it seemed sudden. It magically blotted out the memory of all our disappointments and defeats and carried us up into a region above doubts and fears, to that height where success of itself begets success. There is a line in the blues which runs:

I got de world in a bottle an' de stopper—in-a ma hand.

No single line of poetry that I know of contains a more graphic figure to suggest the reaction to success.

I regard it as pardonable that we were made tipsy; why we did not get drunk I do not know. As for Rosamond and myself, I might definitely attribute our salvation to that precept of Solomon, "Train up a child in the way he should go, and when he is old he will not depart from it," were it not for the fact that so many times its teachings appear to have failed. And, furthermore, Solomon gives not even an intimation of what may happen in the years between. Or I might claim that I was safeguarded by a patent or latent strength of character; but I should be hard put to it to analyze satisfactorily for myself "strength of character." It is probable that one of the reasons why I did not fly off at a tangent was that I was not able to feel completely that our success was real. This trait has persisted in me through all the years of my manhood. When success with me has seemed brightest, there has never failed to lurk somewhere the shadow of doubt. Always, the sense of security is greater in the struggle to succeed. For many years I have been disturbed by a frequently recurring dream, the pattern of which is: I am taking a terribly difficult examination, on the passing of which my future and my means of existence depend; I awake before I know the result of the test, and sometimes seconds pass in the effort to shake off the dream and seize the reality. A psychoanalyst could, I suppose, tell the significance of this dream, but I have never consulted one about it.

With prosperity, we added a degree or so of luxury to our mode of living. We bought furniture, books, and "objects of art," and had the set-up supervised by a professional decorator. Across one wall was stretched a seine, to which was attached with clips our collection of autographed photographs. This collection grew to include nearly all the important persons connected with the musical theater. Our studio now became a center for both Negro and white artists. Among the principals in Broadway musical plays who were singing our music, there were those who found it pleasant to come to the studio to rehearse their numbers. We also began to give parties. Our first big party was given for Miss May Irwin and friends she might wish to bring. She brought eight or ten persons; and we had invited about an equal number of colored guests. The party was a success. One evening we gave a party for G. P. Huntley and principals in the English company playing *Three Little Maids* at Daly's. Several times we entertained Charles Hawtrey, later by the grace of his good friend, King Edward VII, Sir Charles Hawtrey, when he was playing *The Man from Blankney's*. This entertaining entailed considerable expenditure, but we justified it to ourselves under the head of publicity. No doubt, it did bring us returns in publicity, and a certain éclat.

Be that as it may; in the artistic world, anything, from wearing strange-looking clothes to committing manslaughter, may be justified under the head of "publicity."

The fame of the Marshall spread. We lent Jimmie Marshall money to enable him to acquire and adapt the twin house adjoining, and, so, double the capacity of the hotel. Bert Williams and two or three other leading Negro performers and musicians moved in and made the Marshall their home. It was now one of the most interesting places in New York. During this period, Rosamond and I brought our mother and sister north several summers. We brought our father up one summer; he had not been to New York in more than twenty-five years; he had a great time going about with us and pointing out spots where old landmarks used to stand.

We continued to ride the crest of the wave. *The Ladies' Home Journal* then made it a custom to publish musical pieces as a part of the regular edition of the magazine; and Edward Bok, the editor, asked us to contribute. I went over to see Mr. Bok, and made arrangements, with the consent of our publishers, to have certain of our compositions appear in that way. We published, in all, seven or eight pieces in *The Ladies' Home Journal*. Some while after the first conference,

I had another talk with Mr. Bok, and he showed me a letter which had given him, it appeared, one of the biggest laughs of his life. He had accepted a song that had been submitted to him by a young Negro composer in Georgia. Following the acceptance, he announced in the magazine that in a subsequent issue such a song would appear. Promptly he received a letter from a white woman in a little town also in Georgia protesting against it. She declared that no Negro had the musical skill or the artistic taste to interpret even his own race, much less the ability to do anything worthy of going into the pages of *The Ladies' Home Journal.* She ended her letter by imploring Mr. Bok to "give us some more of those little Negro classics by Cole and Johnson Brothers." The very serious-looking Mr. Bok read me the letter and laughed uproariously over it. I laughed too; but my laughter was temperered by the thought that there was anybody in the country, notwithstanding the locality being Georgia, who, knowing anything at all about them, did not know that Cole and Johnson Brothers were Negroes.

We received another call from Klaw and Erlanger; the call this time did not come through Ben Teal, who was no longer with the concern, but directly from A. L. Erlanger himself, the Grand Mogul of the theatrical business. We had a conference with Mr. Erlanger, and he told us pointedly what he wanted, and that was to have us write exclusively for the Klaw and Erlanger productions. There was some question in our minds as to whether it would be more advantageous to do this or remain free lances. Our publishers felt strongly that we should hold ourselves open to work for all producers. We finally did sign a contract for three years, which stipulated the payment to us of a definite sum monthly and, in addition, a flat sum for each ensemble number; the royalty rights in all our numbers being reserved to us.

This arrangement made us members of the Klaw and Erlanger producing staff and brought us into intimate contact with Mr. Erlanger. When a new play was being planned, the staff was called by Mr. Erlanger to meet with him in his offices as often as was necessary—possibly more often than was necessary. We met with John J. McNally, Herbert Gresham, Ned Wayburn, and Fred Solomon. Ernest D'Auban was present if there was to be a ballet in the production. Mr. Erlanger completely dominated these meetings. His word was law, and he brooked no opposition. Members of the staff would offer counter-suggestions but none ever flatly disagreed with him. He was a man of tremendous energy. Short of stature and somewhat portly, he would walk with the pompous strut natural to men of his build and temperament, up and down the room, carrying a lighted or unlighted cigar in his mouth at a forty-five-degree angle, and lay down for us what he wanted done. He impressed me as possessing certain Napoleonic qualities. At times he made himself a bit absurd—a failing common to all Napoleonic figures—by pre-empting more of the creative field of the theater than he could hold, and attempting to picture and outline a whole play in a few words. He would pace up and down saying:—Now, over here I want this— And over there I want that—Then we'll do such and such things— And after that such and such other things. At these times an imperceptible smile ran round the members of the staff, and we made little or no mental note of what he was saying; for these fragmentary suggestions usually had no value.

When a play was nearing the time for production, Mr. Erlanger frequently attended rehearsals; and he carried his dictatorial manner there. He would stand at the back of the theater watching, then suddenly come striding down the aisle to the stage, storming at directors and performers and yelling out his dissatisfaction at the way in which things were being done. These outbursts never failed to upset everybody concerned with the making of the play, but nobody dared to flare back. Only once did I see such an incredible thing take place. We were down to the final rehearsals of *Humpty Dumpty*, another of the Drury Lane Pantomimes, and everybody was on edge. There was a part in the piece that called for a better-trained voice than was, in those days, easily found in the ranks of musical play performers, and a young lady who, as I remember, was the soprano soloist in a prominent church choir had been engaged to sing it. Rosamond had worked with her assiduously, and she knew the score well and sang it beautifully. But in these rehearsals before a cold jury she became timid, nervous, and frightened. Her voice quivered and broke constantly. Mr. Erlanger yelled his dissatisfaction with her several times. Finally, he rushed down the aisle shouting, "Rossmore (the name by which he always called my brother), we'll have to take that woman out and get somebody who can sing the part." Rosamond jumped up from the piano and shouted back, "How in the world can you expect her to sing it when you keep yelling at her?" A silence, I judge, the same in kind if not in duration as that recorded in Rev. viii, 1, fell on the theater. Mr. Erlanger was for that instant the most surprised man in New York. He turned and walked slowly to the back of the theater muttering under his breath something that sounded like "Well, I'll be damned." The silence gave Rosamond opportunity to realize the enormity of his act.

And yet, A. L. Erlanger had a considerate, kindly side. We had been with the K & E institution but a short while when Mr. Erlanger called us for a conference in his offices at eight o'clock in the morning. We got in about fifteen minutes late. As we entered, he took out his watch saying, "Good morning, boys. For what hour did I call this conference?" We somewhat lamely offered as an excuse the fact that we had worked late the night before, feeling that we were in for a sharp reproof. Instead, Mr. Erlanger said to us rather gently, "No matter how late I work, I am up at six, riding in the park at seven, and at my desk at eight. When you are dealing with *busy* men, never be late for an appointment. Try and remember that." I never forgot it. We saw very little of Mr. Klaw, the other half of the firm. I saw him periodically at times when I went to collect money due us. He was a quiet, unobtrusive man, who seemed to hide himself behind the dark luxuriant whiskers he then wore. He had the reputation among his associates of being scholarly. It appeared that he paid no attention to the production of plays, but devoted himself to the business end of the enterprise; and that meant, principally, looking after the percentage tribute that flowed into the coffers of Klaw and Erlanger from companies all over the United States and Canada that had been booked through their offices.

Humpty Dumpty, for which we did the lyrics and music, was the first play produced in Klaw and Erlanger's new New Amsterdam Theater, at the time the last word in New York theaters. We also did the lyrics and music for the show that opened their Aerial Theater, atop the New Amsterdam. In this show Fay Templeton scored a popular success with one of our songs called *Fishing*. Another play for which we did the lyrics and music opened another new Klaw and Erlanger theater; it was *In Newport*, and was produced at the Liberty Theater. In *In Newport* we got the first setback since gaining recognition. The play had a good cast; in it were Peter Dailey, Joseph Coyne, Lee Harrison, the beautiful Virginia Earle, and the temperamental Fay Templeton; but the work had been hastily and carelessly done. Our part of it was pretty far below the standard we had been maintaining. On the opening night I stood back of the orchestra rows and watched the performance; I thought the play was pretty poor. As it went along, I stepped over to where Mr. Erlanger stood and asked him what he thought of it. He answered tersely, "Rotten." For once, at least, his critical judgment was sound. We were called the next day into conference. The case of *In Newport* was discussed and diagnosed, but there seemed to be nothing the doctors could prescribe to save it. Mr. Erlanger decided to withdraw it at the end of the week. In the conference Mr. Erlanger remarked, "We've got some mighty good reports from a show Georgie Cohan has on the road. I think we'll cancel his road dates and bring him in to the Liberty." He did as he said, and George Cohan came to the Liberty Theater with *Little Johnny Jones*. George Cohan's eccentric manner of singing and dancing captured Broadway; and furthermore he had two such songs to sing as *Give My Regards to Broadway* and *I'm a Yankee-Doodle Dandy*. Within forty-eight hours after the closing of *In Newport*, George Cohan had started on his rapid rise in the American theater.

We got an idea for a genuine American pantomime, which we worked on for a while; then took to Mr. Erlanger an outline of the play with some of the musical numbers in a finished state. Our idea was to make a pantomime out of the *Uncle Remus* stories. Mr. Erlanger thought well of it; so well that he said that I should go to Atlanta to talk with Joel Chandler Harris and see if suitable arrangements for rights could be made. I have lost all recollection of what would explain my not going to Atlanta to see Mr. Harris or our failure to push the idea. I am puzzled, because we had the greatest resources in the country back of us, and, without doubt, *Uncle Remus*, made into an artistic music spectacle, would have been successful at that time. The idea still has possibilities.

While we were with Klaw and Erlanger, we observed that through an organized agency—the Southern Society, if I remember correctly —certain leaflets were being placed, before performances, in the seats of New York theaters. The purpose was to disseminate anti-Negro propaganda, and in particular to rouse and strengthen sentiment against Negroes being seated in any part of a theater, except the top gallery. We brought this to Mr. Erlanger's attention, and he at once issued orders that stopped it in all the theaters in New York under his control.

It was difficult to see why this agency should display such solicitude, for the conditions were already humiliating enough. In the "Broadway" houses it was the practice to sell Negroes first balcony seats, but, if their race was plainly discernible, to refuse to sell them seats in the orchestra. (The Metropolitan Opera House, Carnegie Hall, and in general, the East Side and West Side theaters were exceptions.) The same practice was and still is common in most of the cities of the North; it is not necessary to mention the practice in Southern cities. In Washington, where race discrimination is hardly less than in any city in the South, Negroes are not allowed to enter the National Theater; nor was that rule broken when *The Green Pastures* recently played a two weeks' engagement at that house. In that case the colored people made strong protest, and the management compromised by setting aside one night "for Negroes only," stating that even this concession would offend many of their regular patrons. Just how those patrons could feel like that and at the same time be able to feel in any degree the beauty and ecstasy conveyed through the acting of Richard B. Harrison and the great Negro cast of the play presents a mystery of the human soul which only God or perhaps the devil can explain.

Some years ago one of my old Jacksonville friends, a physician, came to New York on a visit. My wife and I thought it would give him a real treat to take him to see a show. We bought orchestra seats several days in advance for an operetta playing at one of the Shubert houses. When we reached the theater, my wife passed through the gate first, I followed with the tickets and my friend followed me. The ticket taker probably was not aware that we were a group of colored people until we had passed through. Inside, each usher we approached was "very busy," and we had to find our own seats. After we were seated, I signaled an usher, asking her to bring us programs. She never brought them. A gentleman seated next to me courteously proffered the use of his program. As the lights were being lowered for the first act, I felt some one tap me on the shoulder from the row behind. I turned. A man from the box office was bending over my chair.

"Have you coupons for these seats?" he asked.

"Yes," I replied.

"May I see them?"

"Certainly."

I held the coupons up to him, displaying the numbers, but kept them tightly gripped between my thumb and forefinger.

"I'd like to look at them."

"You're looking at them."

"You don't think I want to steal them?"

"I don't intend to give you the chance."

He went away. Had I handed him the coupons he would have rushed off with them to the box office, then come back and told us that there had been a mistake made about the tickets and that we would have to give up our seats. I was determined not to undergo that injustice and humiliation, so held fast to my coupons. But I was so blind with anger and resentment that I did not actually see the first act. In relation to the whole scheme of life such an experience appears insignificant, but at the moment it is charged with elements of tragedy.

A marked change in these conditions has taken place in New York City. It began in 1921 with the popular Negro musical play *Shuffle Along* at the 63rd Street Theater, where Negroes in considerable numbers were seated on the ground floor, and increased with *Blackbirds; Porgy; The Green Pastures*, and other Negro plays. It was established more firmly by the big moving picture theaters, which, whatever may have been the reason, never adopted a policy of segregation. At the present time the sight of colored people in the orchestras of "Broadway" theaters is not regarded a cause for immediate action or of utter astonishment.

XIX

IN JACKSONVILLE for a while after my graduation from Atlanta University social life took up a good deal of my time, but as the years went along the additional work that I undertook constantly reduced the margin of time which I felt I could spare for social affairs. Before I left Jacksonville, I had withdrawn almost entirely from such activities.

When I came to New York to live, there was not such a thing as "society" among the colored people who lived in Manhattan. There were, of course, concerts, big dances, the Drury opera performances, and other public events, that anybody who paid the price of admission could attend. In summer there were "picnics" that began at ten o'clock at night. The most popular picnic place was Sultzer's Park out at the Harlem River end of Second Avenue. Many picnics were given there during a season, but there were two that were more select than any of the others: one given annually by the Sons of New York, a society made up of native-born New Yorkers, and another given by the Guild of St. Phillip's Episcopal Church, the richest Negro church in the world. These summer picnics were jolly and promiscuous, but usually quite orderly. But cultivated Negroes living in Manhattan had, for many years, necessarily been going to Brooklyn for the social intercourse that is confined more or less to the people one knows or knows about. Forty years before, there had been a general exodus of the better-off Negroes from Manhattan to Brooklyn. For some years still farther back, there had been the steady lure of the better opportunity to buy homes on that side of the East River; but the Draft Riots in 1863 precipitated a wholesale migration. A number of these older families in Brooklyn were positively rich; their money, made in the days when Negroes in New York were successful caterers, fashionable dressmakers, and the janitors of big buildings, having come down through two or three generations. I knew a family in which, after the death of the parents, four children were left around sixty thousand dollars each in cash and securities, besides valuable real estate.

Rosamond and I knew some of the old families in Brooklyn, and we devoted an occasional Sunday afternoon and evening to paying calls. Naturally, we made the acquaintance of others that we had not known. We got to know the younger people of the "Brooklyn set" and were invited to parties and dances. We went to these when we could make it convenient. I found these social gatherings much the same as those in Jacksonville; the chief difference being that in Brooklyn the number of well-off people was larger, and the houses we went into were more imposing. Today, I should think of those houses as stuffy, too filled with heavy furniture, heavy pictures, heavy curtains, and heavy carpets; then, I thought of them as being very sumptuous.

My social visits to Brooklyn were not regular or frequent, but much more so than Rosamond's, because his vaudeville work left him scarcely any time to use in that way. I went over one night to see an amateur theatrical performance. I have found that amateur theatricals anywhere are generally a bore; and this one was not an exception. After the· performance there was an hour or so of dancing; and that closed the evening pleasantly. Without doubt, the whole affair would have faded completely from my memory had it not been for the fact that it marked the time when I first saw Grace Nail, Jack Nail's sister. She was there with her mother, and was taking, it appeared to me, an initiatory peep at life. Her sensitive response to what she saw was enchanting. She was in her middle teens, but carried herself then like a princess. Her delicate patrician beauty stirred something in me that had not been touched before, and I went away carrying a vivid picture of her in my mind.

I went down to Atlanta University on the tenth anniversary of my graduation to receive an honorary degree. There it was that I first met W. E. B. Du Bois, who was now one of the professors. The year before, he had issued *The Souls of Black Folk* (a work which, I think, has had a greater effect upon and within the Negro race in America than any other single book published in this country since *Uncle Tom's Cabin*) and was already a national figure. I had been deeply moved and influenced by the book, and was anxious to meet the author. I met a quite handsome and unpedantic young man—Dr. Du Bois was then thirty-six. Indeed, it was, at first, slightly difficult to reconcile the brooding but intransigent spirit of *The Souls of Black Folk* with this apparently so light-hearted man, this man so abundantly endowed with the gift of laughter. I noted then what, through many years of close association, I have since learned well, and what the world knows not at all: that Du Bois in battle is a stern, bitter, relentless fighter, who, when he has put aside his sword, is among his particular friends the most jovial and fun-loving of men. This quality has been a saving grace for him, but his lack of the ability to unbend in his relations with people outside the small circle has gained him the reputation of being cold, stiff, supercilious, and has been a cause of criticism amongst even his adherents. This disposition, due perhaps to an inhibition of spontaneous impulse, has limited his scope of leadership to less than what it might have been, in that it has hindered his attracting and binding to himself a body of zealous liegemen—one of the essentials to the headship of a popular or an unpopular cause. The great influence Du Bois has exercised has been due to the concentrated force of his ideas, with next to no reinforcement from that wide appeal of personal magnetism which is generally a valuable asset of leaders of men.

Just before spring in 1905, Bob and Rosamond started again over the Orpheum Circuit; I made the trip with them. Some other performers who were playing the same circuit and who left Denver for San Francisco on the same train with us had planned to stop off for a day at Salt Lake City to visit the Mormon Tabernacle and see the town. They persuaded us to do likewise. We had our tickets adjusted for a stop-over until the next day and got off the train at Salt Lake City. We took a carriage, and directed the driver, a jovial Irishman, to take us to a good hotel. He took us to the best. Porters carried our luggage into the lobby, and I went to the desk, turned the register round and registered for the three. The clerk was busy at the key-rack. He glanced at us furtively, but kept himself occupied. It grew obvious that he was protracting the time. Finally, he could delay no longer and came to the desk. As he came his expression revealed the lie he was to speak. He turned the register round, examined our names, and while his face flushed a bit said, "I'm sorry, but we haven't got a vacant room." This statement, which I knew almost absolutely to be false, set a number of emotions in action: humiliation, chagrin, indignation, resentment, anger; but in the midst of them all I could detect a sense of pity for the man who had to make it, for he was, to all appearances, an honest, decent person. It was then about eleven o'clock, and I sought the eyes of the clerk and asked if he expected any rooms to be vacated at noon. He stammered that he did not. I then said to him that we would check our bags and take the first room available by night. Pressure from me seemed to stiffen him, and he told us that we could not; that we had better try some other hotel. Our bags were taken out and a cab called, and we found ourselves in the same vehicle that had brought us to the hotel. Our driver voluntarily assumed a part of our mortification, and he attempted to console us by relating how ten or twelve years before he had taken Peter Jackson (the famous Negro pugilist) to that same hotel and how royally he had been entertained there. We tried two other hotels, where our experiences were similar but briefer. We did not dismiss our cabman, for we were being fast driven to the conclusion that he was probably the only compassionate soul we should meet in the whole city of the Latter-Day Saints.

We had become very hungry; we felt that it was necessary for us to eat in order to maintain both our morale and our endurance. Our cabman took us to a restaurant. When we entered it was rather crowded, but we managed to find a table and sat down. There followed that hiatus, of which every Negro in the United States knows the meaning. At length, a man in charge came over and told us without any pretense of palliation that we could not be served. We were forced to come out under the stare of a crowd that was conscious of what had taken place. Our cabman was now actually touched by our plight; and he gave vent to his feelings in explosive oaths. He suggested another restaurant to try, where we might have "better luck"; but we were no longer up to the possible facing of another such experience. We asked the cabby if he knew of a colored family in town who might furnish us with a meal; he did not, but he had an idea; he drove along and stopped in front of a saloon and chophouse; he darted inside, leaving us in the carriage; after a few moments he emerged beaming good news. We went in and were seated at a wholly inconspicuous table, but were served with food and drink that quickly renewed our strength and revived our spirits.

However, we were almost immediately confronted with the necessity of getting a place to sleep. Our cabby had another idea; he drove us to a woman he knew who kept a lodging house for laborers. It was a pretty shabby place; nevertheless, the woman demurred for quite a while. Finally, she agreed to let us stay, if we got out before her regular lodgers got up. In the foul room to which she showed us, we hesitated until the extreme moment of weariness before we could bring ourselves to bear the touch of the soiled bedclothes. We smoked and talked over the situation we were in, the situation of being outcasts and pariahs in a city of our own and native land. Our talk went beyond our individual situation and took in the common lot of Negroes in well-nigh every part of the country, a lot which lays on high and low the constant struggle to renerve their hearts and wills against the unremitting pressure of unfairness, injustice, wrong, cruelty, contempt, and hate. If what we felt had been epitomized and expressed in but six words, they would have been: A hell of a "my country."

We welcomed daybreak. For numerous reasons we were glad to get out of the beds of our unwilling hostess. We boarded our train with feelings of unbounded relief; I with a vow never to set foot again in Salt Lake City. Twenty-three years later, I passed through Salt Lake City, as one of a large delegation on the way to a conference of the National Association for the Advancement of Colored People held in Los Angeles. Our train had a wait of a couple of hours, and the delegation went out to see the town, the Tabernacle, and the lake. I spent the time alone at the railroad station.

Concerning this particular lapse from democracy in America, I have heard many people declare that the remedy for the situation is for Negroes to have places of their own. Aside from any principle of common rights, the suggestion is absurd. At the time of which I have been speaking, Negroes in Salt Lake City constituted an infinitesimal element in the community, and Negroes who visited there, a still smaller element; therefore it is evident that no hotel nor even a modest boarding house for "Negroes only" could have been operated on a commercial basis. Such an institution would have demanded a subsidy. Negroes in many localities where their numbers are large have, from necessity, and as often from choice, provided certain places of public accommodation for themselves; but to say that they should duplicate the commercial and social machinery of the nation is to utter an inanity. It takes all New York and its hundreds of thousands of visitors to support one grand opera company. If I want to hear grand opera in New York I must go to the Metropolitan Opera House. To tell Negroes that they ought to get their own opera house in Harlem if they want to hear grand opera would not be less unreasonable than to tell them to get their own railroads if they want to ride in Pullman cars, and just about as reasonable as telling them to have hotels in all cities and towns in which a Negro traveler might, perchance, stop over.

I was delighted with San Francisco. Here was a civilized center, metropolitan and urbane. With respect to the Negro race, I found it a freer city than New York. I encountered no bar against me in hotels, restaurants, theaters, or other places of public accommodation and entertainment. We hired a furnished apartment in the business area, and took our meals wherever it was most convenient. I moved about with a sense of confidence and security, and entirely from under that cloud of doubt and apprehension that constantly hangs over an intelligent Negro in every Southern city and in a great many cities of the North. Bob and Rosamond were booked for four weeks in San Francisco, but were held over for another two weeks; so I, with nothing in particular to do, had time in which to learn the town quite well. At every turn San Francisco roused my admiration; but on one occasion it also gave me proof that I was a good typical New Yorker. The grand opera season was on and an acquaintance invited me to go with him to witness a performance. It struck me as curious to go all the way to San Francisco to attend grand opera; I had heard all the grand operas; there were other things in the Pacific Coast metropolis that would interest me more. My friend insisted that I should hear one of the greatest coloratura sopranos in the world, if not the greatest. This struck me as ridiculous, and I said, "Now, now, if she's all you say she is, what is she doing singing in a small company out here? Why hasn't she been heard at the Metropolitan?" The singer was Tetrazzini; but I did not hear her until she sang in New York.

When I had been in San Francisco a few days I received a cardboard cylinder which contained an ornate signed and sealed commission certifying to my appointment as a "Colonel" in the Roosevelt inaugural parade; the honor being conferred in recognition of services I was adjudged to have rendered in the presidential campaign the year before. Under separate cover I received a letter from a division commander of the Civic Grand Division of the parade, in which he said, "A number of very prominent men have been invited to serve on my staff, and I have every reason to believe that the civic division of the parade will surpass any similar feature on any former occasion. I should like to have you serve on my staff, and, if you accept the appointment, you will be expected to serve rain or shine. Kindly let me hear from you by return mail. The only expense attached to the appointment will be for the hire of a horse." I appreciated the honor and have preserved the commission, but the inducement of being one of a large number of non-equestrian civilians seated for several uncomfortable hours astride an unknown horse was not sufficient to cause me to cut short my stay in San Francisco.

During my stay I made many acquaintances. I was invited to speak in one of the colored churches on a Sunday afternoon, and from that became acquainted with a number of people of my race. The black population was relatively small, but the colored people that I met and visited lived in good homes and appeared to be prosperous. I talked with some of them about race conditions; the consensus of their comment was that San Francisco was the best city in the United States for a Negro. This may, of course, have been in some degree a reflex of prevalent Pacific Coast boosting.

I think the most interesting person I met was Jack Johnson, who was to be, three years later, the champion prize fighter of the world. I saw him first at the theater, where he had come to see Bob and Rosamond. He came frequently to our apartment, and his visits were generally as long as our time permitted, for he was not training. These visits put the idea in my head of improving myself in "the manly art of self-defense"—the manner in which gentlemen used to speak about taking boxing lessons. Jack often boxed with me playfully, like a good-natured big dog warding off the earnest attacks of a small one, but I could never get him to give me any serious instruction. Occasionally, he would bare his stomach to me as a mark and urge me to hit him with all my might. I found it an impossible thing to do; I always involuntarily pulled my punch. It was easy to like Jack Johnson; he is so likable a man, and I liked him particularly well. I was, of course, impressed by his huge but perfect form, his terrible strength, and the supreme ease and grace of his every muscular movement; however, watching his face, sad until he smiled, listening to his soft Southern speech and laughter, and hearing him talk so wistfully about his big chance, yet to come, I found it difficult to think of him as a prize fighter. I had not yet seen a prize fight, but I conceived of the game as a brutal, bloody one, demanding of its exponents courage, stamina, and brute force as well as skill and quick intelligence, and I could hardly figure gentle Jack Johnson in the rôle. Frederick Douglass had a picture of Peter Jackson in his study, and he used to point to it and say, "Peter is doing a great deal with his fists to solve the Negro question." I think that Jack, even after the reckoning of his big and little failings has been made, may be said to have done his share.

Back in New York, Bob and Rosamond found that they were booked for six weeks at the Palace Theater in London. We were all excitement; and at once decided to make of the engagement a tour rather than just a trip. We planned to spend three months. I went to Columbia for the few last lectures that I could attend, and took an opportunity to consult Brander Matthews about our trip abroad. He suggested that we go first to Paris, and radiate out from there to the surrounding places we wished to visit; then to go up through Belgium and Holland, and come back to Ostend for the trip across the Channel. We followed his suggestions.

From the day I set foot in France, I became aware of the working of a miracle within me. I became aware of a quick readjustment to life and to environment. I recaptured for the first time since childhood the sense of being just a human being. I need not try to analyze this change for my colored readers; they will understand in a flash what took place. For my white readers . . . I am afraid that any analysis will be inadequate, perhaps futile. . . . I was suddenly free; free from a sense of impending discomfort, insecurity, danger; free from the conflict within the Man-Negro dualism and the innumerable maneuvers in thought and behavior that it compels; free from the problem of the many obvious or subtle adjustments to a multitude of bans and taboos; free from special scorn, special tolerance, special condescension, special commiseration; free to be merely a man.

On the boat we had made some pleasant acquaintances from among our white compatriots. Of several of these I still have a distinct recollection. One was a West Point cadet; another was a young man going to Paris to study at the *Académie Julien*—the two were relatives, I think, and were traveling with two middle-aged ladies, who were aunts or something of that sort; a third was the fashion plate of the ship, a young man who seemingly had an inexhaustible supply of clothes, and changed four or five times a day. It was this young man who strongly recommended that we put up in Paris at the Hotel Continental. We knew nothing of Paris hotels, and he appeared to know so much; we followed his advice. When we had registered and been assigned to our rooms, we found ourselves in possession of a suite of two bedrooms, sitting room, and bath, opening on the beautiful court. We were appalled in thinking of what the cost would be. What had they taken us for, South American millionaires or what? Bob and Rosamond were inclined to blame me, the one who knew the most about French, with letting the clerk or manager or whoever he was put it over on us. We decided that we should stay at the Continental a day or two for the sake of appearances, then look for a good *pension.*

When we had finished laying out this plan of action, it was near dinner time. We dressed and started out. As we stepped from our rooms a uniformed attendant standing at the door—waiting, it seemed for our exit—bowed low and said, "Messieurs." We walked toward the elevator, and there stood another uniformed attendant, who bowed low and said, "Messieurs." As we entered the elevator, the operator bowed low and said, "Messieurs." As we passed through the office, there came from various functionaries a chorus of "Messieurs." As we went out of the great gate, an attendant uniformed like a major general saluted and said, "Messieurs." We laughed heartily over all this when we got back to our rooms, and declared that whatever it cost to stay at the Continental, it was worth it.

In coming through the office we had been joined by a young man we had met on the ship. He knew his Paris, and we were glad to be taken in tow. After dinner, we went to see the performance at the Marigny; and after the theater our friend piloted us to Olympia. I was amazed at the size of the place, the size of the orchestra seated in the center, and the great gayety of the whole scene. We found a table and were seated. The next number played by the orchestra was *Under the Bamboo Tree.* We attached no particular importance to that; but when it was followed by *The Congo Love Song,* we took notice and sent our compliments to the leader with the request that he and his men order whatever they wished. Soon four girls joined our party; only one of them, a German girl with lovely dark eyes, being able to speak any English, and she knew only a few words. Nevertheless, they all chatted with and at us gayly while they sipped their beer or black coffee drunk from tall, thin glasses. All the while we were in Paris we generally ended up each evening at Olympia; and, generally, this same group of girls joined us at our table. I stopped trying to make an interpreter out of the German girl, and took my first plunge into the practical use of French. My ability to talk the language increased in geometrical progression. I had studied French at school, and had taken the Cortina course in New York, but Olympia proved to be the best school for learning French I ever attended.

A few days after our arrival we were invited to a studio party. Our hostess was an American singer at the Paris Opera House; her husband being the secretary, if I remember correctly, of the American Chamber of Commerce in Paris. Among the guests were the West Point cadet and the art student with their aunts. It was through them that we had received the invitation to the party. There were a number of artists of one kind or another present, and each who could did a turn. This party was our sole opportunity for a peep at Paris on the inside, but, in the short time we had, we saw about all that could be seen on the outside. However, we didn't make a business of seeing Paris; we made a pleasure of it. We looked with something like pity on tourist groups working on a schedule, being hustled from point to point, pausing only while their guide repeated his trite and hasty lecture on this building or that painting or the other monument. I was glad that on my first visit I was able to see what I did see leisurely; not forced to gulp it down but able to take the time to note the taste of it. I kept congratulating myself that I had declined the chance to visit Europe the summer after I graduated from Atlanta as a member of a tourist party of colored Baptist preachers. I quickly discovered that "historical points" interested me less than almost anything else; that a good picture and the facts well told were, generally, as satisfying as the actual sight. What I wanted most, and what cannot be gotten vicariously, was impressions from the life eddying round me and streaming by. I wanted to see people, people at every level, from an élite audience at the Opera House to a group of swearing fishmongers in the market.

I left Paris with few anticipations. It was true that Bob and Rosamond's engagement was still before us in London, but I feared that so far as seeing things was concerned our trip would follow the steps of an anticlimax. I was relieved to find Brussels *un vrai petit Paris*. The city was in gala attire. We learned that the seventy-fifth anniversary of the independence of Belgium was being celebrated. As soon as we were located, we went out to see the sights. We tried to get a street car; we hailed a dozen or more, only to hear the conductor shout back to us, "*Complet, complet.*" Bob looked at me in his quizzical way and asked, "What are they doing, drawing the color line?" The "*complet*" of the conductors did not, so far as our knowledge went, give a clear explanation; for the cars, according to the American practice, were not full, there was lots of standing room. At last, we secured a cab and drove along through the crowded streets. The Belgian peasants, of whom there were great numbers in the city for the festival, made the most picturesque of all the sights. Our cab driver insisted that we go to see the Manneken-Pis. I suppose that every Brussels cabby takes his fares who are strangers to see this famous little statue; we went without any idea of what we were going to see. When we arrived, there were two or three dozen country people looking at the figure. As soon as we stepped out of our cab, we, instead of the Manneken, became the center of their attention. We were at once almost surrounded by them, and they gazed at us respectfully but with undisguised curiosity. Judging that they had never before seen dark people, we stood long enough to enable them to satisfy their eyes; we felt it would be ungracious to rob them of something to tell the folks back home.

We spent our first night in Brussels at the *Palais d'Été*. Nothing on the program particularly interested us until a man in evening clothes stepped before the curtain and made an announcement in French regarding the closing act on the bill. We were confident that the man was colored, but we could not make up our minds whether he was East Indian, West Indian, African, or American. We decided to go to the stage door after the performance and see if we could find out something about him. We met him and found out that he was not only colored, but an American Negro, born in South Carolina. His name was Woodson; he had started out as an acrobat; for eighteen years he had lived in Europe, working as a circus performer the greater part of that time; for seven years he had been stage manager of the *Palais d'Été*. To me, his story was an amazing one. Had it been told to me, I should have taken the "stage manager" climax with a grain of salt. But I myself did see that he held that important and respected position. Mr. Woodson invited us to take breakfast with him at his home the next morning. I was glad to go, for it meant another of those peeps inside, that are rare for a stranger in a strange land. I was not disappointed in Mr. Woodson's home; it was pleasant and tasteful. We met his wife and daughter, a girl about twelve. Mrs. Woodson, like her husband, was brown. She was quite stout but had an extremely nice face. The daughter was brown like her parents, and very vivacious and pretty. I had an immediate foretaste of talking with this little Negro family about Paris and Brussels and Europe and America, too, from a common point of view. We quickly learned that Mrs. Woodson spoke only German. She was born in Germany of a German mother and a Negro father, and had never learned to speak English. We enjoyed the breakfast and the chance

A Childhood Portrait

James Johnson

Helen Louise Johnson

Teachers at Stanton

HELEN LOUISE JOHNSON—SECOND FROM LEFT, BOTTOM ROW
AGNES MARION EDWARDS—FIRST FROM LEFT, CENTER ROW

Atlanta University Quartette

GADSDEN   PORTER   TOWNS   JOHNSON

Bob Cole, James and Rosamond Johnson

Paris

Consulate at Puerto Cabello, Venezuela

Mother Night.

Eternities before the first-born day,
Or e'er the first sun fledged his wings of flame
Calm Night, the everlasting and the same,
A brooding mother, over chaos lay.
And whirling suns shall blaze and then decay,
Shall run their fiery courses and then claim
The haven of the darkness whence they came,
Back to the Nirvanic peace shall grope their way.

So when my feeble sun of life burns out,
And sounded is the hour for my long sleep,
Shall I, full weary of the feverish light,
Welcome the darkness without fear or doubt,
And, heavy-lidded, I shall softly creep
Into the quiet bosom of the Night.

$$\cup - | \cup - | \cup - | \cup - | \cup -$$

Pto Bello.
Dec. 1907.

Facsimile of "Mother Night" Manuscript

Grace Nail

Consul and Sentry, Nicaragua

Negro Silent Protest Parade, July 28, 1917

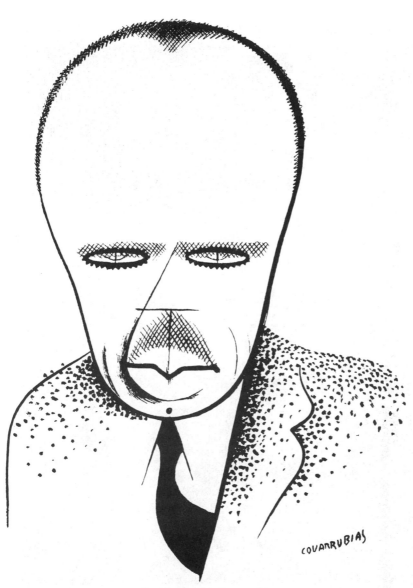

Caricature by Covarrubias

Christophe's Citadel

THE SHAME OF AMERICA

Do you know that the United States is
the Only Land on Earth where human
beings are BURNED AT THE STAKE?

In Four Years 1918-1921, Twenty-Eight People were publicly
BURNED BY AMERICAN MOBS

3436 People Lynched, 1889-1921

For What Crimes Have Mobs Nullified Government and Inflicted the Death Penalty?

The Alleged Crimes	The Victims	Why Some Mob Victims Died:
Murder	1288	Not turning out of road for white boy in auto
Rape	571	Being a relative of a person who was lynched
Crimes against the Person	615	Jumping a labor contract
Crimes against Property	333	Being a member of the Non-Partisan League
Miscellaneous Crimes	453	"Talking back" to a white man
Absence of Crime	176	"Insulting" white man
	3436	

Is Rape the "Cause" of Lynching?

Of 3,436 people murdered by mobs in our country, only 571, or less than 17 per cent, were even accused of the crime of rape.

83 WOMEN HAVE BEEN LYNCHED IN THE UNITED STATES

Do lynchers maintain that they were lynched for "the usual crime?"

AND THE LYNCHERS GO UNPUNISHED

THE REMEDY

The Dyer Anti-Lynching Bill Is Now Before the United States Senate

The Dyer Anti-Lynching Bill was passed on January 26, 1922, by a vote of 230 to 119 in the House of Representatives

The Dyer Anti-Lynching Bill Provides:

That culpable State officers and mobbisters shall be tried in Federal Courts on failure of State courts to act, and that a county in which a lynching occurs shall be fined $10,000, recoverable in a Federal Court.

The Principal Question Raised Against the Bill is upon the Ground of Constitutionality.

The Constitutionality of the Dyer Bill Has Been Affirmed by

The Judiciary Committee of the House of Representatives
The Judiciary Committee of the Senate
The United States Attorney General, legal adviser of Congress
Judge Guy D. Goff, of the Department of Justice

The Senate has been petitioned to pass the Dyer Bill by

29 Lawyers and Jurists including two former Attorneys General of the United States
19 State Supreme Court Justices
24 State Governors
3 Archbishops, 85 bishops and prominent churchmen
39 Mayors of large cities, north and south

The American Bar Association at its meeting in San Francisco, August 9, 1922, adopted a resolution asking for further legislation by Congress to punish and prevent lynching and mob violence.

Fifteen State Conventions of 1922 (3 of them Democratic) have inserted in their party platforms a demand for national action to stamp out lynchings.

The Dyer Anti-Lynching Bill is not intended to protect the guilty, but
to secure to every person accused of crime trial by due process of law.

THE DYER ANTI-LYNCHING BILL IS NOW BEFORE THE SENATE
TELEGRAPH YOUR SENATORS TODAY YOU WANT IT ENACTED

If you want to help the organization which has brought to light the facts about lynching, the organization which is fighting for 100 per cent Americanism, not for some of the people some of the time, but for all of the people, white or black, all of the time

Send your check to J. E. SPINGARN, Treasurer of the

NATIONAL ASSOCIATION FOR THE ADVANCEMENT OF COLORED PEOPLE

70 FIFTH AVENUE, NEW YORK CITY

THIS ADVERTISEMENT IS PAID FOR IN PART BY THE ANTI-LYNCHING CRUSADERS.

*Mr. and Mrs. Johnson at
Fisk University*

*Two Views of
"Five Acres"*

James Weldon Johnson

PHOTOGRAPH BY DORIS ULMANN

to talk with Mr. Woodson. He appeared to know Europe from one end to the other. His memory about his native land was rather faint, but he expressed no desire of reviving it. We left Brussels and hurried through visits to Antwerp and Amsterdam. The London engagement, now only seven or eight days away, was beginning to pull on the nerves of Bob and Rosamond, and they were anxious to get on the ground.

Great, rumbling London; stupendous, overwhelming London gave us, in a manner, a personal reception. Every bus, and there seemed to be thousands of them, carried along its whole length a placard announcing the appearance for the first time at the Palace Theater of "Cole and Johnson, the Great Coloured Comedians" or "Cole and Johnson, the Great American Musicians." Similar announcements were carried on other vehicles, plastered over numerous hoardings, and displayed in many shops. We were astonished, for we had never seen vaudeville performers advertised in such a way in any American city. Bob and Rosamond got a tremendous thrill out of it; they could not help but be thrilled at the thought that probably a million people had noted that Cole and Johnson were coming to London. London blotted out the rest of Europe, for London was a city not to be visited, but to be captured. This inspiriting thought carried, however, a penalty of anxiety that heightened as the opening of the engagement approached. It is needless to say that I shared in the thrill and the anxiety.

A day or two before the opening we met Marie Dressler on the street. She talked with us about the opening night, and radiated buoyancy and confidence in a way that made them infectious. She promised to be present to give the boys a hand. Miss Dressler kept her promise; and, more than that, she rounded up every American performer in London she could get hold of and brought them along to help in "giving a hand." It was a big-hearted thing that she did. We had only two guests that night, Samuel Coleridge-Taylor, the colored English composer, and his wife; they sat with me. I was impressed by the Palace Theater, its splendor, the width and comfort of the seats. I particularly noticed that each chair had two arm-rests, which obviated the American custom of yielding the use of the single arm-rest in common to two chairs to the person who preempts it. When the orchestra filed in, I counted forty men, and made a quick contrast with the scant nine-piece orchestra in the best American vaudeville theaters and with the solitary piano player in a great many of them. I was still more impressed by the audience; all the men and women in the orchestra chairs and boxes were in strict evening dress. The elegance of the whole atmosphere was somewhat like a night at the Metropolitan Opera House.

Bob and Rosamond were the headliners of the bill; so they did not appear until well down the program. I was distrait until they did appear; and, when they did, I was seized with a sort of panic. I stiffened under the tension, and gripped the arms of my chair like a person fortifying himself for the extraction of a tooth. Rosamond's piano solo was courteously received; his song in German more warmly; but I knew, and I knew that they knew, that the audience was not yet theirs. When Rosamond struck the opening bars of *The Congo Love Song*, I knew that the die was about to be cast; that it was now win or lose. They sang the song with flawless artistry, and finished so softly that it induced an intense silence. Then there was an outburst of spontaneous and prolonged applause. They had won; and I was able to let down and enjoy the act as though I had never seen it before.

These states of pain and pleasurable reaction under similar circumstances are more keenly experienced by Negroes, perhaps, than by any other people. For them, the central persons are not individuals, they become protagonists of the whole racial cause. Certainly, all people have similar experiences whenever there are high feelings of partisanship. For example, white Americans who witnessed the recent Olympic Games at Los Angeles experienced the peculiar thrill of the transition from anxiety to elation whenever an American was the victor; but I do not think it possible that any of them experienced in degree what was felt by the Negroes who saw Eddie Tolan, the diminutive black sprinter, win the hundred-meter race by breaking the world record with Ralph Metcalf, another Negro, second, and the two-hundred-meter race by setting a new Olympic record. They saw him gain not only two glorious victories for the United States but a victory of unique significance for them.

We lived in a quite nice furnished apartment, which we had had no difficulty in leasing; it was when we came to give it up that we ran into complications. We had, without anything like exhaustive examination, signed a voluminous document of, I should say, twenty or twenty-five pages written entirely in longhand, never imagining that it was an instrument empowering the landlord to enforce a limitless number of minute exactions, indeed, to make us practically buy the apartment, if he was disposed to press the matter that far.

We had two minor encounters with English business customs. Rosamond went into an exclusive shop to buy a new silk hat for the act. It was handed to him in a box that was constructed, I judge, out of English oak. When Rosamond made what he intended as a jocose remark about the weight of the box, the shopkeeper turned on him and said, "We've been packing our hats in those boxes a hundred and fifty yeahs, sir, a hundred and fifty yeahs," and in a tone that implied, "If you don't like the box, you needn't take the hat." As soon as I could get at it, I made some snapshots of the busses carrying the "Cole and Johnson" placards, and took them to a place to be developed and printed. I went back after four or five days to get the prints; they had not been touched. "But," I pressed, "I left them here four or five days ago." The shopkeeper snapped at me, "If you want them in a hurry, sir, take them to a hurry shop. Take them to an American shop."

I enjoyed my stay in London. I learned to love London. Its gravity in design and temper does not, it is true, allow much for that levity which debonair and sprightly Paris almost forces, but I felt that the spirit of London approached closer to the realities of life. Of course, this feeling may, after all, have been fundamentally a matter of language. In the English city I was able to speak not only the language of words but, more or less, the language of ideas of the people I came in contact with, whether on the streets, in the shops, or in a drawing room. I grew aware of the beauty in the ruggedness of London. I rode atop busses for hours, not knowing or caring where they went, and was grateful for the intrinsic quality in so teeming a city that enabled a man to be alone.

We met a good many people in London, a number of Americans, some of whom we had known in the United States. It is a wise general rule for American Negroes in Europe to steer clear of their white fellow-countrymen, but, although we did not stick to this rule, we ran into no unpleasant or awkward situations. During our stay, Charles Hawtrey made a return of our hospitality to him in New York by inviting us to lunch with him and to go afterwards on an automobile trip to Windsor Castle. That part of the invitation which concerned the trip to Windsor Castle excited us greatly; first, because trips by automobiles were still rare enough to constitute an event; secondly, because we knew of the close friendship between Charles Hawtrey and King Edward. We had no anticipations of supper with the King, but we did feel that we should see the Castle under auspices far beyond the reach of the average tourist. But, alas! those were the automobile days when one merely hoped to get to one's destination and hardly dared to expect to get back. The day was beautiful, and we left the hotel in grand style. We threaded our way out of London and skimmed rapidly over the roads, but not so rapidly that we could not take in the surpassing beauty of the English countryside. As we sped along, our spirits mounted higher and higher. Then suddenly, for reasons that were yet among the mysteries, the car stopped. We went to an inn for a sandwich and a bottle of ale, while the chauffeur would do whatever was necessary to get the car started. When we got back, the chauffeur was still working, but already there were signs of despair on his face. He explained to Mr. Hawtrey what he thought was the trouble; but such terms as "carburetor," "ignition," "sparking plug," "transmission," and "differential" meant less to me then than do the terms of Einsteinian astronomy now. The chauffeur worked on doggedly, but nothing he did started the machine. Finally, we left him and the car and made our way to the nearest railroad station and back by train to London; Mr. Hawtrey and Bob and Rosamond reaching the city just in time to get on the stages of their respective theaters.

One night, walking home from the theater we passed a man standing at a window on the ground floor of a house not far from where we lived. The evening was warm, and he was, presumably, trying to catch a breath of air. We could not see his face very well, but his form was sharply outlined by the light in the room. As we passed, Bob remarked, "That man looks like Gus Kerker." Whereupon, the man at the window put his head out and said, "I am Gus Kerker. Who are you?" We retraced the step or two, and when he saw who we were he invited us in. We sat until long past midnight talking about the theater; or, more exactly, listening to him talk about *The Belle of New York*. He rehearsed the whole history of the show; how they had with trepidation brought it to London; its tumultuous Eng-

lish success; the personal triumphs of Edna May and Dan Daly—and
his own, the triumph of being the composer of the first American
musical play to be unreservedly acclaimed in England. There was
no pose of the braggart in his attitude; his manner was rather that
of one restating incontestable truths. This *magnum opus* of his had
put his name well up in the list of composers of light opera and had
earned him a fortune—a very happy combination; and I judge that
from then until he died his breath of life was the fame of *The Belle
of New York.*

We were short of money on leaving London. Indeed, I had days
before cashed my last American Express Company check. During our
last week we sold for thirty pounds the singing rights of a song to
the producers of a play at the Drury Lane Theatre; and that helped.
Nevertheless, when we boarded the Cunarder at Liverpool, all the
money the three of us could show could be counted in shillings. Getting on the boat with so little cash was easy, but getting off was
another matter. As the ship approached New York, I began to reckon
the smallest possible tips that I could offer to my waiter, the stateroom steward, the bathroom steward, and the deck steward, but by
no shifting of figures could all these items be covered. The situation
began to loom up as something quite serious. I was actually depressed
by the moral element involved. It was something like having a note
fall due at the bank with no funds in sight to meet it. As we steamed
through the Narrows I stood leaning on the rail, reduced to juggling
various plausible subterfuges, when a young man whom I had met
only in a casual manner on board came up and said, "You don't look
very happy about getting back home." "Oh, I'm happy enough on
that score," I assured him, "but the three of us have run short of cash,
and I am wondering how we are going to get off the ship honorably."
He laughed and offered to lend me whatever I needed. I got twenty-
five dollars from him and his address, promising that I should return
the money promptly after I got ashore; which, perhaps I should add,
I did. I could not but wonder why this virtual stranger voluntarily
lent me twenty-five dollars. It was a friendly act of the sort that
lingers warmly in the memory.

XX

IN THE middle of the summer of 1904 Charles W. Anderson had come to me with what struck me as a strange request. Mr. Anderson and I had been friends for a number of years; I considered him one of the ablest politicians in the country. I regarded him as being, beyond any doubt, the very ablest Negro politician. The campaign to elect Theodore Roosevelt to succeed himself in the Presidency was just beginning to warm up. Mr. Anderson dropped in at the studio one evening and revealed to me his plans for establishing a "Colored Republican Club" in West 53rd Street. The plans were: to lease one of the three-story and basement houses across the street from the Marshall; to furnish it in good style, billiard and pool room in the basement, assembly room on the main floor, lounge and card rooms on the second floor, and committee rooms on the top. Mr. Anderson informed me that the money for these initial expenses had already been provided. He said, finally:

"Jim, I've. got to have your help."

"But, Charlie, how can I help you?"

"You can help me in making the club a success; and that's going to be a big job. You can do it better than anybody I know."

"How?"

"I want somebody who'll know where every dollar comes from and where every dollar goes, and who'll keep the records straight. I want a man for chairman of the house committee, and you're the man."

I protested that my work kept me too busy to afford the necessary time; that, in addition, I was studying at Columbia University; that, furthermore, I knew nothing about politics or political organizations. Mr. Anderson summed up his request by saying, "Well, I want you to do it *for me*." The request put in that form I could not refuse. After I had begun, I became enthusiastic about my new job. The club started off with a grand opening. Visitors were surprised at the elegance and completeness of its appointments. The membership increased by leaps and bounds. Big guns of the campaign boomed in its assembly room. I was able to secure a sufficient number of volunteers from amongst the "talent" at the Marshall to have an "entertainment night" once a week; these nights were particularly popular with the New York newspaper men. The trio got busy and wrote a campaign song for "Teddy."

One verse of the song, the verse commenting on Alton B. Parker's famous telegram to the gold standard wing of the Democrats in convention, went the rounds of the press. It ran:

> Oh, Mr. Parker thinks
> That he is like the Sphinx
> But we're inclined to think he is a clam.
> He's bound to get a tilt
> Upon a platform built
> Out of a Western Union Telegram.
>   Chorus
> You're all right Teddy, etc., etc., etc.

Rosamond carefully made a manuscript copy, which was sent to Mr. Roosevelt. He wrote complimenting us on having written "a bully good song."

My new activities gave me a chance to learn something about the workings of practical politics; something about how men deal and are dealt with in this, the greatest American game. I got some understanding of what "political loyalty" is and of its strength as a force in our civic system. I learned that the loyalty of the active, practical politicians—that vast army of actual and prospective holders of political jobs, from street cleaner up—is primarily given not to the party candidate or standard bearer, but to the boss. I learned that the practical politicians who are active in politics three hundred and sixty-five days a year, are those who directly or indirectly gain a living or more than a living from politics. They control the political machinery and, so far as its manipulation is concerned, nobody else really counts. In fact, nobody else is really interested in politics. The contrary premise leads to a great many errors and futile efforts.

Mr. Anderson was the president of the Club. He was the recognized colored Republican leader of New York, an astute politician, keen in his study of men and the uses to be made of them. A versatile man; much more than an ordinary orator, in the style of the day; capable of intelligently discussing the English poets, the Irish patriots, or the contemporary leaders of the British Parliament. A cool, calculating player in the hard game of politics, but always playing the game rather on the grand scale for the higher stakes. On friendly terms with Theodore Roosevelt, Elihu Root, Chauncey M. Depew,

Tom Platt, and other Republican leaders. Nor was there an important Tammany leader who did not know "Charlie" and greet him cordially. He made New York take note of the Colored Republican Club.

The campaign ended. Theodore Roosevelt was gloriously elected, and made that so characteristic expression of thanks to the American people, which was to come up to plague him when later he decided to accept that "third cup of coffee." Within a reasonable time he appointed Charles W. Anderson to the position of Collector of Internal Revenue for that district which includes the Wall Street section of New York City. Mr. Anderson held his office through the Taft administration, and, though his district was changed, through the Wilson administrations; and is, at this writing, still Collector of Internal Revenue—not a slight evidence of political sagacity. After his appointment he decided to resign the presidency of the Club. Again he requisitioned my services. He impressed upon me that the Club was a power and an influence, socially as well as politically, and that it must be kept alive. In accordance with his desires and plans, I became president of the Club. I learned many lessons from this job, some of them hard, all of them valuable.

When I returned from Europe, I sometimes visited Mr. Anderson at his office in the Custom House to talk over Club matters. These visits were generally in the afternoon, and he would, at times, say, "You're not in a hurry, are you? I'll be through in a little while, and we'll walk along and talk." These walks that seemed like nothing to him taxed me terribly. His antidote for fatigue was to stop in somewhere and get a pint of champagne. I frequently had to rebel against walking another step. I remember that on one afternoon we started from Bowling Green and ended up at the Marie Antoinette Hotel at Broadway and 66th Street. In one of our talks, Mr. Anderson suggested that it would be a nice thing for me to go into the United States Consular Service; he felt sure that President Roosevelt would be willing to appoint me. The idea was interesting. I asked some questions. Mr. Anderson supplied me with information: the Service had recently been reorganized by Elihu Root (then Secretary of State); the standard had been raised; applicants were required to pass a real examination and had to possess a knowledge of at least one of the principal foreign languages; the Service had been classified into grades that ranged in salary from two thousand dollars to twelve thousand dollars a year; a new man entered the lowest grade, and would be promoted; the whole Service had been divorced from the spoils system, and consuls henceforth would be secure in their positions and sure of merited promotion. His recital set my imagination in action, but I dismissed the whole matter for the time by laughingly remarking, "But, Charlie, it would take about one-third of my salary just to keep my life insurance going."

During the winter the trio continued to write. Our songs were still selling, with *Lazy Moon* quite popular. Bob and Rosamond were still headliners on the "big time" in vaudeville, but a new idea was working in Bob's mind. He had first let it out in occasional hints, then broached it. The idea was that he and Rosamond drop vaudeville and go out at the head of a theatrical company. His argument was that they should capitalize their reputation; that there was the chance of clearing thirty or forty thousand dollars a year with a company of their own; that, whatever happened, they could always go back into vaudeville. Rosamond was influenced, but I opposed the idea as strongly as I could. I pointed out that their position was unique; that they were independent and free from the responsibilities and worries that a large company would entail; that they played only the best houses in the biggest cities; that this gave them time for composition; and that while they were on the road with a show their Broadway reputation would be fading. I agreed that there would be a chance of clearing thirty or forty thousand dollars a year if they played all New Yorks and Chicagos, but I reminded them that they would have to play a great many second-class houses in one-night stands. I had reasons in addition to those that primarily concerned Bob and Rosamond. I knew that it was in Bob's plans to have me go as business manager of the company, and I had no desire to go trouping around the country and undergoing the hardships that every colored company had to put up with; nor did I have any intentions of doing so, if there was any way to avoid it. The idea was allowed to sleep for a while.

The idea slept, but I knew it would be wakened. I applied myself with more diligence to my work at Columbia and I began planning some more literary work. I found that less and less was I able to go at the work for Broadway on sheer enthusiasm; I had to spur myself forward. Being light enough for Broadway was beginning to be, it seemed, a somewhat heavy task. Unconscious of what was taking place I was actually making a mental shift and adjustment.

The extension of their vaudeville engagements kept Bob and Rosamond out of New York more than ever before. I went to the theater quite regularly, and occasionally to some social affairs. I attended the St. Phillip's Guild picnic, and saw Grace Nail there. She was quite a young lady now. I asked her to dance with me; and I remember distinctly my slight confusion and timidity in asking. I took with me from the picnic an intense vivification of the memory of her that I had taken from the amateur theatrical performance in Brooklyn several years before.

In the spring, D—— came to New York. In the new Jacksonville that rose out of the fire, he had prospered. His law practice had grown; he had accumulated considerable property; he had been elected to the city council, and was counted an influence in politics. For several summers back he had been coming to New York on vacation, so between his trips north and my occasional trips to Jacksonville to visit my parents, we had seen a good deal of each other. But this trip was to be a final one. He had closed his office in Jacksonville, disposed of most of his property, and bought a half-interest in the practice of a colored lawyer in Brooklyn. As D—— had disapproved of my moving to New York, so I had disapproved of his. And I felt that my advice was more disinterested than was his. The personal element could hardly be absent from the advice he had given me: unwillingness to have our companionship and partnership broken, and dislike of my living in the great metropolis and his remaining in the small city. I was glad enough to have D—— in New York, but I felt that, in leaving Jacksonville, he was doing a foolish thing to himself.

Toward the latter part of this same winter, Bob and Rosamond learned that they were booked for a return engagement at the Palace Theatre in London. Bob then again brought up the question of a theatrical company of their own. His plan was to play the Palace engagement as a farewell to vaudeville, and, on their return to the United States in the fall, to start out with their own show. He and Rosamond decided on that plan. Furthermore, Bob had already made an outline of the play. It was to be in three scenes; time, the outbreak of the Spanish-American War; the first and third scenes in a Negro industrial school in the South, the second scene in the Philippine

Islands. The play was to be called *The Shoo-Fly Regiment.* We started writing it at once, and before time for the trip to London, I had done the lyrics and worked with Bob on the dialogue; and Rosamond had set quite a bit of music. I experienced strange emotions while doing my part in creating *The Shoo-Fly Regiment,* for I felt that it was the last piece of work the three of us should do together.

While we were working on the play, Mr. Anderson spoke to me again about going into the Consular Service. I asked him to let me think it over a little while. When I saw him next I said, "Charlie, if the President will appoint me, I'll go." Mr. Anderson started immediately to take the steps to secure an appointment for me. Arriving at this decision was not an easy matter; not nearly so easy as the decision to leave Jacksonville. New York had been a good godmother to me, almost a fairy godmother, and it gave me a wrench to turn my back on her. Over against all that life and work in New York meant, I balanced three things, and they tipped the scales. I put into the scales my desire to avoid the disagreeable business of traveling round the country under the conditions that a Negro theatrical company had to endure; as I proposed to cite, among my qualifications for the Service, Spanish as my foreign language, I expected to be appointed to a South American post, so there was added the lure of the adventure of life on a strange continent; but heavier than either of these was the realization, which came upon me suddenly, that time was slipping and I had not yet made a real start on the work that I had long kept reassuring myself I should sometime do, that the opportunity for seizing that "sometime" had come, and that I ought not let it pass. Then, the feeling came over me that, in leaving New York, I was not making a sacrifice, but an escape; that I was getting away, if only for a while, from the feverish flutter of life to seek a little stillness of the spirit.

I went to Washington and took my examination. My appointment was United States Consul at Puerto Cabello, Venezuela. And so, while D— was setting himself up in New York, I was pulling up my stakes. Once again our see-saw of advice and counter-advice got into action. His expression of opinion, this time, was sharper than it was on my leaving school position and law practice to move to New York. He simply could not accept or understand any reason for leaving New York to go to "the jungle of South America." He dropped into his old racy style of speech and so disparaged the job I had taken and the surroundings in which I should find myself that strictures turned to humor, and the irritation and tension were dissipated. Bob and Rosamond said little; nothing in direct opposition to my plans. I had put these plans before them fully, and they had accepted them. I believe they reasoned that I could always come back to New York; that my sojourn would be brief, and, probably, advantageous, for I should be likely to return with new ideas for Broadway and for Cole and Johnson shows.

Spring came to an end. Bob and Rosamond sailed to fill their return engagement in London; I sailed for my post in Venezuela; and the trio was dissolved.

PART THREE

XXI

I HAVE traveled thousands of miles in ships, but have always been an uncertain sailor. I have crossed a choppy English Channel without the slightest nausea, and been seasick unto death on a Sound steamer, going from New York to Fall River. I was between these two states, a condition worse than outright seasickness, during the entire trip to Venezuela. I went more or less regularly to the dining saloon, but had no relish for food. In the dining saloon I had been given the place of honor, the seat at the right of the Captain. There began at table a friendly relation between him and me that lasted throughout my stay in Venezuela. The ship stopped a day at San Juan, Porto Rico. A friend, Arthur A. Schomburg, who is a native of Porto Rico, had given me a letter to the mayor of the city. I presented the letter and received a cordial welcome. I spent the day ashore, but was seasick, it seemed, even on land. I dreaded going aboard again.

I got my first real relief when the ship entered the quiet waters of the harbor of Curaçao, or Willemstad, as the city itself is known. As a matter of fact, the excitement of approaching the harbor caused me to forget my stomach. The ship pointed her nose directly at what appeared to be an unbroken volcanic shore. It looked as though the Captain was intentionally running his ship aground. It was not until we were close enough to make out a bridge that had been drawn from across the mouth of a narrow channel that we saw any place where it was possible to enter. We steamed through this channel into a spacious landlocked harbor, which, I learned, was the crater of an extinct volcano that had been filled by the sea. It was plain to observe what a perfect pirates' stronghold this most important island of the Dutch West Indies had been in buccaneer days. Around the edges of the harbor and along the sides of several canals formed by inlets from this inner bay, sat the picturesque town of Willemstad, a miniature Amsterdam, dazzlingly clean and bright under a cloudless sky. It seldom, almost never rains in Curaçao, and water is or was then peddled from door to door, like milk. Nevertheless, drawing the conclusion from my observations, there is not a cleaner place in the world. I was told that Willemstad was the origin of Sapolio's popular advertising slogan, "Spotless Town." In this, in particular, its standards were much higher than what I found on the South American continent only twelve hours away.

Dutch is the official language of Curaçao and is, of course, spoken by the Dutch officials, garrison and civilians. But the mass of the population, which is Negro, speaks *Papaimento*. Indeed, everybody who lives in Curaçao knows and uses Papaimento. This is not a mere patois; it is a language, a composite language made up of Spanish, Portuguese, French, English, and a little German and Dutch. It might well serve as a universal medium. It is grammatically constructed, is the language of most of the textbooks used in the public schools, and the language in which the newspapers are published and into which a number of books of literature are translated. It is, probably, for this reason that every Curaçaoan is a linguist. For them, differences caused by language hardly exist. A boatman, an old black man, paddling me across to my steamer, addressed me in four languages in an effort to discover what was my mother tongue. At the club I saw four or five men playing a game of pool, and was astonished at the lightness with which the conversation was tossed from one language to another.

My first sight of South America was that eastern spur of the Andes which rises up, a sheer wall from the Atlantic, where La Guaira stretches along a narrow ledge of shore between mountains and sea. It is a majestic sight—the mountains, not the town. La Guaira, dingy and squalid and fetid, made me decide to stay aboard. But the ship was unbearable; a June sun heated it to the temperature of an oven. We were tied to a wharf with an iron roof, and that radiated heat like a furnace. I couldn't find an endurable spot. My head began to feel strange, and I confided to Captain Crockett my fear that I had symptoms of sunstroke. He said, "The ship will be here two days, loading and unloading; you had better take a train and go up to Caracas and stay there until tomorrow afternoon. Go to the Grand Hotel Klint." The trip from La Guaira is, I should judge, the most wonderful twenty-five mile railroad ride in the world. For more than three thousand feet the train makes its way up over a cogwheel track, and drops into the cup of the mountain, where sits Caracas, the capital of Venezuela. The trip takes about two hours. When I had been riding an hour, I felt a change of climate and like a new man. When I reached Caracas, the temperature was like early June in the Berkshire Hills of western Massachusetts.

I found Caracas not a large city but quite a gay one. A season of Italian Grand Opera opened on the night of my arrival, and I attended. The performance was interesting, but much more interesting to me was a sight of General Juan Vicente Gómez, the Vice-President, and the view which the occasion afforded of Venezuelan rank and fashion on parade. In watching this pageant of Caracas society, I estimated that seven out of every ten women in it under, say, twenty-five years of age, were beautiful. The sight of General Gómez disclosed a calm, stern, morose-looking man. He seemed to bear very little relation to the brilliant military retinue that accompanied him. Between the acts, he came out of the presidential box and moved around or stood in a very sober, almost rustic manner. He was at every point, as I was to learn later, the opposite of the volatile, arrogant, cantankerous Castro. From this glimpse I sensed power in the man—the man who was a brief while later to seize the reins of government from Castro; keep his former chief out of the country for sixteen years, down to an exile's death; and hold Venezuela in his hands for, till now, twenty-five years.

Steaming into the harbor of Puerto Cabello I gained a favorable first impression of my "home." The hills and mountains lay back some distance from the coast and allowed the air to circulate and the town to spread itself out. I caught sight of a pleasant-looking plaza and park just beyond the wharf. The Consulate was an airy, clean, and fairly commodious house. Unlike most houses in Spanish-speaking countries, it was two stories high. Certainly, a big enough house for one man. I kept the Consulate there about a year, then moved it to a better-adapted house. For the first few months, I took my meals at the best of the hotels, but grew tired of that and decided to set up my own establishment. I got echoes of slight censure because, in hiring domestic help, I raised the general wages of three dollars (American gold) a month to four dollars. I engaged and kept four persons, the equivalent, perhaps, of two efficient American servants. I hired a cook, a girl to wait on table and help in the kitchen, a girl to clean the house, and a boy to make himself handy.

I immediately found out that, in addition to being the American Consul, I was consul for Cuba, consul for Panama, and in charge of consular affairs for France, with which country Castro had broken off all relations. I received in fees from these extra duties an amount equal to my salary from the United States. I cleared all vessels bound for any one of the four countries I was representing, and transacted all consular business for their respective citizens. Within a short time Cuba appointed her own consul; and, just before I left Puerto Cabello, diplomatic relations were re-established between Venezuela and France, and the French consul resumed charge of French consular affairs. My duties were not arduous; and even at that, there was a vice consul to perform any or all of them. Most of the routine work and all of the clerical work was done between the vice consul and the clerk; I, however, assumed personal responsibility for writing all consular reports on commercial and political matters. As it was, I had considerable leisure time.

I fell easily into the tropical mode of life; even into the quite sensible habit of taking a siesta. In the better house to which I moved the Consulate, my manner of living was semi-luxurious. The house, evidently, had been built for some Venezuelan grandee. The front faced the plaza and the harbor, and a side overlooked one of the three parks of the town. This was also a two-story house, but the living quarters were confined to the second floor; the ground floor, except for the portion taken up by the bath, being given over to business. The bath was of vast proportions; in it were not only a shower and a large tin tub that I had imported, but also a pool built of concrete in which one could even swim a couple of strokes. The patio of the house was on the upper floor, and so formed a sort of roof garden. It was always cooler there at noon than any other spot in the house, and there I took my siesta. The *sala* was a room capable of accommodating a grand ball. On the park side of the house were three connecting rooms, which I used as office, private office, and bedroom.

I generally got up quite early, as is the custom in Latin America. When I started down to the bath, the housemaid announced to the cook that I was up, and then laid out my fresh clothes—I usually dressed in white from hat to shoes. By the time I put my clothes on, *desayuno*, consisting of coffee, a roll or toast, and an egg, was ready. From eleven o'clock to one, every business door in Puerto Cabello was closed; that was the hour for *almuerzo*, a four-course meal, and the siesta. Five o'clock was the closing hour, and seven o'clock the general hour for dinner. I bought a good horse—horses were comparatively cheap—and learned to ride; and spent many afternoons on horseback until dinnertime. Frequently on Sundays I joined a group of horsemen and rode out to neighboring haciendas.

A few days after my arrival in Puerto Cabello I received a thirty-day card of courtesy from the club and an invitation to join. The club was housed in a low, picturesque building that sat behind a high brick wall with an ornamental gate entrance. In front of the house was a garden, and from the back a wharf extended a little way out into the bay. The wharf was occasionally the landing place for pleasure boats, but it was constantly used as a sitting place on fair afternoons and evenings. But the blades of the club had a sitting place much more popular with them. They would take their chairs and line them along the outer side of the wall, and watch the passers-by, with particular attention to the ladies. That was when I learned of the custom of Venezuelan men of addressing remarks to any pretty woman passing in the streets. Every pretty woman who ran the gantlet of that line of chairs would hear successive explosions of *"Que bonita!"* *"Que linda!"* *"Que hermosa!"* *"Que graciosa!"* An expression I frequently heard was, *"Ah, si tuviera un millón!"* ("Ah, if I only had a million dollars!") I never witnessed an instance in which any lady appeared to take offense at these remarks.

I spent most of my evenings at the club, and used many of those evenings trying to learn to play billiards or chess. I spent enough time in the reading room to go through each monthly issue of the leading French and Spanish illustrated magazines. Often I joined in a discussion or merely listened to one. The common sentiment of the members, as of Venezuelans in general, was anti-American, but I do not remember that it was ever directed against me individually. I had a feeling that I was rather popular. After I had been a member about a year, I was elected to the executive committee. I was aware that the common verdict of the club was that I was *muy simpático*. I was made to feel that there was a special appreciation of the unique experience of having an American consul who spoke the language of the country. The social intercourse that the club afforded me helped very much to make life in Puerto Cabello pleasant. And I am certain that it was the source of the greater part of all I learned about Venezuela that was valuable to me officially or personally.

At the club I observed a confutation of the idea that only women gossip. I heard a great deal of gossip, some of it important, a lot of it idle. But no gossip is unimportant for a man in the foreign service of any country. What might appear to be trivial gossip may shed light on what is serious. Whenever the talk was about Venezuela or Venezuelans I *listened* only. Often gossip gave way to semi-confidential discussions of scandal. Most of these scandalous things that I heard I set down as inventions of the imagination or as malicious lies. I discounted such tales ninety-five per cent; but a friend in whom I had the highest confidence assured me that they were generally ninety-five per cent true, and explained the mystery of how the information was commonly obtained. A Venezuelan matron was forced to be too proud to go to market for herself; such an act was regarded as degrading, and would cause her a loss of caste; but she was not above extracting from a trusted servant every bit of gossip and morsel of scandal that could be gathered. (It should, however, in fairness to the women be said that the men of what we should term the white-collar class were equally careful to avoid in public any task that might be looked upon as menial. The clerk in my office was a young Curaçaoan; I sent him one day to buy something that made a small package weighing not more than a couple of pounds. Imagine my astonishment on looking up the street and seeing him marching proudly ahead of a small boy to whom he had given a penny to carry the package. He did not dare to let it be suspected that he was anything other than a *clerk* at the American Consulate. I tried to teach him a practical lesson by going out and bringing home a ten-pound ham, but it is probable that I merely surprised him as much as he had surprised me.) All the marketing was done by servants. They went out early in the morning, and each one returned with not only the provisions for the day but with every piece of interesting news she had been able to gather from the servants of other households that she had met. Naturally, in getting these items she had to trade her own; and it was through this clearing-house process that every family in Puerto Cabello knew something about what was going on in every other family.

Through Captain Crockett I took up hunting. He wanted to go hunting both because he loved the sport and because he felt it was the best method he could find to keep himself physically fit. He wanted to get out and tramp through the woods. He brought me down a shotgun from New York; and it was understood that, whenever he was in port, he and I should have a morning of shooting, starting out as early as four o'clock. Later, he brought down a canoe so that we could paddle up into the little inlets from the bay and shoot ducks. Our first experience with the canoe came near having tragic results. We started one afternoon from the ship, he in one end of the canoe, I in the other, the guns laid in the bottom, both of us paddling. I considered a canoe a craft for shallow lakes and streams, and was frightened as I thought that it was only a thin, narrow shell that stood between us and the depth of fathoms of water. I felt less nervous when we got up into the inlets. We picked out what we thought was a good spot and beached the canoe; the Captain started round the water's edge in one direction and I in the other. I heard him bang away; then a few minutes later I heard him calling to me for help. There was that in his voice that struck me with terror. I ran back and saw him twenty-five or thirty yards from the shore up to his waist in the mud. He had tried to retrieve a wounded duck by floundering in after it through what appeared to be just shallow water. He had failed to get the duck, and had found that he couldn't get back to shore. He was stuck in a bed of mud, where every effort he made to get out only hastened the process of being sucked down. He directed me to get the canoe. While I was trying in my unpracticed, clumsy way to get the boat into the water, I heard him calling to me frantically to hurry. When I reached him he had sunk to his armpits. He took hold of the front end of the canoe while I sat on the farthest extreme of the other end, in order to provide the greatest leverage possible. The Captain went at the work of extricating himself in a methodical manner, like a man accustomed to dealing with an exigency; had he been panicky, both of us should have been precipitated into the same plight. Gradually, inch by inch, he forced himself up and out and closer to the shore. Before he was completely out, that darkness which comes down so rapidly in the tropics, was beginning to fall and, powerful a man as he was, he was wholly exhausted. I related this incident at the club in the evening and heard in return some weird tales of quicksands abounding in the region, of men disappearing in them, and of their bodies never being recovered. Whether these tales were true or not, I already knew enough to make me vow that I should never let a duck or any other game decoy me to any spot where I could not be sure of my footing.

Yet, the prospects of shooting ducks did lead me into another experience somewhat similar. The Italian Consul and I sat in the club and planned that, as soon as the torrential rains that had been falling for weeks stopped, we should go out to a lagoon twelve or fifteen miles from town, where, it was said, the ducks were plentiful. We started before daylight and used for our transportation a horse and buggy owned by the Consul. We got out into the country and were feeling our way cautiously along the miry road with the aid of a lantern in the buggy, when suddenly and silently, as if by magic, the horse disappeared. We got out to look for him, and found that he had slipped forward into a mud hole and had sunk up to his neck. He was a brave-hearted animal and made heroic efforts to get himself out, but his efforts did nothing more than sap his strength. The Consul got down and helped the horse to keep his nose above the mud, while I ran for help. I came back with a half-dozen *mozos*. They stripped and went into the mud. After hard work the horse was rescued, but he lay panting on the side of the road for, perhaps, an hour before we could hitch him in and start back to town.

The Consul sent out by Cuba was Señor Zangroniz. He was a well-educated man, an engineer by profession. In appearance, he was far from being typically Cuban; his complexion was almost ruddy; his eyes were blue-gray; he cultivated a short but rather fierce mustache; was punctilious with regard to the finer points of Spanish etiquette; indeed, he might easily have passed for a Spaniard of one of the northern provinces. Señor Zangroniz was, I judged, ten years older than I, but our personal relationship somehow adjusted itself in correspondence with the political relationship between our two countries. We became very close friends, and spent lots of time together. We established the custom that regularly he would dine at my house on one night in each week and I at his on another. I do not doubt that one of the strong elements in his preference for my companionship was the fact that mine was the only ear into which he felt he could pour certain criticisms which, otherwise, he would have kept to himself—an element at the base of all close companionship. He never exhausted the subject of the comparison of the standards of civilization and social life in Cuba with those in Venezuela; with the judgment always in favor of Cuba. Particularly enthusiastic and magniloquent did he grow in contrasting the beauty and graces and virtues of Cuban women with those of the women of Venezuela. But this element of the confidential ear was not all on one side; there were some things that appeared to be shortcomings in the Venezuelans and

Venezuela that I felt I could discuss only with Zangroniz, of all the foreign language men in Puerto Cabello. Even so, on my side, I sensed limitations; for I realized that, after all, in language, religion, and traditional background, Zangroniz and the Venezuelans were one.

Our friendship, however, went far beyond the considerations of mutual satisfaction in the freedom to discuss Venezuela. We genuinely liked each other. We talked about many things. Sometimes we took long walks—for the tropics—while we talked. It was on one of these walks that I saw a sight that afterwards gained for me among my best friends the reputation of being, if not a liar, the teller of a very fishy fish story. Zangroniz and I had walked along the edge of the bay until we came to the mouth of a narrow inlet; and there we saw a native fishing. Now fishing, it may be said, is the laziest of all the sports; and here was a fisherman without rod or line or hook, who sat puffing languidly on his cigarette while the fish jumped into his boat. His only effort in the meantime was to observe his catch occasionally to see if it was sufficient. Among my regrets in life, one of the keenest is that I didn't have my kodak with me; for in relating this incident, and I have related it scores of times, I have yet to meet the person who seemed to believe that I was telling the truth. Perhaps, now, since trick photography in the movies has become so commonplace, the proof of the camera would not be regarded as positive. At any rate, this is the inside of the story: The fisherman, just before the tide turned to run out, paddled his boat to the inlet and anchored it across the mouth, which was hardly wider than the length of his craft; then a yard or so on the upstream side of his boat, he stretched a seine entirely across the inlet with about a foot of the net above the water. He then sat in his boat and smoked while he waited. At the turn of the tide, the fish that had been chasing their prey up the bay and into the inlet, started back toward the sea, and found their passage obstructed by the seine; at least a fair number of them simply backed up and took a flying leap over the barrier; some fell short of the boat and others shot over it, but enough of them fell in to reward the fisherman for his ingenuity and patience. We watched until the satisfied fisherman removed his seine, pulled in his anchors, and paddled away; and we agreed that laziness, not necessity, is the mother of invention.

Señor Zangroniz also liked to hunt, and he wanted very much to go along with Captain Crockett and me. On one of his stays in port I informed Captain Crockett that I had invited the Cuban Consul to join us. The Captain expressed great dissatisfaction at this, and declared emphatically that he did not want to be bothered with any "spiggoty." However, the three of us went. All the way out I found myself in the uncomfortable position of mediator and interpreter. The Captain's expressions of his dissatisfaction at the presence of Zangroniz increased in vehemence as we went along; and Zangroniz, noticing the Captain's hostile manner, was concerned about what he was saying. Captain Crockett, although he had been sailing to South American ports many years, spoke only wharf Spanish, and Señor Zangroniz spoke no English at all; so I kept getting from the Captain, "What's that he said?" and from the Consul, "*¿Que dice?*" I translated for each of them, but I took great liberties with the Captain's speeches; for I knew that a true translation might have resulted in a complete break of relations. Of course, Zangroniz was too intelligent not to see that my translations did not always accord with the Captain's tone of voice. When we reached the hunting grounds we set up our blinds at separate points and sat waiting. A flock of ducks alighted to feed and we began banging away. In the midst of the banging I heard Zangroniz yelling to me that the Captain had shot him, and saw him running to the cover of the woods. When I reached him he had taken off his leather puttees, which bore a great many marks of small birdshot, and was searching his legs for wounds. I helped him in the search but we found no marks on his flesh. I was never able to discover to my complete satisfaction whether the Captain had merely shot wild at the rising birds or had in malicious humor discharged a volley at a point close to the Consul's blind. But I do know that Zangroniz expressed no further desire to join any hunting party of which Captain Crockett was a member.

XXII

I N THE tropics, "Do not do today what *can* be put off till tomorrow," is a maxim that contains many grains of wisdom. There have come to the tropics men from a foreign clime who have attempted to put into practice the strenuous life. The effects on them have generally been disastrous. And yet not so disastrous as the effects on those who have yielded too much and become lotus eaters. I saw examples of both classes, and the plight of those who had broken down physically was less pitiable than the plight of those who had broken down spiritually. I strove while taking life easily not to take it too easily. The social day in Venezuela did not begin until five o'clock in the afternoon, and between early morning and that hour there was scarcely ever anything that one could do except attend to one's own business. When I had no official duties to perform, I made it my business to use that period in getting ahead with my writing, to do which had been one of my chief reasons for entering the Consular Service. Before leaving New York, I had made myself known to Richard Watson Gilder, the editor of the *Century Magazine*, and to William Hayes Ward, the editor of *The Independent*. I began mailing manuscripts to them, and my poems began appearing in the two publications. Mr. Gilder and Dr. Ward both evinced personal interest in the work I was doing. Mr. Gilder wrote me enthusiastically about my poem, *O Black and Unknown Bards*.

It was while I was in Venezuela that I had my one and only experience in line with a tradition about poetic inspiration, the tradition of the poet seizing his pen and in "fine frenzy" taking dictation from a spirit hovering about his head. I had come home from the club, and with no conscious thought of poetry in my mind I undressed for bed. When I had finished undressing I turned out my light and threw open the shutters to my bedroom windows. The open windows admitted enough light from the electric light opposite in the park to enable me to see my way about the room. I got into bed and immediately went to sleep. Later in the night, I woke suddenly, completely. For some reason, the light in the park had gone out and the room was in impenetrable darkness. I felt startled; then the darkness and silence combined, brought down on me a feeling of uttermost peace. I lay thinking for a long while; then I got up and fumbled for the light, took pen and paper, and almost without hesitation wrote a sonnet which I called *Mother Night*. Hardly bothering to read it over, I got back into bed and at once went off to sleep. The next day I made one or two slight revisions in the poem, typed it, and sent it to *The Century*. Promptly I got a letter from Mr. Gilder in which he said, "We are overwhelmed with poetry but we must take *Mother Night*."

I began earnest work on *The Autobiography of an Ex-Colored Man*, of which I had already made a first draft of the opening. The story developed in my mind more rapidly than I had expected that it would; at times, outrunning my speed in getting it down. The use of prose as a creative medium was new to me; and its latitude, its flexibility, its comprehensiveness, the variety of approaches it afforded for surmounting technical difficulties gave me a feeling of exhilaration, exhilaration similar to that which goes with freedom of motion. I turned over in my mind again and again my original idea of making the book anonymous. I also debated with myself the aptness of *The Autobiography of an Ex-Colored Man* as a title. Brander Matthews had expressed a liking for the title, but my brother had thought it was clumsy and too long; he had suggested *The Chameleon*. In the end, I stuck to the original idea of issuing the book without the author's name, and kept the title that had appealed to me first. But I have never been able to settle definitely for myself whether I was sagacious or not in these two decisions. When I chose the title, it was without the slightest doubt that its meaning would be perfectly clear to anyone; there were people, however, to whom it proved confusing. When the book was published (1912) most of the reviewers, though there were some doubters, accepted it as a human document. This was a tribute to the writing, for I had done the book with the intention of its being so taken. But, perhaps, it would have been more farsighted had I originally affixed my name to it as a frank piece of fiction. But I did get a certain pleasure out of anonymity, that no acknowledged book could have given me. The authorship of the book excited the curiosity of literate colored people, and there was speculation among them as to who the writer might be—to every such group some colored man who had married white, and so coincided with the main point on which the story turned, is known. I had the experience of listening to some of these discussions. I had a rarer experience, that of being introduced to and talking with one man who tacitly admitted to those present that he was the author of the book. Only two or three people knew that I was the writer of the story—the publishers themselves never knew me personally; yet the fact gradually leaked out and spread. The first printed statement was made by George A. Towns, my classmate at Atlanta University, who wrote a piece in which he gave his reasons for thinking I was the man. When the book was republished,[1] I affixed my name to it, and Carl Van Vechten was good enough to write an Introduction, and in it to inform the reader that the story was not the story of my life. Nevertheless, I continue to receive letters from persons who have read the book inquiring about this or that phase of my life as told in it. That is, probably, one of the reasons why I am writing the present book.

At the end of the year I was granted the statutory sixty-day leave of absence. I spent about a week in Washington, during which I visited the State Department several times. I went to Jacksonville for a brief stay with my parents; then returned to New York. In Washington, I found myself a non-resident member of the "Black Cabinet." This was a group made up of colored men who held important federal positions in the capital. At the time, it included the Register of the Treasury, the Recorder of Deeds for the District, the Auditor of the Navy Department, an Assistant United States Attorney General, a Judge of the Municipal Court, and the Collector for the Port of Washington. Charles W. Anderson was a member of the group, and so was P. S. B. Pinchback, former Lieutenant Governor of Louisiana. Those of the group who lived in Washington customarily met at lunch and discussed the political state of the nation, with special reference to its Negro citizens. On such matters, Booker T. Washington was chief adviser to President Roosevelt, and became the same to President Taft; but the "Black Cabinet" was not without considerable influence and power. The "Cabinet" no longer exists, and for the reason that Presidents since Taft have adopted a policy of appointing fewer and fewer Negroes to important positions; the lowest mark, close to zero, being reached in President Hoover's administration.

In New York, I found Bob and Rosamond back from their tour with *The Shoo-Fly Regiment*. They had started out with a company of sixty people, with some fairly good bookings and promises of more;

[1] Alfred A. Knopf, New York, 1927.

but the bulk of it all turned out to be in one-night stands in popular-price theaters. Not yet had the fight for colored companies to play first-class houses been won. A good part of their tour had been laid out to cover small towns in the South. With a large and expensive company, it was impossible for them to make money at the prices to which they were compelled to play. Indeed, they lost money; so much that the management under which they were booked failed them and left the show to shift for itself somewhere in the far South. Bob and Rosamond used their own money to keep their company intact and bring it back to New York. A short engagement at the Bijou Theater in New York had the result of bringing them under the more reliable management of Stair and Havlin for the coming season.

New York did not seem the same to me. Some of the shine seemed to have come off. I enjoyed going to the theater again, especially because most of the times I went with Grace Nail. She had been a theater-goer since childhood, and was well informed about plays, players, and playwrights. The performances that we saw together we talked over from the three angles. But my enthusiasm about being back in my old surroundings was not as high as I had expected it would be. Bob and Rosamond were in low spirits over the financial failure of the *Shoo-Fly Regiment*, and worried about the prospects and outcome of the approaching season. The wear and tear of "trouping" coupled with anxiety had worn on Rosamond physically and showed particularly in the almost complete loss of his singing voice. Bob, more used to the ups and downs of theatrical life, showed no marked ill effects, and, probably because the plans gone awry were chiefly of his making, maintained a defensive show of optimism. But neither of the two, though they were sincerely happy to see me back, were in the mood or condition to kill a fatted calf. The studio was changed, and I could not feel at home in it. During the months that Bob and Rosamond had been on the road, D— had used it as living quarters; it was rearranged and cluttered up; it had lost its air. The Marshall itself seemed to have deteriorated. There was still a large clientele of patrons and sightseers, but I missed the Broadway stars, the important newspaper men, and other writers that had been frequent visitors. There seemed to me to have been an all-round cheapening process going on. Some of these reactions may have been due purely to subjective causes, but they were not for that reason any less real.

When Bob and Rosamond came back to town, D—— moved out of the studio, but he took another room in the Marshall, so I saw him every day. I found that he had dissolved his partnership with the Brooklyn lawyer and had set up for himself, with offices downtown in Beekman Street. I visited him there several times. He kept a suite of well-furnished rooms, and appeared to be building up a good practice. He was surely far from being discouraged and I was forced to admit that my advice to him not to leave Jacksonville had apparently been no sounder than his to me. From what I saw, his clientele was almost entirely white. In taking lunch or dinner downtown with him, I found that he was on terms of breezy intimacy with a number of professional and business men in his district. On one occasion when I was in his office, a strikingly beautiful woman came in. She was young, about twenty-two, and her face was symmetrically perfect. She was tall and slender, but with that breadth of shoulders that presages an Amazonian air in middle life. But middle life to her was a long way off, and I recognized her beauty for what it was in the present. D—— took in the homage I silently paid her, I could see from the way he smiled that he relished it. It did not require the slight proprietary air that he assumed for my benefit to make me perceive that the young lady's visit was not that of a client to her lawyer. When she had gone, D—— proceeded to enlighten me fully on what I had already guessed to be the main point. The young lady was a Jewess; she belonged to a very nice family; she knew that he was colored but her family did not; he was deeply in love with her; she was in love with him. He enlarged on the last two points.

Throughout our lives, D—— in all his love affairs had sooner or later made me a sort of confessor. He frequently did something that I should rather have lost a finger than do, he would read me most ardent letters from his lady loves; I recall, in particular, letters he received for several years from a girl he met at the University of Michigan, letters too tender, too sincere, yes, too sacred to be seen by a third pair of eyes; yet he read them to me. It may have been an injustice to him, but I always suspected that the act was not purely confidential in its nature, but was more or less mixed with vainglory. A confession about a great love from D—— had for some time since ceased to strike me as a crisis in his life; so I took no extreme heed of this latest one.

I would not say that I was pleased to get away from New York, when my leave was over; but when I got aboard ship it was with a feeling of relief that I was bound for my great house, where I commanded not only my time but my actions and my near surroundings, where I should not be so tightly wedged in by the will and presence of others.

I think I have indicated that the little city of Puerto Cabello constituted a man's world. The women of Puerto Cabello had very little part in that world, and where they did touch it they did so mainly through contact with men of their immediate families. Business, politics, community activities, were wholly and exclusively masculine provinces. Even social life was preponderantly the affair of men; directly the opposite of what it is in the United States, where "society" is run and ruled by women.

But in 1908 Puerto Cabello was the scene of two consecutive weeks of social activity in which the women played a full part. Late in August, *El Restaurador* steamed into port. *El Restaurador* was the flagship of the Venezuelan Navy; in fact, almost the whole Navy. Formerly a steam yacht belonging to one of the Goulds, she had been purchased by the government, converted into a war vessel, and named in honor of President Castro, who had assumed the title, *El Restaurador de Venezuela* (The Restorer of Venezuela). On board were General Cipriano Castro, President of the Republic; his wife, Doña Zoila de Castro; numerous military aides; a full military band, and an entourage of several dozen pretty young women. It was said that the General never traveled without a large number of maids-in-waiting, as it were.

General Castro was by no means universally popular among the Venezuelans, but he was universally feared; and for the good reason that his power and his ruthlessness were both unbounded. There was, in fact, great opposition to Castro; there was opposition to him among the men I knew in Puerto Cabello, but it was never expressed openly. No one would be foolhardy enough to oppose a dictator like Castro through the expression of opinion; opposition had to be kept covert until it was able to manifest itself in armed rebellion. And, even then, one must feel fairly certain of the chances for success, because no imaginable fate could be worse than being made a political prisoner. I used to talk with a man who had lain for months in a filthy dungeon, weighted down in *grillos* (irons). In his case, he and another man were bound together by heavy shackles that were riveted on their ankles and connected by a short chain; they were never able to be more than three feet apart. His story caused me nausea. So, in the welcome to Puerto Cabello given to General Cipriano Castro, *Restaurador de Venezuela*, there was no voice of audible dissent. Men who bitterly hated Castro, though they took no active part in entertaining him, hardly dared to decline to attend affairs to which they were bidden.

But no one, friend or enemy to the Dictator, could escape the intoxication engendered by the festivities. Various officials invited guests *a tomar una copa de champagne* in honor of the General. The presidential band, a good one, played every afternoon in the principal park, while the populace and society promenaded round and round. A special *Te Deum* was sung at the church. The high spot, however, came at the beginning: it was the grand ball given by the Collector of the Port. All of Porteña society was present. I was surprised that it could boast so many lovely women. The orchestra had been brought down from Valencia. I have not yet heard a finer orchestra for the kind of dances it played. It was composed entirely of strings and woodwinds, and played only waltzes and quadrilles. I danced most of the waltzes— they were played ravishingly—and omitted all of the quadrilles. The women were beautiful, the music enchanting, and the champagne, unusual for the tropics, was dry—a trinity that left little for a man's attention elsewhere. I could not help but note that one of Castro's generals present at the ball was a gigantic, full-blooded Negro; and I was mildly surprised, because there were, comparatively, only a few Negroes in Venezuela. But something else made a still stronger pull on my attention—General Castro.

This was the first good opportunity I had had to observe the man— this man who for seven years had been the absolute master of Venezuela; who had snapped his fingers at the power of England, of Germany, of Italy, of France, and of the United States; who compared himself with Napoleon, slightly to the latter's disadvantage; this man who had risen from the bottom level of his country's peasantry to be the overlord of all; who until he was thirty had never worn a pair of shoes and now lived the life of a sybarite; who was a superlative combination of vanity, arrogant ignorance, cruelty; and of courage, too;

this despot who was able to decree the prosperity or the ruin of any Venezuelan citizen, under whose disfavor security crumbled away, in whose hands life and death actually lay. It was like seeing the sinister hero of some barbarous page in history brought to life.

During the early part of the evening, General Castro sat in a high-backed chair, where he received those who were presented to him. I was presented as the American Consul. He extended his hand to me with the palm turned down and the fingers hanging limp. He took my hand with the ends of those limp fingers and expressed a perfunctory greeting, taking no pains to disguise the contempt he had for all foreigners. He was an exceptional figure in the throng of men about him. Short in stature—his height, within a fraction of an inch, was that of Napoleon's—he, nevertheless, did not look small in the great chair in which he sat; his haughty and disdainful manner filled it up. His complexion showed his Indian ancestry, but he had a sallow hue. His head was square rather than round. Looking at his face, it appeared that from the line of his eyes the length to the extremity of his forehead was much greater than it was to the point of his chin. This appearance was magnified by the top of his head being bare, except for a very thin and rat-like growth of hair. A jet-black, luxuriant beard and mustache did not entirely cover a sensual mouth. But the dominant feature was the eyes; black, hard, unresponsive, impassive, they darted a quick glance here or there, but immediately recovered their insensitivity. I had seen such eyes in some animal, somewhere.

There was a note on the invitation to the ball saying, full dress *es de rigor*; but General Castro did not comply with the requirement. He was attired neither in full dress nor, like his aides, in uniform. He wore a long, fawn-colored Prince Albert coat, with vest and trousers of the same material, patent leather shoes, and on his head a dark velvet skull-cap embroidered with a wreath pattern in gold. This cap was his only insignia of rank. He took it off frequently to mop his face and brow and the top of his head with his handkerchief. The manner in which he was arrayed seemed to me to be strangely at variance with his known vanity. At any rate, he was dressed more sensibly than any other man present; for one of the follies of man in tropical America is the slavish fashion of wearing black clothes at state and high official affairs, a folly that is an actual hardship. The man in equatorial America who will design a light and cool style of dress for such occasions will be a benefactor worthy of a monument.

Toward the middle of the evening, the announcement ran round in whispers that the President would dance. No one could stay in Venezuela thirty days and not learn that Castro was a remarkable dancer; but I was not prepared for the exhibition I witnessed. He took part in a quadrille, and for a while went through the figures in the customary manner. By degrees, the spirit of the dance seemed to get into his blood, to run through his nerves, to seize and control his muscles. He became more and more animated, and finally took the center of the floor to himself. He chasséd right and left, forward and backward. He pranced round and round, spreading out the skirts of his coat with his hands. No other dancer in the set was now making any move. He executed fantastic figures and steps, at one time squatting on his haunches and kicking out his feet alternately, somewhat after the manner of a familiar Russian folk dance movement. His dancing quickened the tempo of the music; he jumped, he leaped, he pirouetted, he spun himself round like a whirling dervish. He was, it was evident, bordering on a state of frenzy. When he stopped, wet with streaming perspiration, the set in which he had been dancing ended; but he danced again in the same manner many times before the ball was over, coming up, seemingly fresh, for each new dance. I was told that at a ball he always had on hand a supply of extra shirts, at least a dozen, and made changes whenever the moisture of a garment reached the point of saturation. Without doubt, it was these extraordinary antics that had led to his being dubbed *El Mono de los Andinos* (the Monkey of the Andes). It was difficult for me to reconcile these grotesqueries with the air and actions of the man I had an hour before been observing as he sat in his high-backed chair.

This series of festivities was brought to a close with a grand ball given by General Castro himself in honor of *la sociedad carabobeña*. The ball was given in Valencia, the chief city of the State of Carabobo. A number of invited guests went up from Puerto Cabello. I went for a double reason; I wanted to attend the ball and I wanted to see Valencia, where I had not yet been, although it was in my consular district. I found it a beautiful little city of about thirty thousand, twice the population of Puerto Cabello, with some very nice shops and a great many fine dwelling houses. It was more typically Spanish than the Port, because foreign interests and influence were not so strong there as they were in the city on the coast. I liked Valencia so much that I decided to be a frequent visitor; but I never got back. The ball was similar to the one given in Puerto Cabello; the difference being in degree rather than in kind. In each particular it was on a grander scale because of the larger number of persons of wealth and culture in Valencia. The President danced with even wilder energy than he had displayed on the former occasion. I began to suspect that he was dancing against death. Castro was then forty-eight, and at the peak of his power, a comparatively young man, who had conquered the world about him; but, as some knew, he was also a sick man. A close study of his face in repose, the deep lines, the weary mouth, the cadaverous aspect lurking just behind the countenance, revealed even to the unpracticed eye that the dread hand was preparing to strike. Beyond a doubt, Castro had forebodings of this; but it is improbable that he had a single inkling that it was the hand of political fate that was to strike first.

Several months passed, and Puerto Cabello had entirely settled back to its leisurely pace. Then, suddenly, there was excitement at the club. Rumors and more rumors came down from the capital regarding the President's health: that his physical condition was approaching a critical point; that his doctors had informed him that only a surgical operation, one which they did not dare to perform, could save his life; that he had cabled to Germany for the services of a great specialist; that the German specialist was willing to take the case, but declined to operate in Venezuela; that this disinclination developed into a blank refusal in the face of a proffered fee of fifty thousand dollars. This last item in the succession of rumors was hotly discussed at the club; some asserting that the German was unwilling to risk his reputation with the hospital facilities of Caracas; some that he feared he would never get out of Venezuela alive if the operation was not successful; and still others that he probably knew, if he came and performed even a successful operation, Castro would bilk him.

In the end, General Castro reluctantly yielded to the pressure of his advisers and decided to go to Germany for the operation. He took nearly all the space on a large French liner; for, with him went not only a full complement of aides and friends, but also, as the reports had it, more than a hundred of the most beautiful young women of Venezuela. As the ship prepared to get under way, Castro sat dejectedly on a great strong-box, which contained, as other reports had it, an immense amount of money in gold currency. It is more than probable that many of the friends who accompanied Castro felt that they would be safer on the ocean with him than in Venezuela without him. Among these was one, Gumersindo Rivas, the editor of Castro's personal organ, *El Constitucional*. In the field of press agency, American journalism has never produced anything to compare with this man Rivas. His praise of Castro strained even the grandiloquence of the Spanish language. Venezuelans read daily about "The Restorer," "The Invincible Hero," "The Supreme Leader," "The Savior of His People." Frequently Rivas listed in an ascending scale the names and deeds of the world's great heroes, sages and saints, including the name of Jesus, and rose to a climax with the name and deeds of Cipriano Castro. When Castro was making the tour that took in Puerto Cabello and Valencia, the progress of his itinerary was published in a series of articles under the title, "The Apotheosis of the Hero." I used to read *El Constitucional* every day, not omitting to read Rivas's leading editorial. The man's ingenuity and his ability to ring in Castro's name, no matter upon what subject he was writing, was astonishing. If he wrote an article, say, on the solar system, he would end it by declaring that as the sun is the center of the solar system, so is Castro the center of Venezuela. I took up *El Constitucional* one Sunday morning and read an eloquent, perfervid article on Easter. And that article did end: "As Christ rose to save the world, so has Castro risen to save Venezuela." For Gumersindo Rivas, Castro was the breath of life and the staff of life, so it was natural that he could not exist separated from him.

The ship had hardly cleared the harbor of La Guaira before the university students of Caracas rose in revolt against the Castro administration. General Vicente Gómez, Vice President of the Republic, promptly put down the "revolution," and as promptly took over the Presidency. There is no doubt that Castro got the news on shipboard by wireless. What were his thoughts? Did he have full confidence in the lieutenancy of Gómez? Did he believe that the subordinate had merely taken strong measures to hold the power until the return of his chief? Or did he have misgivings and doubts? There must have occurred to Castro's mind the success of a most simple expedient which he had himself employed a few years before. At that time he had wanted very much to get rid of the French Minister to Venezuela. One day that official went down to La Guaira and made a visit aboard a French steamship. Now, there was a regulation in Venezuela that no one was allowed to go aboard a vessel without an authorization signed by the officer of the port. The French Minister, relying on the courtesy usually accorded to foreign representatives with regard to the ships of their own nations, simply walked aboard. When he started off, Castro's soldiers, under orders from Caracas, asked to see his permit and, when he was not able to show one, refused to let him go ashore. The Minister was obliged to sail without bag or baggage.

Castro's operation was successful. He came through in better health than he had had for years. When he sought to return to Venezuela, Gómez would not let him land; an eventuation that produced satisfaction, even if disguised, in our Department of State. Castro retired long enough to raise an expedition of several thousand men, and effected a landing on the north coast of the country. But Venezuelans did not flock to his standard, and in a single battle he was defeated. He spent the remainder of his life in efforts to regain his lost power. He had an idea that he might further his cause among Venezuelan expatriates in the United States, through a visit to New York; but our government detained him at Ellis Island and finally denied him admission. He hovered round Venezuela as closely as he could, and finally died, an exile, at San Juan, Porto Rico, in 1924.

XXIII

LIFE in Puerto Cabello ran along evenly. I enjoyed it, but I didn't want to slip so deep into the rut of it that I shouldn't be able to get out. The consulship at this indolent little port afforded ideal conditions for me to carry on my principal aim in entering the service; but I had grown ambitious as a consul, and I worked to make a record that would entitle me to promotion. I did my best to make my commercial reports more than perfunctory communications. I kept both eyes open as wide as possible for opportunities for American business. I sent in frequent suggestions gathered in the method pursued by the Germans, who did the greater part of all the foreign business done in Venezuela. Actuated by the fact that baseball was so popular and well played in Cuba, I promoted the idea of organizing two clubs in Puerto Cabello. There was, at least, the result of an order for complete outfits from a New York sporting goods house. I can't ever forget the first game they played; it was so much more vocal than athletic. When I left Puerto Cabello there were indications that our national game was gaining a foothold in that section of Venezuela. The gathering of commercial information and a supervision over American ships and seamen are prime duties of a consul. However, when the post lies within the sphere of American influence, the gathering of political information and the protection of American citizens also become prime duties.

I sent in frequent political reports, because our State Department had more than the conventional interest in the internal political situation of Venezuela. But, because there were practically no American citizens resident in Puerto Cabello and the only American visitors were passengers en route who came ashore while their ship was in port, I had little or nothing to do about the protection of American citizens. "Protecting American citizens" is the bane of a consul's life; and the point of the difficulty is not that of seeing that an American citizen's rights are not violated, but of seeing that his physical needs are taken care of. This is especially true in many of the Latin American countries, where there are so many destitute Americans. Among the beachcombers in these countries, applying to the consul for aid is a regular "racket." A consul is authorized to draw on the Treasury of the United States for any necessary amount to aid destitute seamen, to provide them with food, shelter, clothes, medical treatment, and passage back to an American port, if the situation warrants; but he is not allowed a penny for the aid of mere citizens; any financial aid that he gives them comes out of his own pocket. Not in my entire experience, however, did I meet a fellow consul who could say that he had ever been able to convince an applicant of that fact. The applicant, when he failed to receive as much as he thought he was entitled to, usually expressed his doubts as to the consul's interest or his sincerity or his honesty. Sometimes an outspoken individual would express his opinion about his country, declaring that he didn't consider it worth a damn.

Among the American visitors to Puerto Cabello came a shipload of Congressmen headed by "Uncle" Joe Cannon. As I remember, they were on their way to see how the digging of the Panama Canal was coming on. I knew that the party had been touring around the Caribbean several weeks, so I met the ship with my latest batch of *New York Heralds*, which I placed in Mr. Cannon's hands. He expressed great appreciation of this; and I felt sure there was nothing I might have done for him in Puerto Cabello that would have pleased him more. He came ashore and, running his arm through mine, walked along to pay a short visit at the Consulate. He asked me a number of pointed questions about Venezuela and about myself. Strangely, with him, I felt no reticence in answering the latter questions. I put him down as a fine, democratic old gentleman. The only other member of this junketing party that I recall was Congressman, later Senator, William B. McKinley.

The visitor at the Consulate who caused me the greatest excitement was an officer from aboard an American man-of-war that had just anchored in the harbor. He presented me the compliments of the Captain, and advised me that the launch would be at my service at the hour when I wished to pay my official visit aboard. I appointed the hour, then set myself to reading over the regulations governing the conduct of a consul paying an official visit aboard an American war vessel. Both the launch and the ship flew the consular flag; the ship was manned as I went aboard; the Captain met me at the gangplank and escorted me to his cabin. When the visit was concluded, he escorted me back to the gangplank. When the launch cleared the ship, I was given the consular salute of seven guns, which I received standing with bared head. This ceremony was, later, to become rather commonplace with me, but this first experience was the thrill of a lifetime.

After I had served two years at Puerto Cabello, my thoughts turned more and more to the matter of a promotion. It was not that I was dissatisfied with Puerto Cabello; I was simply anxious to go up in the Service, and I knew that a consul who stayed too long a time at one post was likely to become regarded as a fixture there. Before my first year was up, President Roosevelt had expressed a willingness to name me as consul at Nice, but Secretary Root had said that it simply could not be done. Consideration of me for the post at Nice was a by-product of the riot at Brownsville, Texas, August 1906, in which a battalion of the Twenty-fifth Regiment (Negro) United States Infantry was implicated. In November, the President issued an order dismissing the entire battalion without honor and disqualifying its members from military or civil service thereafter. This order aroused a wave of disapproval and criticism. But from the colored people came a storm of protest which burst over the President with a force that must have shocked him, for he was genuinely proud of the fact that he held a greater degree of the confidence and affection of the Negro people than had been given to any president since Abraham Lincoln. A Congressional investigation smoothed the matter out somewhat by opening a way for members of the battalion to re-enlist, and the President revoked the civil disability order, but he was still disturbed by the resentment of the colored people, and was ready and willing to do anything he properly could to allay that feeling.

When the matter of a promotion was uppermost in my mind, I awoke to find that I was trapped in Venezuela. An epidemic of bubonic plague broke out, and every American representative got out of the country, except me. Certainly, I did not stay on because I wished to; but there I was, the only one left. I suffered no great fright; I felt that my habits of living secured me more than a fair degree of immunity. I, of course, kept clean and I took the further precaution of not going to any place where there was likelihood of contagion. But those were dreary weeks. Shipping fell off to a minimum. The few ships that did put in guarded against rats going aboard by placing midway up their hawsers metal disks a foot and a half or two feet in diameter. I spent much of my time reading about rats. I was surprised at the large amount of literature on the subject, and to find that it was so interesting. In the spring of 1909, a cable from the State Department came advising me that I had been appointed Consul at Corinto, Nicaragua, and that I should proceed to my post by way of Washington. My new post carried a promotion to the next grade above and an increase in salary of a thousand dollars a year. But when the moment came, I felt some keen regrets at leaving Puerto Cabello. I had established many kindly associations, and life had been very pleasant. I confess that the biggest emotional strain came in saying good-by to my ménage; two of the women had been in my employ for three years, and they wept as though I was going to my death. A group of the men I knew best were at the ship to see me off; and bade me good luck and Godspeed in, as is the custom in Latin America, many a glass of champagne. When the ship touched at Curaçao I went ashore and to the shop of a filigree worker, where I purchased one of his masterpieces, a heart done in gold, to be worn as a pendant. I made it a gift to Grace Nail.

XXIV

WHEN I reached New York, I went directly to Washington to report at the State Department and receive instructions. My instructions were brief; they were that I should proceed to my post as promptly as possible, with the added instruction that my duties would be more diplomatic than consular. I took the time to run over to Baltimore for a night to see Bob and Rosamond; they had written a new show called *The Red Moon*, and were playing there. My two former partners were enthusiastic about the future under their new managers. I returned to New York and spent a feverish ten days or so in preparations to sail.

I felt less at home in the city than ever before. The studio was closed. Bob had bought a house in West 136th Street, in Harlem, and moved his family in. He was, I believe, the first colored person to buy a home in Harlem, west of Lenox Avenue. Rosamond had taken an apartment in West 99th Street, and I stayed there. I went down to The Marshall only once; it seemed like a place I had known and almost forgotten. West 53rd Street was already beginning to lose its place as the Negro center, and the trek to Harlem was taking on significant proportions. D—— had married; he had married the beautiful Jewess I had seen at his office on my former visit to New York. But his marriage made no change in his relations toward me; nor, in fact, any marked change in his relations with his other Negro friends. D—— was, so far as I can remember, the only man I have known to "pass"—and I have known numbers of them—without feeling it was necessary to "pass up" his colored friends. One of his first acts was to have me up to his apartment for dinner with him and his wife.

During the time I was in New York I saw Grace Nail as often as I could. We went many places together, to the theater a number of times. I remember, specifically, that we saw *Anna Karenina* at the old Herald Square Theater; but clearer than any memory of the play is my memory of the fact that, through my clumsiness, one of her hatpins was lost under the seats. I replaced the pin, and was superstitious enough to exact a penny from her in payment. She was at the steamer to see me sail; and, as the ship slipped out from her pier, the thought came down on me heavily that I was a lonely man; and I knew that I was really and deeply in love.

The voyage was uneventful, except that I got my initiation into the science and art of poker. A quartet of young men insisted on my taking the fifth hand at table, and we played every night in the smoking room. I liked the game, and also I was lucky enough to get my lessons at small cost. I had reasons, later, to be thankful for this primary instruction. Our vessel docked at Colon—which reminds me that there was a man on board who got lots of fun out of inveigling victims into making the losing bet that Colon, on the Atlantic, was east of Panama, on the Pacific. The Panama Canal was still in course of construction; so, transportation across the Isthmus had to be made by train. I had considerable baggage to be transferred, because I was taking with me a good many articles that I needed and which I doubted could be obtained in Nicaragua. But the manager of the Panama Railroad was good enough to extend to me the courtesies of the company, and all my baggage was carried across without trouble or expense on my part.

I was glad to get out of Colon; the town was utterly unattractive and unbearably hot. Panama was an agreeable change. I found this old city, originally built by the Spaniards in 1518, exceedingly interesting and charming. As soon as I was installed at my hotel, I drove the several miles to Ancon, the port, to verify the arrangements for my passage to Corinto. At the offices of the Pacific Mail Steamship Company, I learned that the ship on which I was to sail had sunk at the dock. True it was; I went down on the dock and looked at her, or rather, at what could be seen of her. I learned, further, that I should have to wait fully two weeks for the next ship. This was not a pleasing prospect; that length of time was more than I required for seeing Panama; moreover, in view of my instructions, I was anxious to get to my post. But there was no way out of the dilemma. While I was at the offices of the Pacific Mail Steamship Company talking with the agent, I became aware of the presence of a dozen or more

Negroes in the large counting room back of the outer office. Now, Negroes were not a rare sight in Panama; they were almost as ubiquitous there as they are now in Harlem; the spade work on the Canal was being done mainly by Negroes. So these that I saw in the Pacific Mail office made no special demands on my attention until I gradually perceived that they were not working as janitors or laborers, but doing clerical work. I noted that they were making entries in the big ledgers and handling stacks of bills of lading and other shipping documents. I was particularly impressed by their nonchalant skill in the trick of making pen and pencil racks of their ears. I could not refrain from asking the agent about them. He informed me that the very best accountants and bookkeepers to be found in Panama were educated Jamaican Negroes.

I spent the time seeing Panama. In the afternoons I took a drive. In the evenings I listened to the band play in the park and watched the crowds or explored the places of amusement—some of them tough places. I did not omit seeing the world-famous Panama "red light" district. I had only two or three more days to wait. I went out on a morning to make some purchases: Panama hats, which, as ought to be known, are made in Ecuador, not Panama, and some trinkets from the Chinese shops. I had hitherto avoided going out in the heat of the day; and, when I got back to the hotel about noon, I was wet with perspiration and felt extremely fatigued. I took off my coat and threw myself on the bed under a window through which a delightful breeze was blowing. I intended to relax only a few minutes before going down to lunch, but I fell sound asleep. I got up in time for dinner, and after dinner went out to the band concert. In the night I woke with terrible pains in my chest and back, which were intensified each time I breathed. I managed to ring for a bell boy. When he came, he grew quite concerned about my condition. I asked him to call me a doctor at once. He left and came back with two porous plasters, one of which he applied to my chest and the other to my back, and told me that the doctor was out but would come as soon as he got the message. I asked him if he could not call some other doctor, but he seemed to go on the assumption that there was only one doctor in Panama—this probably was the one who had special arrangements with the hotel.

The doctor came the next morning. I had one additional symptom, I could not swallow. He took my temperature and examined me; it was four or five, I don't remember exactly how many, degrees above normal; I had a severe case of tonsillitis; and symptoms of pleurisy. The doctor urged me to go to the hospital immediately. I told him that it was impossible; my ship sailed within thirty-six hours, and I could not miss it; I'd stay, at least, through the day at the hotel and see how I felt. He shrugged his shoulders, prescribed for me, and said that he would come again in the evening. The next morning I felt no better and the rain was coming down as it can only in the tropics. On his visit the doctor again advised my going to the hospital. I declined to go. I lay in bed weighing the situation; sick in Panama, no friends, not a single person interested in me, not sure even that I had a competent physician; I had better take my chances on board an American ship with the ship's doctor. I made the decision. With the aid of a bell boy I got dressed and packed. I then hired a wagon and drove through the rain to the Pacific Terminals of the Railroad, where I picked up my goods being held in storage for me there, then to the docks, and, soaking wet, caught my ship within fifteen minutes of her sailing time. I don't know what to attribute it to, but this rash action had none of the results to be expected. I felt better as soon as I got aboard, and I improved rapidly each day at sea. It was only the tonsillitis that hung on and made swallowing uncomfortable for six or seven days.

My first view of Corinto sent my heart down like a plummet. What I saw was not a city or a town, but a straggling, tropical village. H. H. Leonard, the Vice-Consul, came aboard and courteously took charge of my belongings. When I got ashore, I found that the close-up was less flattering than the view from the bay. The bay itself was beautiful; landlocked by several islands, with Cardon, a great rock, standing up in strong relief. Directly across the bay, three or four miles, was a large, finely wooded island, and along the left ran the shore of the mainland with its skyline of five volcanoes. Of the surroundings, only what man had done in making Corinto was vile. It was a shanty town, built entirely of wood. There were less than a half-dozen attractive houses in it. The streets were unpaved; there was no electricity. Except for a couple of primitive grocery stores, there was not a shop in the place. There was a rambling old building on the waterfront, the Hotel Papi, run by a fat Italian of that name. It was a wooden structure, built largely of mahogany, and in a more or less tumbledown condition; but its airy *cantina* and dining room made it the pleasantest place in Corinto. Adjoining the Hotel Papi were the comparatively splendid houses of the brothers Palacio, also Italians and the leading importers and exporters in Nicaragua. A block back was another hotel, a crude, new building, which lacked the picturesqueness that the old Hotel Papi possessed. It was run by a tall, gaunt but handsome old Irishman, whom the English-speaking people called Dan Finnegan. Dan wrote his last name "Finucane," pronouncing it as a three-syllable word with the accent on the "u." The natives made it a four-syllable word, with the accent on the "a." Dan, with his aristocratic face and soldierly bearing, running a crude hotel in Corinto, never, during the four years I knew him, ceased stirring my curiosity as to the whys and wherefores of his being there.

As soon as I had settled myself at the Hotel Papi, I went to the Consulate. It was located in a room that was part of a private dwelling adjoining Dan's hotel. I was the first consul appointed to Corinto; the office up to that time had been in charge of a vice-consul who was under the Consul at Managua, the capital. I saw at once that it would not be possible to organize the office properly in the limited quarters it occupied; so I signed a lease for the third-best house in town, which, fortunately for me, had just become vacant. The house consisted of three rooms built in a straight line facing the street. Two of the rooms were each twenty by twenty. There was an ell on the back that contained the kitchen and quarters for servants. There was an elevated porch on the front, that also served as a sidewalk for the public; and on the back was a wide veranda that looked out over a very lovely flower garden. At the far end of the garden was a shower bath, supplied with water from a tank which was filled by a force pump at the well. One of the large rooms I took as an office, the other for my personal use, and the third as a filing room. I requisitioned office furniture from Washington, bought a commodious, native-built cedar wardrobe, and some other pieces for myself; and in a short while the Consulate was presentable and I was comfortable.

When I arrived at Corinto, there was an American warship anchored in the harbor. I was prompt in paying my official visit aboard. She was in command of Captain William S. Benson (later, the American representative in drawing up the naval terms of the Armistice with Germany and the Central Powers, and naval adviser to the American Commission to Negotiate Peace). Captain Benson was glad to talk with someone who had recently come from Washington. He had been anchored in Corinto bay several months, and he was anxious to get some sign, however slight, as to why he was being held there and when he would be relieved. I could give him no sign that was hopeful; but a little while after, he was relieved, when another warship came in and took his place.

Within my first few days in Corinto, I paid another official visit. I learned that President Zelaya was living at his summer house on Cardon Island. I went over to pay my respects to him, and was cordially received. Here was another famous dictator, the man who had held autocratic power in Nicaragua for sixteen years. It was inevitable that I should compare him with Castro. He was like Castro, in that he was a ruthless tyrant and also "in bad" with the United States. In every other respect he was unlike the Venezuelan. Castro was boorish, and took refuge in his ignorance; Zelaya was urbane and well educated. He spoke three languages; his English was very good. Castro made a boast of his provincialism; whenever he might be asked why he never visited Paris, he would answer sarcastically that he had no need to go to Paris, Caracas was in every way as fine a city as Paris, only smaller. Zelaya was a cosmopolite who knew his Paris and the Riviera. The President of Nicaragua was light bronze in color, slightly bald, rather stout, and possessed of perfect poise and charming manners. He chatted with me without constraint for half an hour. I do not question that he had as great distrust of the United States and dislike for its citizens as Castro, but he was too suave to make any exhibition of it under the circumstances. I left carrying a pleasant impression of Zelaya although I already knew that, officially, my hand was to be against him.

I quickly found that Corinto was not to be at all so close to a sinecure as Puerto Cabello had been. There were more ships to be cleared, and the seamen on the American ships were different from those I had been dealing with; many of them were Mexicans, and they gave considerably more work and worry. Occasionally, there were fights among them, in which someone was seriously hurt. In one instance there was a killing. In such cases, the Consul has preliminary extraterritorial powers, which he is called on to exercise. The American warships, always present in the harbor, entailed another set of duties. Then there were duties involved in protecting American citizens, of whom there were, relatively, a great many in Nicaragua:

American businessmen, American plantation owners, American concession hunters, prospectors, adventurers, soldiers of fortune, beachcombers, and a steady stream of tourists. An American citizen, dead, in a foreign country and without adult next of kin, puts a heavier responsibility on the Consul than any live one could. The Consul at once becomes the custodian and administrator of all his possessions, whether they consist of gold and lands or only a valiseful of old clothes. There was a coffee planter living in Nicaragua with his wife and two grown sons. The wife and both sons, within a matter of months, died under tragic if not suspicious circumstances. The coffee planter decided to go back to the United States. He was making his way on muleback down from the far interior, but was taken sick and got no farther than the city of Leon, where he died. I had to take charge of all his affairs and property at once. (The Consular Regulations are extremely rigid on this point.) I held ten thousand dollars in my safe and looked after the income from a coffee plantation worth fifty thousand dollars or more, while search was being made for heirs of the dead man in the United States. Inquiries by the State Department brought no results; but, in going through the planter's papers, I found a letter written to him by a brother living in Philadelphia. It was a letter in which the writer stated that two of his daughters would be unable to attend school because he could not buy shoes for them, and begged for a small sum of money. I cabled the news of the planter's death to this brother, then wrote and told him about the estate, directing him to come to Nicaragua immediately with proof of his kinship so that I could turn the property over into his hands. He replied saying that he could not come to Nicaragua; that I could send the ten thousand dollars to him (I suppose he meant by mail), and implying that he had no particular use for a coffee plantation; that if I sent him the cash I could keep the plantation. I do not know what perils this man thought lay in traveling from Philadelphia to the interior of Nicaragua. I promptly informed him that he would have to come in person or through a proper power of attorney. He gave his power of attorney to a lawyer—a Philadelphia lawyer—who came down at once, and to whom I turned over the property with feelings of great relief. In addition to these duties, there was the one of keeping both eyes and ears open for political developments, to interpret them correctly and keep the State Department informed.

I found, too, in Corinto—unlike in Puerto Cabello—that occasionally race prejudice bumped into me. I mean to indicate specifically that I did not bump into it. In other words, I was not concerned with its stupid outbursts or with how it bruised its own head. A man, from South Carolina, came into the Consulate on a matter of business. His gaze at once met a white man (the Vice-Consul) seated at a long table just to the right of the entrance. And, up center of the room, a Negro (myself) seated at a desk, just back of which an American flag draped the wall. This set-up evidently did not accord with his sense of the fitness of things, for he stood perplexed for a moment. But conditioned reflexes forced him over to the Vice-Consul, to whom he made known his case. The Vice-Consul informed him that it was a matter which he had better take up with the Consul, and directed him to me. The man's perplexity gave way to confusion, perhaps to something worse; he appeared incapable of taking the three or four steps over to my desk. I went on with what I had been doing, allowing him all the time he needed to make up his mind whether he would ask for what he wanted or not; to adjust himself to meet the humiliation which confronted him or avoid it by walking out. He finally came over to me, and I dispatched the business he had come to have done. He went out—having slain a bugbear or sustaining a smarting wound to his Nordic pride?—I don't know which. There were several other cases of individuals, caught unawares and psychologically unprepared to meet the situation. I found it best always to let them work out their own recovery from the shock and embarrassment.

In October, news flashed across the country that a revolution to overthrow Zelaya had been started on the east coast at Bluefields, under the head of General Juan B. Estrada. I easily put together all the intimations I had gathered; and the import of the instructions given me at the Department of State became perfectly clear. I had not asked for further instructions from the Department, because I had been in the Service long enough to learn that in certain phases of diplomacy definite instructions are not given, and an officer is valuable only so far as his ability to divine the main objects of his government goes. I knew that our government would be glad to see Zelaya overthrown. He had been an energetic and capable administrator of Nicaraguan affairs, but his hostility to the United States had made him a thorn in the thumb of the Department of State. The American Minister had thrown up his hands and his commission, saying that he could not deal with such an uncivilized ruler as Zelaya. On the surface was his hostile and tricky attitude toward American concessionaires; and deep down at the center was his attitude regarding the Nicaragua Canal route. And now I saw that our government had had foreknowledge that this revolutionary blow against him was to be struck, and that it stood definitely on the side of the revolutionists.

The revolutionists had a great advantage and a great disadvantage in starting their operations in Bluefields. They were relatively close to New Orleans and New York, their main bases of supplies and resources, and were free from any danger of their line of communications being cut or interrupted. On the other hand, they were some two hundred miles from the real Nicaragua; for the capital, the government, the overwhelming portion of the population and wealth of Nicaragua—as in each of the Central American republics—are on the Pacific rather than the Atlantic side. The comparatively wide stretch between the Caribbean and the two great lakes of Nicaragua was a wild region without a railroad or even adequate roads. To march and sustain an army through this jungle and over an intervening range of mountains called for tremendous courage and endurance. The revolutionists did make and fight their way toward the lakes, and almost within striking distance of Managua. But, for the reason that the American interests in control of the great Deitrick concession, which was a big part of the milk in the revolutionary coconut, were still not quite sure where Estrada stood on the question of concessions (the insurgent leader had declared himself opposed to all "monopolistic" concessions; later, upon inquiries from the United States, he had declared that he would protect "lawful American interests"), negotiations in New York for money to finance the revolution came to a standstill, and the revolutionists, who had advanced on promises of forthcoming support, found themselves in the interior without ammunition. General Chamorro, the commander in the field, thus caught, was defeated by the government forces, and compelled to fall back on Bluefields.

The fighting in eastern Nicaragua was farther away from Corinto than the fighting in the World War was from San Francisco. Business and life at the port went on as usual. I made trips up to Leon, the largest city; to Managua, the capital; and to Granada, the third city in importance, in order to get in closer touch with what was taking place. Very little authentic news could be gained; there were rumors aplenty, but they had to be weighed, compared, and sifted. The safest method was to infer what was going on from the action of government and military officials. At any rate, from these trips, I got a view of the cultural life of Nicaragua. Leon was an old, sleepy, typical Spanish-American city, of about forty thousand inhabitants, very proud of its primacy in distinguished families and culture. On these two points, there was a fierce rivalry between the people of Leon and the people of Granada. In fact, this rivalry widened into a breach that constituted the political cleavage in Nicaragua. The struggle for the control of the government was a fight waged between *Los Liberales* (the Liberals) of Leon and *Los Conservadores* (the Conservatives) of Granada. The terms, it hardly needs to be said, had no more of intrinsic significance than the terms "Republicans" and "Democrats" in the United States. Indeed, it seemed to me that it would have been more fitting if these two cities had exchanged their political labels; for Leon was much less modern in its attitude toward politics and everything else than Granada. Thus it was that the political division of the country was also a geographical division, and it was, to say the least, politically uncomfortable for persons of one party to live in the geographical territory of the other.

In the political sense, Managua, lying between these two cities, was the territory to be captured. Managua was a smaller city than Leon, but was more of a metropolis. In the capital there was considerable movement and some approach to the gayeties of life. This aspect was heightened by the presence of the foreign representatives and a fairly large number of foreign residents. A good club and the Grand Hotel Luponi, the latter kept by an Italian, afforded meeting places of a fashionable air. At the brewery there was an outdoor beer garden which was popular in the afternoons and evenings. The National Band gave concerts in the park. In Leon, as I remember, the most popular diversion was a walk on Sunday afternoons out to the cemetery. I used to visit Leon often, because it was near to Corinto. I was an accepted visitor at a number of houses there, and became acquainted with members of Leon's literary group. Among the boasts of Leon was its leadership in literature; and it was not an empty boast; Leon was the birthplace and home of Rubén Darío (1867–1916), the foremost and widest known figure in Latin American letters in his generation, and a world influence on modern literature in the Spanish language.

I could not help but note, as I had done in Venezuela, the strong position of the Germans in business. I saw that in both countries they did not limit their relationships and activities to business; they entered fully into the social life. The unmarried men connected with the German commercial houses were more than likely to marry into the native families. This unified social relationship gave them an inside advantage over the English and Americans, their chief business rivals. I think it was true of all Latin American countries that Englishmen and Americans were unable to enter the social life without reservations and reticences. A solitary individual might approach doing so, but whenever either nationality numbered as many as three, there was inevitably formed a group within a group; wherever the number was sufficient, a separate and distinct group was formed. This seemed to be especially true of the English. Marrying into a native family appeared to be no part of an Englishman's stock of ideas. He might keep a low caste native woman as a mistress, and raise a family by her, but, when it came to marriage, he chose an Englishwoman of any class in preference to the highest-class woman of the country in which he was only sojourning.

When I moved into the new Consulate, I did not hire a cook; I took my meals at Dan's, which was only two doors away. At Dan's there was one long table at which twelve to sixteen men sat (rarely was there a woman), and served themselves from large dishes that were passed round. Dan's table gave me some degree of the opportunity to keep an ear open to local reports and opinions that in Puerto Cabello had been afforded me by the club. There was no social life in Corinto, no places of amusement. This monotony was broken by invitations to dine with the Commander or at the officers' mess aboard our warships. I followed more or less regularly the custom for the Consul to dine with the captains of American merchant vessels in port. Occasionally the officers of one of the ships would give a dance aboard, and invite persons from as far away as Leon. There was but one important social event given in the town of Corinto during my whole stay there. An Italian cruiser put into harbor, and the Comandante of Corinto tendered the officers a banquet. The leading local men were invited, as were the officers of the American warship then in port. I was among those asked to speak. I spoke in Spanish because none of the Italians were familiar with English. I remember two ensigns from our ship endeavoring to hold a conversation across the table with one of the Italian officers, who sat beside me. One of these ensigns was using his

Annapolis Spanish and the other his Annapolis French; meanwhile the Italian sat smiling suavely and nodding his head. A dispute, stimulated by the champagne, arose between the two Americans as to which of them the Italian understood better. The dispute developed into a wager, and I was called on to act as referee and stake-holder, two five-dollar gold pieces being posted in my hands. I rendered the decisions by returning the stakes, because it turned out that the Italian didn't understand either one.

Often for recreation I sat with the Vice-Consul late in the afternoons on the front porch of the Consulate and watched the people go by and the trains from Managua come in. The railroad terminus was the open street directly in front of the Consulate. Across the street from the Consulate was a long, low, frame building which contained the municipal headquarters and the school for boys. Frequently there was excitement at the headquarters caused by the *policia* bringing in arrested persons; and periodically from the school came outbursts of sing-song recitations in concert. I finally got so used to hearing these recitations that I did not hear them, but I never got accustomed to the sight of the teacher patrolling his schoolroom with a big stick in his hand and a long cigar in his mouth.

One afternoon as I sat on the porch, three ragged fellows came along and offered to sell me a pearl. I had not then been long in Corinto and asked Mr. Leonard where these fellows would get a pearl. I learned that pearls were found just off Cardon Island, and that the soldiers of the garrison there dove for them. The leader of the trio unwrapped a soiled bit of newspaper and showed me a pear-shaped pearl about three quarters of an inch in length. I asked him how much he wanted for it, and he named a price equal to about twenty dollars gold. Mr. Leonard, seeing my willingness to make the purchase, shook his head violently and said to me in English, "Don't appear so anxious. Offer him half; he may go off, but he'll come back in five minutes, and you'll save six or seven dollars, at least." I knew that the Vice-Consul had had years of experience in Nicaragua, but I yielded to his advice with great reluctance. The fellows did go off, but they did not come back in five, nor ten, nor fifteen minutes. I grew panicky and sent the office boy to find them and bring them back. He met them returning from a steamer lying at the wharf, where they had sold the pearl to one of the passengers. I was very much vexed, and Mr. Leonard very much mortified. The men passed the Consulate, and I told them, if they would give me first choice, I'd buy whatever catch they made. Carrying out this agreement, I bought nearly a tumblerful of baroque pearls; which, however, cost me only a few dollars. But one day the leader came in with a broad grin on his face and said: "*Ah, señor Consul, tengo una cosa muy bonita.*" On my desk he slowly unwrapped his little package and out rolled two evenly matched, almost perfectly round pearls of beautiful luster. I could scarcely conceal my delight and anxiety. His price was twelve dollars gold, which I paid without hesitation. The pearls later became a pair of ear rings for Grace Nail.

From time to time, I ran across some persons among the people making the trip up and down the Pacific who interested me. On one ship was the daughter of Lillian Russell, Dorothy, whom I had known in New York, a young woman who had her mother's beauty and a great deal of talent. On another was Mrs. Luders, the wife of the composer of *The Prince of Pilsen*, and still on another day, the wife of George Primrose, the famous minstrel, who had sung many of our songs. On one ship I found Peter Clark MacFarlane, at that time a well-known story writer. He was seated on deck in the coolest spot he could find, banging away on his typewriter. He asked me if he could pick up any worthwhile material in Nicaragua. I told him that he might if he took a trip up into the interior. He followed my suggestion. In his going up and back, I made him my guest for a couple of days; it was so good to have a writer to talk with. But he taught me an unforgotten lesson about talking too freely with anyone of that unscrupulous tribe—from which I do not exclude myself. I told Mac-Farlane my choicest South American story about the value and fluctuations of exchange. I told him I had stopped off at Baranquilla, Colombia, and that when I asked a porter at the wharf how much he would charge to take my bags up to the hotel, the fellow had looked at them and answered, "*Tres cientos pesos, señor.*" (Three hundred dollars, sir.) I didn't know what the rate was in Colombia, but I took a chance and proffered the man an American dollar in payment; and he promptly returned to me in the paper currency of the country, seven hundred dollars in change. MacFarlane enjoyed the story immensely; but imagine my chagrin when later I saw in *Collier's Weekly* an article on Nicaragua by him, in which he related the story as having happened to him, and without even so much as intimating that he knew there was an American consul at Corinto.

XXV

IT APPEARED that the insurrection against Zelaya had collapsed. Some weeks dragged along, and I resolved to ask for a leave of absence to visit the United States. I had a decided reason for wanting to get back to New York. I cabled my request to the Department and it was granted by cable. I made immediate preparations to sail; among my preparations was arranging with the owner of the house in which the Consulate was located to have two rooms added to it and the whole house repainted. Aboard the Pacific Mail Steamer, I made a change in my itinerary. In order to see a new country, I decided to cross to the Atlantic side by way of Costa Rica instead of Panama, so I debarked at the port of Punta Arenas. The change from Nicaragua to Costa Rica was comparable to a change from Costa Rica to France. The difference was immediately noticeable. Even in the small port there were cleanliness and order and, in every respect, a higher plane of civilization was obvious. One of the boasts of Costa Rica at that time was that she spent more money on her schools than on her army. The pleasurable anticipations of my trip across the country received a shock, however, when I learned that between Punta Arenas and San José, five thousand feet up in the mountains, there was a gap in the railroad—perhaps it was twenty miles—that had to be covered on horseback. I looked in dismay at my two very big trunks and three or four bags and packages; nevertheless, there was nothing for me to do but go ahead. My train left the next morning and made very good speed over the coastal plain, but soon began puffing laboriously up the grade of the mountain. In the early afternoon we came to a stop at a long steel bridge over a river; and the conductor came through advising the passengers that they should get off and precede the train across the bridge on foot; that those who remained aboard did so at their own risk. It was in the rainy season and the river, which in the dry season was a beautiful little mountain stream, was a swirling, foaming, rushing, roaring flood that every moment threatened the utter destruction of the bridge. Several men passengers were foolhardy enough to stay on the train; I was not of their number. Walking across the quivering bridge, I could not keep my eyes off the ominous torrent rolling below, and I had as little sense of security as I should have had in walking a tightrope over Niagara Falls. We anxiously watched the train come over like a snail, then again got aboard. We reached the terminus of the first section of the railroad and I went with some other passengers to an inn for the night. I learned that to catch the train at the other end of the gap, the start would have to be made before daylight. I hired a horse and engaged a man to transport my baggage. This man used two mules. Of course, they were not the big Missouri breed, common to the United States, but the Spanish breed, small but strong, willing, and sure-footed on mountain trails. My porter showed astonishing skill in strapping the baggage on the backs of the mules, but an old-fashioned, sky-scraper wardrobe trunk that I had seemed to be beyond his ingenuity. When daylight broke, a mountain scene of great beauty was revealed; I should have enjoyed the thrill of the rest of the ride had not my wardrobe trunk kept slipping and the continual delays to readjust it kept me in a state of apprehension about missing my train. The other travelers, with their lighter packs, forged ahead. We got in sight of the station just in time to see the train for San José pulling out; and I was forced to spend twenty-four hours in a little mountain village with nothing I could do but nurse my chagrin. I found the capital of Costa Rica the finest Spanish-American city that I had seen. I was sorry that my sailing schedule allowed me only one full day to see it; but promised myself to come again. I left to catch my steamer down at Limon, taking one of the most amazing railroad rides in the world.

After I reached New York, I went directly to Washington and made in person as full a report as I could on the political situation in Nicaragua. Then I returned to New York on what was to me a more important and delicate mission. I went back to New York to ask Grace Nail to be my wife. There was one consideration that disturbed me in an increasing measure, one that could not be removed or escaped; that consideration was Corinto itself. Before I left Nicaragua I questioned myself whether I had any sort of right to ask a girl who had lived all her life in New York to come and live in Corinto. I justified myself, saying: I had no idea of spending the rest of my days in Corinto; yet, I don't know how much longer I may be held there; and there is only one girl I want to marry; and she is more than three thousand miles away. I tried sincerely to paint Corinto for her in true colors, but, it is probable that, in spite of myself I threw some splashes of light upon its dull, drab background. We became engaged.

I took the opportunity to go out to Chicago and spend a few days with Bob and Rosamond, who were playing *The Red Moon* there. I also made the trip to Jacksonville to see my parents. On my trip up from Jacksonville I stopped in Washington and visited the Department. Things had been happening in Nicaragua—the revolution was in full swing—Zelaya had committed an inexplicable blunder, for so astute a statesman, in sanctioning the execution of Groce and Cannon, two Americans charged with filibustering—the United States had severed diplomatic relations, dismissed the Zelaya representatives in Washington, and declared it would hold those concerned in the killing of the two American citizens personally responsible—Zelaya, recognizing the hopelessness of the situation, had "deposited the power" in Doctor José Madriz, and fled; taking refuge with his friend Porfirio Diaz, President of Mexico.

It was plain to those familiar with the situation that Zelaya's move of self-elimination was made not only to save himself but in the hope of robbing the revolution of its reason for being; that it was made with the intention of reserving the power to his régime, possibly, with the hope of reserving it for himself in a happier day. It was a highly strategic move, but it did not win; the revolution, backed by the resources and power of the United States, continued; not against Zelaya but against "Zelayaism." Doctor Madriz was a fine man, a scholarly man, an honest man; at some other period he might have made a good president for Nicaragua; but he did not possess the dominating strength to hold the reins that had just been held by Zelaya's hands.

It was necessary for me to get back to my post as quickly as was convenient. I induced the Department to furnish a reception room at the Consulate, and I purchased in New York furniture, rugs, and curtains to fit out the large room I had been using as a bedroom. At the same time, I bought on my own account bedroom furniture and household utensils. Grace Nail and I were married, and with the good wishes of many friends sailed for Corinto. The trip down was now an old experience for me, but it became fresh and new, seen through Grace's eyes. It was her first ocean voyage, but she proved a first-rate sailor. We had some stormy weather, but she never tired of standing where she could watch the big waves break over the prow of the ship. Kingston, Jamaica, with its black custom house officials, black soldiers, black policemen, black street car conductors, black clerks in the big shops, black girls in the telegraph office and at the news-stand of the fashionable Myrtle Bank Hotel, struck her as white civilization turned topsy-turvy. She was fascinated with old Panama; and in the flying fish and phosphorescent waters of the Pacific she took almost childish delight. But I was anxious about her first view of Corinto, the place that was to be home. On the morning that our steamer slipped into the harbor, I wondered that I had not before noticed how miserable an appearance Corinto could present. I plainly saw that Grace was dazed with disappointment; and that, as we made our way over the long, hot wharf, through the unlovely streets to the Consulate, her disappointment increased. Mr. Leonard had the office spick and span. The floor had been scrubbed until the boards shone white; there were flowers on my desk and flowers in the bedroom; but the carpenters had not quite finished the addition they were building, and the new part of the house was still littered with tools and lumber and sawdust and shavings. I was smitten with an agonizing sympathy for my young wife. But she quickly recovered herself and immediately made a display of the courage that she showed under trying conditions for the next two years. Within a few days, the carpenters cleared out, and we excitedly unpacked and set up our new furniture. Into the living room went the cool, green, grass-woven furniture, and rugs of the same material; into the larger new room, opening off the living room, went the new bedroom furniture; and into the smaller went the bedroom furniture I had been using. Into the living room went also what proved to be the greatest pleasure-giving piece of all, a fine victrola with a large supply of records, a wedding present from Bob Cole. The curtains were hung and some water colors and prints placed on the walls. With the portières of the living room and front bedroom undrawn there was a vista straight through the four rooms that faced on the street. Set up in this manner, the Consulate gained the reputation of being the most charming house in Nicaragua.

Grace took great pride in her house, and with the help of two girls kept it immaculate—"immaculate" is a word with great religious but little domestic significance in Latin America. She started in earnest to learn Spanish, and in a month or so was able to give all the directions to her two maids. I was her teacher, but, as I frequently said to her, she made remarkable progress because she had to talk Spanish with her domestic help, and because with them she was not held back by the fear of making mistakes. Her absorption in acquiring the language went far toward making many of the discomforts of life in Corinto less apparent. She enjoyed the trips we made to Leon and

Managua, and meeting people there; to be able to talk with them better on each succeeding visit became an interesting game. Her first big excitement came, however, one night when we were sitting quietly in our living room reading through a batch of New York newspapers that had just come down. Suddenly, the lamp on the table began to shiver and the pictures on the walls to sway. I had learned the meaning of these signals, and said to Grace as quietly as possible, "Get out into the street. Get out into the street." We ran out of the house and found the streets filled with people. The ground was heaving under our feet and the birds and fowls, shaken out of the trees, were flying around and making weird noises. In cataloguing for Grace the things she might expect in Nicaragua, I had failed to include the item of earthquakes; and my statement that it was because of their very frequency that they were not regarded with great concern did not, for the time, wholly reassure her. In truth, the question, "Did you feel the earthquake last night?" was asked with scarcely any greater agitation than, "Did you hear the rain?"

But at Corinto itself there was an occasional social flurry. Because of the impending crisis of the revolution, there were, at times, two and even three United States naval vessels in port, and my wife and I were frequently invited aboard for luncheon or dinner. And there came down to spend a season at the shore and take the baths, Mrs. Madriz, the wife of the President, and a party of ladies from the capital. In total disregard of the political factors at work, a couple of dances were given aboard ship in honor of the President's wife. Certainly we could not be merely recipients of hospitality. The Consul was a standing host for the officers of the warships; whenever they called, they met a hospitable welcome. This was pleasant, officially and socially, but financially it was quite a burden. It was a case of one hundred to one; all the officers entertained the Consul, and the consul entertained all the officers. Champagne and other French wines were comparatively cheap, but the price of American whisky was exorbitant. Champagne was an indispensable element in diplomatic and official intercourse with the Latin Americans, but U. S. Americans preferred to drink to each other's health in something less effervescent.

A good many of the naval officers seemed to enjoy the Consulate. Every once in a while, a group of them would say, "Consul, wouldn't it be possible for us to have a little game of poker ashore tonight?"

And the Consul would answer, "Why, certainly." I remember vividly the first of these parties. Five officers came ashore to play. I provided the sandwiches and the beverages. When we sat down one of them asked, "Well, what shall we make it?" And another answered, "Let's make it ten dollars a stack." I felt a cold moisture on my brow. I was no poker player; my highest flying had been a penny-ante game with a ten-cent limit; and here, as the host, with no way of escape, I faced the possibility of losing a half month's pay as well as the cost of the refreshments. This thought might not have been so appalling in former days, but now with a wife to take care of, it was a serious matter. I must have had extraordinary luck, or the officers were no better players than I, for I came out just about even, counting the refreshments. In self-defense, I showed the naval men after that how much more fun there was in playing for Nicaraguan instead of American money—enjoying the thrill of high bets without the danger of large losses, for often a pot ran up to several thousand "dollars."

For a long while back, American soldiers of fortune have played parts in Central American history. In the time of which I am writing, the two most famous were "General" Lee Christmas and "General" H. O. Jeffries. I never saw "General" Christmas, but one day in the latter part of March 1910, "General" Jeffries landed at Corinto and handed me a letter of introduction written by the American consul at Panama. I was curious about this man because he had been one of the chief factors in the revolution that separated Panama from Colombia and made the Panama Canal possible. He had also been the principal actor in a tragedy of private life that had shaken Panama City. In appearance he was disappointing. There might have been a time when, as an adventurer staking his life against long odds for big gains, he had looked the part of the gaunt, picturesque, rakish soldier of fortune; if so, ease and prosperity had changed all that. He was now inclined to portliness, was well fed and well dressed, almost sleek—the image of a successful American businessman. But under this commonplace surface was the "General" Jeffries of other days—venturesome and daredevilish, taking the hazards of life as a joke. During a whole evening he was the center of a small group that he kept hanging on the tales of his exploits. He told about his revolutionary activities, and he told how he had gone into the office of a Panama editor to avenge a woman's honor. One of the charms of his recital was that he took none of these episodes over-seriously. He related how once, at the head of a band of insurgents, he was surprised by a superior force, and gave commands for an orderly retreat back down the railroad track; how the speed of the retreat increased under the increasing pressure and fire of his pursuers, until, finally, "we were going down that railroad track so fast that the telegraph poles looked like teeth in a fine-toothed comb." "General" Jeffries told a great many things, but he did not tell just what his mission to Nicaragua was. I judged that it was not simply a matter of pleasure.

The revolution against "Zelayaism" continued. On December 18, 1909, the commander of the U.S.S. *Des Moines* had declared Bluefields a neutral zone and thereby, to the great advantage of the Conservatives, prevented Zelaya forces from attacking revolutionary forces in that territory. On December 23, the revolutionists had defeated Zelaya's troops at Rama; and on the next day Zelaya "deposited the power" in José Madriz and fled to Corinto, where he boarded a Mexican gunboat and took refuge in Mexico. Later, he went to Paris. But the United States refused to recognize Madriz, and the revolution continued. President Madriz, perplexed and harassed, did all he could to work out an adjustment and maintain the power of his party. He canceled the government's procedure initiated by Zelaya to void the Deitrick concession; but that action did not avail, and the United States continued to withhold recognition. In August of 1910 he fled to Corinto and with a large party of followers boarded a Pacific Mail steamer and sailed away. The flight of Zelaya and of Madriz constituted the only close-ups that Corinto got of the revolution.

General Juan B. Estrada, the political head of the revolutionary party, and provisional President, was later chosen President—his official term of office beginning December 31, 1910—and was recognized by the United States. Estrada proceeded to the capital over land from the east coast, but Adolfo Diaz, who was later chosen Vice-President, came by way of the Panama Canal and Corinto. In the group that accompanied him was Thomas W. Moffat, the American Consul at Bluefields. I had known Mr. Moffat in Venezuela; he was consul at La Guaira while I was at Puerto Cabello; we had both been transferred to Nicaragua at the same time and with the same instructions. I entertained Señor Diaz and Mr. Moffat at the Consulate until they left for Managua. Don Adolfo was a quiet-mannered man, rather small of stature and quite dapper. He spoke English very well, but had little to say. I was to know him better and to learn that, despite his slight figure and gentle demeanor, he was a man of iron nerve.

Estrada, formerly a Liberal, now a Conservative (he was in command of the Bluefield District, under Zelaya, when he turned revolutionist), a man of no exceptional force or qualifications, was President, but the chief factors in the future of Nicaragua were Don Adolfo Diaz, General Emiliano Chamorro, and General Luis Mena. Of this trio, Diaz was the intellectual, the student, the diplomat. General Chamorro, a Granada aristocrat, proud of his almost pure Spanish ancestry, was a man of courage and much military resourcefulness. The strong man of the trio was General Mena, a giant of a man, a man of great physical magnetism, showing a large proportion of Indian blood and, apparently, a tinge of Negro, rough, audacious, fearless, and the idol of his soldiers. Each of the three was ambitious; and, unfortunately for Nicaragua, the ambition of each had the presidency as its goal. Suspicion and mistrust developed into open hostility first between President Estrada and General Mena, Minister of War. Estrada tried the iron hand and threw Mena into prison. The latter's soldiers, hearing that the life of their hero was in danger, marched from all sides, several thousand strong on Managua. Estrada became panic-stricken. At three or four o'clock in the morning of May 12, I was wakened by the whistling and rumbling of a train. I did not understand it, for no regular trains ran at night in Nicaragua. A moment later, there was a loud knocking at my door. When I opened it, a lone, terror-haunted man stood there. He was President Estrada. He asked for asylum. On the first ship leaving Corinto, after only four months in office, he fled in fear of his life. Adolfo Diaz succeeded to the presidency amidst shouts of "Viva Diaz!"

In the midsummer I received sad news from New York. Bob and Rosamond had closed the season in the spring with *The Red Moon.* They had come to the conclusion that they could neither make money nor break even playing the popular-price theaters, the only ones in which they could get bookings, and determined to go back into vaudeville. They went back at a salary of $750.00 a week, and made their reappearance on the vaudeville stage at Keith's Fifth Avenue Theatre. On the last night of their engagement there, Bob was stricken with a mental breakdown. His condition continued to grow worse for several weeks. Then his mother took him to a little resort in the Catskills, where, it was hoped, the quiet and rest would do him good. The first few days seemed to benefit him a great deal. He enjoyed going for a swim in a nearby lake; he was an excellent swimmer. He and his mother were sitting on the porch of the house. A lady arrived, passed them by, and entered. In the hallway she remarked to someone, loudly enough to be overheard, "Isn't that Bob Cole? Poor fellow. Too bad, isn't it?" Bob got up and said to his mother that he was going to take his swim. She did not see him again until his body was dragged from the bottom of the lake.

I was shocked and disturbed beyond measure. I had lost one of the closest friends of my lifetime, a friend whom I loved not only for his unchanging fidelity, but whom I admired for his unquestionable genius. I thought back over the twelve years of our relations; I again lived through experiences that we had suffered or enjoyed together; I tried to reckon the degree of his influence on the course my life had taken; and I felt only deep contentment in the fact that we had been friends and co-workers. Bob Cole's death was a vital loss to the Negro stage.

The year was coming to a close. My wife had been more than twenty months in Corinto. She had not been sick a day, but I was anxious for her to have a change, for I knew that no woman from a northern climate ought to stay longer than two years at a time in the tropics. There was some political unrest; General Mena, through control of the Assembly, had in October had himself elected President for four years, his term of office to begin in 1913. Our government looked on this action with grave concern. Mena had been one of the strongest forces in making the revolution successful, but formerly he had been a stanch supporter of Zelaya. Pressure was brought to have him renounce the election; our representative at Managua pointed out that the Assembly under the new Constitution had not the right to elect the President. Mena acquiesced but sulked in his tent. He remained, however, in control of the army.

In the lull, I requested a leave of absence. It was granted, and Grace and I sailed for a visit to the United States. Remembering my promise to myself to visit San José again, and wanting Grace to see Costa Rica, I arranged our passage that way. Certainly, I should not have done this had I not known that the Costa Rica railroad was now complete from Punta Arenas to San José. I did not dream that, even so, Grace would be in for trunk trouble. The harbor of Punta Arenas is an open road-stead, and passengers going ashore must be transferred into small boats. On the day that we arrived a very heavy swell was running in, and that made getting off the ship into a small boat an uncomfortable if not risky feat. All of the passengers got ashore without mishap, but when the trunks were being swung over the side, one slipped out of the sling and fell into the water. It proved to be one of Grace's, the one in which she had packed the light pretty things she expected to wear in San José and on the Atlantic trip during the warm days. The news reached us at the hotel, when we were getting ready for dinner. Grace was heartbroken. We got the trunk and opened it; everything in it was water-soaked. The hotel proprietor secured us first-aid in the shape of a Chinese laundryman, who promised to have everything "back fine" in time for us to catch our train in the morning. He got the things back on time, but Grace declared that their present was worse than their former state. She and the laundryman had a stiff row. The pidgin Spanish of the Chinese amused me, but the scope, color, warmth, and volubility of Grace's Spanish completely astounded me. Parts of her vocabulary did not come out of any textbook she had studied.

The elegance of the hotel in San José, its air of urbanity, its fault-less menu and service, its well-dressed, well-mannered patrons, were our first taste of metropolitan life in nearly two years; and it affected Grace like wine. I had achieved the ability to make the best of almost any conditions, but I could not help catching some of her intoxication. When we went to our room to change, we heard the Band of the Republic, a band of nearly a hundred pieces, marching through the street on its way to the park for the *retreta* that evening. I became as excited as Grace, and we hustled into our clothes like eager children. The band was an excellent one, but good bands may be heard in many places; on the other hand, in no place in the world, so far as I know, can such rapturously beautiful women be seen as in San José, Costa Rica. The park was crowded; all San José seemed to be out. The people did not sit down and listen to the music, but, in the Spanish-American custom, the men and youths promenaded round and round the park on the outer side of the walk, while on the inner side, the *señoritas*, accompanied by the older women of their families, or by their *dueñas*, promenaded in the opposite direction. The chatter made the music sound far away; very red lips constantly disclosed very white teeth, and very dark eyes constantly flashed all the signals of coquetry and love. Grace's comment was that the girls were too beautiful to seem real. She said that the scene was like a multiplied Ziegfeld chorus out of doors. And, although the prevailing type was brunette instead of blond, that was an apt comparison.

We spent a week in San José seeing the shops and places of interest. We went to the National Theater, which cost something like a million dollars and is probably one of the finest theater buildings on the western continent. One night while walking through a lesser street, we heard a strange but familiar sound. It was nothing other than the singing of a Methodist hymn, led by a lusty voice. We drew alongside the house whence the singing came and found that it was an improvised church. The preacher was just about to begin his sermon, and the preacher was a jet-black Negro. The congregation was composed of a few Negroes and overwhelmingly of Costa Ricans. That constituted the most curious sight we saw in Catholic San José.

We spent a while in New York, then went to Jacksonville; Rosamond joined us there. The Jacksonville people made quite a to-do over the three of us, and we stayed through two lively and happy weeks. On the way back to New York, Grace and I stopped in Washington, where I had several conferences with members of the Department. I received assurance that I should soon be transferred to a pleasanter post; perhaps to a post in France. The intimations were that my transfer would be made in three or four months; and Grace and I decided that the best plan would be for her to remain for that short time with her parents in New York, while I went back and closed up affairs. So, when I sailed for Corinto, I sailed alone.

XXVI

IT WAS now 1912. I arrived back in Corinto near the end of March. The town was just as I had left it; my house was very different. But the expectation of an early transfer kept me in high spirits. A month passed; two months passed. In the latter part of June I received a cablegram. I held it in my hands for a moment, experimenting with the powers of second sight. Was it France? If not, where? I opened the message and found that it was from my brother, telling me that our father was dead. This was the closest that death had yet struck at me. The day's work was over; it was night; I stood leaning against the door-post with the thin slip of paper in my hand, weeping quietly. Nothing else could have served me so well at that moment as the opportunity to weep quietly and alone. I went to bed with memories of my days of childhood unreeling in my mind.

The third month passed, and the fourth month was passing; it was surely now but a matter of days before I should receive my transfer. On July 29 word reached me of a ministerial crisis in Managua. President Diaz had dismissed General Mena from the Ministry of War. Mena had refused to hand over his authority and had withdrawn the armed forces and taken up positions around the capital. I immediately cabled this news to the Department of State and telegraphed it to Commander Terhune of the U.S.S. *Annapolis*, who, a few days before, had sailed down to San Juan del Sur, the cable station. On the morning of August 1, the *Annapolis* was back at Corinto. General Mena, in the meantime, was fortifying the positions that commanded Managua, and the situation was unquestionably serious.

President Diaz did not follow the example of his predecessor and flee; instead, he called upon the United States to maintain him in the position in which it had placed him. On August 3, Commander Terhune, under orders, landed with one hundred bluejackets and five officers from the *Annapolis*, and with arms and ammunition proceeded to Managua to act as a Legation guard. The *Annapolis* remained at her anchorage with twenty-odd bluejackets left aboard under the command of a young lieutenant named Lewis. One other American ship, the collier *Justin*, was in port. On the sixth, the *Justin* received orders from Washington to proceed to Panama for a force of marines. On the eleventh the American minister called me on the telephone and informed me that General Mena had begun bombarding Managua.

The bombardment of the capital continued. Refugees began pouring into Corinto. The American members of the Mixed Claim Commission and other Americans from Managua made the Consulate their headquarters. Many refugees coming down reported that the rebel fire was centered on the Legation. One significant rumor was that the old Zelaya followers in the district of Leon would rise and array themselves under the Mena standard. On the fourteenth the *Justin* returned to Corinto bringing three hundred and fifty-six marines under the command of Major Smedley D. Butler. This entire force entrained for Managua to reinforce the Legation guard.

On the sixteenth, Dr. Toribio Tijerino, Delegate of the President in the Departments of Leon, Chinandega, and the Segovias, arrived in Corinto. (The President had delegated his authority in the areas which he could not control from the capital.) Dr. Tijerino reported that the situation in Leon was critical; that General Mena had succeeded in supplying arms and ammunition to los Liberales in that stronghold of Zelayaism, and that an uprising in that city was imminent. After making this report, Dr. Tijerino returned to Chinandega, a fair-sized city fifteen miles up the railroad from Corinto. I at once called the Legation on the telephone to give the Minister this information, which was of particularly vital importance because of Leon's position, halfway between Managua and the port of Corinto. The Minister was inclined to pooh-pooh the report. The bombardment had subsided, and he felt that the situation was well in hand. Quite naturally, with a Legation guard of nearly five hundred American marines and sailors, he had a sense of security. Nevertheless, I continued and told him that I had heard that a large quantity of arms and ammunition had been smuggled into Leon in wagons, under cover of being farm produce. While I was talking with the Minister, the telephone wire snapped. A few minutes later I learned that the telegraph wires had been cut. Corinto had no direct communication with Managua by telephone, telegraph, or rail for the next two weeks.

Two days later, Dr. Tijerino came down again to Corinto, bringing with him three hundred government troops as far as Paso Caballos. (Paso Caballos was the narrow inlet and wide salt marsh, three or four miles above the town, that separated Corinto from the mainland and made it actually an island. The railroad ran over a long bridge across the pass.) Dr. Tijerino reported that there had been an uprising in Leon and the insurrectionists had taken the city with great slaughter; that they were on their victorious way to the port; and that they were now approaching Chinandega and would soon get to Corinto. It was a day or two before we got full news about the capture of Leon. There had not been a battle but a massacre. The insurgents had fallen on the government garrison, numbering five or six hundred, and killed them to a man. No quarter was allowed. Two American soldiers of fortune, Dodd and Phillips, were fighting with the government forces; wounded, they were taken to the hospital; but the rebels attacked the hospital, killing every wounded soldier in it, including the two Americans. Thus Managua was cut off from Corinto, and the American forces forming the Legation guard from their base.

Dr. Tijerino's report created great excitement. The Comandante addressed a communication to me stating that he did not have a sufficient force at his command to maintain peace and order and protect lives and property at the port, and requested that the American forces assume that responsibility. I conferred with Lieutenant Lewis and a six-pounder was taken off the ship, mounted on a flat car, manned, and placed at the juncture of the railroad and the main street. A machine gun was mounted at the corner of the custom house. A patrol consisting of fourteen bluejackets from the *Annapolis* was detailed for duty at night. Several times each night, for ten nights, I made the rounds of this patrol with the ensign in command. During that period, I did not take off my clothes for the purpose of going to bed. American and foreign women and children I had placed each night aboard the *Annapolis* and *Justin*. I kept the Consulate open all night as headquarters for the American landing force. All the Americans and most of the foreigners made it their headquarters. There were thirty to forty men there every night during the "siege." The stewards of the *Annapolis* kept a caldron of coffee for the patrol. I drank, I judge, a couple of quarts a night. Dr. Tijerino resented the establishment of the American patrol. His plan was to bring his troops in and himself take military control of the port. The Comandante stood by his request to the American Consul. Thereupon, the General (he was a general as well as a doctor) threatened to put the Comandante and all his staff in prison on Cardon Island. I advised Dr. Tijerino that the American force, small as it was, was better able to hold the port without bloodshed than any force he could bring in. The next day he took his soldiers and went back to Chinandega. I was glad to see him go. For the time, the responsibility for Corinto rested on me, and I was determined that there should be no bloodshed there if I could prevent it. The horror of what had happened in Leon made my determination stronger.

But I was not yet rid of Tijerino. The next day he was back in Corinto, and sent a note through me to the commanding officer of the *Annapolis* requesting that he be furnished with a hundred rifles and ammunition and provisions from the ship. He became very indignant when he was informed that it was not possible to grant his request. On the following morning, he sent me a note requesting that I call a conference of all the consuls in Corinto, to be held at the Comandancia at three o'clock, to consider the best means of maintaining peace and order at the port. I replied to him that I should be glad to request the consuls to meet at the American Consulate at the hour indicated. I did that, and informed the General. He sent back word that he would not attend the conference but would transmit a note in which he would state his intention of sending the Comandante with all his force, including the police force, to the front, and installing himself as the chief local authority at the port; leaving the maintenance of peace and order and the protection of lives and foreign interests to the American forces. The hour for the meeting arrived and with it the consular representatives at Corinto of England, France, and Italy. Every American in Corinto was present. Dr. Tijerino had not put in his appearance; so I requested Lieutenant Lewis to go across the street, where the General had his headquarters, and urge him to come over to the meeting, since there was neither time nor necessity for diplomatic correspondence. A half-dozen bluejackets were on guard in front of the Consulate. The Lieutenant took them with him and made his way through the gathering crowd across to Dr. Tijerino's office. The General refused to come over, whereupon Lieutenant Lewis became out of patience, placed him under arrest, marched him between the bluejackets across the street, and delivered him to me in the Consulate. Of course, the Lieutenant had been far more urgent than I had intended or anticipated.

The news spread like wildfire. Instantly, it seemed, the street in front of the Consulate was jammed with a surging crowd. The six American bluejackets with an ensign stood lined across the entrance of the Consulate with fixed bayonets. Every American present realized that the moment was charged with every possibility of danger; for the crowd continued to press forward. General Tijerino approached me, and with a dramatic gesture unbuckled his sword, took his revolver from its holster, laid both weapons on my desk and said, "Sir, I am your prisoner." Then immediately he launched into an eloquent and incendiary speech, in a voice loud enough to reach the already excited crowd outside. He began by charging me with having placed under arrest the President of Nicaragua; the which was virtually true. He declared that he would protest to the Central American governments and to the world. (He did send protests to the Presidents of Guatemala, Salvador, and Honduras, but none of those rulers took any action, so far as I ever learned.) He called on patriotic Nicaraguans to resent the indignity to which he had been subjected. There were *vivas* from the crowd. At the beginning of the General's speech, I had hastily called Lieutenant Lewis and asked him to take personal charge of the bluejackets and to use every means to avoid anything like a clash. I then cut the General's speech off by attempting to make as dramatic a gesture as he had made on his entrance. I gave him back his revolver and with my own hands rebuckled his sword upon him; at the same time declaring that he was in no sense a prisoner; that no indignity was intended to him personally or in his capacity of Delegate of the President; that the American officer had only been over-zealous in the desire that the conference have the benefit of the General's wisdom and judgment in the vital matters to be discussed. The gesture ended the speech, but I am sure it did not fool the General; he was too intelligent a man for that. And the gesture also ended the conference. The consular representatives went away; Lieutenant Lewis personally conducted the General back to his headquarters, and the crowd dispersed.

General Tijerino spent all of the next day in his office. He was busy getting his protests out to the world. On the following day, he sent me another request. This time it was that he be furnished with a train in order that he might go back with his troops for the defense of Chinandega. Now this was a serious request. When the uprising in Leon cut the railroad line in the middle, there was a train standing in Corinto that would make the trip the next morning to Managua and on to Granada. Of course, it did not start. That train was vital to Corinto; more vital than the American ships and guns; for every day it went up as far as Chinandega and brought back vegetables, chickens, eggs and milk, and a huge tank on a flat car filled with water. Nothing to eat was grown on the island that was Corinto; and every hole dug in the ground gave only brackish water. That train was Corinto's guaranty against a food and water famine.

I debated the matter, and talked with Lieutenant Lewis and Mr. Leonard about it. Two reasons inclined me to grant the General's request; I was anxious to make amends as far as I possibly could for the affront he had received, and I was equally anxious to embrace any plan by which I should never again lay eyes on Tijerino. I let him have the train on his solemn and many-times repeated oath that he would send it back immediately. I later called in the engineer in charge of the train and impressed on him the vital necessity of bringing it back to Corinto. The engineer, I saw, understood the seriousness of the matter. He was a bright man, much too bright to be running a train in Nicaragua; he should have had Tijerino's job. The General loaded his troops on. They filled the four coaches inside, outside and on top. They left Corinto with many *vivas*. The General did not keep his word. When he reached Chinandega, he refused to let the train come back. The engineer was powerless; but, while he waited, a train pulled in from the direction of Leon, and the locomotive stood panting with the cowcatcher pointed toward Corinto. Then my engineer and his fireman conceived and carried out a plot in which they risked their lives. They watched and saw that everybody, including the crew, got off the train that had just arrived; then they hopped aboard the locomotive, opened the throttle, and brought the train down to Corinto. Had it been in my power, I should have awarded the engineer some kind of a cross. As it was, we were better off; the kidnaped train had five coaches and a newer and bigger locomotive.

The entire plan, after all, worked out; for I never again laid eyes on Tijerino. Two days after he left Corinto, the rebel forces came down from Leon and captured Chinandega. In the fight, Tijerino's son, who was his adjutant, was killed; and he himself lost an eye, was captured and made a prisoner. With the fall of Chinandega, rumors came down to Corinto that the rebels would next attack and capture the port. The port and custom house constitute the grand prize in every Latin-American revolution. On receipt of the news from Chinandega, we transferred the six-pounder to Paso Caballos, where it would command the railroad, and placed Captain Meriwether of the collier *Justin* and a guard of five in charge. News also leaked down to us that Captain

Terhune had attempted to come from Managua to Corinto with a force of his bluejackets, and had been met at Leon by the rebel army, forced to detrain and march back to the capital. Following the outbreak of the insurrection, the Department cabled that the U.S.S. *Denver* had been ordered to Corinto; more than sufficient time had passed for her to make the trip, and we were much puzzled as to where the *Denver* could be.

Late in the afternoon, two days after the capture of Chinandega, Captain Meriwether telephoned me from Paso Caballos that a locomotive carrying a flag of truce had approached the other end of the bridge and was waiting for a signal to cross the pass. He asked what he should do. I asked him how much of a train the locomotive had. He answered that he could not tell, as only the engine could be seen from the Corinto side, but that he would find out. He did, and telephoned down that there was only one coach. I told' him to let them cross. The train brought a commission of seven or eight civilians, representing the rebel forces at Chinandega, who stated to Captain Meriwether that they had come to confer with the Comandante of Corinto. Captain Meriwether telephoned to ask if he should allow them to come down into town. I answered, yes, but not without having hesitated. When the train came down, I met the commission and invited them to hold the conference in the Consulate. They thanked me politely, and politely informed me that, since their business was not with the American officials but with the local Nicaraguan authorities, and concerned only Nicaragua, they would prefer to meet in the Comandancia. These interchanges were taking place in the middle of the street; the commission would not enter the Consulate even for a preliminary conference. The Comandante, almost crouching behind me, begged piteously that I prevent the conference from being held in the Comandancia; with or without good reason, he was in fear for his life. I pressed my invitation, and the commission firmly declined. They pointed out to me that the matter in hand was purely internal, one in which the American government had no concern or authority. The commission was composed of educated men; the spokesman was a lawyer and a graduate of the University of Pennsylvania; they had come down armed with a great array of books on international law; however, without these books they knew, probably, ten times as much international law as I did; and aside from their overlooking the existing facts, they were in every respect right. I reminded them that it was upon my word that they had been allowed to come down into Corinto to confer. They bowed, and countered by saying that they could have made the entry by force had they so decided.

I realized that, in permitting the commission to come down into the town, I had committed a tactical blunder. I knew that the insurrection, begun by Mena, had in Leon and the districts to the west developed into an uprising of the old Zelaya element; that it required only a spark to convert Corinto into an exploded powder magazine. The crowd in the street had grown to a dense throng that kept pressing in. The firm stand taken by the commission brought forth loud cries of "*Viva la revolución! Viva la república! Viva Zelaya! Abajo los americanos!*" I had before me a problem in extrication.

I stood firmly against the commission, on such grounds as I had; and we finally reached the compromise that the conference would be held on neutral territory. We agreed upon the house of the Italian Vice-Consul. It was nearly dark. I said to the trembling Comandante that there would be no danger in going into the conference as arranged; that he should not, however, take any definite step before he had apprised me of the demands made by the commission.

We waited anxiously. The Consulate was crowded. Every American man and many of the foreign men in Corinto were there. It was nearly ten o'clock when a messenger came from the conference bringing a note for me from the Comandante. The note stated that the commission had served an ultimatum on him to the effect: If the port is not turned over within six hours, beginning from midnight, General Vaca, of the revolutionary army, will come down with a force of three thousand men and take it. From the Americans who crowded the Consulate came the many-times repeated expression, "Where in the hell is the *Denver?*"

I had to think fast, if my thinking was to serve my purpose. I was fundamentally aware that the whole mess was, strictly, Nicaragua's business; that it would be better if we were entirely out of it, or better still if we had never gotten into it. But I was also aware of the fact that we were in it. The plan I intended to stick to was to do my utmost to prevent bloodshed and looting, perhaps massacre, at Corinto and to hold the port open, at least, as long as the American forces were cut off in the interior. However, I was not fully aware of another element that had entered—the fascination of the game I had been called on to play. I formed a little inner council consisting of Lieutenant Lewis, Captain Meriwether, Mr. Leonard, and Judge Shoenrich and Judge Thompson, members of the Mixed Claim Commission, who had fled from Managua and were among the refugees at the Consulate. We decided upon a reply that the Comandante should make to the commission, and we drafted it at once. The reply stated that the Comandante would, in order to avoid violence and bloodshed, be willing to turn the port over to the revolutionists; but having already, for the purpose of preserving peace and order, invoked the aid of the American forces present, he did not feel that he could comply with the demands of the commission, unless the American Consul was brought into the conference.

An hour later, we received a message that the commission desired to confer with the Comandante and the American Consul at the Consulate. At this point, Lieutenant Lewis, a very zealous young man, as we have seen, but not an exceptionally brilliant one, devised a bit of strategy that gave all of us a laugh for many a day thereafter. Indeed, it was a stroke that entirely redeemed him from mediocrity in our eyes. Requested to escort the commission to the Consulate, he suggested that he station the whole of his patrol of fourteen blue-jackets at intervals between the Consulate and the place where the conference was meeting. The night was dark; there were no street lamps in Corinto, and the Lieutenant and an ensign took their lanterns and started out to station the patrol and fetch the commission. A few steps from the door of the Italian Vice-Consul, the commissioners discerned by the light of the lanterns the glimmer of a white uniform and the glint of a rifle, and heard a sharp challenge, "Halt! Who goes there?" Lieutenant Lewis approached the sentry, gave the satisfactory information, and received the order to "Pass on." Fourteen times within the distance of four blocks the party was thus challenged; and, it is probable that, by the time the commissioners reached the Consulate, Lieutenant Lewis's plan to give them a magnified idea of the American force in Corinto had worked.

I welcomed the commission and listened to its demand for the immediate surrender of the port. I told them that I felt they had forestalled any awkward complications by asking the American Consul into the conference; that, however, by their own declarations on arriving in Corinto, they had neither instructions nor authority to deal with the American officials; that, therefore, I did not see how there could be any guarantee of the terms we might arrive at in the present conference; that before I could take any steps it would be necessary for them to secure from the military leader of the revolution instructions and authority for them to deal with the American Consul. Earlier in the evening, I had ordered Dan to prepare a bountiful roast beef supper, with no limits on the supply of beverages. Our impasse was forgotten in the feast that followed. Party lines, political antagonisms, individual and national aspirations were all melted down into one strong current of fellowship and brotherhood. Liberales and Conservadores actually shed tears on one another's shoulders at the woes of their common country. The American consul was a "prince," and *los americanos* were "all right." At about two o'clock in the morning we succeeded, not without physical difficulties, in loading the commissioners on their train and starting them back to Chinandega.

But the commissioners were sober the next day; and in the afternoon, Captain Meriwether telephoned that they were again at the pass under a flag of truce. We had decided the night before that all future conferences would be held at Paso Caballos. I asked Captain Meriwether to inform the commission that I should be up at Paso Caballos as soon as I could and confer with them. The Captain told me that they were much disappointed at not being allowed to come down into the town. I took my time about getting up to the pass; for I realized that time was the most important factor in the game I was playing. I went up to Paso Caballos weighing in my mind the statement I intended to make, and wondering what the result of it would be. I stood on a little knoll under a tree; the commission was in front of me; at my side stood the ensign whom Lieutenant Lewis had sent to accompany me to the conference; around me were grouped the men in charge of our six-pounder. When I began to speak I realized suddenly that I was very tired. Ten nights out of bed, running on black coffee, was telling on me. The men who had been keeping the vigil with the six-pounder were haggard. The commissioners appeared obnoxiously fresh and alert. The scene took on an air of unreality, the air of opéra bouffe, and I was merely playing a part, a rather ridiculous part. I did not state the points succinctly that I had come to lay down. I made an address to the commissioners, bringing the points in as I went along: Any transfer of the port to the revolutionists must be made in an orderly manner—No armed force, except the necessary police force, must be installed in Corinto—Whatever authority and government was set up would have to be purely civilian. When I had finished talking, the commissioners agreed to the terms. Their decision instantly brought back the realities. I was again face to face with the impending actualities of the situation. I ventured one more stroke to gain time: I required of the commissioners that they get from General Vaca a written communication addressed to me and over his own signature, stating that he held himself bound by the terms, before any of their conditions could be entered upon. The commissioners willingly promised to do this and to return with the required document the next day. They boarded their train and returned to Chinandega. The ensign who accompanied me to Paso Caballos, a young Southerner, was the only officer on the *Annapolis* with whom my relations were not fully cordial—he himself had pointedly indicated that he did not wish them so. After the parley he came up to me and wrung my hand. He appeared to be proud that we were both Americans. But things around me had already slipped back into the realm of unrealities, and his gesture and words seemed merely parts in a play.

On the next morning Captain Terhune with a force of one hundred marines and bluejackets from the Legation guard was in Corinto, having made his way down from Managua. Before the morning passed the U.S.S. *Denver* arrived with five hundred marines. When the commissioners from the revolution came back in the afternoon, I had them brought down into the town, and the conference was held at the Consulate between them and Captain Terhune of the *Annapolis*, Captain Washington of the *Denver*, and myself. We refused to turn over the port. I went to bed that night and slept soundly; and, of course, without any thought that I was having a hand in establishing a precedent that Japan was to cite to us twenty years later.

On the following day, the U.S.S. *California* arrived with Rear Admiral W. H. H. Southerland. Four hundred marines were landed from the *California*, and the cruiser proceeded to Panama for an additional force. The Admiral transferred his flag to the *Annapolis*. Marine Headquarters were established at the Consulate, and in an open space in the town a marine camp was set up under the name of Camp Dixie. During the day Captain Terhune said that he wanted to talk with me. He told me how, when he was making his way with his small force from Managua to Corinto, one of his men had shot and killed a young Nicaraguan. This was the first bloodshed by an American, and the Captain, who was a fine, generous-hearted man, was deeply disturbed by it. The Nicaraguan had been seen under a bridge where the rail-

road crossed a small river; the American shot him on the supposition
that he was tampering with the bridge; Captain Terhune was of the
opinion that the young fellow was only trying to catch some fish. I
said to the Captain that he was right in feeling that it was a terrible
thing to have killed a boy who was, probably, innocent even of mischief; but that, under the circumstances, I did not think that he should
assume the guilt personally. For nearly an hour, midst the clatter and
clutter of the landing forces, he and I paced back and forth on the
waterfront, while he tried to work the matter off his mind and conscience. I know he did not succeed in doing it then; because he
brought it up again and talked it over with Admiral Southerland and
me. The Admiral assured him that what had happened was in the
course of military action, and advised him to put the incident out of
his mind. Whether Captain Terhune was ever able to do this, I cannot
know.

While the marines were setting up camp, Mr. Palacio ran to me with
the complaint that they were taking mahogany that he had on the
waterfront ready for shipment, and using it for firewood. I at once
reported his complaint to the Admiral. The marines themselves were
astonished to learn that they were burning mahogany. This action,
however, was something less than vandalism; for among the uses to
which mahogany is put in Nicaragua is the making of cartwheels and
railroad cross ties.

On September fourth, the *California* came back from Panama with
seven hundred and fifty marines aboard. Within a few days, there was
a fleet of eleven warships under command of Admiral Southerland.
Captain Halstead, whom I had known since my first year at Corinto,
was in command of the *California*. The Admiral assigned to me a
bluejacket as a guard. Wherever I went, my "naval attaché" followed
a few paces behind. I am sure this measure was not taken for my
protection—I needed no protection—but to impress the native population. The population was likewise duly impressed when I paid my
official visit to Admiral Southerland. As I left the flagship, every vessel
in the fleet, one after another, boomed a salute of seven guns, seventy-
seven in all. The thunder startled the country for miles around. It
threw the dogs of Corinto into a panic; the whole canine colony of
the port started yelping and running as though they were mad. If any
of them are still alive, they are, I judge, running yet.

On September twenty-sixth, General Mena surrendered. On the

twenty-seventh he was brought to Corinto, and on the next day deported to Panama aboard the U.S.S. *Cleveland*. On October third, the American forces began bombarding Barranca. On the following day Barranca and Coytepe were taken by assault, with four Americans killed and eight wounded; forty Nicaraguans killed and seventy-five wounded. On October sixth, American forces entered Leon, the last stronghold of the Mena revolution. The first step of the American intervention was finished. Admiral Southerland was ready to transfer his flag back to the *California* and return to the United States. He had been a frequent visitor at the Consulate, and so much admired a gray parrot which I owned that I made him a present of the bird. Before the *California* sailed, Captain Halstead gave a breakfast for me aboard, that was attended by the other captains in the fleet. The marines remained and had their base at Corinto.[1] But excitement and tension subsided, and affairs fell into the course of daily routine.

On the surface, the reasons for armed intervention of the United States in Nicaragua appear to be based solely on considerations of concessions and loans. Those who have opposed the imperialism of the United States in the Caribbean region have, for the most part, opposed it on those grounds. I am sure that the reasons go deeper; that they are based upon a policy of government that has been running and growing stronger since 1826, a policy of government that is a part of the tradition of the State and Navy Departments (and, as to foreign affairs, Administrations may come and Administrations may go, but the State and Navy Departments go on forever). This policy held that the security of the United States depended upon controlling an inter-oceanic canal across Central America. For more than fifty years, the United States made tentative efforts for a Nicaragua Canal. Down to the purchase of the unfinished Panama Canal, it was agreed that the Nicaragua route was the most practicable and feasible of all. This policy of government now holds that, even with the American ownership of the Panama Canal, the security of the United States still depends upon domination of the very possible route across Nicaragua. Only a year or so before the 1909 revolution, Zelaya was endeavoring to open secret negotiations with Japan for the acquisition of the Nicaragua route, and a copy of his letter broaching the matter was in the hands of the State Department. This policy embraces also

---

[1] Just before writing these lines I read that three months hence seven hundred American marines will be withdrawn from Nicaragua, ending the occupation begun in 1909.

the control of certain potential naval bases guarding the sea paths on the Atlantic side to any canal across Central America. The State and Navy Departments may feel that they can rest easier, since now a treaty with Nicaragua has been negotiated and proclaimed by both countries granting the United States rights in perpetuity to construct, operate, and maintain a canal across Nicaragua. These are, I believe, fundamental facts in the Caribbean policy of the United States; and, I think, those who oppose that policy should take these facts into consideration and not lay all their stress upon the profits made by holders of concessions and clippers of loan coupons. I leave it to a financial accountant to compute how long it will take before the expenditures for intervention will begin to show a strictly business profit. Concessions, loans, and revolutions are important factors, but, for the government, their chief importance lies in their connection with its fundamental policy. It is my opinion that the relations of the United States to all the islands of the Caribbean and to Panama, Nicaragua, and the other Central American countries, as well, depend almost entirely upon how far we can go toward abolishing the possibility and fear of war between the United States and any other great power; and that, of course, comprehends the complete abolishment of war.

XXVII

The *Autobiography of an Ex-Colored Man* was brought out in Boston while the revolution was in progress. Copies were sent to me, and the book was read by many of the naval and marine officers. But I had written scarcely a line of new work in my more than three years in Nicaragua. For some time I had been carrying in my mind the plan to write a poem in commemoration of the fiftieth anniversary of the signing of the Emancipation Proclamation. By some mental twist I had kept thinking that the anniversary would fall in 1915. In early October, I read in my copy of *The New York Age* that colored people in various parts of the United States had been celebrating the fiftieth anniversary of the preliminary proclamation, which Lincoln signed September 22, 1862; and I suddenly found that I had three months, instead of three years, in which to write my poem. I went to work feverishly, but under some disadvantages; one room in the Consulate was still used as marine headquarters; there were two machine guns on the front porch with marine guards; at night, thirty or forty marines slept on the porch at the rear of the house; of quiet, privacy, or peace, I had little. Nevertheless, I did manage to work. I found the hours after midnight best. But throughout the day, my mind was so absorbed with making the poem that the affairs of Nicaragua and of the United States, too, took a secondary place. I finished the poem in about six weeks and mailed it to Brander Matthews. He, feeling that it ought to appear on the exact date of the anniversary, submitted it to the *New York Times*, where it was printed January 1, 1913. On the following day *The Times* printed a fairly long and quite laudatory editorial comment on the poem. The writer of the editorial went so far as to say, "While there would be hesitation in pronouncing this poem a work of genius, there would be difficulty in explaining why it did not deserve to be so described."

The poem as originally written consisted of forty-one stanzas. After a struggle in which my artistic taste and best judgment won, I cut off the last fifteen stanzas—something which I did not find easy to do. The main theme of the poem, as I had carried it in my mind, was fifty years of struggle and achievement. As the poem took form, it made a rapid sweep back over the two hundred and ninety-four years between 1619 and 1913, and, beginning with the eleventh stanza—

> This land is ours by right of birth,
> This land is ours by right of toil;
> We helped to turn its virgin earth,
> Our sweat is in its fruitful soil

it affirmed our well-earned claims to a share in the commonwealth; reaching in the twenty-sixth stanza a note of faith in the future. At that point, it took a turn and brought into view the other side of the shield, ending on a note of utter despair. I saw that I had written two poems in one. I saw that the last third of the composition, though it voiced the verities, was artistically out of place, and, moreover, that it nullified the theme, purpose, and effect of the poem as a whole. I recognized that the last fifteen stanzas required another and different setting.

I decided to make a separate poem out of the deleted fifteen stanzas, but I never attempted to have them printed. I grew, more and more, to fear that they contained an element of empty rhetoric that was absent in the major portion of the original poem. However, if I were today writing that "major portion" of the poem, I should question the superiority in the absolute of so-called white civilization over so-called primitive civilization.

President Taft was defeated in the November elections. After his defeat he sent a long list of nominations to the Senate; in the list I was named as Consul to the Azores. I was disappointed that I had not been named for a post in France, but I was too glad to get away from Corinto to feel the disappointment very keenly. I knew nothing about the Azores, but, looking the islands up in the catalogue of consular posts, I found that the climate was pleasant, and the standards of living far above those of Nicaragua. I knew that my duties would not be of the kind required at Corinto, and I anticipated the opportunity to go on with my writing. I also calculated that I would be within rather easy distance of Europe. I saw that I should be faced with a new language, Portuguese; but I felt sure that I should have little trouble with it, since it was allied so closely to Spanish. But the Democratic majority in the Senate, having in mind the fifteen hungry years endured by their constituents and the fat years just ahead, refused to confirm the nominations made by an outgoing Republican president. And that was the status of my case when I reached the United States.

When I got to New York, I found Rosamond on the eve of sailing for Europe. He had been serving as the executor of our father's estate, and had waited only to talk with me about certain matters in connection with it. I went first to Washington and talked with the officials at the State Department with respect to my appointment to the Azores. They seemed to feel optimistic about the list of nominations being sent back to the Senate and being confirmed. Grace and I went to Jacksonville. I found my mother cheerful but looking much older.

My father had left, in addition to several parcels of real estate, fifteen thousand dollars in mortgages, negotiated through a local house of which a Judge W. B. Owen, a man in whom he had entire confidence, was the head. I was in Jacksonville only a week or two before I heard that the Florida Realty Trust Company was on the rocks. I attended a meeting called by the investors in the concern, but I felt safe because my father's investments were secured not by bond or stock issues of the company, but by individual first mortgages locked up in his safe at home. As I was leaving the meeting, a lawyer whom I knew well called me aside and whispered in my ear that I had better look into my "first mortgages." The company went smash. Judge Owen, it appeared, lost his mind. I talked with the business manager, who declared to me over and over that the only way he saw out for himself was to commit suicide. I engaged a lawyer and he uncovered the divers methods these financial second-story men had employed to fleece their clients. They had, in my father's case, in two instances, recorded a mortgage on a piece of property twenty-four hours before they delivered to him a document purporting to be a first mortgage deed. After three or four years of litigation, we recovered only a fraction of my father's investments with this company; hundreds of others lost all they had. I don't think Judge Owen went to an asylum, and the business manager did not have the decency to commit suicide. Not a step was ever taken to punish a single one of the respectable scoundrels connected with this concern.

I remained in Jacksonville six or seven months on leave of absence; then I went back to Washington. The heads at the Department of State with whom I talked were not so optimistic now. Wilbur J. Carr, who examined me for my entrance into the Service, and who became First Assistant Secretary of State, suggested that I go and have a talk with the Secretary of State. As the reader knows, the then Secretary of State was William Jennings Bryan, a man who superficially was a statesman, but fundamentally was a political spoilsman. He was the Secretary of State who wrote to the newly appointed Receiver General of Customs for the Dominican Republic:

My dear Mr. Vick:

Now that you have arrived and are acquainting yourself with the situation, can you let me know what positions you have at your disposal with which to reward deserving Democrats? Whenever you desire a suggestion from me in regard to a man for any place there call on me.

The same who had written to President Wilson:

We have so many deserving Democrats and so few places to give that I would like if all of them would be willing to serve for a short time so that we could pass the offices around. . . . If you do not approve of the suggestions in regard to George Fred Williams, would you like to have me look for a good Democrat who would like a winter's stay in Greece?

Nevertheless, I went to see him to press my case and to ask if my name would again be sent to the Senate for the post at the Azores. I had not seen Mr. Bryan since the days of the Spanish-American War. Then I saw him a number of times, a handsome young colonel, still in his thirties, marching at the head of his Nebraska regiment, which was in camp at Jacksonville. There, because he had already been the national standard bearer of the Democratic Party, he attracted more attention than did even General Fitzhugh Lee; now, I saw him still young in years, but old in looks. His antique aspect was emphasized by his wearing clothes that literally flapped about him. Mr. Bryan received me cordially and I stated my errand. With much arching of the eyebrows, drawing down of the corners of the mouth, and many gesticulations, he informed me without words directly to the effect that I, as a Republican appointee, ought to feel grateful if I was left in the Service at all. Mr. Bryan seemed to have no idea that the plan he had in mind would be blocked by the merit system, so far as the Consular Service was concerned. I left the Secretary of State with this clearly in mind: I was up against politics plus race prejudice; I might be allowed to remain at my present post; if so, I should be there for another four years at least, perhaps for another eight. I came to the definite conclusion that life was too short for me to spend eight years more of it in Corinto. I wrote out my resignation. The problem was more serious than my resignation from Stanton School; notwithstanding, it caused me only little more hesitation. I dropped my letter in the mail box, and marked another turn on the way along which I have come.

PART FOUR

XXVIII

I RETURNED to Jacksonville discouraged and disturbed. I had burned my bridges, but I could not entirely keep down the question as to the wisdom of my action. I had given up a secure position carrying retirement and a pension, and placed myself where I had to make a new start, without knowing what direction I should take. Nevertheless, deep down I felt sure that, if the question was still open, I should close it as I had already done. Several colored citizens approached me with respect to the principalship of the New Stanton. The idea did not appeal to me. It struck me that to become principal of Stanton again would be to make a complete circle of my life path, ending where I had begun. I thought seriously about resuming the practice of law. Jacksonville had become a bustling, go-getter, money-mad city; it was, at the time, a boom town; and I figured that it would offer me a good field as a lawyer. Most of the colored men I talked with had caught the get-rich-quick fever; they told me many marvelous tales of fortunes suddenly made, of how such and such a person had bought a piece of property for a few hundred dollars and, within a short time, sold it for many thousands. This sort of talk was substantiated by considerable material evidence; a number of these colored men lived in finer houses than were occupied by anybody, except the quite rich white citizens, in the Jacksonville I had formerly known. Among them, the ownership of automobiles had passed the stage of being a novelty. And they were as loud in their praises and as firm in their faith in the future of Jacksonville as was the local board of trade or club of Rotarians. I could not help but be infected by their enthusiasm and, from the advice they gave me, I gathered that among the very few things that Jacksonville lacked was just such a lawyer as I should be. The Negro Masons of the state were building a five- or six-story Masonic Temple, and I went so far as to speak tentatively for office space.

Jacksonville was also making a bid for the moving picture industry; there were three or four studios already located there. While I was floundering, I thought to make a try at this new art field. I wrote a half-dozen short scenarios, Grace working with me on them, and promptly sold three of them, at prices ranging from twenty-five to fifty dollars each. We saw the exhibition of the first picture, and were so disappointed in it that we were actually ashamed to see the others.

Grace was having her first experience of really living in the South. The colored people we knew were very nice to her; they gave dinners and receptions and parties; they took us on long automobile rides; all of which she enjoyed. But those affairs, naturally, subsided; and, even had they not, it was not possible to live wholly within that circumscribed world. Many things on the outside, notwithstanding her hearsay knowledge of conditions, she resented so strongly that it was plain that she would have the greatest difficulty in adjusting herself to them. Some of these things seemed, in themselves, trivial; so trivial as to be ridiculous; but the truth is, these trivialities, taken with what they signify, are often vital and far-reaching. Grace and I were walking along the street one day, and, passing a man whom I knew, I raised my hat. He, in turn, smiled pleasantly but sheepishly, and nodded his head. Grace asked me, "Who is that man?" "He is Mr. Bours," I replied. "He was a member of the school board when I was principal of Stanton." A little farther along, I saw two men approaching. One of the men I did not know, the other I had known for twenty years. The man I knew was "Colonel" Carter, the editor of one of Jacksonville's newspapers. The "Colonel" was a fine man, and, speaking from a racial point, an *exceptional* Southern white man. One day, during the time I was running *The Daily American*, I was in his office when his wife came in. He said at once, "Mr. Johnson, do you know Mrs. Carter?" She interrupted by saying, "Why, I've known him nearly all my life." And this was true and, furthermore, meant that she had known me before the "Colonel" had come to Jacksonville. During the time I was writing for the theater in New York, a very beautiful and socially prominent Jacksonville young lady decided to go on the stage. "Colonel" Carter gave her a letter to me in which he asked me to use my best efforts in her behalf. The young lady presented the letter, and I introduced her at the offices of Klaw & Erlanger. She did go on the stage, but before the end of a full season she married one of the outstanding light opera stars. At that happy event, she did not forget my efforts; she sent me an invitation to the wedding. None but an exceptional Southern white man would or could have done either of these two things. As the distance between the two approaching men and Grace and me lessened, I began to speculate upon what the "Colonel," in the presence of another white man and on the public highway, would do. He had seen us, and, I judge, his brain was working faster than mine. When he was within, say, fifty feet of us he did an amazingly quick-witted thing; he took his hat entirely off and began scratching his head violently. As he passed, he smiled, bowed, and said, "How do you do?" I had felt like kicking myself for having "seen" Mr. Bours at all. I felt a bit sorry for "Colonel" Carter.

Certainly, the refusal to tip one's hat to a colored woman and to address a Negro as Mister or Missis are trivialities, but they connote the whole system of race prejudice, hatred, and injustice; their roots go to the very core of the whole matter. I have heard many Negroes brush aside these trivial things. The position they take is: What does it matter?—It doesn't hurt us—We should be foolish to endanger our economic and financial good or, it may be, our security of life and limb, by taking umbrage at these trifles. All of which is true enough, if nothing can be done to alter the situation. But there are instances in which it can be altered, if only by taking one's self out of it. These are trivialities, but for myself, I wish as little dealings or relations as possible with a man who will expect me to tip my hat when he is with his wife and will refuse to do the same thing when I am with mine. This mere trifle declares that, actually, there is no common ground on which we can stand; and I shall, whenever it is possible for me to do so, avoid standing on any ground with him.

On another day, I was standing in the bank with which my father had done business when Dr. John C. L'Engle, the white-haired, aristocratic president, beckoned me to his desk. He talked to me for some minutes about my father, in the characteristically terse manner for which he was well known in Jacksonville. He told me, too, that he had attended my father's funeral, and how much he had been affected by the singing of *We'll Understand It Better By and By.* Then quite abruptly he asked, "Do you intend to stay in Jacksonville?" I replied that I was not sure. He then said, "You can't do it. If you had never gone away, it would be a different matter. But Jacksonville is not the Jacksonville you used to know. Don't try it." These words from a wise man added to the doubts which for weeks had been gathering and growing thicker and darker.

D—— made a flying visit to Jacksonville. He brought with him his little daughter, a cute child three or four years old. She made a remark that circulated in town for days afterwards. D——'s stepmother had taken her to church; it was, probably, the first time the child had ever been in a church, and of course she had not seen *The Green Pastures*. On a front seat sat William De Lyon; he it was who had been a partner in the brickmason firm that gave me my first job. He was now a very old man with beautiful, silvery hair that he wore reaching down to his shoulders. The child nudged her guardian and asked in an awestruck whisper, "Is that God?" I saw little of D——; he was in town only a few days. When I talked with him he exhibited much interest in my situation, mixed, it seemed to me, with a degree of sympathetic condescension. But I may have been sensitive on the point.

Rosamond was in London. When, on the death of our father, he had gone to Jacksonville, he had become engaged to Nora Floyd, who as a small girl had been one of his piano pupils. The date set for their wedding was approaching, but Rosamond was supervisor of music at Hammerstein's Opera House in London and could not afford to leave to come to Jacksonville. It was finally arranged that the marriage would take place in London. Nora went over with her mother. The news that Rosamond's fiancée was going to Europe to be married grew into a sensation in Jacksonville when clippings that my brother sent over showed that news and pictures of the wedding had been given front page space in three or four of the London dailies.

Secretary Bryan had small success in his efforts to oust men from the Consular Service in order to make places for "deserving Democrats"; but Secretary Burleson had wholesale success with domestic patronage. This whole patronage business, as it developed under the new administration had, it seemed to me, a significance beyond the substitution of one set of partisan officeholders for another set. The South, it appeared, had taken the election of a Southern-born president, the first (to be elected) in sixty-four years, together with a Cabinet in which the proportion of Southern-born portfolio holders was one-half, as a signal that the country had been turned over not only to the Democratic Party in general, but to the South in particular. One of the effects of this impression held, I should say, by a majority of Southern white people, was a determination to nullify what remained of the Negro's national citizenship. Going back to the days of Reconstruction, the Negro in the South had always felt, no matter what his local status might be, that he was a citizen of the United States. This feeling was manifest especially when such a Negro entered a federal building. There he felt that he was on some portion, at least, of the ground of common citizenship; that he left most of the galling limitations on the outside. This, in reality, was only little more than a feeling; but, at that, it was worth something. The only place in the South where a Negro could pretend to a share in the common rights of citizenship was under the roof of a federal building. In parts of Florida, at any rate, efforts were made to take even that away from him. In several communities near Jacksonville, newly appointed postmasters cut "Jim Crow" windows at the side, through which Negroes were to get their mail, *without coming into the post office*. There they had to stand in sun or rain until the last white person on the inside had been served. The steps begun during President Wilson's first term to sweep away the remaining vestiges of the Negro's federal citizenship would have gone far had they not been halted by the World War.

Rosamond's absence in London added to my dilemma about my future. Property affairs needed the attention of one of us; and I saw more plainly each day that it was my mother's desire for me to remain in Jacksonville; she wanted one of us near her. My mother's desire tugged unremittingly at my heartstrings. I struggled through many indecisions, lying awake, at times, for hours in the night. I was at the fork, at the crossroads; no, I was standing lost in the woods. I did not know which direction to take, but I knew whichever I took would be fateful. I finally arrived at a fixed purpose. Just how I reached it I cannot tell. Was I governed by prescience or led by the wish? Was it blind luck or just a good guess? Someone has said that a large part of the whole business of life is good guessing. That someone was, I think, pretty close to the truth. I had a tearful parting from my mother when I carried out my purpose of returning to New York. I reassured her with the promise that I should come back to

Jacksonville as often as I possibly could. Toward the end of the summer of 1914 Grace and I started north.

New York was more changed for me than ever. Grace's parents had followed the tide flowing uptown and moved to Harlem. And in Harlem we made our home. It was now that I came to know well my wife's parents. My mother-in-law, a lovely, intelligent, and cultured woman, took, for me, all the point out of the ancient joke. In time, through mutual affection, she grew to take, very largely, the place of a mother in my life. I found in my father-in-law a good friend and, moreover, an exceedingly interesting character: a man without a day of formal schooling, but full of wisdom and a knowledge of the world. He had a collection of books that made one of the best small libraries I ever saw, every book an important one. He is still an insatiable reader and still maintains a disdain for "trash." His reading makes conversation and discussion with him, sometimes, an exciting experience. He has a philosophy of life, to which he attributes the fact that he has reached the age of eighty, hale and hearty; and its main elements are moderation and regularity. He gets up every morning at the same hour, a very early one, drinks a cup of coffee and, no matter what the weather, goes out. It is jokingly said that he opens up Harlem. He comes back and by breakfast time has read the morning paper. He takes a nap at a certain hour; must have his dinner precisely on the minute; has certain evenings for the movies, certain nights for reading, and a certain hour for going to bed. For years he has gone every Sunday morning to the Ethical Society. Nothing less than some *force majeure* can change this schedule. Notwithstanding this seeming inflexibility, he is a man of tender sympathies. For many years he has been a generous contributor to causes, especially to Negro causes and institutions. I have never ceased to find him interesting and stimulating.

My sole justification to myself in making the decision to return to New York was that I should have opportunity to make my way by writing. I had done it once; why couldn't I do it again? At all events, I should be exerting my efforts in a field where the goal was great enough to call up all my energies and enthusiasm. My first opportunity came from a quarter which I had not given consideration. I had been in New York only a few weeks when Fred R. Moore, the owner and publisher of *The New York Age*, the oldest of the New

York Negro newspapers, offered me the position of editor of the paper. I agreed to write the editorials, but made the arrangement to have what I wrote in the main appear under my name as contributing editor, a title I copied from Theodore Roosevelt. I wrote *The Age* editorials for ten years; those that I signed being printed in double columns under the caption, "Views and Reviews." I got great gratification out of the fact that the articles in those double columns quickly began to attract the attention of readers and also of other Negro editors.

But writing the editorials for *The New York Age* neither took all my time nor paid me as much as I needed to earn. I tried again for Broadway. I wrote the words for a half-dozen or so popular songs, collaborating with various composers, and I did some work with Jerome Kern on a new play for Marie Cahill; but I found that I had lost the touch for Broadway. I simply couldn't turn the trick again; I don't think that anybody else has ever been able to do it. A vogue of that kind is a vogue, and is about as exempt from recapture as past time. My failure to effect a "comeback" on Broadway led to some extremely blue days for me. For the first time in my life I was confronted with the actual want of money. I turned to writing "art songs," and did a number of them with Harry T. Burleigh, with Will Marion Cook, and with my brother. *Sence You Went Away,* which I wrote with Rosamond, was sung by John McCormack and made some money. At this point, I took a part in the organization of the American Society of Composers, Authors, and Publishers. We gave an organization dinner at Luchow's in Fourteenth Street. I sat at the speakers' table next to Victor Herbert, whose music I had so long admired but whom I had not known personally. The Society has grown to be the richest and most powerful organization of its kind in the world. Its membership fee is ten dollars a year, and it distributes something like a million and a half dollars to its members annually. This it can do because through a law it succeeded in having passed by Congress it is enabled to collect a royalty on all mechanical, electrical, and radio reproductions and also upon the professional use of the music written by its members. Then the chance came for me to put into English the libretto of *Goyescas,* the Spanish grand opera produced at the Metropolitan Opera House in 1915. In doing this piece of work I kept two objects (not always attained in the translations of grand opera librettos) in mind: to make it singable and sensible. Seeing my name and work in the program of the Metropolitan gave me a new sensation.

Señor Periquet, the librettist of the opera, and I got to be very good friends. He was sufficiently impressed with my work on *Goyescas* to enter into a contract with me to be the English translator of his plays for the United States. I did translate one of them, but was not able to find anyone willing to produce it, so I never did another. Periquet was ruddy, with light hair and gray eyes and of a gay temperament. Enrique Granados, the composer of the opera, was a directly opposite type. He was olive in complexion, with black hair and dark, sad, dreamy eyes. His manner was quiet, almost apologetic. He had a high reputation as a composer in Spain, but he had always been poor and struggling. He had come to New York to witness the American première of his work, bringing his wife with him and leaving their six children at home. The opera was not a startling success, but Granados was quietly happy; it had made his fortune. He had never thought, perhaps, of there being so much money in the world; at any rate, of so much of it coming to him. Prospects of simple but secure life in Spain for himself and family were rosy.

The night before Granados sailed for home, I took dinner with him and his wife and Periquet at the Hotel Claridge. After dinner, he played for us—he possessed remarkable virtuosity. His wife sat demurely listening; Periquet, between the numbers and after Granados had finished playing, continued his importunities for the composer and his wife to give up their plan of returning to Spain by way of England, and to wait for the Spanish steamer on which he, Periquet, was going to sail. But Granados in his quiet way clung to his plan. He then had something like ten thousand dollars in gold and banknotes in a belt strapped around his waist, and he was eager to get back home and to his children. It may have been that he needed to count his fortune over in his own country before he could feel that it was real money and really his. He pressed Periquet to change and sail with him, but the latter was explosive in the expression of his determination to sail on none other than a Spanish steamer. He did not consider it safe, he said, to return over the more northern route. Granados and his wife sailed. They were crossing the channel in the *Sussex* when she was torpedoed by a German submarine, and both of them were lost. The treasure that he was carrying home helped to carry him down. It took me a long while after the news to get that evening at the Claridge out of my mind. If Periquet could have been only a little more persuasive; or if Granados had been only a little less eager to get home.

Naturally, I turned my hand also to literary writing. This was nearly a decade before the big magazines threw their pages open to Negro writers and principal publishers had begun to feel that they would like to have at least one Negro author added to their lists. I greatly missed Richard Watson Gilder and Dr. Ward, both of whom had always been ready to talk with me and to consider my work for publication. However, I did establish cordial relations with Robert Underwood Johnson, who had succeeded Mr. Gilder as editor of *The Century*, and went often to see Brander Matthews.

The first new contact I made was with H. L. Mencken, then one of the editors of *Smart Set*. Mr. Mencken had made a sharper impression on my mind than any other American then writing, and I wanted to know him. As a reason for going to see him, I took along a one-act play, *Mañana de Sol*, which I had translated from the Spanish of Serafín and Joaquín Álvarez Quintero. I sent my name in, feeling not entirely confident that I should see Mr. Mencken, but he came out almost promptly. We sat and talked for thirty, forty, perhaps, forty-five minutes; and I kept wondering how a man as busy as he could give so much time to a mere stranger. I had never been so fascinated at hearing anyone talk. He talked about literature, about Negro literature, the Negro problem, and Negro music. He declared that Negro writers in writing about their own race made a mistake when they indulged in pleas for justice and mercy, when they prayed indulgence for shortcomings, when they based their protests against unjust treatment on the Christian or moral or ethical code, when they argued to prove that they were as good as anybody else. "What they should do," he said, "is to single out the strong points of the race and emphasize them over and over and over; asserting, at least on these points, that they are *better* than anybody else." I called to his attention that I had attempted something of that sort in *The Autobiography of an Ex-Colored Man*. He was particularly interested in Negro music, and I afterwards sent him copies of songs by Burleigh and Cook and Johnson. Through some correspondence which we had about the songs, I discerned that his chief interest in them was not that of an editor but of a musician. Mr. Mencken did not accept the play, but my visit was the beginning of a very pleasant relation. His parting advice was that I center my efforts on prose rather than poetry; I gathered that his opinion of poetry and poets was not exceedingly high. When I left him I felt buoyed up, exhilarated. It was as though I had taken a mental cocktail.

In the meantime, I contributed some poems to *The Crisis*. One of these, "The White Witch," a poem that puzzles many people who read it—I consider its meaning quite plain—figured rather sensationally in a court scene in Boston, where colored citizens were attempting by legal steps to prohibit the exhibition of the moving picture, *The Birth of a Nation*. One of the attorneys for the picture people rose in court, waving a copy of *The Crisis* in his hand, and tried to make the poem evidence that such a picture as *The Birth of a Nation* was an absolute necessity in the United States.

With the coming of the presidential campaign of 1916, I found myself again taking a hand in politics; but this time I had a deeper interest and a stronger influence. I felt convinced that the maintenance of such national citizenship rights as the Negroes still held depended upon throwing the Southern oligarchy at Washington out of power; and I bent all my energies, especially through my editorials in *The Age*, toward that end. My distrust and dislike of the attitude of the Administration centered upon Woodrow Wilson, and came nearer to constituting keen hatred for an individual than anything I have ever felt. In addition to writing as strongly as I could, I volunteered as a speaker and campaigner for Hughes through New York and Massachusetts. In the midst of the campaign, the *Philadelphia Ledger* offered two thousand dollars in prizes for editorials on the candidates of the two major parties; one thousand dollars in three prizes for editorials on "Why Hughes Should Be Elected," and similar amounts for editorials on "Why Wilson Should Be Elected." By the terms of the contest, only bona fide editors of newspapers could enter; about eight hundred editors took part. The time limit had nearly expired before it struck me that I was a bona fide editor, and might take a chance. I wrote my article, and was compelled to send it by special delivery in order to get it to Philadelphia in time. I was awarded the third prize for a Hughes editorial. The Negro press gave me unanimous congratulations and hailed my success as a feather in the cap of Negro journalism.

On the day before election, I was at Republican headquarters in New York when Mr. Hughes came in to pay a visit. I was introduced to him as the man who had written one of the prize-winning editorials on "Why Hughes Should Be Elected." He graciously expressed his appreciation; though, in all probability, he had not read the article. That night he made the closing speech of his campaign at Madison Square Garden. I was among those seated on the platform. Mr. Hughes did not make a back-stage entrance; he strode down the long center aisle, Mrs. Hughes swinging on his arm, and tripping along at his side as gayly as a girl, while the thousands stood up and cheered. It must have been a tremendous moment for them both. On election night I was with those invited to listen to the returns at headquarters—no broadcasting in those far-off days. A committee of gentlemen received returns as telegraphed in, and chalked them up on a blackboard. At about ten or ten-thirty o'clock the great states east of Mississippi had been heard from, and enthusiasm reached the point of jubilation. The word went out "Hughes elected!" Newsboys were shrilly crying up and down the streets, "Extra! Hughes elected!" The crowds shouted "Hughes elected!" The committee telephoned the news to Mr. Hughes at his hotel, and he went to bed, President of the United States.

I felt jubilant, too. Had I not had a hand in overthrowing the Southern oligarchy? Toward midnight a lull came over Republican headquarters. It appeared that returns from the far western states were coming in rather slowly. A little after midnight, I went upstairs, where I found a vacant room and sat down to write my editorial on the election, which would go to press within twenty-four hours. I put down the heading, "Thank God for Hughes," and under that caption wrote my article. When I had finished, I came down and peeped into the large room. A good part of the brilliant assemblage had left, and the lull that I had noted before seemed to have deepened. However, I did not stop to ask any questions; I slipped out and started for Harlem. When I got out of the Subway at 135th Street and Lenox Avenue, I felt hungry and I stopped in a restaurant to get something to eat. Before I came out, I heard newsboys crying, "Extra! Wilson elected!" I thought it was a hoax, but I bought a newspaper and read it avidly. After the first shock of amazement, the thought that struck me most forcibly was that I should have to get to work and write another leading article to fill my column.

XXIX

EARLY in the summer of 1916 I was in Jacksonville on a third visit to my mother since I had moved to New York. While there I received a letter from J. E. Spingarn, inviting me to be a member of a conference on questions relating to the Negro, which would be attended by both white and colored people, and would be held at his country place, Troutbeck, at Amenia, New York. At the bottom of the letter, W. E. B. Du Bois had scribbled, "Do come." I wrote back that I gladly accepted membership in the conference and that I should certainly attend. The meeting was held in August and lasted three days. Mr. Spingarn, then Chairman of the Board of Directors of the National Association for the Advancement of Colored People, was host to the conference. A half hundred of the most influential and progressive Negroes in the country, and of white people interested in the cause of Negro rights, participated in the sessions. At one of these, the group was dazzled by the beauty and fired by the crusading zeal of Inez Milholland. Another session was attended and addressed by the Governor of the state, Charles S. Whitman. I was chosen, through the suggestion of Mr. Spingarn, I am sure, to make the remarks introducing Governor Whitman. During the conference I had a talk with Oswald Garrison Villard, in which he said that one of the most effective steps the Negro in New York could take would be to march down Fifth Avenue in a parade of silent protest.

The conference was held at a time when the fundamental rights of the Negro were in a state of flux. At no time since the days following the Civil War had the Negro been in a position where he stood to make greater gain or sustain greater loss in status. The great war in Europe, its recoil on America, the ferment in the United States, all conspired to break up the stereotyped conception of the Negro's place that had been increasing in fixity for forty years, and to allow of new formations. What new forms these conceptions would assume depended largely upon what attitude and action the Negro himself and the white people willing to stand with him would take. Those gathered at the conference determined to help shape them more in accordance with real democracy and the heart's desire of the Negro. The Amenia Conference came at an hour of exigency and opportunity, and took its place in the list of important events in the history of the Negro in the United States.

Late in the fall, I received another letter from Mr. Spingarn. In this letter he asked me if I would not take a place in the National Association for the Advancement of Colored People. The offer was a genuine surprise. I had not received the slightest intimation of its likelihood; nevertheless, under my surprise I was aware that what had come to me was in line with destiny. Out of such tenuous stuff had it come—the unspoken reactions between me and two other men, J. E. Spingarn and W. E. B. Du Bois—that it could not have been other than the resultant of those mysterious forces that are constantly at work for good or evil in the life of every man. A short while before, a tentative offer, and a flattering one, had been made to me, which, I am confident, I could have taken up; but I hesitated and doubted and did not make an attempt to do so. When I received Mr. Spingarn's letter, it at once seemed to me that every bit of experience I had had, from the principalship of Stanton School to editorship on *The New York Age*, was preparation for the work I was being asked to undertake. The Board of Directors created the position of Field Secretary, and in that capacity I began work with the Association in December 1916.

Our offices were situated in two small rooms at 70 Fifth Avenue. The office staff consisted of four persons, Roy Nash, secretary; myself; Frank M. Turner, bookkeeper; and Richetta G. Randolph, stenographer. Both Mr. Turner and Miss Randolph, the best confidential secretary I have known or known of, are still with the Association. Across the hall, Dr. Du Bois, the editor of *The Crisis*, had quarters occupying considerably more space. *The Crisis* was the organ of the Association, but was maintained as a distinct business entity, with a separate staff, then numbering eight or ten persons. The magazine had been established five years before, and in that time had grown to have a circulation of thirty thousand. It was, I believe, the only radical publication in the country that was self-supporting. And here the word "radical" is used in a relative sense. *The Crisis* voiced the protests of the Association, but in the English-speaking world, most of those protests had passed out of the radical program with the signing of the Magna Charta at Runnymede seven hundred years before. The central purpose of the National Association for the Advancement of Colored People was nothing more nor less than to claim for the Negro common equality under the fundamental law of the United States; to insist upon the impartial application of that law; to proclaim that democracy stultified itself when it barred men from its benefits solely on the grounds of race and color. And yet, things relative are as real as things absolute. In parts of the country—say, for example, darkest Mississippi—it was, and still is, actually radical to hark back to the demands made by the barons on King John, and insist upon the right of Negroes to enjoy common security of life and property; upon their right, when charged with crime, to a fair trial by a jury of their peers before a duly constituted court of justice; upon the application for them of the principle, "No taxation without representation"; upon the right of qualified Negro citizens to cast a vote. "Negro radicalism" that went no farther than this has times without number been met with violence and even death. Communists, who advocate and work for the overthrow of the entire governmental system, run no such risks as the Negro "radical" who insists upon the impartial interpretation and administration of existing law.

In 1916, the Association was a small organization. It had its inception in a call issued February 12, 1909, the one-hundredth anniversary of the birth of Abraham Lincoln, for a conference to consider the civil state of the Negro. In the following year a temporary organization, composed of both white and colored people, was formed; and in 1911 the Association was incorporated under the laws of New York, with a board of thirty directors, constituted of about equal numbers of white and colored members. From its beginning, the organization took an unequivocal stand against disfranchisement, against inequitable public schooling for Negro children, against segregation and all forms of public discrimination based on race or color, and against mob violence and lynching. For thirty years past the accepted status of the Negro as a citizen had been steadily declining. In some respects it was lower than it had been at the close of the Civil War. In the whole South, the home of the overwhelming masses of the race, he had been completely disfranchised, segregated, and "Jim Crowed" in nearly every phase of life, and mobbed and lynched and burned at the stake by the thousands. There had been the isolated declarations of the Afro-American Council in 1890 and 1898; and the pronouncements of the Niagara Movement in 1905 and the several years following, pronouncements on which the program of the National Association for the Advancement of Colored People was based;

but the race as a whole had adopted soft-speaking, conformity, and sheer opportunism as the methods for survival. Concerted effort inspired by high courage and idealism seemed to be wholly lacking. It looked as though the Negro would let his rights and his claim to rights go by default. In that quarter, whence came the champions of justice to the Negro from the whites, there had been a shifting of front, and there was a more or less general admission that the noble crusade had been undertaken in vain. Most of what had been gained as a result of war had been yielded in the struggle on the field where public sentiment is won or lost.

And so, when the National Association for the Advancement of Colored People announced its platform of Equality for the Negro, a great many people were startled. Such a platform, as was to be expected, aroused fierce antagonisms to the organization. It was denounced as radical, revolutionary, subversive; and those at its head were branded as dangerous busybodies or idealistic fanatics. But the most telling attack on the Association was made by those who called it a "social equality" society; for that had the effect of making a good many white friends of the Negro's cause uneasy, and of placing Negroes themselves on the defensive. This term, "social equality," is, at the same time, a most concrete and a most elusive obstacle in the Negro's way. It is never defined; it is shifted to block any path that may be open; it is stretched over whole areas of contacts and activities; it is used to cover and justify every form of restriction, injustice, and brutality practiced against the Negro. The mere term makes cowards of white people and puts Negroes in a dilemma.

Very few, even among the most intelligent Negroes, could find a tenable position on which to base a stand for social among the other equalities demanded. When confronted by the question, they were forced by what they felt to be self-respect, to refrain from taking such a stand. As a matter of truth, self-respect demands that no man admit, even tacitly, that he is unfit to associate with any of his fellow men (and that is aside from whether he wishes to associate with them or not). In the South, policy exacts that any plea made by a Negro—or by a white man, for that matter—for fair treatment to the race, shall be predicated upon a disavowal of "social equality." Booker T. Washington, in his great Atlanta speech, felt the necessity of declaring, "In all things purely social we can be as separate as the five fingers, and yet one as the hand in all things essential to material progress." It was this figure of speech, this stroke of consummate diplomacy, that made the whole of his eloquent plea swallowable for Southern throats, and straightway brought him recognition as a statesman. And a fine figure of speech it is, but it does not stand logical analysis. Beyond the ineptitude of its implication that separated fingers (though separated only socially) can constitute an efficient hand, is the fact that it raises an illimitable question: of what do "all things essential to material progress" consist? An elimination of the things deemed "purely social" by Dr. Washington's white hearers, would have left a very narrow margin, perhaps only a mudsill level of things on which to co-operate like one as the hand.

There ought not to be any intellectual dilemma in this question for a self-respecting Negro. He can, without apology to himself or to anyone else, stand for social equality on any definition of the term not laid down by a madman or an idiot. Certainly, he does not mean that he is watching to sneak or break into somebody's parlor, or to present himself uninvited for a dinner or a party, or that he has intentions of seizing some Nordic maiden by the hair and dragging her off to be his woman. Certainly, he knows that nothing can compel social intercourse. He sees many Negroes that no force within the race can compel him to invite to his house; and he sees many white people that he would not, under any circumstances, have in his house. But he holds: There should be nothing in law or public opinion to prohibit persons who find that they have congenial tastes and kindred interests in life from associating with each other, if they mutually desire so to do.

But I am fully aware that in writing as I have in the last page or two I have been arguing about "social equality" only from the surfaces of the question. And these surfaces give the whole matter the aspect of a preposterous and absurd farce; especially in the region where "social equality" is talked about most. For, in that region, a white gentleman may not eat with a colored person without the danger of serious loss of social prestige; yet he may sleep with a colored person without incurring the risk of any appreciable damage to his reputation. But behind and under the paradoxes lies a definite significance, a significance so seldom allowed to come into the open that most Negroes have not even thought about it; that white women, even those in the South, are, probably, not entirely aware of it; but which every thinking Southern white man understands clearly: *"Social equality" signifies a series of far-flung barriers against amalgamation of the two races; except so far as it may come about by white men with colored women.*

The platform of the Association startled a great many Negroes. Many there were who, while longing for the objectives set forth, felt timid about the methods proposed for attaining them. They feared that a full statement of the Negro's case, and an open avowal of the determination to prosecute it, would retard rather than hasten the results aimed at; that a frontal attack would do the Negro's cause more harm than good. And many there were who definitely opposed the association, who fought it covertly and openly. This particular opposition to the organization was, in a large degree, an inheritance from the Niagara Movement. It was the Niagara Movement, inaugurated by Dr. Du Bois in 1905, that marked, with respect to the question of the Negro's civil rights, a split of the race into two well-defined parties—one, made up from the preponderating number of conservatives, under the leadership of Booker T. Washington and the other, made up from the militant elements, under the leadership of W. E. B. Du Bois. Between these two groups there were incessant attacks and counter-attacks; the former declaring that the latter were visionaries, doctrinaires, and incendiaries; the latter charging the former with minifying political and civil rights, with encouraging opposition to higher training and higher opportunities for Negro youth, with giving sanction to certain prejudiced practices and attitudes toward the Negro, thus yielding up in fundamental principles more than could be balanced by any immediate gains. One not familiar with this phase of Negro life in the twelve- or fourteen-year period following 1903 (the year of publication of *The Souls of Black Folk*) cannot imagine the bitterness of the antagonism between these two wings. When the National Association for the Advancement of Colored People was organized, the Du Bois wing merged to help form the new organization, and the old antagonism, in a considerable measure, was transferred. In 1916, the situation, in brief, was as follows: Booker T. Washington had died the year before, but the conservative mass of Negroes, together with a large part of the white South and the greater proportion of the Northern whites at all interested in the Negro, stood firm under the banner of the Tuskegee Idea; Negro militants and white champions of equal rights for the Negro were grouped together in the National

Association; in addition, there was a third group, under the leadership
of Monroe Trotter, editor of the *Boston Guardian*. Mr. Trotter, in
many respects an able man, zealous almost to the point of fanaticism,
an implacable foe of every form and degree of race discrimination,
waged, during this period referred to, a relentless and often savage
fight through his newspaper against Dr. Washington and the Tuskegee Idea. Mr. Trotter, however, could not work, except alone; and,
although there were numbers of people who subscribed to his opinions,
he lacked capacity to weld his followers into a form that would give
them any considerable group effectiveness.

During the first seven years, the growth of the Association was
slow and the result only of continual effort. The organization was
lacking in funds and the strength that comes from numbers, but it
made a valiant use of the only effective weapon available—agitation.
It agitated through mass meetings, through leaflets and pamphlets,
The Crisis, and any other publication that would open its pages. It
had sent Elizabeth Freeman, a young white woman, exceptionally
fitted for the job, to investigate the burning alive of a Negro in Waco,
Texas, and had published to the world the gruesome details of her
findings. Later, Roy Nash went to Abbeyville, South Carolina, and
investigated the lynching of Anthony Crawford, a prosperous Negro,
who was lynched mainly because of the fact that he was well-to-do
and independent. I threw myself wholeheartedly into this work. In
1916 there were sixty-eight branches in Northern and Western cities.
There were three branches in three Southern cities, New Orleans,
Shreveport, Louisiana, and Key West, Florida, with a total of three
hundred and forty-eight members. My first step as Field Secretary
was an effort to organize in the South. It was my idea that the South
could furnish numbers and resources to make the Association a power.
This idea did not meet with the unqualified approval of all the members of the Board of Directors. There were some who feared that a
large membership in the South might cause the organization to modify
its position; they felt that it could be freer to speak and act if not
hampered by responsibility for Southern branches. It was, however,
my deep conviction that the aims of the Association could never be
realized by only hammering at white America; I felt convinced that
it would be necessary to awaken black America, awaken it to a sense
of its rights and to a determination to hold fast to such as it possessed

and to seek in every orderly way possible to secure all others to which it was entitled. I realized that, regardless of what might be done *for* black America, the ultimate and vital part of the work would have to be done by black America itself; and that to do that work black America needed an intelligent program. A large majority of the Board agreed with me in my plan for organizing the South. I took the preparatory step of drafting a manual for branches, setting forth the aims of the Association, the plan for organizing branches, and the laws by which branches would be governed; then I wrote a letter stating my purpose to key persons in some twenty cities, and asking them to call a conference of twenty-five representative people to meet with me on a date specified. I started on the actual work early in January 1917; beginning at Richmond, Virginia, and going as far south as Tampa, Florida. At each conference, with the exception of one city, a branch organization was set up and arrangements planned for a mass meeting at which a drive for members would be made. On my way back, I retraced the ground I had covered and addressed these mass meetings.

The results of the trip were not overwhelmingly successful, but, at least to me, they were encouraging. They did, in fact, lay the groundwork for what, two years later, the Association called its "Southern Empire." By that time, through supplementary work done by Mary E. Talbert in the Southwest, there were alert, aggressive, intelligently directed branches in almost every Southern state, and the South was contributing an amount for the national work greater than what had been the total general fund of the organization in 1916. At the close of 1919, there were three hundred and ten branches in the Association, one hundred and thirty-one of them being in the South.

Nor were the results of the trip uniform; in some cities the idea of making a united stand and a concerted effort for citizenship rights was seized upon more enthusiastically than in others. But I was impressed with the fact that everywhere there was a rise in the level of the Negro's morale. The exodus of Negroes to the North, pulled there to fill the labor vacuum in the great industries, was in full motion; the tremors of the war in Europe were shaking America with increasing intensity; circumstances were combining to put a higher premium on Negro muscle, Negro hands, and Negro brains than ever before; all these forces had a quickening effect that was running through the entire mass of the race. This effect was especially noticeable in

Atlanta. The mass meeting I addressed in that city was held in the splendid Negro theater. The meeting had been well advertised, and the crowd took up every available bit of space in the auditorium. As I sat on the platform, I noticed that a number of policemen were stationed in the theater. In other days, this would have placed a hand of chilling restraint on the proceedings, but now it had no such effect. Each person who took part spoke out frankly and courageously about the business that had brought the people together; and the more frank and courageous the utterance, the louder and longer was it cheered and applauded. I don't know what those Atlanta policemen thought about the meeting, but, so far as I could see, they did nothing more than look and listen. Atlanta grew to be one of the strongest branches in the Association; reaching a membership of more than a thousand.

The organization conference which was held at Atlanta was unique; it was the only one in which no woman was invited to take part. There were present fifty or so of the leading colored men of the city; lawyers, doctors, college professors, public school teachers, editors, bankers, insurance officials, and businessmen. Some of these men I had known before, but most of them were strangers. From the whole group, a very young man who acted as secretary of the conference became singled out in my mind. I saw him several times and was impressed with the degree of mental and physical energy he seemed to be able to bring into play and center on the job in hand. I did not need to guess that the representative conference and the extraordinary mass meeting were largely results of his efforts. I left Atlanta having made a strong mental note about him.

Within a few weeks after I got back to New York, the United States entered the World War. Shortly thereafter, Mr. Nash resigned the secretaryship and entered the army, and I took the place of acting secretary. In the fall, I put before the Board what I believed to be the qualifications of the young man I had met in Atlanta and urged that he be offered a place in the national office. Many of the members of the Board were somewhat doubtful about a very young man from the deep South, and utterly unknown; and, furthermore, they were thinking in terms of a new secretary. Nevertheless, I pressed the case of my candidate, and was finally authorized to write to him. I did so. He hesitated for a while, and I could not blame him, for he had a position and a promising outlook with an insurance company; and the salary that we offered him was very small. However, in the end he wrote that he would accept the offer. So, at the beginning of 1918, Walter White came to New York to be assistant secretary of the Association, and to carry through, later, the series of lynching investigations that were to make his name nationally known. A few days later, John R. Shillady, the newly elected secretary, took up his work.

The months between the resignation of Mr. Nash and the coming of Mr. White and Mr. Shillady were strenuous. The organization was beginning to show signs of greater growth, and there were only three of us at the office to do the necessary work. I spent part of my time in the office and part of it on the road. But Mary White Ovington, who was one of the founders of the Association, and who had been its volunteer secretary at the beginning, when there were no salaried officers, came in almost daily and helped.

It was in this period that I rushed to Memphis to make an investigation of the burning alive of Ell Persons, a Negro, charged with being an "ax murderer." I was in Memphis ten days; I talked with the sheriff, with newspaper men, with a few white citizens, and many colored ones; I read through the Memphis papers covering the period; and nowhere could I find any positive evidence that Ell Persons was the man guilty of the crimes that had been committed. And, yet, without a trial, he was burned alive on the charge. I wrote out my findings, and they were published in a pamphlet that was widely circulated.

On the day I arrived in Memphis, Robert R. Church drove me out to the place where the burning had taken place. A pile of ashes and pieces of charred wood still marked the spot. While the ashes were yet hot, the bones had been scrambled for as souvenirs by the mobs. I reassembled the picture in my mind: a lone Negro in the hands of his accusers, who for the time are no longer human; he is chained to a stake, wood is piled under and around him, and five thousand men and women, women with babies in their arms and women with babies in their wombs, look on with pitiless anticipation, with sadistic satisfaction while he is baptized with gasoline and set afire. The mob disperses, many of them complaining, "They burned him too fast." I tried to balance the sufferings of the miserable victim against the moral degradation of Memphis, and the truth flashed over me that in large measure the race question involves the saving of black America's body and white America's soul.

It was in this period that the Association won the first of its victories in reaffirming the Negro's constitutional rights. From the United States Supreme Court it gained, in the Louisville Segregation Case, a unanimous decision declaring that laws which established residential segregation by race were unconstitutional. It is true that the Association, through its president, Moorfield Storey, had had a hand in winning the decision handed down by the Supreme Court in 1915 declaring "grandfather clauses" unconstitutional;[1] but the Segregation Case was the Association's case from the beginning; with its Louisville branch it fought that case through all the courts of Kentucky, up to and through the Supreme Court. In the Supreme Court, the case was argued by Mr. Storey; I had the privilege of hearing him.

It was also in this period that the Association, under the lead of J. E. Spingarn, undertook to see that provision was made for the training of colored men to be officers in the army.[2] Mr. Spingarn made efforts to have them admitted to the regular training camps; on one occasion I went with him as one of a committee to see Secretary of War Newton D. Baker about their admission to the regular camps; but such an arrangement "simply *could not be made.*" This decision could not be charged to any personal attitude of Mr. Baker; for not even Secretaries of War can override a fixed policy of the army bureaucracy at Washington. The arrangement finally made was for a special training camp at Des Moines.

This arrangement brought down on Mr. Spingarn some sharp criticism, criticism from within and without the Association. He was denounced by some as going back on a basic principle of the organization of which he was a high officer. At any rate, his critics could

---

[1] Speaking generally, these grandfather clauses in the amended constitutions of the Southern states enumerated as necessary to the rights of suffrage a list of property, literacy, and character qualifications of high standard; and then provided that none of these qualifications need be met by any persons who had the right to vote or who had an ancestor who had a right to vote before the time of the close of the Civil War. There were, of course, numbers of colored people who could have qualified under the ancestor proviso, but the right was not worth the risk of attempting to establish it.

[2] There were four Negro regiments in the regular army, but, practically, no commissioned officers. 2,290,527 Negroes were registered, 458,838 were examined, and 342,277 were accepted and drafted for service. Of the total number of registrants in the United States, 26.84 per cent of the whites were accepted for full military service, and 31.74 per cent of the Negroes. Including the regular army regiments and National Guard units, 380,000 Negro soldiers were mobilized for the World War.

not charge him with being a doctrinaire; he had faced a situation—several hundred thousand Negroes in the armies of the United States, and not a chance for one of them to be an officer, unless he had already received the required training—and he met it practically. Mr. Spingarn is one of the most finely sensitive souls that I know, and, probably, he was wounded by some of the criticisms hurled at him, but he never showed it. From the Des Moines Camp, 678 colored men received commissions as officers in the army. The common sense of the matter and the pride the race took in the results snuffed criticism out.

When I went with the committee to see Secretary Baker, it was my first visit to Washington after our declaration of war. As I passed the White House and entered the State, Army, and Navy Building, I saw a sight which gave me food for thought. Those were the days when the nation was in a panic over the rumors of pro-Germans and spies in our midst, and troops were thrown around these two buildings for their protection. And every man of the troops guarding the home of the President and the offices of the three principal departments of the government was a black man.

In the middle of this same summer, on July 2, the colored people of the whole country were appalled by the news of the East St. Louis massacres, a riot in which four hundred thousand dollars' worth of property was destroyed, nearly six thousand Negroes driven from their homes, hundreds of them killed, some burned in the houses set afire over their heads. This occurrence was the more bitterly ironical because it came when Negro citizens, as others, were being urged to do their bit to "make the world safe for democracy."

But the reaction to the East St. Louis Massacre was widespread. Congress passed a resolution calling for an investigation. At a hearing before the Committee on Rules of the House of Representatives, Congressman Dyer, of Missouri, among other things, said:

I have visited out there and have interviewed a number of people and talked with a number who saw the murders that were committed. One man in particular who spoke to me is now an officer in the United States Army Reserve Corps, Lieut. Arbuckle, who is here in Washington somewhere, he having come here to report to the Adjutant General.

At the time of these happenings he was in the employ of the Government, but he was there on some business in East St. Louis. He said that he saw a part of this killing, and he saw them burning railway cars in yards, which were waiting for transport, filled with interstate commerce. He saw members of the militia of Illinois shoot Negroes. He saw policemen of the city of East St. Louis shoot Negroes. He saw this mob go to the homes of these Negroes and nail boards up over the doors and windows and then set fire and burn them up. He saw them take little children out of the arms of their mothers and throw them into the fires and burn them up. He saw the most dastardly and most criminal outrages ever perpetrated in this country, and this is undisputed. And I have talked with others; and my opinion is that over five hundred people were killed on this occasion.

Congressman Rodenberg, of Illinois—East St. Louis is in Illinois— in his remarks before the Committee said:

Now, the plain, unvarnished truth of the matter, as Mr. Joyce told Secretary Baker, is that civil government in East St. Louis completely collapsed at the time of the riot. The conditions there at the time beggar description. It is impossible for any human being to describe the ferocity and brutality of that mob. In one case, for instance, a little ten-year-old boy, whose mother had been shot down, was running around sobbing and looking for his mother, and some members of the mob shot the boy, and before life had passed from his body they picked the little fellow up and threw him in the flames.

Another colored woman with a little two-year-old baby in her arms was trying to protect the child, and they shot her and also shot the child, and threw them in the flames. The horror of that tragedy in East St. Louis can never be described. It weighted me down with a feeling of depression that I did not recover from for weeks. The most sickening things I ever heard of were described in the letters that I received from home giving details of that attack.

As is usual in such occurrences, Negroes were singled out and held legally responsible. The Association secured a staff of lawyers headed by Charles Nagel, Secretary of Commerce under Taft, for their defense, and it also raised a fund for the relief of those who had been made destitute by the riot.

I attended a meeting of the executive committee of our Harlem branch. They were discussing plans to register a protest against the East St. Louis massacre; the plan most favored was a mass meeting at Carnegie Hall. Recalling Mr. Villard's remarks at the Amenia Conference, I suggested a silent protest parade. The suggestion met with immediate acceptance. It was agreed that the parade should not be made merely an affair of the Association and the Harlem branch, but of the colored citizens of all Greater New York. A large committee, including the pastors of the leading churches and other men and women of influence, was formed, and preparations were gone about with feverish enthusiasm. On Saturday, July 28, nine or ten thousand Negroes marched silently down Fifth Avenue to the sound only of muffled drums. The procession was headed by children, some

of them not older than six, dressed in white. These were followed by
the women dressed in white, and bringing up the rear came the men in
dark clothes. They carried banners; some of which read:

MOTHER, DO LYNCHERS GO TO HEAVEN?
GIVE ME A CHANCE TO LIVE.
TREAT US SO THAT WE MAY LOVE OUR COUNTRY.
MR. PRESIDENT, WHY NOT MAKE AMERICA SAFE FOR DEMOCRACY?

Just ahead of the man who carried the American flag went a streamer
that stretched half across the street and bore this inscription:

YOUR HANDS ARE FULL OF BLOOD

The streets of New York have witnessed many strange sights, but,
I judge, never one stranger than this; certainly, never one more
impressive. The parade moved in silence and was watched in silence.
Among the watchers were those with tears in their eyes. Negro Boy
Scouts distributed to those lined along the sidewalks printed circulars
which stated some of the reasons for the demonstration:

We march because by the Grace of God and the force of truth, the dangerous,
hampering walls of prejudice and inhuman injustices must fall.

We march because we want to make impossible a repetition of Waco, Memphis,
and East St. Louis, by rousing the conscience of the country and bringing the
murderers of our brothers, sisters, and innocent children to justice.

We march because we deem it a crime to be silent in the face of such barbaric
acts.

We march because we are thoroughly opposed to Jim-Crow Cars, Segregation,
Discrimination, Disfranchisement, LYNCHING, and the host of evils that are forced
on us. It is time that the Spirit of Christ should be manifested in the making
and execution of laws.

We march because we want our children to live in a better land and enjoy
fairer conditions than have fallen to our lot.

Within less than a month after the silent protest parade, news flashed
up from Texas about the "Houston affair." A battalion of the Twenty-
Fourth Infantry, one of the Negro regiments of the regular army,
was stationed at Fort Sam Houston. Late in the night of August 23,
the city of Houston was "shot up"; two Negroes and seventeen white
people, five of the latter being Houston policemen, were killed. The
Negro soldiers were charged by the local authorities with being re-

sponsible for the killings, but the whole incident seemed somewhat wrapped in mystery. Great pressure was brought to have the soldiers tried in the courts of Texas on charges of murder, and, at one time, it looked as though the government might yield to it, but the men were tried by court martial.

The Association promptly sent Martha Gruening to Houston to get at the facts. Miss Gruening found that there had been cumulating bad feeling between the soldiers and the Houston police; that the friction was due chiefly to the fact that the local authorities had objected to the policing of the men while in the city by the usual methods of establishing a provost guard, and had insisted on that duty being placed in the hands of the local police; that the police had been insulting and brutal in enforcing their powers; that, without need, the police had cruelly clubbed a number of soldiers; that on the day preceding the shooting, Corporal Baltimore, the most popular noncommissioned officer and one of the most experienced soldiers in the regiment, had been seriously beaten; that the news reached the camp that he had been killed.

The Association attempted to assist in the defense of the men through the services of a white Texas attorney, A. J. Houston, son of Sam Houston. Sixty-three members of the regiment were court-martialed, and on December 11, early in the morning before it was quite daylight, almost surreptitiously, thirteen of them were hanged. The Negroes of the country were agony-stricken. Not that they questioned the findings of the court, but they felt that the fiendish baitings by which the men had been goaded should have been taken as extenuating circumstances, and, too, that the men should have been afforded their right of appeal to their Commander-in-Chief, the President. They thought back over the fifty years of the Negro regiments in the regular Army; how in that time those regiments had been stationed in every section of the country without ever a serious blot on their record for discipline and soldierly conduct, except in two incidents, and both of those incidents had happened in Texas; and they felt that the primary cause of the trouble lay not in the Negro soldiers, but in Texas.

In a second court martial, five more of the men were sentenced to be hanged, fifty-one to life imprisonment, and five to long terms. Before the court was finally discontinued, eleven more of the men received the death sentence, bringing the number condemned to die up to sixteen.

A committee of four, consisting of the Rev. George Frazier Miller, Frank M. Hyder, F. A. Cullen, representing the Harlem branch of the Association, and myself, hastened to Washington to see President Wilson, taking a petition of twelve thousand signers, asking executive clemency for the condemned men.

A short while before, I had gone to Washington with a delegation to see the President, but his secretary, Mr. Tumulty, acted as a buffer. This time the President received us graciously. He asked us to be seated. Mr. Wilson did not sit behind his desk, he sat out from it in a comfortable chair, and we sat grouped in a sort of semi-circle in front of him. But almost immediately I rose, as spokesman for the committee, and presented the petition. In presenting it I said:

We come as a delegation from the New York Branch of the National Association for the Advancement of Colored People, representing the twelve thousand signers to this petition which we have the honor to lay before you. And we come not only as the representatives of those who signed this petition, but we come representing the sentiments and aspirations and sorrows, too, of the great mass of the Negro population of the United States.

We respectfully and earnestly request and urge that you extend executive clemency to the five Negro soldiers of the Twenty-Fourth Infantry now under sentence of death by court martial. And understanding that the cases of the men of the same regiment who were sentenced to life imprisonment by the first court martial are to be reviewed, we also request and urge that you cause this review to be laid before you and that executive clemency be shown also to them.

We feel that the history of this particular regiment and the splendid record for bravery and loyalty of our Negro soldiery in every crisis of the nation give us the right to make this request. And we make it not only in the name of their loyalty, but also in the name of the unquestioned loyalty to the nation of twelve million Negroes—a loyalty which today places them side by side with the original American stocks that landed at Plymouth and Jamestown.

The hanging of thirteen men without the opportunity of appeal to the Secretary of War or to their Commander-in-Chief, the President of the United States, was a punishment so drastic and so unusual in the history of the nation that the execution of additional members of the Twenty-Fourth Infantry would to the colored people of the country savor of vengeance rather than justice.

It is neither our purpose nor is this the occasion to argue whether this attitude of mind on the part of colored people is justified or not. As representatives of the race we desire only to testify that it does exist. This state of mind has been intensified by the significant fact that, although white persons were involved in the Houston affair, and the regiment to which the colored men belonged was officered entirely by white men, none but colored men, so far as we have been able to learn, have been prosecuted or condemned.

We desire also respectfully to call to your attention the fact that there were mitigating circumstances for the action of these men of the Twenty-Fourth Infantry. Not by any premeditated design and without cause did these men do what they did at Houston; but by a long series of humiliating and harassing incidents, culminating in the brutal assault on Corporal Baltimore, they were goaded to sudden and frenzied action. This is borne out by the long record for orderly and soldierly conduct on the part of the regiment throughout its whole history up to that time.

And to the end that you extend the clemency which we ask, we lay before you this petition signed by white as well as colored citizens of New York; one of the signers being a white man, president of a New York bank, seventy-two years of age, and a native of Lexington, Kentucky.

And now, Mr. President, we would not let this opportunity pass without mentioning the terrible outrages against our people that have taken place in the last three-quarters of a year; outrages that are not only unspeakable wrongs against them, but blots upon the fair name of our common country. We mention the riots at East St. Louis, in which the colored people bore the brunt of both the cruelty of the mob and the processes of law. And we especially mention the savage burnings that have taken place in the single state of Tennessee within nine months; the burnings at Memphis, Tennessee; at Dyersburg, Tennessee; and only last week at Estill Springs, Tennessee, where a Negro charged with the killing of two men was tortured with red-hot irons, then saturated with oil and burned to death before a crowd of American men, women, and children. And we ask that you, who have spoken so nobly to the whole world for the cause of humanity, speak against these specific wrongs. We realize that your high position and the tremendous moral influence which you wield in the world will give a word from you greater force than could come from any other source. Our people are intently listening and praying that you may find it in your heart to speak that word.

The presentation of the petition was finished; the President did not rise, and I retook my seat. He talked with us about the mission that had brought us to the White House. We were surprised when he admitted that he had not heard of the burning at Estill Springs. He asked us to give him the facts about it; and declared that it was hard for him to think that such a thing could have taken place in the United States. We pressed him for a promise to make a specific utterance against mob violence and lynching. He demurred, saying that he did not think any word from him would have special effect. We expressed our conviction that his word would have greater effect than the word of any other man in the world. Finally, he promised that he would "seek an opportunity" to say something.

Mr. Wilson talked on with us in a sociable manner. He sat with his knees straight, his elbows resting on the arms of his chair, his hands joined at the tips of his fingers and thumbs, and pointing in front of him in the shape of a wedge. I had seen him only once before, and then at a distance, when he had marched in a preparedness parade in New York; now I was sitting within six feet of him and regarding him intently. I had thought of him as an extremely austere man; as he talked, I realized that the official air had been dropped, and that he was, as we say, very human. His head, no longer inclined forward, rested back easily, and the sternness of his face relaxed and, occasionally in a smile, became completely lost. He asked us questions about the colored people, and we answered them as wisely as we could. He chatted a short while longer, even recounting one or two slight reminiscences of his youthful days in the South. We had been with the President a few minutes longer than a half-hour when he rose, signifying that the interview was at an end. We left with a last plea in behalf of the condemned men of the Twenty-Fourth Infantry. When I came out, it was with my hostility toward Mr. Wilson greatly shaken; however, I could not rid myself of the conviction that at bottom there was something hypocritical about him.

The President did take some action. He prohibited the execution of any more American soldiers—except in the forces at the front—before the sentences of the courts martial had been reviewed by the War Department; and of the sixteen men of the Twenty-Fourth condemned to die, he, after a review of their cases, commuted the sentences of ten to life imprisonment, and affirmed the death sentences of six. He also did "find an opportunity" to make a strong utterance against mob violence and lynching. (So it may be that my estimate of Mr. Wilson was actually colored and twisted by prejudice.) The Association continued its efforts for the men in prison; it secured the commutation of sentences of some and, finally, the release on parole of the entire number.

All that happened in Houston just before and on that night in August will probably never be known. The nineteen executed men went to death and the fifty-odd others to prison without "talking." Barlett James was one of the white officers of the regiment, the Captain of Company L, a West Pointer and an experienced soldier. The military investigation showed that on the night of August 23 he was in the company street with the men of his company gathered round him. It showed that a detail from the men who had left camp came back to induce the main portion of the battalion to join them; that an appeal was made to Company L, and that Captain James said, "The men of Company L are going to stay with their captain." Captain

James was in the list of witnesses for the court martial; but seven days before the date set for the opening of the trial, he went to his quarters and blew out his brains. And so, a witness who might have shed light on the mystery as to why sixty-odd men of the regiment were not prevented from leaving camp with arms and ammunition did not testify.

XXX

NINETEEN seventeen was a busy year for me. Yet I made the time to collect my published and unpublished poems and issue them in a little volume entitled *Fifty Years and Other Poems*. Brander Matthews wrote a word of introduction for the book. In the middle of the summer, I attended a three-day conference of the Intercollegiate Socialist Society that was held at Belleport, Long Island. I was on the program, but I did not make a talk on economic or social conditions; instead, I read a paper on the contribution of the Negro to American culture.

Some of the contributions that the Negro has made to America are quite obvious—for example, his contribution of labor—and their importance, more or less, has long been recognized. But the idea of his being a generous contributor to the common cultural store and a vital force in the formation of American civilization was a new approach to the race question.

The common-denominator opinion in the United States about American Negroes is, I think, something like this: These people are here; they are here to be shaped and molded and made into something different and, of course, better; they are here to be helped; here to be given something; in a word, they are beggars under the nation's table waiting to be thrown the crumbs of civilization. However true this may be, it is also true that the Negro has helped to shape and mold and make America; that he has been a creator as well as a creature; that he has been a giver as well as a receiver. It is, no doubt, startling to contemplate that America would not and could not be precisely the

America it is, except for the influence, often silent, but nevertheless potent, that the Negro has exercised in its making. That influence has been both active and passive. Any contemplation of the Negro's passive influence ought to make America uneasy. Estimate, if you can, the effect upon the making of the character of the American people caused by the opportunity which the Negro has involuntarily given the dominant majority to practice injustice, wrong, and brutality for three hundred years with impunity upon a practically defenseless minority. There can be no estimate of the moral damage done to every American community that has indulged in the bestial orgy of torturing and mutilating a human being and burning him alive. The active influences of the Negro have come out of his strength; his passive influences out of his weaknesses. And it would be well for the nation to remember that for the good of one's own soul, what he needs most to guard against, most to fear, in dealing with another, is that one's weakness, not his strength.

My paper, despite the fact that it was removed from the main topic of the conference, was received well, and gave rise to some interesting discussion. A young man, Herbert J. Seligmann, who was reporting the conference for the *New York Evening Post* was enthusiastic about it. He asked for my manuscript and made a summary of it for his newspaper. Paragraphs of his summary actually went round the world; they were copied in American and European periodicals, and I got clippings from as far away as South Africa and Australia. The statement that evoked the greatest interest—and some controversy—was that the only things artistic in America that have sprung from American soil, permeated American life, and been universally acknowledged as distinctively American, had been the creations of the American Negro.

I was, of course, speaking of the principal folk-art creations of the Negro—his folklore, collected by Joel Chandler Harris under the title of *Uncle Remus*, his dances, and his music, sacred and secular. Some years later, I modified that statement by excepting American skyscraper architecture. In making the original statement I certainly had no intention of disparaging the accomplishments of the other groups, the aboriginal Indians and the white groups. The Indians have wrought finely, and what they have done sprang from the soil of America; but it must be admitted that their art-creations have in no appreciable degree permeated American life. In all that the white groups have wrought, there is no artistic creation—with the exception noted above —born of the physical and spiritual forces at work peculiarly in America, none that has made a universal appeal as something distinctively American.

One other statement in Mr. Seligmann's summary of my paper which was widely copied was that the finest artistic contribution that this country could offer as its own to the world was the American Negro spirituals.

It is, however, in his lighter music that the Negro has given America its best-known distinctive form of art. I would make no extravagant claims for this music, but I say "form of art," without apology. This lighter music has been fused and then developed, chiefly by Jewish musicians, until it has become our national medium for expressing ourselves musically in popular form, and it bids fair to become a basic element in the future great American music. The part it plays in American life and its acceptance by the world at large cannot be ignored. It is to this music that America in general gives itself over in its leisure hours, when it is not engaged in the struggles imposed upon it by the exigencies of present-day American life. At these times, the Negro drags his captors captive. On occasions, I have been amazed and amused watching white people dancing to a Negro band in a Harlem cabaret; attempting to throw off the crusts and layers of inhibitions laid on by sophisticated civilization; striving to yield to the feel and experience of abandon; seeking to recapture a taste of primitive joy in life and living; trying to work their way back into that jungle which was the original Garden of Eden; in a word, doing their best to pass for colored.

It was early in 1917 that a number of liberals organized the Civic Club. In the discussions of the plans, the question of Negro membership was brought up. Finally, after considerable debate, it was settled upon that there would be no bar to membership on account of race or color. Dr. Du Bois and I were invited to become charter members, and we did. The Club had quarters, at first, in the Hotel Marquis; later, it moved into leased quarters on 12th Street, just off Fifth Avenue. The organization quickly became an influence in civic matters. One of the first of the special committees formed was one on The Negro in New York, under the chairmanship of Marie Jenney Howe. Other members on that committee that I remember were Fola

LaFollette, Paula Jacobi, and Mary White Ovington. The first case undertaken was that of admittance to interneship at Bellevue Hospital of a young colored woman doctor. Mrs. Howe worked earnestly on the case and it was won, but the young lady did not take the interneship; she got married.

The Civic Club grew to be a strong influence in the life of Negro New Yorkers. The Negro membership increased to twenty-five or thirty. I served for a number of years on the executive committee and, finally, served as president.

XXXI

WITH the opening of 1918, Mr. White, as assistant secretary, and Mr. Shillady, as the new secretary, came to the Association; and my individual responsibility and work were lessened. Mr. Shillady had great ability as a systematizer and organizer. He laid out the work of the increasing staff according to the most modern and approved methods. He planned a national drive for membership that was eminently successful. And he conducted the first adequate statistical study of lynching ever made. He sent two research workers to the Congressional Library at Washington, who read the newspapers back over a period of thirty years and extracted the data regarding every lynching that had been published. They set down the names, sex, and age of the victim; the place, date, and manner of each lynching; and the charge upon which each victim was lynched. These data were compiled and tabulated by Mr. Shillady, and published in a book of over a hundred pages, under the title of *Thirty Years of Lynching in the United States*. The most startling fact revealed was that the common opinion that Negroes were lynched only for rape was without foundation. The figures showed that of the more than three thousand Negroes lynched in the thirty-year period, less than seventeen per cent had even been charged with rape. They showed that Negroes had been lynched for "talking back" to white persons, for "not driving out of the road" to let white persons pass. They also showed that more than fifty Negro women had been lynched; against whom, of course, the "usual crime" could not be charged. This publication was of a value beyond estimation in the Association's fight against lynching. The Association began to take on magnitude. The office staff was added to. H. J. Seligmann was taken on as Director of Publicity, and William Pickens, already widely known as an orator, was taken on as Associate Field Secretary. The clerical staff in the office was increased to a dozen or more persons.

Very early in the year I went on the road speaking and organizing. The field was ready to be harvested. The war and the exodus had shaken the Negroes of the entire country loose from their traditional moorings of standpatism and timidity. They were awake and eager. My speaking was not confined to the colored people; in the North, I addressed many white audiences.

The experiences that came to me through these meetings were varied; some of them thrilling, some pathetic, and some humorous. I remember how the pathos of one situation gripped me. I was addressing a white forum in a Mid-Western industrial city, which, at that time, had only a very small Negro population. As is generally the case under such conditions, these people were disoriented. But a delegation of them waited on me when I had finished my address, and asked if I would not come and speak to a meeting of colored people and organize them into a branch of the Association. It was late, but, when I learned that an audience was waiting for me in the little colored church, I went. When I reached the church, I found it jammed to suffocation. As I went up the aisle to the pulpit, there was no applause—a demonstration I had become accustomed to—the people seemed to regard me with a worshipful silence, as though I were some sort of messiah. When I spoke to them, they hung on my words with such confidence and childlike faith that I could have wept, wept because of my own lack of power to deliver them.

In my trip through the Middle West, I reached a large colored church one Sunday morning and found that the whole service had been turned over to me. I was sitting with the pastor in his study waiting for the time to begin, when he asked me what my text was to be. I stammered that I really had no text, and that I was going to make a talk, not deliver a sermon. "But," he demanded, "aren't you a preacher?" I had to admit that I was not. He grew angry at my admission, and spoke to me as though he had been taken in. He declared that he could not allow any secular topic to take the place of the regular morning service. I told him there were phases of my subject that had a decidedly spiritual bearing, and that I did not think his congregation would consider them out of place. He reluctantly yielded, and did so, I felt, really because he had counted on a Sunday morning off and had not prepared a sermon.

The error this pastor had made in considering me a clergyman was based on a double confusion. I was frequently referred to in the newspapers, and introduced to audiences (incorrectly) as "ex-Minister to Venezuela and Nicaragua," and to many people, "preacher" comes up spontaneously as the synonym for "minister." In fact, after my engagement to Grace became known, one of her admirers called her up to josh her about the absurd rumor he had heard that she was going to marry a preacher.

I found that the matter of professional titles was not a minor one in many a place where I spoke. At a meeting in a Southern city, the preacher who was down on the program to make the remarks that would introduce me to the audience, leaned over, as we sat on the platform, and whispered. "What might be your entitlements?" "No entitlements," I whispered back, "just Mister. Introduce me as Mr. Johnson." With deep sincerity he whispered back again, "I can't do it. I can't introduce you to these people as just Mister." And he didn't; he introduced me as "Professor Johnson."

My meetings quite commonly served a double purpose; an occasion for me to make a speech on the work of the Association and to organize a branch or add to membership; and an opportunity for local talent, especially musical talent, to display itself. Good music helped a meeting, if it was not too good, and if there was not too much of it. For the main purpose of the meeting I preferred spirited singing by the audience to solos by individual artists. One soloist, however, I shall never forget. He was a powerful, ebony-hued baritone who unwittingly metamorphosed *Danny Deever* into a stirring race song by dramatically declaiming:

> "'What makes that rear-rank breathe so 'ard?'
> Said Files-on-Parade.
> 'It's bitter cold, it's bitter cold,'
> The *colored* sergeant said."

I received once a laboriously written and marvelously spelled letter.

The writer assured me that he had heard a great deal about me and the wonderful society for the advancement of colored people of which I was "the head." He informed me that he was colored and that the state of his affairs had reached a point so low as to be critical; and concluded with the request that I *advance him* about ten dollars.

My work on the road carried me into the far South, and I had opportunity to observe closely the operation of two powerful forces that were at work on the Negro's status—the exodus and the war. Negroes were migrating to the North in great numbers, and I observed the anomaly of a premium being put on this element of the population that had generally been regarded as a burden and a handicap to the South. Here, it seemed, was a splendid chance to get rid of a lot of "lazy, worthless people," but some communities were so loath to lose them that they obliged railroad ticket agents to adopt a policy of not selling tickets to Negroes to go North. In many instances Negroes were forcibly restrained from leaving.

The demands of the war were also working great changes. A train that I was on stopped at Waycross, Georgia. I saw a great crowd around the station and on the tracks, and got out of my coach to see what it was all about. I found a long train loaded with Negro troops who were on their way "over there," and witnessed the incredible sight of white women, together with colored women, all dressed alike in a Red Cross looking uniform, busy distributing to the men neatly wrapped packages of whatever things such committee gave to soldiers leaving for the front.

I reached Jacksonville a day or two before the date of a mass meeting that was being held in the National Guard armory. Let me here go back to a time when I was in Jacksonville three or four years prior to this meeting. The armory, built, of course, out of the tax funds of Duval County, was then brand-new. The drill room was the finest and largest auditorium in Jacksonville; its use as a municipal auditorium was among the advantages set forth in the project for building the armory. Its first use under this head was for a musical affair that had been promoted by a committee of white women. These ladies had arranged to have Coleridge-Taylor's *Hiawatha* sung, and for the principal rôle had engaged a tenor from Atlanta. A small group of colored people wanted very much to hear the cantata, and they asked me if I would not see if it could be arranged for them to do so. I telephoned Mrs. Lund, who was on the committee, and stated the case. She seemed very much pleased that there were colored people who wanted to hear the class of music that was to be sung. She asked how many there would be. I told her, probably twenty-five. She assured me that seats would be arranged for them and they would be welcome. The group was delighted. They asked me if I was going with them. I answered that I had been lucky enough to hear *Hiawatha* under better circumstances, and would not go. The next day, Mrs. Lund rang me up. She was very much perturbed. She gave me to know that the militia officer in charge of the armory had countermanded the arrangements that had been made; he had declared that Negroes could not be allowed in the armory. I asked Mrs. Lund if she thought the militia officer knew that the music to be sung was the work of a Negro composer. She did not answer that. Indeed, it is doubtful whether Mrs. Lund, as competent a musician as she was, or any other lady of the committee, knew that Coleridge-Taylor was a Negro.

The mass meeting that was to be held at the armory was for the purpose of stimulating the sale of Liberty Bonds. Fully a half of the auditorium was filled with colored people, and they subscribed liberally. On the platform was a large committee composed of white and colored citizens. Both white and colored speakers addressed the audience. By the white speakers, especially, great emphasis was laid on "*our* country" and "what *we* must do" to win the war for democracy. I don't know whether the same militia officer was still in charge of the armory or not.

But all of the forces were not favorable. These changes that I have alluded to were, after all, slight in proportion to the underlying mass of prejudice and bigotry. The Ku Klux Klan was beginning to gain the tremendous power it possessed a year or so later; and clouds were gathering that, within twelve months, would blot the light from the skies for the Negro. It was while I was in Jacksonville on this trip that I received a letter from Mr. Shillady asking me to go to Quitman, Georgia, and talk with a young colored man who knew a great deal about the "Mary Turner lynching," and to try and have him come on to New York. Walter White had, a short while before, investigated this lynching and reported that this young colored man had driven the wagon of the white undertaker who took charge of the bodies of the victims; and that he, probably, could divulge the names of some of the members of the mob. Mr. White's investigation of this lynching, one of the most monstrous in all the records, made a national sensation. It was his first important job in this work for which he was so well fitted; not the least of his advantages being that his race could not be detected from his appearance.

I proceeded to Quitman, arriving late in the afternoon. I went to the house of a colored doctor. He was fearful; so much so that he communicated his fears to me. He said that the town was still alive over the lynching, and much incensed over Mr. White's disclosures; and that it would not be safe for me to go out that night, because my appearance in a town the size of Quitman would be sure to arouse suspicion. He put out all the lights in the house at about nine o'clock and we went to bed. I did not sleep. The slightest sound gave me a start, for I could not but judge that the doctor's precautions were necessary. The very fact that he had taken me in was proof that he was no coward.

The next day I started out to find my young man. I found him in one of those dingy restaurants for Negroes, common in the South. He told me that his mother ran the place. It was located in the Negro quarter. There were ill-kept tables in the front, and a battered pool table in the back. I talked with him a long while, using all the persuasion I could bring to bear to have him consent to come North and state all he knew about the lynching, or give me the names of such members of the mob as he knew. He refused to do either. He said that if he went North, he would leave his mother at the mercies of the lynchers; and if he gave me the names, suspicion would point directly to him. The common sense of the position he took was unassailable.

While I was talking with him, an automobile drove up at the front. It was a small roadster or coupé, but it was loaded down with six men, all white. They were a pretty tough-looking lot. They called for the young fellow to come out. He said to me, "There they are now. What'll I tell 'em if they ask about you?" I did not see how they could know that I was in town, but I told him to say what I had told the doctor to say, in case of any questions—that I was taking subscriptions for a colored newspaper. He went out, and remained talking with the men longer than was pleasant for me. When he came in, he summed up what the men had said to him into—"They asked me what you were doing here, and I told them you were taking subscriptions. They told me to keep my damned mouth shut."

I got out of Quitman that afternoon and I did not feel safe or comfortable until the train had crossed the Florida line.

At a meeting that I addressed in one of the Western cities, I received the impulse to make a definite start on a piece of literary work I had long been nursing in my mind. I had long been planning that at some time I should take the primitive stuff of the old-time Negro sermon and, through art-governed expression, make it into poetry. I felt that this primitive stuff could be used in a way similar to that in which a composer makes use of a folk theme in writing a major composition. I believed that the characteristic qualities: imagery, color, abandon, sonorous diction, syncopated rhythms, and native idioms, could be preserved and, at the same time, the composition as a whole be enlarged beyond the circumference of mere race, and given universality. These ideas I had revolved, but I had not yet set myself to the task of working them out. For several years, I had been excusing myself on the ground of not having time.

It was Sunday, and I had been addressing meetings in various colored churches. I had finished my fourth talk, and it was after nine o'clock at night. However, to my surprise and irritation, the local committee informed me that I was scheduled for still another address. I protested the lateness of the hour, but was told that for the meeting at this church we were just in good time.

When we reached the church an "exhorter" was concluding a dull sermon. I was ushered to the platform, where I sat and listened to two more short, uninteresting efforts. These were but preliminaries, curtain-raisers, for the main event, a sermon by a famed evangelist.

At last he rose. He was a dark brown man, handsome in his gigantic proportions. I think the presence of a "distinguished visitor" on the platform disconcerted him a bit, for he started in to preach a formal sermon from a formal text. He was flat. The congregation sat apathetic and dozing. He must have realized that he was neither impressing the "distinguished visitor" nor giving the congregation what it expected; for, suddenly and without any warning for the transition, he slammed the Bible shut, stepped out from behind the pulpit, and began intoning the rambling Negro sermon that begins with the creation of the world, touches various high spots in the trials and tribulations of the Hebrew children, and ends with the Judgment Day. There was an instantaneous change in the preacher and in the congregation. He was free, at ease, and the complete master of himself and his hearers. The congregation responded to him as a willow to the winds. He strode the pulpit up and down, and brought into play the full gamut of a voice that excited my envy. He intoned, he moaned, he pleaded—he blared, he crashed, he thundered. A woman sprang to her feet, uttered a piercing scream, threw her handbag to the pulpit, striking the preacher full in the chest, whirled round several times, and fainted. The congregation reached a state of ecstasy. I was fascinated by this exhibition; moreover, something primordial in me was stirred. Before the preacher finished, I took a slip of paper from my pocket and somewhat surreptitiously jotted down some ideas for my first poem.

It had been thirty years since I had heard such a sermon. I still had my somewhat vague, youthful memories; but this fresh exhibition of the potentialities of the material I planned to use was just what I needed to start me on the work. In the course of several weeks, I finished "The Creation" to my satisfaction. It was published in *The Freeman.*

In writing "The Creation," I had to consider a question that had to be settled then and there for the whole group of poems—the question of form and medium. I at once discarded the use of conventionalized Negro dialect, for reasons which I set forth fully in the Preface to the poems when they were published in book form.[1] Furthermore, it was not my intention to paint the picturesque or comic aspects of the old-time Negro preacher—I considered them extraneous—my aim was to interpret what was in his mind, to express, if possible, the dream to which, despite limitations, he strove to give utterance. I chose a loose rhythmic instead of a strict metric form, because it was the first only that could accommodate itself to the movement, the abandon, the changes of tempo, and the characteristic syncopations of the primitive material.

In "The Creation" I was happy over the results of my experiments. Following its publication in *The Freeman*, it received numerous commendations. It has since been included in a dozen or more anthologies. One of the first to pronounce the poem an excellent one was William Stanley Braithwaite, with whom in these years I had formed a close and helpful friendship. I was happy, too, over the fact that I had at last made an opening on this piece of work; but seven years

[1] *God's Trombones—Seven Negro Sermons in Verse.* New York, The Viking Press, 1927.

elapsed before I formulated the subject matter and chose the title of the second poem of the group that I wrote—"Go Down, Death."

I addressed a mass meeting in Carnegie Hall and made the most effective speech of my whole career as a platform speaker. It was a great meeting; and the famous auditorium was packed to capacity. As I sat on the platform I felt depressed, almost listless. When I rose, every nerve in my brain and body was quickened by the intensity of feeling that came across the footlights from the audience to me. As I talked, I was lifted up and swept along by that sense of demi-omnipotence which comes to a speaker at those moments when he realizes that by an inflection of the voice or a gesture of the hand, he is able to sway a mass of people. It is a sensation that intoxicates; and it carries within itself all the perils of intoxication. Words surged to be uttered; and uttered, they were effective beyond their weight and meaning. One passage of my speech had an electrical effect:

I can never forget what I felt on the day I saw "The Buffaloes," New York's own black regiment swing out of Madison Square into the most magnificent street in the world. They were on their way to receive a stand of colors to be presented by the Union League Club. I followed them up Fifth Avenue as they marched, with a vision in their eyes and a song on their lips, going to fight, perhaps to die, to secure for others what they themselves were yet denied. They halted in front of the club, and in a mighty chorus sang *The Star Spangled Banner*. Then from the balcony the Governor of the state came down and presented the colors. As he gave the flag into their keeping, he raised his voice, trembling with emotion, and cried out, "Bring it back! Bring it back, boys! Bring it back!" And the answer welled up in my heart: Never you fear, Mr. Governor, they will bring it back; perhaps tattered and torn, but they will bring it back. And they will bring it back as they have always done whenever it has been committed to their hands, without once letting it trail in the dust, without putting a single stain of dishonor upon it. Then it is for you, Mr. Governor, for you, gentlemen of the Union League Club, for you, the people of America, to remove those stains that are upon it, upon it as these men carry it into battle, the stains of Disfranchisement, of Jim-Crowism, of Mob Violence, and of Lynching. . . .

The emotional tension of the audience snapped with an explosion of cheers and applause. I continued, finishing the passage:

The record of black men on the fields of France gives us the greater right to point to that flag and say to the nation: Those stains are still upon it; they dim its stars and soil its stripes; wash them out! wash them out!

But I do not think my voice reached farther than the length of my outstretched arms. I stood silent and waited for the tumult in the audience and the tumult within me to subside.

I read these words over now. They are cold. They strike me as a rather flamboyant piece of oratory. If it were not for my own memory, I should doubt that they ever possessed the power to do what they did do. So I come back to my theory that the inner secret of sheer oratory is not so much in the *what* is said as in the combination of the *how*, *when*, and *where*. The *how* is the most important of these factors, and its chief virtue lies in "timing"; that is, in the ability of the speaker to set up a series of rhythmic emotional vibrations between himself and his hearers. I have witnessed the accomplishment of this feat by oldtime Negro preachers using pure incoherencies.

At the beginning of the fall of 1918, Rosamond and I received a telegram from Jacksonville stating that our mother had been taken sick. We at once put into execution what we had been planning, to have her and our sister come to New York to live. Rosamond was at this time director of the New York Music School Settlement for Colored People. The school was located in two imposing adjoining houses in 130th Street, between Lenox and Seventh Avenues. My mother arrived very ill, but in a few weeks she rallied, and we had hopes of her recovery. Then she had a relapse and began to sink, and day by day our hopes grew fainter. I spent every hour with her that I possibly could; often sitting by her bed through the night. She had heard talk about the meeting that was to be held at Carnegie Hall; and she kept repeating how sorry she was that she could not go to hear me speak. I told her that I might not go to speak. She insisted that I should; and she urged my sister to go also. Christmas came drearily for us, and New Year's still more drearily; for we now knew that death was distant only in days. On the night of January 6, I went to Carnegie Hall to speak; my sister remained at home. After my speech, I went back to my mother's bedside. She died early the next morning. Of this, the most poignant sorrow in my life, I am unable to write.

After my mother's death, Rosamond and I had our father's body brought to New York and buried in the same plot with hers. We both gained a deep sentimental satisfaction in knowing that, after the many and varied intervening years, they rested together in a piece of the soil of the city where they first met.

XXXII

IN THE late spring of 1919, I spoke at another mass meeting in Carnegie Hall. It was a meeting in protest against lynching, and Charles Evans Hughes was the chief speaker. Immediately after this meeting, I started on a speaking tour of the branches of the Association on the Pacific Coast and to organize new branches there. I talked from San Diego to Seattle. Many of the meetings were large and enthusiastic, but, on the whole, the trip was uneventful. It was, however, interesting to meet large numbers of worthwhile colored people; something I did not have the opportunity of doing on my visit to California fourteen years before. And now there were so many more of them.

On the trip I had to bear with a certain amount of lionizing. Toward the end it began to wear on me. In one of the large cities of the Northwest, I arrived at about eight o'clock in the morning after ten hours of effort to get some sleep on a train that was swaying and bumping over mountains. A committee met my train, and I was informed that a breakfast would be given for me at ten o'clock. There were twelve people at the breakfast. Immediately after breakfast, we piled into three or four automobiles and drove, it seemed to me, over the whole county, a county larger, I judge, than some of the Eastern states. When we drove back into the city I was taken to see a number of prominent citizens, among them, the editors of the daily newspapers. I protested gently. I was met by "just one more," and "just one more," and "the dinner will not be until six o'clock." I knew the meeting that night was to be an important one. I knew, too, that I should be up against what a public speaker is always up against, his record of past performances. Certainly, I could not end a speech by saying, "I wasn't as good tonight as you may have been led to expect, but the committee kept me on the go all day, and wore me out."

I finally lost the restraint that I usually try to maintain, and commanded the committee to take me to my stopping place at once, and told them not to expect me at the dinner before the meeting, to be given in my honor. They all seemed hurt; the chairman acted as though I had struck him in the face. I was sorry afterwards, for it is a terrible thing to wound friends who are sincerely endeavoring to be kind. But my action was in sheer self-defense. After that experience I could understand what Elbert Hubbard meant by what he was said to have included in his printed terms: "One hundred dollars a lecture. One hundred and fifty dollars if entertained."

I addressed a meeting in Spokane. Just before leaving the next afternoon for Seattle, I was walking up and down the railroad station platform, talking with two gentlemen who had come to see me off. My train came in and stood at the station for a quarter of an hour or so. A porter from the train approached me and said, "This is James Weldon Johnson, isn't it?" I was accustomed to having porters and waiters on trains address me by name; and always regarded it as a high mark of distinction. The porter added: "Madame Schumann-Heink is on the train, and she asks if you won't come to her drawing room when you come aboard."

I judged that she had seen me from her window and, out of curiosity, had asked the porter who I was. However, when I went to her drawing room, she talked as though she knew something about me. I stayed with her more than an hour. She did most of the talking and talked most of the while about the war. Her emotions, it appeared, were still torn by the fact that she had sons who had found it necessary to fight each other. Her words manifested the heart of the infinite mother, and I was deeply moved. She talked a little about music and art, and mentioned the fact that she had given her old home on Michigan Avenue in Chicago for a conservatory of music for Negro students. I left Madame Schumann-Heink feeling that I had had the opportunity of being in the presence of not only a great artist but a grand woman.

I returned east by way of Vancouver and the Canadian Rockies, reaching Cleveland, the latter part of June, to attend the first of the larger annual conferences of the Association. At the Cleveland conference, the Southern branches made themselves felt. Their delegates were among the most aggressive and outspoken. They proved their sincerity by demanding that the next conference be held in the South. They declared that the Association should demonstrate its own sincerity and courage by stating the case for equality of all the rights of citizenship in the South as well as in the North. They argued, and soundly, that the branches in the South should not be expected to do this if the national body refrained. Such a challenge could not be brushed aside. Atlanta made the bid for the conference, and the bid was backed up by an official invitation from the city. The national body voted that it would meet there the following May (1920).

The Red Summer of 1919 broke in fury. The colored people throughout the country were disheartened and dismayed. The great majority had trustingly felt that, because they had cheerfully done their bit in the war, conditions for them would be better. The reverse seemed to be true. There was one case, at least, in which a returned Negro soldier was lynched *because of the fact* that he wore the uniform of a United States soldier. The Ku Klux Klan had reached ascendancy. Reports from overseas had come back giving warning that the returned Negro soldiers would be a dangerous element and a menace; that these black men had been engaged in killing white men, and, so, had lost the sense of the inviolability of a white man's life; that they had frequently been given the treatment accorded only to white men in America, and, above all, that many of them had been favorably regarded by white women. One of the chief recruiting slogans of the Klan was the necessity of united action to keep these men in their place.

During the summer, bloody race riots occurred in Chicago, in Omaha, in Longview, Texas, in Phillips County, Arkansas, in Washington, and other communities. The riot in the national capital lasted three days, during which Negroes were hunted through the streets, dragged from street cars, beaten, and even killed. These pogroms brought from Claude McKay this cry of defiant despair sounded from the last ditch:

> If we must die—let it not be like hogs
> Hunted and penned in an inglorious spot,
> While round us bark the mad and hungry dogs,
> Making their mock at our accursed lot. . . .
>
> Oh, Kinsmen! We must meet the common foe
> Though far outnumbered let us show us brave,
> And for their thousand blows deal one death-blow!
> What though before us lies the open grave?
> Like men we'll face the murderous, cowardly pack,
> Pressed to the wall, dying, but fighting back![1]

The riots in Phillips County, Arkansas, were the most brutal of all these outbursts of violence, and the most memorable, because out of

---

[1] Quoted from *Harlem Shadows*, by Claude McKay, New York, 1922, Harcourt, Brace and Company.

them came a law case in which the Association won its second important constitutional victory. Early in 1919, when the price of cotton
had soared to undreamed-of heights, Negro farmers in and about
Elaine, Arkansas, who were realizing no greater profit than when
the price of cotton was at its nadir, organized to see if they could not
by legal steps force a statement of accounts and a fair settlement from
their landlords. They were holding a meeting one night in a little
church at Hoop Spur in an effort to raise the fee of a Little Rock
firm of white lawyers—father and son—which they had engaged to
take their case. Without warning the church was fired upon by a
deputy sheriff and his posse. In the mêlée, the deputy sheriff was
killed. The church was burned to the ground.

A reign of terror followed. Between two hundred and three hundred Negroes were hunted down in the fields and swamps to which
they had fled, and shot down like animals. Many of them had no idea
of what the trouble was about. The two white lawyers barely escaped
violence. They fled the state and settled in Detroit. Then, in accordance with common policy, the onus of what had taken place was put
on the Negroes. A large number of them were indicted on the charge
of conspiracy to massacre the whites and seize the land. A farcical
trial lasting three-quarters of an hour was held in a courthouse that
was filled with and surrounded by a mob. The jury, after being out
five minutes, brought in a verdict that condemned twelve of the Negro
farmers to death. Sixty-seven others received sentences of life imprisonment and long terms. What they were all actually guilty of was
attempted assault on the peonage system—the system by which the
Negro in the agricultural South is as effectively robbed of his labor as
ever he was under slavery.

The Association took up the defense of these men and, after fighting
their cases for five years through the courts of Arkansas and twice up
to the United States Supreme Court, won a decision from the latter
court in which it virtually reversed itself. The decision declared that
the Negroes, though tried in a duly constituted court, had not had
a trial according to due process of law, because the court had been
dominated by a mob. This was the reverse of the position taken by the
Supreme Court in the famous Leo Frank case. Ultimately, the twelve
farmers condemned to die were freed, and the sixty-odd others released
from prison.

Early in August of the Red Summer, our national office received a letter from the president of our branch in Austin, Texas, a branch of more than three hundred members, stating that he had been cited to appear in court and to bring all books and papers and correspondence belonging or pertaining to the National Association for the Advancement of Colored People; and that he had complied. Mr. Shillady telegraphed the Attorney General of Texas offering any information concerning the Association that might be desired. He then left immediately for Austin. On arriving there, he first met with a committee of the local branch, then called at the Governor's office, but that office was closed. At the Attorney General's office he had an interview with the acting Attorney General and gave him full information as to the purposes and methods of work of the Association, together with copies of its principal publications. The object of Mr. Shillady's visit to Austin was to ascertain why the books and papers of the local branch had been subpœnaed and to give the state official a fuller record than could be obtained from an examination of those documents. On the morning of his arrival he was haled before a local judge and examined in camera, being subjected to many questions, pertinent and impertinent, by a group of inquisitors. When he left this secret court of inquiry, he started for his hotel, and just across the street from it he was overtaken by a group of men who had been present at the inquiry. They quickly surrounded him and beat him severely. Mr. Shillady was a non-resistant and during the assault did not raise a hand. Of course, it is possible that he would have been killed had he defended himself. Among Mr. Shillady's assailants were a constable and a county judge. The Governor of Texas publicly expressed his satisfaction at the treatment Mr. Shillady had been given.

When this attack on Mr. Shillady took place, I was at Hampton Institute, where I had gone for a brief vacation. I had been there but two or three days before I received the telegram informing me of what had happened. I left immediately for New York. I met Mr. Shillady when he arrived at the Pennsylvania Station. His face and body were badly bruised; moreover, he was broken in spirit. I don't think he was ever able to realize how such a thing could happen in the United States to an American, free, white, and twenty-one. He never fully recovered spiritually from the experience.

We, the Association's officers, found ourselves faced by two disturbing conditions: We realized that there was a campaign of considerable proportions on to intimidate our members in Southern communities and stamp out the organization; in a number of instances this campaign was successful. We also found that there had arisen a division throughout the whole membership as to the wisdom of holding the next annual conference in Atlanta. Many felt that the meeting should be canceled, postponed, or transferred to a Northern city. The officers and the majority of the Board of Directors, together with the greater part of the membership, stood for the decision made at Cleveland. The Atlanta branch stood firm; so the national officers could not have done less, even had they wished to. As the Atlanta conference drew nigh, in the same degree it became a test of courage.

XXXIII

THE United States had seized Haiti in 1915. For the seizure of an independent nation, we offered the stock justifications: protection of American lives and American interests, and the establishment and maintenance of internal order. Had all these reasons been well founded, they would not have constituted justification for the complete seizure of a sovereign state at peace with us.

But they were not all well founded. American lives were not and never had been jeopardized in Haiti; and, if American business ventures were not as profitable as had been expected, that could not be wholly charged to the Haitian government. Nor could it be said that the United States or any other country had sustained loss through any default of Haiti on its foreign obligations. It is true, there was internal disorder; but that disorder was not so great or so menacing to us as the disorder then prevalent in our next-door neighbor across the Rio Grande. Perhaps the distinction lay in the difference in size between Haiti and Mexico. The underlying reasons were not given. They were, however, those involved in long-standing policies of the State and Navy Departments at Washington.

An army of marines had been landed in Haiti, as had been the case in Nicaragua. In Nicaragua, however, the American forces were there in accordance with the wishes of the government; they were there to sustain that government in power. In Haiti, the American forces seized the power and made themselves the government. Haiti was quickly developed into a very nice job-holding colony for "deserving Democrats." Harsh conditions resulted from this situation because a number of Haitians were deluded by the idea that they had the patriotic right to arm themselves and defend their native land against the invaders. Probably, they thought that the majority of the people in the United States who were at all familiar with American history would recognize them as patriots. The term that the majority of the American people learned to apply to them was, "bandits."

In spite of the fact that the lid was kept down tight, reports of the harsh conditions due to the American occupation kept leaking through to us. The Association considered having me go to Haiti and make an investigation. I went to see Theodore Roosevelt and talked the matter over with him. He was enthusiastic about such a mission, and thought I ought to be able to do a good job. He talked in his naturally energetic manner, snapping out the words and biting them off. He talked for quite a while about the weaknesses of the Administration at Washington. He was especially strong in expressing his opinion about its refusal to accept his offer to raise a division of volunteers for the war. He made no effort to conceal the deep disappointment he felt. He told me that it was in his plans to have one brigade made up of Negro troops and to place it under the command of Charles Young as a brigadier general.[1] I expressed myself bitterly about the retirement of Colonel Young and the shunting of him off from a generalship. Mr. Roosevelt dictated and signed a letter for my use; and, as I left him, he slapped me on the shoulder and wished me good luck. I did not go to Haiti, however, until February 1920. Herbert Seligmann sailed with me, but after several weeks there he was taken seriously ill and returned home.

I had been reading up on Haiti on the trip down, but I was not quite prepared for my first sight of the country. I had, of course, seen enough of the tropics to know that every island there is not a palm-covered coral bed jutting only from a few feet to a few hundred feet

[1] Charles Young was the third Negro to graduate from West Point (1889) and was a splendid soldier and officer. At the outbreak of the World War he held the rank of major. Over his protest and despite his desire for service, he was retired in 1917 with the rank of colonel; but was detailed to organize a constabulary in Liberia. He died there, but his body was brought home and buried with military honors in the Arlington National Cemetery.

above the ocean's level; but I was surprised at the high ranges of purple-colored mountains that we saw as we ran down the Haitian coast. The city of Port-au-Prince surprised me still more, for it is not only situated on one of the most beautiful bays in the world, but I found it the finest city of all the Latin-American seaports that I had seen. I had also been familiarizing myself with Haitian history, and in doing that I met with other surprises. I learned that Haiti was the second independent republic in the Western Hemisphere; the United States being the first. I learned that its aid had made possible the independence of the third republic, Venezuela, as early as it was achieved. I learned that the war in Haiti by which black slaves liberated themselves worked a more complete social revolution than the war by which the slaves were freed in the United States. Our Civil War freed the slaves in name only. It left them, illiterate, homeless, and penniless, and at the economic mercy of their former masters. Masses of them merely entered a new slavery in which there was neither legal nor moral obligation on the masters; there was not even so much as a financial interest in the "new slaves." In Haiti, the large plantations were cut up into small parcels, and the former slaves settled on plots of ground, which they cultivated, perhaps poorly, but as independent farmers. Some families had cultivated the same plot of ground for a hundred years or more; and so there was no such thing in Haiti as a peon class, a class, the creation of which is one of the curses of Mexico.

For a while, I was something of a "man of mystery" in Port-au-Prince. I was stopping at the best hotel; I entertained important people there and at the Café Dereix; I cashed drafts at the bank; and I appeared to have important business. What that business was remained, on the whole, a question; for nobody knew just what it was, except the people with whom I discussed it, and they were, if anything, more anxious than I to have the matter considered confidential.

My aim was to gather information and shades of opinion from as many sources as I possibly could; and in trying to carry it out, I talked with a large number of persons. I talked with almost every important Haitian, many of them men of wide political knowledge and experience, who realized the difficulty of the situation, but were determined to take every feasible step for the restoration of Haitian independence. I talked also with members of the radical group, the group whose slogan was, "Down with the Americans!" and which stood for taking steps, feasible or not.

I called to see ex-President Légitime, a grand old gentleman; indeed, a jet-black Frenchman of the courtly school. He returned the call, taking lunch with me at my hotel. He spoke frankly of the wrongs and evils that had resulted from American rule. I saw President Sudre Dartiguenave twice. I believed that he was a patriot at heart, but he was in a delicate position and was extremely guarded in what he said to me. It seemed to me to be his intention to have me form my opinions from what he did not say. I spent an evening with Louis Borno, who succeeded M. Dartiguenave in the presidency. M. Borno, a lawyer, was a former Secretary of State for Foreign Affairs. He was one of the most accomplished men I have met; tall, slender, bronze-colored, with the face and hands of an artist; a linguist, a fine poet, and a very astute statesman. Our conversation lasted a couple of hours and was genuinely pleasant, but on every vital topic M. Borno was guarded. I saw a great deal of M. Sanon, who had resigned as Secretary of Foreign Affairs rather than sign the Haitian-American Convention by which Haiti was forced to abdicate its sovereignty. A huge man, pure black, and with exceptional intellectual powers. I saw as much of M. Price-Mars, formerly Secretary of the Haitian Legation at Washington, a gentle scholar, as slight in bulk as Sanon was huge, and also pure black. I frequently saw most of the men who are today reassuming the control of their country.

But the man with whom my visit to Haiti had the most far-reaching relations was the least pretentious of all that I met. He was Georges Sylvain, small and shy, but quite distinguished. He was a well-known lawyer, a former Haitian minister to France, and a man of letters. Some of his literary work had been crowned by the French Academy; he had addressed the Sorbonne and had been made a member of the Légion d'Honneur. With him, the cause of Haiti seemed to dominate every other interest. He gave me a good deal of information about Haiti, and about American misrule, which he knew I was going to make use of in the United States in the interest of the Haitians. In return, he asked me what I thought the Haitians themselves ought to do. All the Haitians I talked with complained bitterly of conditions; they had learned that I had been named as a member of the Republican National Advisory Committee for the approaching presidential

campaign, and they piled these complaints up for me, seeming to feel
that, if the Democratic administration, under which the oppressive
conditions had been put upon them, was replaced by a Republican
administration, I, by laying their complaints before the new régime,
could have those conditions removed. They reckoned not at all how
infinitesimal was the influence that my position carried. M. Sylvain was
the first to ask me what I thought were some of the things the
Haitians themselves could do.

The plan I suggested to M. Sylvain was one for organizing sentiment among the Haitians and for setting up machinery by which they
could take united action. I told him that external help could not be
effective unless the Haitian people were active. I gave him a full
explanation of the central idea and the working methods of the National Association for the Advancement of Colored People, and urged
upon him that a similar organization be established in Haiti, with
headquarters in Port-au-Prince, and branches in the other important
cities and towns. He followed the suggestion, and at a mass meeting
held in the theater at Port-au-Prince the Union Patriotique was organized. This organization exerted a vital force in advancing the restoration of Haitian independence to the point it has reached. It is sad that
M. Sylvain did not live to see the fuller realization of his hopes and
efforts.

I talked with foreigners as well as Haitians. I made a point of seeing
the several Americans who were conducting mercantile businesses in
Port-au-Prince; without exception, they expressed sentiments that
leaned toward the Haitians. I also talked with a number of our marine
officers. I now knew their language; and in my talks with them I spent
a tidy sum in *goutte d'or* (a famous brand of Haitian rum). I found
that the rum had the effect of lessening restraint and inducing frankness. The effect was so potent in several instances that my marine
friends appeared to become oblivious to the fact that they were talking with a Negro—an American Negro. One of them summed up the
situation for me by declaring, "The trouble with Haiti is that these
niggers down here with a little money and education think they are as
good as *we* are." Another one related to me an incident that occurred
at a fire. He told me that the fire was gaining headway, and they were
calling on everybody to give a hand; that standing on the sidewalk
was a Haitian dressed in a silk hat, Prince Albert coat, and patent
leather shoes; that when his command to this Haitian to take hold of

the hose was ignored, he "gave him a kick that landed him one way in the gutter and his silk hat another." A gentleman, black or white, dressed in a silk hat, Prince Albert coat, and patent leather shoes, under a tropic sun, has always struck me as ludicrous, but this incident did not strike me as humorous.

Some of the marines related to me details of their fights in the hills and back country with the "bandits." One of them told me about a "bandit hunt"; how they finally came upon a crowd of natives engaged in the popular pastime of cock-fighting, and how they "let them have it" with machine gun and rifle fire. It was evident that for many of the American boys who had enlisted in the marines and been sent to Haiti, "hunting bandits" was a great adventure and a very thrilling sport. I used these accounts given me by the marine officers, together with other reports that I gathered, as the basis for an estimate of the number of Haitians that had been killed by the American forces of the occupation.

I had the opportunity to take a peep into social life in the Haitian capital. I visited a number of the beautiful villas on the heights above Port-au-Prince. I had the privilege of going to the Cercle Bellevue, the leading club, where the men talked understandingly about world affairs. I attended the closing exercises of the Normal School, where the girls acted one of Molière's plays with a verve and finish that was surprising to me. And I was present at a charity ball given at the French Legation, the grandest affair of the kind I had ever witnessed. I was forced to conclude that Haitian society in Port-au-Prince moved on a level that for wealth and culture could not be matched by the colored people in any city in the United States.

In my last two weeks in Haiti I made a ten-day trip in a Ford through the country, as far north as Cap Haïtien. I satisfied my curiosity to see the inside of some of the native huts. These huts were ingeniously built of thin strips of wood plaited about the heavier uprights and plastered outside and inside with clay, the whole covered with a thatched roof. There were generally two rooms or more. The floor was usually of hard clay. In almost every instance the outer walls were whitewashed or tinted blue, or pink, or yellow. On the inside, the cabins were kept very clean and the yards about them were swept daily. An æsthetic touch, flowers or a gorgeous shrub or vine, was common. Nowhere did I see the filth and squalor that is hardly ever missing in and around the log cabins of the South. And yet, some

Americans, who were, doubtless, sincerely anxious to see the Haitians make progress, felt that they would be essentially advanced if, instead of living in these native huts—so well adapted to their needs and their environment—they lived in American-built cottages with glass windows and a front porch, and covered by a tin roof and a mortgage. The Haitian peasants were kindhearted, hospitable, and polite. They were, naturally, ignorant of a great many things, but far from being stupid; indeed, they were rather quick-witted and imaginative. The countrywomen were magnificent as they filed along the roads by scores and by hundreds, taking farm and garden products to the town markets. Their baskets balanced on their colored-turbaned heads, the large, gold loops in their ears pendulating to their steps, they strode along lithe and straight, almost haughtily, carrying themselves like so many Queens of Sheba. The weather was fine, and I enjoyed the trip as though it were only a pleasure jaunt. I stopped in a village where they were celebrating a feast day, and saw a native dance. The men and women danced in a thatched-roof pavilion without walls. They danced in a ring, to the music of drums of various sizes and pitch. There was the same ring going round and round on shuffling feet, one heel stamping out the rhythm of a monotonous chant, in the same manner that I had seen as a child in the African village in Nassau, and observed later in the "ring shouts" in Negro churches in the South. When I crossed the mountains, I saw scenery as wonderful as any my eyes had beheld.

The sensation of my trip to Haiti came in my visit to Cap Haïtien. I telegraphed to Lemuel W. Livingston that I was coming. Up to a short time before, he had been the American Consul at Cap Haïtien, having served about twenty years at the same post. He had also during nearly all that time been the correspondent of the Associated Press. Livingston and two or three of his friends met me on the road ten or fifteen miles out of Cap Haïtien, and I drove into the city with them. I took dinner with my old friend. I had not seen him for many years. I was glad to talk with him about past things; but, more important, there were things I wanted to ask him about Haiti that I did not feel I could ask anyone else. He had married a charming Haitian woman, whose father, I learned, was a man of some wealth. Livingston's marriage furnished his main reason for never wishing to be transferred from Cap Haïtien. After dinner we went to the club, a spacious and well-appointed building. There, he introduced me to a number of men, some of them white. White men having residence or business in the Cape were glad to have the privileges of the club. While Livingston and I were playing billiards, I told him what the chief desire was that had brought me to Cap Haïtien—to make the trip up to Christophe's citadel. He told me it was a strenuous trip, and would require some preparation, but that there was no reason why I could not make it.

I drove, starting at daylight, in my Ford to the little village of Milot. There at the inn I met the man with whom I had arranged to furnish me with three horses and six men. Two of the horses turned out to be mules, but a mule is much superior to a horse for mountain climbing. We started out supplied with food and coffee. Just beyond the village, at the foot of the mountain, are the ruins of Sans Souci, Christophe's palace. The palace of the great black king of Northern Haiti was a copy, more or less and on a smaller scale, of Versailles. It was the work of French architects and builders; and when it was finished it was, beyond question, the most palatial residence in the Americas.

Christophe built his citadel in the first decade of the nineteenth century on the top of a mountain more than three thousand feet high, which dominates the fertile plains of Northern Haiti. He built it as a last stronghold against the French if they attempted to retake Haiti. The trip up took a little more than two hours and was over a narrow, precipitous, at times dangerous path. After I had ridden an hour and a half, I reached a sudden turn in the path and caught the first view of the great fortress. The sight was amazing, it was dumbfounding, I could scarcely believe my own eyes. There, from the pinnacle of the mountain, rose the massive walls of brick and stone to a height of more than one hundred feet. On three sides the walls are sheer with the sides of the mountain; the other side is approached by the path.

The first sight to attract my attention after I entered the citadel was fifty long, solid brass cannons, with which Christophe had commanded the path. How he ever got those cannon up there, nobody seemed to know. I was told that the Haitian government had had offers for them as metal, but that nobody seemed to know how to get them down. I explored the vast structure for several hours, its storerooms, its dungeons, its subterranean passages, its chapel. There was a fountain from which the water still bubbled up—a sort of physical mystery to me, as I saw no greater height from which it could come—and there was a dark opening into which one dropped a stone without ever hearing it strike bottom. In places the walls were from eight to twelve feet thick. Some idea of the size of the citadel may be gained from the statement that Christophe built it to quarter thirty thousand soldiers. The more I saw of it, the more the wonder grew on me not only as to the execution but as to the mere conception of such a work. I should say that it is the most wonderful ruin in the Western Hemisphere, and, for the amount of human energy and labor sacrificed in its construction, can be compared to the pyramids of Egypt. As I stood on the highest point, where the sheer drop from the walls was more than two thousand feet, and looked out over the rich plains of Northern Haiti, I was impressed with the thought that, if ever a man had the right to feel himself a king, that man was Christophe when he walked around the parapets of his citadel.

I did my best to get some pictures with my small kodak, but without much success. Since that time many photographs have been made of it from airplanes. Christophe's citadel had been written about, but forgotten. I think I may claim that I rediscovered it for the United States. When I returned home, I lectured about it and wrote about it, publishing with some of my articles the snapshots I had taken. What I said and wrote was in some degree responsible for a new literary interest in Haiti. John W. Vandercook talked with me about Christophe and his citadel before he went down and wrote his book, *Black Majesty*[1]; and William B. Seabrook talked with me about Haiti before he went down and wrote *The Magic Island*.[2] Among my friends and acquaintances, my trip started a sort of pilgrimage to the black republic.

When I got back to Port-au-Prince, I went directly to the steamship office to arrange for my passage to New York. I was told that there was nothing I could get on the next ship nor on the next. There was only one line of steamships touching Haiti, the United States-owned Panama Line; the Dutch and German lines had been suspended. It was May, and the Panama Canal employees were going home as fast as they could on the vacations allowed them by the government. The ships reached Port-au-Prince loaded beyond capacity. I waited, but without any assurances that I could get passage.

While I was waiting, a farewell luncheon was given me at Pétionville, a village up on the mountainside above Port-au-Prince. About a

[1] Harper & Brothers, New York, 1928.
[2] Harcourt, Brace & Co., New York, 1929.

dozen prominent Haitians were present, including M. Sanon and M. Price-Mars. The luncheon gave me an opportunity of emphasizing to this group the necessity for organization of the Haitians. I also made it an opportunity to offer a gratuitous suggestion. My suggestion was that Creole be made a written language. I said that in my opinion one of the greatest handicaps of Haiti was the fact that her masses, though possessing native intelligence, were absolutely illiterate. They had no means of receiving or communicating thoughts through the written word. For a reason that I cannot explain, the French language in the French-Colonial settlements in America containing a Negro population divided itself into two branches, French and Creole. This is true of Louisiana, Martinique, Guadeloupe, and Haiti. I think it is strange, because nothing like it happened with the Spanish language. Creole is an Africanized French, but it must not be thought of as a mere dialect. The French-speaking person cannot understand Creole, excepting a few words, until he learns it. It is a distinct, grammatically constructed, graphic, and very expressive language. A merchant woman, following the native idiom, will say, "You do not wish anything beautiful if you do not buy this."

I elicited from the group, that, possibly, less than a half-million Haitians knew and used French in addition to Creole, while more than two million knew and used only Creole; that the children of the masses studied French for a few years in school, but it never became their everyday language. I expressed as strongly as I could my belief that, while French should be retained as the language of literature and culture, Creole should be made the common written and printed tongue; that it be used in much the same way that Papaimento is used in Curaçao. I emphatically declared to my listeners that books and newspapers made available to the masses through Creole would be a greater power for liberating and raising up the Haitian people than any other I could think of. My suggestion was politely received, but aroused no enthusiasm. For the educated Haitians are exceedingly proud of their French traditions and of the fact that French is their tongue. They consider the French language a precious heritage and their strong link with world culture. On this latter point, they are, of course, right.

The middle of May was approaching, and I was growing desperate. I simply had to get back to the United States; and not because I could not have spent the time pleasantly waiting for a ship, but because the

Atlanta conference of the Association was set for the latter part of the month, and I *had* to be there. I had been one of those at the national office who had most loudly proclaimed that the conference should not be postponed or transferred to some other city; that it should be held in Atlanta, despite any risks. I now plainly saw that if I were absent it would be a thing that I could not explain away in a lifetime; that the most polite response the explanation of not being able to secure passage on a ship would receive would be a smile, which in words would take the form of that very expressive vulgarism, "Oh yeah?"

In my extremity, I made arrangements with a native fisherman to take me in his boat from Port-au-Prince to Santiago, Cuba, a distance of about two hundred miles. I planned to take a train from Santiago to Havana, and to go from there to Key West or New York.

My next-room neighbor at the Hotel Bellevue was a Mr. Cochran. He was the owner of a large tobacco shop in Washington. He had been the owner of a hotel there, but had sold it at a high profit during the war, when hotel space in the capital was worth anything a proprietor had the lack of conscience to charge for it. With the money from the sale he had come to Haiti and made investments. He showed a decided liking for me. One day he apologetically confessed that I was the "first educated colored man" he had ever known. He backed up his sentiments by making me a very good offer to remain with him in Haiti as a kind of manager for his ventures—an offer I, of course, had to decline.

Mr. Cochran and two of his American friends and I were playing bridge on the upper piazza of the Hotel, when I disclosed to him my plan for getting back to the United States. He became greatly concerned. He declared that I shouldn't think of carrying out any such plan; that the trip from Port-au-Prince across the Mona Passage in a small boat would be not only very uncomfortable but hazardous. There was a Panama Line steamer bound for New York in port that morning. Mr. Cochran stopped the bridge game, went to his room and got two boxes of cigars, and asked me to come along with him. We went aboard the ship and into the captain's cabin. The captain seemed glad to see Mr. Cochran and gladder to get a supply of cigars double the quantity he had usually received. My friend quickly came to the point—wouldn't the captain take me to New York—business of the most urgent sort. The captain came back just as promptly—it was impossible—the ship was loaded to the gunwales—not an inch of space left—there were already more passengers aboard than she was chartered to carry—if anything happened to her on the trip, he would be in danger of losing his master's license. But Mr. Cochran was a determined man; he would not accept a refusal. Finally, the captain said that I might come aboard and go up as a deck passenger, for there were no accommodations. I was overjoyed and thanked him. Mr. Cochran, I hardly knew how to thank.

I hurriedly packed and got aboard, and began the most uncomfortable four or five days that I can remember. I, of course, had no stateroom; not a bunk; not even a steamer chair. The voyage was rough, and I was in that state of constant semi-nausea which is many times more disagreeable than outright seasickness. The ship was far from being a vessel de luxe, and often I had no place where I could sit down. I paid the steward to place a makeshift bed for me on one of the wooden benches in the smoking room, and there I slept. But I could never get to bed before twelve or one o'clock, for until that hour the room was filled with men gambling. They used all the tables for gambling, and shot dice on the floor. These men who crowded the smoking room were Canal employees of the artisan class—engineers, machinists, plumbers, electrical workers, and helpers. They were rough; their language was coarse and profane. But I gave the best attention I could to what they said, because it presented an interesting and important view of life, a view that I was unfamiliar with, a view that disclosed one of the most discouraging aspects of the racial situation. One expression that they constantly used brought to me more vividly than anything else ever had a realization of the Negro's economic and industrial plight, of how lean a chance was his with his white brothers of the proletariat. The expression which I heard at least a hundred times was, "Never let a nigger pick up a tool." "Never let a nigger pick up a tool." "Never let a nigger pick up a tool."

This expression echoed in my mind for a long time, and the answer to it was, I knew, that in the practical processes of dealing with the race question there is nothing more fundamental and vital than the lowering and sweeping away of economic and industrial barriers against the Negro. For no condition under which he struggles oppresses the Negro more than the refusal of a fair and equal chance to earn a living—to say nothing of earning it in ways in which he is able to prove himself well fitted. It is at once unfair, unreasonable, and cruel to declare to the Negro that, when he has grown to the stature of a full American citizen, he will be acknowledged as such, and at the same time to deny him the basic means of accomplishing the very thing demanded. And of this unfairness, this unreasonableness, this cruelty, the American people as a whole are guilty.

When economic and industrial avenues are open to the Negro, many of the most perplexing phases of the race question will automatically disappear.

XXXIV

I GOT back to New York just in time to go to Atlanta. I was disturbed at hearing of the number of persons who had decided not to go. Mr. Shillady himself had decided not to attend the conference. He confessed to me, "I think I have the moral courage, but I find that I have no physical courage." Mr. Seligmann was not yet fully recovered from his Haitian illness and so could not go; Edward Bernays took his place and handled the publicity for us. Miss Ovington, Mr. White, and Mr. Pickens of the national office had already gone. Arthur B. Spingarn, chairman of our legal committee, and I made the trip down together.

When Mr. Spingarn and I reached Atlanta, the Pullman porter put our bags out, and, when we alighted, both his and mine were in the hands of one and the same red-cap. As we followed this red-cap along the platform and up the stairs, I could see through the back of his head how his brain was working on a serious problem which increased in imminence with each step that he took. And the problem was whether to break the laws of Georgia by taking the white man through the Jim-Crow exit with me, or by taking me through the white folks' exit with him. I was so curious about his mental processes and their probable result, that I lost sight of the fact that the poor fellow and ourselves were between the upper and nether millstones of all the power of the sovereign State of Georgia. I could not help but muse over the paradoxicalness of the situation; for Atlanta, like every other Southern community, was a city in which there was not a white household worth going into in which Negroes did not go and even live and sleep. The finer and wealthier the household, the more certain was this to be true. Negroes kept such houses clean, they took care of the children, they nursed the sick, they were entrusted with the family treasures and family secrets, and with their own black hands they prepared the food; yet, the entrance to the Union Station, as wide as a city street, was too narrow for the two races to pass in and out of together. The superficial observer will, quite naturally, conclude that the so-called race problem in the South is based upon an innate racial antipathy; indeed, the opposite is more nearly true. The red-cap showed real courage and successfully risked the chance of taking us both through the main entrance.

The Northern members of the Association who went down to Atlanta did so feeling that they were performing a rather heroic action, but it developed that the feeling was not warranted. Of course, it is true that they went without knowing what might happen. There was considerable tenseness at the first session, a mass meeting held on Sunday afternoon at the largest colored church in the city. The mayor of Atlanta was present and made the address of welcome; and, after making allowance for the strong implications that we would not have any trouble so long as we remembered that we were in Atlanta and not in New York or Boston, it was a very good address of welcome. In lieu of Mr. Shillady, I was on the program for the keynote speech, the speech in which the aims of the Association would be set forth and its achievements rehearsed. I was in a position where I did not dare to pussyfoot, even if I wanted to do so. The conference ran along easily and quite pleasantly. I believe that the authorities of Atlanta felt that the city was on trial, and I think that some special instructions must have been given to policemen, street car conductors, and such others as might come in direct contact with the delegates, for there was more than the wonted public courtesy and a noticeable elasticity in the traditional racial bounds.

Back in New York, I began at once to get my Haitian material into shape. But I interrupted this work long enough to go to Chicago and, armed with a badge and a pass as a member of the National Advisory Committee—insignia of quite an empty honor—attended the Republican Convention which nominated Warren G. Harding for president and broke General Leonard Wood's heart. In fairness, I should modify the "empty honor" stricture; for Herbert Parsons did write me a letter asking that I prepare some material on the Negro for inclusion in the campaign book. The letter followed me to Haiti and back to New York.

Shortly after my return to our office, Mr. Shillady resigned, and I was appointed, for a second time, Acting Secretary. At the meeting of the Board of Directors in October I was elected Secretary, and became the first Negro to hold that position. Early during my secretaryship Mrs. Addie W. Hunton and Robert W. Bagnall were added to our staff.

Immediately upon getting back from Chicago, I again took up work on the data I had gathered in Haiti. I wrote a series of four articles for *The Nation*, single articles for several other publications, and prepared a lecture on Self-Determining Haiti. In the meantime, I made a trip to Marion, Ohio, and talked with Senator Harding. I calculated that the most advantageous break possible to be gained for Haiti could be secured through him as the Republican presidential candidate. I found Mr. Harding an exceedingly busy man; Republican politicians from all over the country were flocking to Marion to see him; but, when he learned the nature of my visit, he became instantly interested and gave me plenty of time. I went over the whole Haitian situation, going back to the efforts of the Washington Administration at the close of 1914 to force American control on Haiti; I rehearsed the steps taken later through the Ford Mission and those taken still later through the Fuller Mission; I pointed out that the overthrow and assassination of President Guillaume and the attending consequences did not constitute the cause of the American occupation of Haiti in July 1915, but merely furnished the long-awaited opportunity; I spoke of the influence upon the actions taken by the United States in Haiti that Roger L. Farnham, Vice-President of the National City Bank of New York had exercised. I stressed that, in establishing the occupation, American marines had killed three thousand Haitians, many of them unarmed persons; I emphasized the contradiction in the preachments of President Wilson about the self-determination of small nations and the military seizure under his administration of a weak but friendly republic.

Mr. Harding was quick to see the importance of this data as campaign material, but he was cautious. He wanted me to give him the fullest verification possible of all the facts, in order that he might be on solid ground in using them. I said to him that in addition to the statement I was presenting, I could furnish him with copies of documents that would substantiate all the charges except one; and this I did do on a second visit to Marion. Regarding the charge that American marines had killed three thousand Haitians, I told him that I had arrived at the number after the widest inquiry I could make and upon what I believed was a conservative estimate.[1]

Mr. Harding's handsome face was a study while I talked with him. Despite his occasional grave and cautious protestations, I could see that he looked upon the Haitian matter as a gift right off the Christmas tree. He could not conceal his delight. I sat directly opposite him at a flat-top desk. In my anxiety to impress him, I leaned forward with my arms on the desk. He sat in a swivel chair, smoking cigarette after cigarette, and listening intently. From time to time he leaned back in his chair and blew clouds of smoke upward. Once, toward the latter part of the interview, when he came back down into position, he reached into his hip pocket, brought out a big plug of tobacco and, cutting off a generous mouthful, began to chew. After he became president, the W.C.T.U. sent him a petition requesting that he discontinue smoking cigarettes as an example to the youth of the country. I wonder what the dear ladies would have done had they known he was a tobacco chewer. I left the Senator satisfied with the results of my mission.

Mr. Harding made of the Haitian matter a campaign issue that struck Washington like a bombshell. The Administration was thrown on the defensive and, through Secretary Daniels, a naval investigation was promptly instituted. The prime purpose of this investigation was to give a whitewash to the marines; nevertheless, the light had been turned on, and some of the more brutal abuses in Haiti were abolished. The bombshell hurled by Mr. Harding brought out return fire from those on the defensive:—the Haitian government was so rotten with graft that our government was compelled to take charge in order to straighten out and purify things—the people of Haiti had sunk to such depths of degradation that it was our moral duty to step in and lift them up—they had regressed to cannibalism—there was a case in which

---

[1] This estimate was, a short while later, more than confirmed by General Barnett, of the marines, who in a published report put the number of "indiscriminate killings of Haitians" at 3250; the number of marines killed at 13; and the number of Haitians wounded "impossible to estimate."

an American marine had been killed and his vital organs taken out and eaten raw. This tale of atrocity logically raised a question that the naval inquiry did not go into. The question as to which was more reprehensible, the alleged custom in Haiti of eating a human being without cooking him, or the authenticated custom in the United States of cooking a human being without eating him. The Haitian custom would have, at least, a utilitarian purpose in extenuation.

Under President Harding, a Senate investigation was held. This investigation also, on the whole, was a whitewash. The Senate Committee felt that there should be a liberal civil government in Haiti, but under the tutelage of the United States for a period of years; however, some further reforms were effected. The latest governmental step taken was the appointment of the Forbes Commission to Haiti by President Hoover. This Commission recommended a number of reforms and broader policies, and the final withdrawal of American military authority. President Hoover also sent down a commission headed by Dr. R. R. Moton, of Tuskegee, which made valuable recommendations for the betterment of educational and social conditions. And so, during these more than twelve years, through the efforts of the Haitians themselves, and their friends in the United States, the restoration of Haitian independence has been going forward by degrees. The work is not yet completed, but a great deal has been done. All this while the Association has kept up its fight for a free Haiti. We have held mass meetings, we have disseminated publicity, we have appeared at the hearings of Senate committees, and we have brought all pressure we possibly could to bear on both the Senate and the President. Haiti freed will owe a great debt to the National Association for the Advancement of Colored People.

My two interviews with Mr. Harding at Marion established a cordial relationship. I saw him a number of times in Washington after he became President. On my first visit, he shook hands with me as I was leaving and laughed as he said, "We certainly made a good shot with that Haitian material." I replied, "We certainly did."

XXXV

IN THE latter part of 1919 I had taken the first steps for the Association toward securing the enactment of a federal law against lynching. In this period, the number of lynchings was not so high as it had been in former years, but the barbarous manner in which victims were being put to death could not have been surpassed by the fiends in hell. The colored people of the whole country agonized over these recurring outbreaks of inhuman savagery. As an example, merely: Henry Lowery, a Negro, shot and killed a white man and his daughter at Nodena, Arkansas; the killings resulting from a dispute about money that the white man owed the Negro. Lowery escaped but was captured by officers of the law. These officers surrendered him to a mob. The mob chained him to a log and lynched him. A part of the account of the lynching given in the Memphis, Tennessee, *Press*, in its issue of January 27, 1921, by one of its special correspondents who was an eye witness, reads:

More than 500 persons stood by and looked on while the Negro was slowly burning to a crisp. A few women were scattered among the crowd of Arkansas planters, who directed the gruesome work. . . .

Not once did the slayer beg for mercy despite the fact that he suffered one of the most horrible deaths imaginable. With the Negro chained to a log, members of the mob placed a small pile of leaves around his feet. Gasoline was then poured on the leaves, and the carrying out of the death sentence was under way.

Inch by inch the Negro was fairly cooked to death. Every few minutes fresh leaves were tossed on the funeral pyre until the blaze had passed the Negro's waist. As the flames were eating away his abdomen, a member of the mob stepped forward and saturated the body with gasoline. It was then only a few minutes until the Negro had been reduced to ashes. . . .

Even after the flesh had dropped away from his legs and the flames were leaping toward his face, Lowery retained consciousness. Not once did he whimper or beg for mercy. Once or twice he attempted to pick up the hot ashes and thrust them in his mouth in order to hasten his death. Each time the ashes were kicked out of his reach by a member of the mob. . . .

Words fail to describe the sufferings of the Negro. Even after his legs had been reduced to the bones he continued to talk with his captors, answering all questions put to him. . . .

This incident was not unique; the national office of the Association had dealt with a number of cases equally atrocious, and had tried through publicity and protest to make them means of arousing the conscience of the nation against the Shame of America, the shame of being the only civilized country in the world, the only spot anywhere in the world where such things could be. These happenings caused in me reactions that ran the gamut from towering but impotent rage to utter dejection, and always set me wondering at the thoughtlessness of people who take it as a matter of course that American Negroes should love their country.

I had gone down to Washington to see if Senator Capper, at that time the President of our Topeka branch, would introduce a bill in the Senate for us. He expressed complete willingness to do so, but suggested that the measure would stand a better chance if we could get his colleague, Senator Curtis, to sponsor it. He took me over to Senator Curtis's office and gave me a very favorable introduction to him. Senator Curtis said that he would be glad to introduce a resolution in the Senate that would call for an investigation of lynching. An investigation was less than we wanted; we had in our office a record of the facts for thirty years back, but I felt that a Senate investigation would be a beginning, at least. When I left Senator Curtis, I went over to the House Office Building and saw Representative L. C. Dyer, who had made efforts to bring before Congress a bill to make lynching a federal crime. Mr. Dyer said that he believed an anti-lynching bill could, eventually, be passed in the House if it could be gotten out on the floor; that the first great difficulty was to get such a bill reported out favorably from the committee. I told him that I believed the National Association for the Advancement of Colored People could stir the Judiciary Committee to favorable action on an anti-lynching bill. Mr. Dyer welcomed our co-operation.

Nothing definite was done, however, until the opening of the Sixty-seventh Congress in the spring of 1921. On April 11, Mr. Dyer introduced H.R. 13, a bill "to assure to persons within the jurisdiction of every state the equal protection of the laws, and to punish the crime of lynching." The bill was at once referred to the Committee on the Judiciary and ordered to be printed. We joked a bit about it, but neither Mr. Dyer nor I was dismayed at the number 13, which the bill had drawn. We dug up notable precedents in which 13 had proved lucky. Within a short time, the entire machinery of the Association, its full organized strength and all the collateral force it could marshal, were thrown behind the measure.

The length of anything like a detailed account of the fight for the passage of the Dyer Anti-Lynching Bill, would, for inclusion here, be too much out of proportion to the length of this story. For nearly two years, during the periods when Congress was in session, I spent the greater part of my time in Washington. I tramped the corridors of the Capitol and the two office buildings so constantly that toward the end, I could, I think, have been able to find my way about blindfolded. I could say almost as much for the trip up Pennsylvania Avenue to the White House. My experience as a lobbyist brought me into personal contact with almost every outstanding man in both branches of Congress, and with a great many who were not outstanding. In seeing some of them I was often given precedence over people who had been waiting long before I arrived. Martin B. Madden, Chairman of the Appropriations Committee, arranged with me for a signal on the door to his private office that gave me access while others were waiting in the reception rooms. Once when I went in to see Senator Medill McCormick, one of his clerks, after taking in my name, told me that the Senator wanted me to come around and into his private office. When I got in he said, "Come on, let's take a ride and talk things over." And, leaving a half-dozen or so people waiting, we got into his car and rode out into the country, then back to the Capitol. He was a thin, nervous, high-strung, and, I thought, somewhat erratic man, but he was often impulsively warm-hearted. Once, when the filibuster was on in the Senate, and the supporters of the Dyer bill had gained a point, he waved to me from his place on the floor to where I sat in the gallery as though we were alumni of the same college and our football team had just scored. Theodore Burton, of Ohio, gave me the privilege of his office as a place where I could write or read or just sit down and rest; Senator Calder, of New York, did likewise. I always felt fully at ease in the offices of Senators Capper, Curtis, Shortridge, Willis, and Watson, and of Frank W. Mondell, majority leader in the House, and Congressman Dyer, and Hamilton Fish. Matters concerning the bill frequently made it necessary for me to see Andrew J. Volstead, who as chairman of the House Judiciary Committee exercised great influence in having the bill reported favorably; also Nicholas Longworth, then on the House Steering Committee, and Senators Lodge and Borah.

I saw and talked with every man in Congress who was interested in the bill or who, I thought, could be won over to it. Early I learned the trick of sitting in the Senate lobby and sending my card in to members I wanted to see. At times when the Senate was in session, this saved considerable energy; and I found it an easy method of catching men who were hard to see in their offices. I discovered, to my surprise, that a Senator who was not making a speech, or waiting to make one, welcomed any good excuse to come off the floor. But it was not all easy sailing. Many of the men I tried to reach were cold. Often my tower of hopes came crashing down and had to be built up all over again. Sometimes my heart was as sore and weary as my feet.

The Anti-Lynching Bill was reported out of the House Judiciary Committee on October 20. This meant that the bill would be placed on the calendar; but being placed on the calendar did not mean that it would be reached promptly; nor even that Congress might not adjourn without reaching it at all. Mr. Dyer informed me that the only method of securing prompt action was to have the Steering Committee place the bill among other measures to be considered, and then to have a special rule made on it by the Committee on Rules. He advised me to get to work on the influential Republican members of both Committees. I did. I saw them many times and brought to bear on each one all the suasion and pressure I could command. I kept in touch with our New York office by mail, telegraph, and telephone; and members of the Committee who needed greater suasion and pressure began to receive letters and telegrams from their constituents back home.

On December 19, Mr. Campbell, Chairman of the Rules Committee, rose on the floor and moved the adoption of a special rule. The Democrats, led by the Southern Representatives, immediately began filibustering tactics by walking off the floor and leaving the House without a quorum. Finally, Speaker Gillette ordered the doors locked and the arrest of members by the Sergeant-at-Arms. By eight o'clock at night, after a three-hour wait, enough members were found and brought in to make a quorum. A vote on the special rule was then taken, and the rule adopted. On the following day, Mr. Volstead attempted to have the House go into Committee of the Whole for consideration of the bill. The opposition repeated its tactics of the previous day. But the Speaker repeated his methods and a quorum was obtained. The House went into Committee of the Whole and the bill was read. The leaders hesitated to attempt to push the measure any further before the holiday recess. Forty Republicans had gone on a junketing trip to Panama, and twenty others had been sent to convey the body of Representative Elston, of California, who had died, back to that State (I don't know whether the latter trip came under the head of junketing or not). These absences reduced the Republican working majority to so narrow a margin that the leaders feared to try a definite test of strength. However, the groundwork was now fully laid for bringing the measure properly before the House of Representatives when Congress reassembled in January. The Association had been working at high pressure. It had roused the colored people of the country; it had secured the co-operation of the Negro press, and enlisted the aid of many influential agencies and individuals. A constant shower of communications urging the passage of the bill was being poured on members of Congress. The Dyer bill brought out the greatest concerted action I have yet seen the colored people take.

I was back in Washington on January 10. The Anti-Lynching Bill was taken up on that day, but side-tracked for a week for the Post Office Appropriation Bill. On the seventeenth, debate was resumed; then consideration was postponed another week for another appropriation bill. I began to suffer qualms of anxiety. I wondered if the men with whom I had been dealing were merely giving me and the Association and the Negroes of the country a little "run-around." In the morning on the twenty-fourth, I went to see Mr. Mondell. He told me that the Dyer bill would not be taken up because there was another appropriation bill to be disposed of. He said that some of the leaders wanted more time, and that it might be best to leave it until the thirtieth, then keep it up until it was passed. He added that he had called a meeting of Republican leaders in the Speaker's room, to discuss the matter, and was on his way there. We came out of his office together; he went to the Speaker's room, and I went to my accustomed place in the gallery to sit and read the morning papers, while waiting for the opening hour. While the roll was being droned out, I saw Mr. Mondell beckoning me from the floor to meet him in the lobby. When I reached him, he told me rather excitedly that the Dyer bill would be taken up the next day, whether the appropriation bill was out of the way or not, and pushed through to a finish.

Debate opened on the next day and grew more bitter as it went along. Speeches of the most truculent character were made by Representatives Sisson, of Mississippi, and Blanton, of Texas, both of whom spoke not only in favor of mob rule, but in utter defiance of anything the federal government might propose to do about it. Most of the

Southern opponents of the bill argued that rape was the cause of lynching, and that, in such cases, the white community simply went mad and was not accountable for its acts which, after all, were in fulfillment of a "higher law." Mr. Sisson put it more crassly when he declared that lynching would never stop until black rascals kept their hands off white women. It had been part of my work to keep the sponsors of the bill supplied with facts and figures. They had the figures from me showing that less than seventeen per cent of the victims of lynching in thirty-three years had even been charged by the mob with rape. But the piece of data that completely swept away the "usual crime" argument, was a list of dates and places, and of the names of sixty-four Negro women who had been lynched. The supporters of the bill made some good speeches and used the statistics that had been furnished to them with telling effect. The most eloquent of these speeches was made by Burke Cochran, a Democrat.

The news that the Anti-Lynching Bill was being debated jammed the galleries on the following day; the majority of the crowd being Negroes. There was intense excitement. At a point in one of the speeches, the Negroes in the galleries broke the rules and rose and cheered. A voice from the floor shouted, "Sit down, you niggers!" And a voice from the galleries shouted back, "You're a liar! We're not niggers." The Speaker announced that he would have the galleries closed if there was any further applause. At three o'clock the bill went to a vote, and at three-thirty the Speaker declared it passed by a vote of 230 to 119.

A wave of thanksgiving and jubilation swept the colored people of the country. I was exceedingly happy. But I realized that the fight in the Senate would be harder; and without pausing I started on this second part of my task. The bill was promptly referred to the Senate Committee on the Judiciary; the formation of that committee at once presented the practical difficulty of most of the influential Republican members being men who were not sensitive to Negro votes. On the committee were Chairman Knute Nelson, from Minnesota; Senator Cummings, from Iowa; Senator Brandagee, from Connecticut; Senator Borah, from Idaho; Senator Dillingham, from Vermont; Senator Colt, from Rhode Island; Senator Shortridge, from California; and Senator Sterling, from South Dakota. But the greatest difficulty was the overwhelming number of constitutional lawyers in the Senate, very few of whom seemed willing to leave a decision on the constitutionality of the bill to the Supreme Court.

This question of constitutionality stood highest between Senator Borah and the support of the bill; and the bill had been placed in the hands of a sub-committee of five, three Republicans and two Democrats, of which he was chairman. I talked with the Senator. He said to me at the beginning that he did not require any further facts about lynching; that he was convinced of its infamy and the necessity for its abolishment. He went on to say that the problem before him was the constitutionality of the measure, and the more he studied it, the greater was his doubt. He asked to be provided with briefs on the bill by lawyers who considered it constitutional. Such briefs were prepared by Moorfield Storey, Herbert K. Stockton, W.H. Lewis, Butler R. Wilson, and James A. Cobb, and given to Senator Borah. In the meantime, the bill hung in his sub-committee. At another time when I saw him he said with warmth that he would do anything in his power, as a Senator, to save the life of a single Negro from a lynching mob, but he could not support a measure that he did not believe was constitutional. He stated that he would try to find a way to make the legislation constitutional as well as adequate, and that a refusal on his part to champion the bill would come only from a decision that it was totally unconstitutional. Once when I saw him he looked at me squarely from under his shaggy eyebrows, but with that expression characteristic of him, which makes you uncertain as to whether he is in earnest or laughing at you, and said, "Let me give you a suggestion. Lay this bill aside and try for an Amendment to the Constitution that would enable its enactment." He indicated that he would be willing to draft the resolution. I emphatically expressed my doubt that any such amendment could ever be ratified by a sufficient number of states for its adoption.

I kept pressing Senator Lodge, the Republican leader in the Senate, for a report of the bill out of committee. The Association doubled its efforts. A memorial to the Senate urging the enactment of the Dyer Anti-Lynching Bill was prepared. This petition was signed by twenty-four state Governors; thirty-nine mayors of cities; forty-seven jurists and lawyers; eighty-eight bishops and churchmen, including three archbishops; twenty-nine college presidents and professors; thirty editors, and thirty-seven other prominent and influential citizens. A committee of three, Archibald H. Grimké, president of our Washington branch; Butler R. Wilson, president of our Boston branch; and myself, waited on Senator Lodge and requested him to present the memorial. He consented to do so, and did on May 6. But the bill still hung in the sub-committee.

On May 18, Senator Borah telegraphed me that the report of his committee on the bill was being urged and asked that all briefs not yet filed be sent at once. I went immediately to see the Senator, and found him in no pleasant mood. He informed me that Senator Lodge had ordered a report on the bill, and that he intended to hold it no longer, but to report it to the full committee the following Monday. He complained that sufficient time for a thorough study of the constitutionality of the measure had not been allowed, and therefore he would report the bill in accordance with the only opinion he had up to the time been able to form. He added, as though talking to himself, that he would get out of the Senate before he would do anything to pull anybody's political chestnuts out of the fire. This remark, perhaps, referred to the coming election in which Senator Lodge would be up for return to the Senate. I was dismayed by this sudden turn in the prospects of the legislation. I recognized that Senator Borah was the most commanding figure in the Senate, and I had been nurturing the hope that he would, in the end, take upon himself the championing of the bill. I felt that that would mean the battle already half won. But the mischief had been done, and I realized that, if the bill went along, it would go without his help. He did report the bill back to the full committee when he said he would, and the report was adverse; the Senator voting with the two Democrats. On the first of June, I directed a letter to each member of the Senate, calling attention to the fact that in the single month of May, twelve Negroes had been lynched, five of them burned alive; that on May 6, the day on which Senator Lodge presented the memorial to the Senate, a mob at Kirbin, Texas, had burned three Negroes alive, one immediately after another.

On June 27, I received a letter from Senator Lodge, marked "Confidential," in which he advised me that the Judiciary Committee was preparing to report the bill out. The committee reported it out on the twenty-ninth, and set a date for hearings. I appeared before the committee at these hearings and, in addition to the other things that I had to say, took my one fling at setting myself up as a constitutional lawyer. The gist of the argument against the constitutionality of the measure was that lynching is murder, and, therefore, the federal government has no more constitutional right to step into a state and punish lynching than it has to do likewise and punish murder. In my statement to the Committee I said:

The analogy between murder and lynching is not a true one. Lynching is murder, but it is also more than murder. In murder, one or more individuals take life, generally, for some personal reason. In lynching, a mob sets itself up in place of the state and acts in place of due processes of law to mete out death as a punishment to a person accused of crime. It is not only against the act of killing that the federal government seeks to exercise its power through the proposed law, but against the act of the mob in arrogating to itself the functions of the state and substituting its actions for the due processes of law guaranteed by the Constitution to every person accused of crime. In murder, the murderer merely violates the law of the state. In lynching, the mob arrogates to itself the powers of the state and the functions of government. The Dyer Anti-Lynching Bill is aimed against lynching not only as murder, but as anarchy—anarchy which the states have proven themselves powerless to cope with.

The bill was put into the hands of Senator Shortridge to be brought up on the floor. My heart sank as I thought of the gap between a Borah and a Shortridge. Mr. Shortridge, as a Senator, was rather pompous of style; he seemed to have schooled himself in the graces of the statesman of a former generation. I judged that Daniel Webster was his model, for in speaking he employed the Websterian tone, and even wore his right hand in the bosom of his long coat. Late in August, I was assured by Senator McCormick, and also by Senators Curtis and Watson, that the Senate Steering Committee would meet within a day or two, and that the Anti-Lynching Bill would be placed on the program of measures to be taken up for consideration before Congress adjourned. The committee did meet on the thirtieth and place the bill on the program.

I kept urging upon the Senate leaders personally that the bill be taken up for consideration, and our national office kept up organized pressure. On September 21, at the noon hour—the hour for the opening of regular sessions—I walked with Senator Curtis from his office over to the Capitol. At the entrance we met Senator Lodge and Senator Watson. A hurried conference was held, and Senator Lodge, addressing his colleagues as "Charlie" and "Jim," gave orders for the recognition of Senator Shortridge and the taking up of the bill for consideration at two o'clock. At two o'clock Senator Shortridge was recognized and given the floor. Before he proceeded, he was interrupted by Senator McNary, who asked to be allowed to place before the Senate, House amendments to a certain resolution. Senator Short-ridge, with exceeding courtliness, yielded to "the gentleman from Oregon." Immediately thereafter, he was interrupted by Senator War-ren, who asked to be allowed to report on a joint resolution from the Committee on Appropriations, and he likewise yielded to "the gentle-man from Wyoming." The opposition had not anticipated the move for the bill, but they quickly sensed why Senator Shortridge was on the floor. At this point, Senator Pat Harrison, the keenest parliamen-tarian in the upper house, I think, raised the point of order that the resolution reported by Senator Warren was debatable. A long and complicated parliamentary wrangle ended in the ruling by the Chair that Senator Harrison and *not* Senator Shortridge was entitled to the floor. Senator Harrison took the floor and proceeded to hold it for nearly two hours, and the Democratic filibuster was on.

When Senator Shortridge regained the floor, he did what he should have done in the first instance; without a preliminary word or gesture he said, "I move that the Senate proceed to the consideration of House Bill 13, being Calendar Number 822—" Before he could give the title of the bill, Senator Harrison raised the point of no quorum. The roll call showed a quorum. Senator Heflin made a motion to adjourn, which was voted down. (Here it was that Senator McCormick waved to me in the gallery.) Senator Shortridge then went on with his speech in support of the bill. It was an eloquent speech, a logical speech, a good speech; but on his call for a vote, the point of no quorum was sustained. I felt that a bit of stupid courtesy had cost us the opportunity of having the bill taken up for consideration.

The Senate adjourned until November 20. At the opening of Con-gress, the Association had had placed in the hands of each member of the Senate a copy of a full-page advertisement which had been inserted in *The New York Times* and seven other daily papers in various cities, including the *Washington Star* and the *Atlanta Constitution*, with a total circulation of 1,633,803. The advertisement, which was published at a cost of $5136.93, set forth the salient facts about lynching, and probably caused more intelligent people to think seriously on the shame of America than any other single effort ever made.

Senator Shortridge again made the motion to take up the bill for immediate consideration, but now the Democratic filibuster was or-ganized, and under the leadership of Senators Underwood and Harri-son, with Heflin butting in, was at once put into operation. The tactics embraced leaving the chamber without a quorum, raising points of order, and making extended speeches, the subject matter of which was limited only by the limits of the universe. The filibuster was not met by any determined aggression on the part of the Republicans. Except by Senators Shortridge, Edge, Willis, and New, no actual fight for the consideration of the bill was made on the Republican side. The majority leaders seemed to feel that they would have done their duty and cleared their own skirts when they allowed the Southern Democrats to "put themselves on record" and, in doing so, assume responsibility for the failure of the measure. Senator Underwood, the Democratic leader, laid down an ultimatum to the Republican leaders; namely, that the opposition would not allow any government business whatsoever to be transacted until the Anti-Lynching Bill was withdrawn, not only for the remainder of the extra session, but for the entire remaining term of the Sixty-Seventh Congress. Such a withdrawal would, of course, necessitate a repassage of the bill by the House. Once or twice during the fight, I caught a glance from Senator Borah. This time I felt sure he was laughing at me, and somewhat maliciously.

At the close of the week, Saturday, December 2, the Republican leaders felt that the "record" had been made and they were ready to abandon the Anti-Lynching Bill. On that morning, I conferred with Senator Lodge, with Senator Curtis, and with Senator Watson, and pleaded with each of them not to abandon the bill on the terms laid down by the filibusters. Each of them said to me that the bill would not be abandoned on any such terms. That night the Republican Senators held a caucus to discuss the question. The morning papers announced that the caucus, after a heated session of more than two hours, had voted to abandon the bill; that nine Senators, however, did vote to keep up the fight until the fourth of March if necessary.

It would be difficult for me to tell just what my feelings were. I think disgust was the dominant emotion. What I had for a week been sensing would happen—the betrayal of the bill by Republican leaders —had happened. I knew that they had been making no determined effort to have the bill taken up for consideration. My thoughts were made the more bitter by a fact which I knew and which every Senator admitted, the fact that the bill would have been passed had it been brought to a vote.

I immediately sent to Senator Lodge, to Senator Curtis, and to Senator Watson the following telegram:

IN MY TALK WITH YOU SATURDAY MORNING REGARDING DYER ANTI-LYNCHING BILL I URGED THAT MEASURE BE NOT ABANDONED ON TERMS OF DEMOCRATIC FILIBUSTERS EVEN THOUGH EXIGENCIES REQUIRED THAT IT BE LAID ASIDE FOR PRESENT STOP YOU SAID TO ME BILL WOULD NOT BE ABANDONED ON TERMS LAID DOWN BY FILIBUSTERS STOP MORNING PAPERS STATE THAT AT CAUCUS YESTERDAY IT WAS DECIDED THAT BILL BE PERMANENTLY WITHDRAWN AND NOT BROUGHT UP AGAIN BETWEEN NOW AND MARCH FOURTH STOP WILL YOU PLEASE LET ME KNOW IF NEWSPAPER REPORTS ARE CORRECT

JAMES WELDON JOHNSON

By Special Delivery I received from Senator Lodge the following reply:

Personal

United States Senate
Committee on Foreign Relations,
December 4, 1922.

Dear Sir:

I received your telegram of last evening. I do not know what you mean by saying that I said to you in our conversation that "the bill would not be abandoned on terms laid down by filibusters." I never said anything of the kind. I never mentioned terms to you in any way. There was no question of terms. The bill was either to be laid aside or kept before the Senate. There was no question of terms at all. I explained to you that the bill could not become law even if the effort to take up the bill was continued until March 4th, that it was equally impossible to change the rules, and that the only question that the conference would decide was whether they would give up all business of the session—put aside the ship subsidy bill, the farmers' extension of credits bill, and all the supply bills, and in addition a large number of confirmations—or whether they would withdraw the Dyer bill and not press it during the coming session, which begins today. The conference agreed not to press the bill further and instructed me to say precisely what I said in the newspapers, so far as I have seen the newspaper report. I wish to repeat to you that I said nothing whatever about terms because nothing of that sort arose, and the words you attribute to me were never uttered by me. Nothing of that sort was said.

Very truly yours,

H. C. LODGE.

James Weldon Johnson, Sec'y
National Association for the Advancement of Colored People,
1333 R Street, N.W.
Washington, D. C.

It is, of course, possible that Senator Lodge forgot what he said to me. Almost as promptly I received from Senator Watson the following note:

United States Senate
Committee on Finance,
December 4, 1922.

Hon. James Weldon Johnson
Nat'l Assn. for the Advancement
  of Colored People,
Washington, D. C.

Dear Johnson:
  If you will come to my office, I will tell you what happened. There is too much about it to place within the limits of an ordinary letter.
                    Yours, etc.
                              JAMES E. WATSON.

The Dyer Anti-Lynching Bill did not become a law, but it made of the floors of Congress a forum in which the facts were discussed and brought home to the American people as they had never been before. Agitation for the passage of the measure was, without doubt, one of the prime factors in reducing the number of lynchings in the decade that followed to less than one-third of what it had been in the preceding decade—to one-tenth of what it was in the first decade of the keeping of the record. It served to awaken the people of the Southern states to the necessity of taking steps themselves to wipe out the crime; and this, I think, was its most far-reaching result.

I went to Washington occasionally after my period of lobbying for the Dyer bill on various other matters. I went down to see young Theodore Roosevelt, then Assistant Secretary of the Navy, and talked with him about the barriers that were being raised against Negroes enlisted in the Navy, a service in which they had a long and praiseworthy record. When I had about finished with the interview, I mentioned to Mr. Roosevelt that I was going over to see Mr. Slemp, secretary to President Coolidge, on a matter. Mr. Roosevelt asked, "Do you know Mr. Slemp?" I replied that I did not know him personally. He then said, "Wait a moment." He called Mr. Slemp on the telephone, and with some highly complimentary remarks about me, said that I was coming over to the Executive Offices. When I got over, Mr. Slemp was prepared to meet me and gave me a hearty welcome. We talked over the matter in hand; then he said to me, "I'd like to have you meet the President." This looked as though the procedure of official form was being turned round. I don't know how many American citizens have had an official say to them, "I'd like to have you meet the President." Mr. Slemp took me in and gave me a rather flattering introduction to President Coolidge, and withdrew. The President was, I think, more embarrassed than I. He, it appeared, did not want to say anything or did not know just what to say. I was expecting that he would make, at least, an inquiry or two about the state of mind and condition of the twelve million Negro citizens of the United States. I judged that curiosity, if not interest, would make for that much conversation. The pause was painful (for me at least) and I led off with some informational remarks; but it was clear that Mr. Coolidge knew absolutely nothing about the colored people. I gathered that the only living Negro he had heard anything about was Major Moton. I was relieved when the brief audience was over, and I suppose Mr. Coolidge was, too.

XXXVI

I GOT immense satisfaction out of the work which was the main purpose of the National Association for the Advancement of Colored People; at the same time, I struggled constantly not to permit that part of me which was artist to become entirely submerged. I had little time and less energy for creative writing, but in 1921 I began work on an anthology of poetry by American Negroes. My original idea was extremely modest; I planned to start with Paul Laurence Dunbar and sift the work of all the Negro poets from him down to Claude McKay and his contemporaries, with a view to publishing in a small volume thirty or forty of the poems that I judged to be up to a certain standard.

Before I had gone very far with the work, I realized that such a book, being the first of its kind, would be entirely devoid of a background. America as a whole knew something of Dunbar, but it was practically unaware that there were such things as Negro poets and Negro poetry. So I decided to write an introduction; and the introduction developed into a forty-two page essay on "The Creative Genius of the Negro." In that essay I called attention to the American Negro as a folk artist, and pointed out his vital contributions, as such, to our national culture. In it I also made a brief survey of Negro poetry. I began with Phillis Wheatley, who, brought in 1761 on a slave ship from Africa to Boston when she was nine years old, became the second woman in America to publish a volume of poetry, and touched on the most significant work from among the thirty-odd Negro poets between her and Dunbar. I also went a little afield and mentioned some of the Negro poets of the West Indies and South America, giving most space to Plácido, the popular poet of Cuba. My selections for the anthology proper increased to three or four times the number I had originally planned for, but I felt that in the case of this particular book, there was more to be gained by being comprehensive than would be lost by not being exclusive. The use of "Aframerican" in the introductory essay to designate Negroes of either North America, South America, or the West In lies gave some currency in this country to the term as a substitute for "Negro" or "colored" or "Afro-American." The word was coined, so far as I know, by Sir Harry H. Johnston. It is on all points a good word, but in its use in this country it quickly acquired a slightly derisive sense, a sense due mainly, perhaps, to the stamp put upon it by H. L. Mencken. Mr. Mencken and George S. Schuyler, the Negro satirist, are the only American writers who continue to make frequent use of it. Many white people, when they wish to be especially considerate, are in doubt about the term most acceptable to Negroes. There are indeed puzzlingly subtle distinctions, to which colored people are more or less sensitive. The adjective "colored" and the generic designations "Negroes," "the Negro," and "the Negro race" are always in order; but, "a Negro man," "a Negro woman," etc., are somewhat distasteful. "Negress" is considered unpardonable. *The Book of American Negro Poetry*[1] was published early in 1922.

Later in the same year, Claude McKay published his *Harlem Shadows*. He did not follow up this book of poems, but turned to prose. That, together with his long absence from the United States, has caused him to be partially forgotten as a writer of verse, but *Harlem Shadows* proclaims him one of the finest of modern American poets. Jean Toomer followed with *Cane*, a series of realistic stories of Negro life, interspersed with original lyrics of great beauty. Strangely, he never worked further the rich vein he had struck; this single book, however, made a deep impression on the critics and is still referred

[1] Harcourt, Brace and Company, New York, 1922.

to as one of the best pieces of latter-day American prose. The extraordinary poems of Anne Spencer attracted attention; there were beginnings by others, and the Negro "literary revival" was under way.

Shortly after the publication of *Harlem Shadows*, Claude McKay decided to go to Russia. He had for a time been associate editor with Max Eastman of the *Liberator*, and was familiar with and interested in the Soviet experiment. Grace and I gave a farewell party for him at our apartment in Harlem. There were present seven or eight white persons prominent in the literary world and a dozen or so colored guests. News about the party leaked out. Harlem was not yet accustomed to social gatherings of the sort, and the local Negro papers referred to it as the "black and white" party.

In 1924, Jessie Fauset published *There Is Confusion*,[1] a novel of life among intelligent and fairly well-to-do Northern Negroes. Almost simultaneously, came Walter White's *The Fire in the Flint*,[2] a novel that gave a sectional view of life in the South, and aroused wide comment and sharp controversy. In this period literary prizes were awarded for several years through *The Crisis*, edited by W. E. B. Du Bois, and *Opportunity*, edited by Charles S. Johnson. The *Opportunity* awards were each time made at a dinner attended by two or three hundred people, many of them white writers and others interested in literature. In 1924 and 1925 came volumes of poetry by Countee Cullen and Langston Hughes, followed by novels by Nella Imes and Rudolph Fisher and by books of prose and poetry by a dozen other writers. The leading publishers opened their doors and the important magazines opened their pages to these writers—and the Negro "literary revival" was in full swing.

In 1925, with my brother, who made the piano arrangements, I collected a group of sixty-one Negro spirituals. For the collection I wrote forty pages of preface in which I gave the history of the spirituals, the probable theories as to their origin, and an estimate of them as music and poetry. The collection was published under the title of *The Book of American Negro Spirituals*.[3] It was an instantaneous success, and is still in demand. It is, I believe, probably the best collection of Negro spirituals in print, and would have made headway under any conditions; but we were fortunate in having it come out just at the

[1] Boni and Liveright, New York.
[2] Alfred A. Knopf, New York.
[3] The Viking Press, New York.

propitious moment. We followed the next year with a second collection; and although it contained as many numbers as beautiful and interesting as those in the first collection, it has not approached the success of its forerunner.

The research which I did in collecting the spirituals and gathering the data for my introductory essay had an effect on me similar to what I received from hearing the Negro evangelist preach that Sunday night in Kansas City. This work tempered me to just the right mood to go on with what I had started when I wrote "The Creation." I was in touch with the deepest revelation of the Negro's soul that has yet been made, and I felt myself attuned to it. I made an outline of the second poem that I wrote of this series. It was to be a "funeral sermon." I decided to call it "Go Down, Death."

On Thanksgiving Day, 1926, I was at home. After breakfast I went to my desk and began work in earnest on the poem. As I worked, my own spirit rose till it reached a degree almost of ecstasy. The poem shaped itself easily and before the hour for dinner I had written it as it stands published. Grace had as dinner guests Lucile Miller and Crystal Bird. I read the poem to this little group. Between Thanksgiving and the Christmas holidays, I wrote the prayer, "Listen, Lord." My plan was to write seven "sermons," and I had finished only two. I decided to go to Great Barrington, Massachusetts, and write the other five. I found the thermometer there around 18 below zero, but I stayed two weeks and brought the finished poems back with me to New York. The poem that gave me the hardest work was "The Crucifixion." I realized that its effectiveness depended upon a simplicity which I found more difficult to achieve than the orotundity of "The Creation" and "The Prodigal Son" or the imagery of "Go Down, Death" and "The Judgment Day."

When I had finished the poems, I decided that they needed a preface; and I wondered if I was condemned to do a preface for every book that I should write. I did a preface, telling something about the old plantation preacher and setting forth at some length my reasons for not writing the poems in conventionalized Negro dialect. Next to writing "The Crucifixion," my greatest difficulty was in finding a title for the book. I toyed and experimented with at least twenty tentative titles. I narrowed them down to *Listen, Lord*; *Cloven Tongues*; *Tongues of Fire*; and *Trumpets of the Lord*, or *Trumpeters of the Lord*. I liked the last two titles, but saw that "Trumpets" or

"Trumpeters" would be a poetic cliché. Suddenly, I lit upon "trombone." The trombone, according to the Standard Dictionary, is: "A powerful brass instrument of the trumpet family, the only wind instrument possessing a chromatic scale enharmonically true, like the human voice or the violin, and hence very valuable in the orchestra." I had found it, the instrument and the word, of just the tone and timbre to represent the old-time Negro preacher's voice. Besides, there were the traditional jazz connotations. So the title became *God's Trombones—Seven Negro Sermons in Verse.*[1]

In 1925 I was awarded the Spingarn Medal. The Spingarn Medal, established by J. E. Spingarn, has now for eighteen years been awarded annually for "the highest or noblest achievement by an American Negro during the preceding year or years," and is the most distinguished badge of merit that an American Negro may wear. The Medal was awarded to me as "author, diplomat, and public servant." *God's Trombones* won for me the Harmon Award, consisting of a gold medal and a check for four hundred dollars. I was elected a member of the Board of Trustees of Atlanta University, and became a member of the committee that brought about the merger of Atlanta with Morehouse College and Spelman College to form the greater Atlanta University. Talledega College and Howard University conferred on me the degree of Litt. D.

During this period, I went to a great many "literary" parties. At such gatherings I met and came to know a large number of American literary and artistic celebrities—great and near-great—and some of the stars of the theater and of Hollywood. I also made the acquaintance of a few European celebrities. At the Van Vechtens' I met Theodore Dreiser. I had formed a stern mental image of Mr. Dreiser, picturing him as a morose and dour individual. But at dinner he impressed me as being more jovial than somber; indeed, he contributed a full share to the jollity of the occasion. In the home of Alma Wertheim, I became acquainted with several of the foremost composers, musicians, and conductors of the modern school. It was there that I met Louis Gruenberg, who had already, while living in Vienna, made a setting of "The Creation," scored for voice and orchestra. It was partly through Mrs. Wertheim's interest in modern music that the work was given a production at Town Hall under the direction of Sergei Kous-

[1] The Viking Press, New York, 1927.

sevitzky, with a portion of the Boston Symphony Orchestra, and Jules Bledsoe as soloist. At a dinner at the Lewis Gannetts', I met Count Karolyi, former President of Hungary, and his wife. The Count, much to my surprise, was deeply interested in the American race question, and talked to me earnestly to learn what I could tell him about the Negro in the United States. He was particularly curious about race intermixture and amalgamation as a solution of the problem. The guest of honor and his wife left earlier than the others of us. When our host, who had seen them out, came back into the room, he laughingly related that the Count, in saying good-by, had expressed satisfaction at the apparent confirmation of his idea of race intermixture and social intermingling as a way out; for he had gained the impression that my wife was white and that another of the guests, a beautiful brunette, was colored. Between me and the people to whose homes I went and those I met in them, there grew some friendships, several of them deep and abiding. I went to two or three parties in Greenwich Village. At one of these, I remember, costume of some kind was *de rigueur*. I was taken in hand by a Russian who had been connected with the theater in his own country. My regular clothes were discarded; then the Russian took a single narrow length of an oriental-looking fabric, and with amazing deftness wound it round my head as a turban, passed it under my arm, around my waist, draped my loins, and, presto, I was some sort of denizen of the desert. The transformation pleased me highly, despite some disturbing qualms about exhibitionism.

In turn, Grace and I entertained occasionally at our home in Harlem. And so did Walter White and his wife at their home. Some of the parties we gave were gay; more than once we closed the evening, or began the morning, by all going to one of the Harlem cabarets to dance. But the most lasting impression I have of any of the gatherings at my home is of Clarence Darrow, sitting under a lighted lamp, the only one in the room left lighted, reading in measured tones from his book, *Farmington*. I retain a memory of the Lincoln-like beauty of the man, the beauty of sheer simplicity of his prose, the rising and falling melody of his voice, and the group seated about him drinking in the three elements combined—Ruby Darrow, no doubt, musing, "This wonderful man is my husband"—Carl Van Vechten, the most sophisticated of American novelists, sitting back in the shadow, but not so far back that his face does not show emotions straining for tears— Fania Marinoff, seated on the floor, her head thrust slightly forward, her lips parted, her dark eyes glistening, herself unconsciously revealing an unblemished line of beauty of head and face and throat—the whole group silent, as the words falling, falling, slip through their minds and lodge in their hearts with strange stirrings. Then to change the mood, Mr. Darrow takes up Newman Levy's *Opera Guyed*,[1] and reads "Samson and Delilah," then "La Traviata," and then "Thaïs"; his sober voice and manner against the wit and ribald humor of the poems make us chuckle and roar. The author of the poems tries to maintain a becoming modesty, but we are ready to forgive him for chuckling as heartily as the rest of us. Mr. Darrow, for his own delight, repeats the concluding lines of "Thaïs" several times over. Now, in partial repayment, Paul Robeson gives a reading of "The Creation," and "Listen, Lord," and Clarence Darrow quotes to him the words of Agrippa to Saint Paul, "Almost thou persuadest me to be a Christian."

This was the era in which was achieved the Harlem of story and song; the era in which Harlem's fame for exotic flavor and colorful sensuousness was spread to all parts of the world; when Harlem was made known as the scene of laughter, singing, dancing, and primitive passions, and as the center of the new Negro literature and art; the era in which it gained its place in the list of famous sections of great cities. This universal reputation was the work of writers. The picturesque Harlem was real, but it was the writers who discovered its artistic values and, in giving literary expression to them, actually created the Harlem that caught the world's imagination. Very early, Langston Hughes discovered these values and gave them their first expression in poetry. The prose about this Harlem is voluminous. The writers who came to parties and went sight-seeing in Harlem found stimulating material for their pens. Then other writers flocked there; many came from far, and depicted it in many ways and in many languages. They still come; the Harlem of story and song still fascinates them.

But there is the other real and overshadowing Harlem. The commonplace, work-a-day Harlem. The Harlem of doubly handicapped black masses engaged in the grim, daily struggle for existence in the midst of this whirlpool of white civilization. There are dramatic values in that Harlem, too; but they have hardly been touched. Writers of fiction, white and black, have limited their stories to Harlem as a play-

[1] Alfred A. Knopf, New York, 1923.

ground, and have ignored or not recognized the fundamental, relentless forces at work and the efforts to cope with them. This is, of course, understandable; picturesque and exotic phases of life offer the easier and more alluring task for the fictionist. But the sterner aspects of life in Harlem offer a unique and teeming field for the writer capable of working it. Under these aspects lie real comedy and real tragedy, real triumphs and real defeats. The field is waiting, probably for some Negro writer.

The two books about Harlem that were most widely read and discussed were Carl Van Vechten's *Nigger Heaven*,[1] and Claude McKay's *Home to Harlem*.[2] Mr. Van Vechten's novel ran through a score of editions, was published in most of the important foreign languages, and aroused something of a national controversy. For directly opposite reasons, there were objections to the book by white and colored people. White objectors declared that the story was a Van Vechten fantasy; that they could not be expected to believe that there were intelligent, well-to-do Negroes in Harlem who lived their lives on the cultural level he described, or a fast set that gave at least a very good imitation of life in sophisticated white circles. Negro objectors declared that the book was a libel on the race, that the dissolute life and characters depicted by the author were non-existent. Both classes of objectors were wrong, but their points of view can be understood. Negro readers of the book who knew anything knew that dissolute modes of life and dissolute characters existed in Harlem; their objections were really based upon chagrin and resentment at the disclosures to a white public. Yet, Mr. McKay's book dealt with low levels of life, a lustier life, it is true, than the dissolute modes depicted by Mr. Van Vechten, but entirely unrelieved by any brighter lights; furthermore, Mr. McKay made no attempt to hold in check or disguise his abiding contempt for the Negro bourgeoisie and "upper class." Still, *Home to Harlem* met with no such criticism from Negroes as did *Nigger Heaven*. The lusty primitive life in *Home to Harlem* was based on truth, as were the dissolute modes of life in *Nigger Heaven*; but Mr. Van Vechten was the first well-known American novelist to include in a story a cultured Negro class without making it burlesque or without implying reservations and apologies.

[1] Alfred A. Knopf, New York, 1926.
[2] Harper & Brothers, New York, 1928.

Most of the Negroes who condemned *Nigger Heaven* did not read it; they were estopped by the title. I don't think they would now be so sensitive about it; as the race progresses it will become less and less susceptible to hurts from such causes. Whatever the colored people thought about *Nigger Heaven*, speaking of the author as a man antagonistic to the race was entirely unwarranted. Carl Van Vechten had a warm interest in colored people before he ever saw Harlem. In the early days of the Negro literary and artistic movement, no one in the country did more to forward it than he accomplished in frequent magazine articles and by his many personal efforts in behalf of individual Negro writers and artists. Indeed, his regard for Negroes as a race is so close to being an affectionate one, that he is constantly joked about it by his most intimate friends. His most highly prized caricature of himself is one done by Covarrubias in black-face, and presented to him on his birthday. Mr. Van Vechten's birthday, that of young Alfred Knopf, and mine, fall on the same day of the same month. For four or five years we have been celebrating them jointly, together with a small group of friends. Last summer we celebrated at the country place of the Knopfs. In a conversation that Blanche Knopf, Lawrence Langner, and I were carrying on, something about the responsibility for children came up. Mr. Van Vechten interrupted Mrs. Knopf with an opinion of his own on the subject, to which she retorted, "Carl, you don't know anything about it, because you are not a parent." Mr. Van Vechten responded with, "You're mistaken; I am the father of four sons." And Alfred Knopf flashed out, "If you are, they must be the four Mills Brothers." Mr. Van Vechten joined in the outburst of laughter. From the first, my belief has held that *Nigger Heaven* is a fine novel.

My own literary efforts and what part I played in creating the new literary Harlem were, however, mere excursions; my main activity was all the while the work of the Association. But doubled activities began to tell on me, and my doctor began to give warning. I had been helped to keep the pace because Miss Ovington had generously given me and Grace the use of her place, Riverbank, in the Berkshire Hills, for several summers. In 1926 I bought a little place in the township of Great Barrington, Massachusetts. I rode one day by an overgrown place where a little red barn was all that stood out amongst the weeds; the house on the place had burned down. A bright little river ran under a bridge and circled round behind the barn. On inquiry, I learned that there were five acres in the tract, and I said, "This is just the place for me." Grace and I studied the possibilities and decided that we could remodel the barn, keeping the interior, with the old hand-hewn beams, just as it was. We did; and named the place Five Acres. There, we have made our home ever since for a part of the year.

To get outdoor exercise I took up golf. For four or five years I was a votary of the game—though remaining a dub. One day in September, 1925, I was on the links of a club over in New Jersey, when a messenger ran up and told me that I was wanted for a long-distance telephone call. I rushed to the clubhouse and found that the call was from Detroit. I talked for a half-hour with the officers of our branch there.

The Negro population of Detroit had in a little over a decade increased from some ten thousand to some seventy-five thousand or more. This had brought about an actual physical pressure in their housing conditions. Several Negroes, to escape this pressure, bought homes in new neighborhoods, but were evicted from them by organized violence; in several instances the houses being practically destroyed by bombs. Dr. Ossian Sweet, a Negro physician, had bought a house in a modest white neighborhood of mechanics, clerks, and small tradesmen, but he hesitated for several months about moving in because of the assaults that had been made on the homes bought by other Negroes in white neighborhoods. Finally, he asked for police protection and with his wife moved in. With his household goods, he took in guns and a supply of ammunition. There also went in with Dr. Sweet his two brothers and some of his men friends, making eleven in all in the house. The police guarded the house that night and the next day. Late in the afternoon a crowd began gathering, and the police guard was increased; but the police did not disperse the crowd. As darkness came on, the street became jammed with people and others were constantly arriving. Later, stones began to hit the house; there was no interference from the police; a rifle cracked, and Leon Breiner, a white man in the crowd, fell dead. All of the inmates of the house, with the exception of the doctor's wife, were taken to jail and held without bail. The situation in Detroit was inflammable. Our branch officer there was calling on the national office for counsel and assistance.

I hurried back to the city and consulted with Arthur B. Spingarn. Walter White was dispatched immediately to Detroit and there he took the first steps to allay passions and arrange for legal defense. The Association engaged a staff of six lawyers, headed by Clarence Darrow and Arthur Garfield Hays. The eleven defendants were indicted for first-degree murder. During the trial, Mr. White spent most of his time in Detroit, and Mr. Spingarn made several trips there. I undertook to raise money for the defense of the case. The issue was segregation by mob violence and the simple question was: Does the common axiom of Anglo-Saxon law, that a man's house is his castle, apply to a Negro American citizen? We set our organization machinery in motion, and I issued an appeal to the country in which we called for the raising of a Defense Fund, a fund for the Detroit cases and any other cases that would involve the Negro's constitutional rights. The response was spontaneous; within four months a sum in excess of $75,000 was raised. (A third of this amount was contributed by the American Fund for Public Service.) The trial of the eleven defendants resulted in a disagreement.

The second trial began in the following spring. In this trial the defendants demanded to be tried separately, and the state elected to proceed against Henry Sweet, the doctor's youngest brother, who admitted that he had fired the shot from the house. I attended the second trial. We had three lawyers, Clarence Darrow and two local lawyers. The courtroom was filled each day; and on the last day, when Mr. Darrow addressed the jury, not another person could have been squeezed in. The doors were jammed and the corridors packed. I had the opportunity of hearing Clarence Darrow for the defense, at his best, in a famous case. He talked for nearly seven hours. I sat where I could catch every word and every expression of his face. It was a wonderful performance. Clarence Darrow, the veteran criminal lawyer, the psychologist, the philosopher, the humanist, the apostle of liberty, was bringing into play every bit of skill, drawing on all the knowledge, and using every power that he possessed upon the twelve men who sat in front of him. At times his voice was as low as though he was coaxing a child. At such times, the strain upon the listeners to catch his words made them appear rigid. At other times, his words came like flashes of lightning and crashes of thunder. He closed his argument with a plea that left no eyes dry. When he finished, I walked over to him to express my appreciation and thanks. His eyes were wet. He placed his hands on my shoulders. I tried to stammer out a few words, but broke down and wept. The jury brought in a verdict of "Not guilty," and the Association had won another victory in its fight to maintain the common rights of citizenship for the Negro.

Before the Detroit case was over, the Association undertook another case involving the Negro's constitutional rights. In a section of the Texas law regulating primary elections, was the following clause: "However, in no event shall a Negro be eligible to participate in a Democratic Party primary election held in the State of Texas, and should a Negro vote in a Democratic primary election, such ballot shall be void, and election officials are herein directed to throw out such ballot and not count the same." Similar provisions in most of the Southern states constitute the "white primary," which, due to the one-party political system, is the most effective method of disfranchising the Negro. In these states, there is no law that prohibits Negroes from voting in the general elections, but the functions of the general elections have been transferred to the primary election. The persons winning nominations in the primary election are already elected, and the general election becomes merely perfunctory. For example, in the Texas gubernatorial campaign of 1926, in the first Democratic primary, with six candidates in the field, 735,186 votes were cast; in the run-off, with the candidates narrowed down to Dan Moody and Governor "Ma" Ferguson, 793,766 votes were cast. But in the general election in the same campaign, only 89,263 votes were cast.

The Association undertook a test of the Texas law, taking up the case of Dr. A. L. Nixon, a Negro physician of El Paso, who, though qualified as a Democrat, was denied the right to vote in the Democratic primary. This case was fought for two years, through the courts of Texas to the Supreme Court. At the end, the Supreme Court handed down a unanimous decision declaring white primary laws unconstitutional.

The scope of my activities had widened; I had become a member of the national committee of the American Civil Liberties Union and had taken an earnest part in the fight in behalf of minority groups in general and in the fight for the restoration and maintenance of free speech, which was still circumscribed by the wartime prohibitions that had been placed on it. When Charles Garland refused to accept an inheritance of a million or more dollars, the American Fund for Public Service was organized and chartered, mainly through the efforts of Roger N. Baldwin, who was a friend of Mr. Garland, for the express purpose of taking over and administering this money. I was made a member of the board of twelve directors charged with the duty of disbursing the fund; later, I was chosen president of the board. Once, when the Fund was being organized, Mr. Garland lunched with us. He was an uncommonly handsome young man and extremely reticent. He turned his inheritance over merely with the request that it be given away *as quickly as possible, and to "unpopular" causes, without regard to race, creed, or color.* In doing this, he made no gesture of any kind. He simply did not want the money, and refused to take it. He wished only to be left free to follow the life he had planned to live. It was a strange experience to look upon a man in the flesh and in his right mind who could act like that about a million dollars. For a while the fund, which was for the most part in First National Bank stock, increased faster than we could get rid of it, and I was surprised at learning that giving away money, if it is done at all judiciously, is a difficult job.

Shortly after my return from Detroit I found myself at the center of a sensational fight for free speech. Three organizations, the League of Neighbors, the Union of East and West, and the Fellowship of Faiths, had planned to celebrate Peace Week. For the close of the week a mass meeting was scheduled to be held at the Morris High School; the speakers to be Judge Jacob Panken, Rev. Albert Thomas, Arthur Garfield Hays, and myself. The permission for the use of the school was revoked because Mr. Hays and I were among the speakers. The American Civil Liberties Union immediately took up the matter, and in a letter to the Board of Education charged that Mr. Hays and I had been barred from speaking because our names were on a black-list kept by the board. This the school board denied. The Union decided to bring a test case to determine the right of the Board of Education to maintain a blacklist against public speakers, and promptly filed an application for the use of the auditorium of the Stuyvesant High School for a discussion of "Old-Fashioned Free Speech," with John Haynes Holmes, John Nevin Sayre, Arthur Garfield Hays, and myself as the speakers. The application was denied. The case was taken before the Board of Education and into the courts, with Samuel Untermeyer and Morris Ernst representing the Union. After con-tinual efforts extending over more than two years the case was won, and the Board of Education approved the application for the meeting in the auditorium of the Stuyvesant High School. By that time I had recovered from the shock of being classed as a dangerous and un-American character. I felt fully reinstated when I was invited to take part in the unveiling of the bust of Whittier at the Hall of Fame.

My work as secretary of the Association, together with the books I had published, caused an increasing demand for me on the lecture platform. Calls for me came from forums, women's clubs, and from colleges and universities. I filled as many of these as time and energy permitted. Some of the forums I addressed had always a goodly number of wild-tongued radicals in the audience. These, I discovered, loved nothing better than having a speaker to bait. During the period for questions they often "treated me rough" because I did not hold that all of the ills and disadvantages suffered by the Negro could be wholly accounted for by the theory of economic determinism. At times, I encountered churlishness. Once a man rose and said, "I want to ask you a frank question. Isn't the chief objection to the Negro due to the fact that he has a bad odor?" In reply, I agreed that there were lots of bad-smelling Negroes; but, in turn, I asked my questioner if he thought the expensive magazine advertisements about "B.O." were designed to attract an exclusive Negro patronage. I remarked that I did not think so, since they were generally illustrated with pictures of rather nice-looking white girls.

I learned that by keeping my temper I could deal with irrationality, even with cases of violent race prejudice, but I was completely nonplused by the gentle old lady who would come up after a talk before a woman's club and dilate to me on the qualities of her colored butler or cook, as evidence of the high opinion she held of the Negro. I did not question that her colored help possessed all the excellencies she ascribed to them, but I was, nevertheless, at a loss for just the proper comment to make about it. My embarrassment was the greater because I knew that the gentlewoman was being actuated by a sincere desire to say something nice to me. And yet, as I think of it, there perhaps is no good reason why I should not always express to the gentle old lady my appreciation of the fact that she is providing one or two Negroes with jobs. I enjoyed talking before women's clubs, because that gave me frequent opportunities to talk about literature and art, and to read my poems. At a number of colleges and universities I talked about the æsthetic as well as about the sterner factors in the race question. Through arrangements made by Helen R. Bryan of Philadelphia, I spoke before the high and normal schools of that city on Negro art and literature. I think that the students and teachers in general gained information from these talks; I am sure that at least one result was a marked psychological effect on the few colored students in the overwhelming mass of white students—the emergence of a new pride and self-respect, which I could not help but note in their words and in their faces as they grouped around me after each talk. In the spring of 1927, I was invited to the University of North Carolina to hold seminars for a week on the sociological and artistic phases of Negro life. I believe this invitation was unprecedented. This was one of the most interesting episodes in my whole career. As I faced those groups of Southern white young men, I felt a greater desire to win them over than I had felt with any other group I ever talked to; and to win them over by the honest truth. I was not sure that I could do it, but, I think, to a good extent, I did. My course increased in popularity; so much so that my last talk was adjourned from the classroom to one of the assembly halls because of the additional number of students in English who attended. At the end of the week, I addressed the student body and citizens of Chapel Hill in the University Chapel.

On this visit to the University of North Carolina I formed some friendly relations. I met Paul Green, the playwright, and Elizabeth Lay Green, his wife. It was very interesting to talk with them about Negro literature and drama. I talked, too, with Howard W. Odum and Guy B. Johnson, who were directing the work at the University in digging up and making a record of Negro folk material, a work second only to that done by Fisk University in preserving and bringing to the attention of the world the Negro spirituals. After my address in the University Chapel, a young lady introduced herself to me as Mrs. Katherine Elmore. Her husband, Lee Elmore, was connected with the Department of Dramatics at the University. She asked me if I would come to her home and meet some friends. I was happy to go. A dozen or so people came in, and the evening was a delightful one. There was talk about a great many things, with the race problem left out. I read from *God's Trombones*—the book was just coming off the press. In a letter that Mrs. Elmore wrote to her mother, Mrs. Laura T. Huyck, in Albany, she spoke about me. I was in Albany to make an address the following winter and met Mr. and Mrs. Huyck. Since then, among the pleasantest days that Grace and I have passed have been the week-ends that we have spent each summer at their beautiful place at Rennselaerville, New York. On one of these visits I was talking with Mrs. Huyck, who is a constant reader, and suggested an idea I had by asking her why, instead of always taking in, she did not cultivate an art-means of giving out, of giving expression to herself. She put the question back to me somewhat quizzically: "Why, what shall I do? I believe I am too old to start to take up the piano again." I ventured, "Well—why not try painting?" She laughed the suggestion away as preposterous, saying that she had never had a pencil or brush in her hand. But her secretary gave her a set of pastel colors and boards as a present the following Christmas, and she did, without any instruction or direction, begin to work with them. Grace and I were at her home in Albany in the spring and both of us were surprised by the pictures she had made. I could hardly credit my eyes. Since then she has held two exhibitions at the Durand-Ruel Galleries in East Fifty-Seventh Street, New York City, and received the praise of the art critics. One of her pictures was bought by the Brooklyn Museum of Art.

I regard it as curious, almost as a matter of destiny, when I think of the number of times my life has touched the life of some other individual in an apparently cursory and transient way, and then consider how that contact marked the beginning of an important phase in my own life. I have no intention of depreciating my own intelligence and industry, but the farther back I am able to look, the more clearly I discern that such results as I have gained may be, in a fair degree, traced to "lucky breaks." If I were giving an exhortation on the subject to young people, I should say, "*Do not trust to luck*, but be, in every way, as fully prepared as possible to measure up to the 'lucky breaks' when they come."

I attended another important conference on the race question. It was held for three days at New Haven in one of the fraternity houses of Yale University. Twenty-five men, white and colored, made up the conference. Arthur B. Spingarn and I represented the National Association for the Advancement of Colored People. At this conference I met Edwin R. Embree, then Vice-President of the Rockefeller Foundation, and Dr. Thomas Elsa Jones, the new President of Fisk University. In the remarks that I made introducing the round-table discussion which I led, I said, "It is a common error to think of the race situation as static, as a problem that will remain fixed until it is solved. What we call the race problem is not what it was a hundred years ago, or fifty years ago, or twenty or even ten years ago. The situation is constantly shifting and changing. It has never remained the same in any two generations. And it has never shifted more rapidly than it is shifting at the present time. The situation is a shifting one, therefore the means and methods of meeting it must also change." Mr. Embree made a summary of the conference, and commented with emphasis on that statement. A while later, I saw Mr. Embree again at dinner at the house of Julius Rosenwald, in Chicago, but I had no idea then what this association would lead to.

I spoke one Sunday morning for the Ethical Culture Society in New York. As I sat on the platform, I noted D— in the audience. He waited until the exercises were over to speak to me. I was glad of this because I had seen only little of him during these busy years. He introduced me to a very beautiful girl who was with him, as the young lady he was going to marry. I didn't fear that he was going to commit bigamy because I knew he had had matrimonial difficulties and that he and his wife were divorced. As soon as the young lady opened her mouth, I noted her Southern drawl. D—, always quick-eyed and mentally alert and, without a doubt, a mind reader with regard to me, promptly gave me the information that she was from Louisiana. The information surprised me in no manner. D—, in the confessions he used to make, had more than once confided to me the strange and strong attraction that Southern white women possessed for him. There was certainly nothing unnatural in his experience. A situation which combines the forbidden and the unknown close at hand could not do less than create a magnified lure. White men, where the races are thrown together, have never, for themselves, taken great pains to disguise that fact. There is no sound reason to think that this mysterious pull exerts itself in only one direction across the color line, or that it confines itself to only one of the sexes; the pull is double and inter-crossed. It is possible that Dame Nature never kicks up her heels in such ecstatic abandon as when she has succeeded in bringing a fair woman and a dark man together; and vice versa. Nor are there any facts on which to base a belief that, under comparable conditions, it would be more difficult for a colored man to win the love of a white woman (I am not here considering marriage, which is governed by a number of things aside from love) than for a white man to win the love of a colored woman. This is a thought well nigh impossible for the average white man to think; at least, with any equanimity. The primitive spirit of possessive and egotistic maleness is broad enough to embrace the women of other men, but its egotistic quality brooks no encroachment on the women of the clan. This primitive maleness is not limited to the white man, it is a masculine trait that may be traced back through many ages and among many races. The Negro, the Negro in the South possesses it; the difference being his lack of power to give it authority. In this whole situation, further complicated by the primitive antagonisms of femaleness, the sensitive nerve of the race problem in the South is embedded.

I saw D—— and his fiancée occasionally after they were married, they seemed perfectly happy. I enjoyed hearing her talk. In that delicious drawl she informed me: "I never knew that colored people had any problem till D—— told me about it. I used to see lots of them where I lived; sometimes I used to go to the quarter of the town where most of them lived, and they always seemed so happy to me." The three of us were at dinner one night at the Civic Club, when she proudly told me that she was going to have a baby; that she hoped it was going to be a boy, and that he would be the first colored president of the United States. I gave her my best wishes, but added that, according to rumors that had been current, Warren Gamaliel Harding had beaten her prospective heir to that distinction. The baby was a boy; and a girl followed, both of them lovely children. I did not see D—— frequently, but our old intimacy was in some measure reestablished. He had made considerable money. He told me that it cost him twenty thousand dollars a year to live. He had put nearly all he could get together in the then recent Florida real estate boom and the burst of the bubble had hit him hard. One day in the summer of 1930, Grace, who was reading the *New York Times*, startled me with the cry that D—— was dead. I snatched the paper, and read that he had risen early, gone into the bathroom, and shot himself through the heart. At the hospital, where he died a few hours afterwards, his last words were that he was just tired of life.

Death has grieved me more deeply, but never has it more terribly shocked me.

In the elections of 1928, an effort was made to draft me as a candidate for Congress from the district in which the majority of Negroes in Harlem lived. I spent a disagreeable couple of hours at the rooms of the County Committee. Samuel Koenig, Chairman, and members of the committee made a strong attempt to impress on me that it was my duty not only to the Republican Party but to my race to accept the nomination. I had no more ambition to be a Congressman than I had to be a prize fighter; and—in other words—I told them so. They would not take "No" for an answer then and there, and urged me to consider the matter for a few days. I consented to do that, but my mind was quite made up. I did not see that I owed the Republican Party any duty that called on me for such a disruption of my plans and violation of my tastes. But I realized how important a thing it would be to have a Negro in Congress, and at the end of a few days, I wrote Mr. Koenig a letter definitely declining the nomination and urging the naming of some other colored man. A colored man was nominated but failed by a narrow margin to be elected.

My fervor as a Republican partisan had for some time been cooling off until now it was quite cold. Indeed, five years before, in speaking at the annual conference of the Association that was held in Kansas City, I had said:

As soon as the Negro is able he should go into the Democratic primaries and vote for what he believes to be the best men for the local offices. For a long time, he should not bother himself about helping to elect Republican presidents —or Democratic ones either. By eschewing national Republican politics he will undermine all arguments about his being a mere tool and monkeypaw of alien Yankee domination. By such a course, he will be building from the ground up. In common sense, the chief concern of a Negro in the South is to have a voice in electing the judges of the local courts, the county prosecuting attorney, the sheriff, the members of the school board. Unless he holds a federal job, it is sheer nonsense for a Negro in Mississippi to boast that he voted for Harding. If he can't get equitable school facilities for his children, or is in danger of being railroaded in the courts, or mobbed, or lynched, President Harding can't help him—in Mississippi. Of course, if the same Negro were in China, the President could send the entire navy to his assistance.

This statement did not meet with enthusiastic applause. To a gathering of Negroes, at that time, it sounded like heresy. Today, it is precisely what a great proportion of the race is attempting to do.

XXXVII

IN THE spring of 1929, Mr. Embree, who had become the President of the Julius Rosenwald Fund, offered me a Fund fellowship that would enable me to devote a year exclusively to writing. Nothing could have been more welcome, and I gratefully accepted the fellowship and planned to enter on it in the fall. I had just decided on this arrangement, when I received a telephone call from E. C. Carter, editor of *The Inquiry*, and secretary of the American Council of the Institute of Pacific Relations. I had had the opportunity of getting to know Mr. Carter through serving with him on a committee at the National Interracial Conference that was held in Washington the previous winter. Mr. Carter was calling to ask me if I wouldn't go as a member of the American group to the third biennial conference of the Institute. I don't think I quite caught the import of the invitation, so Mr. Carter said he would run down to my office and talk the matter over. He told me about the Institute—and I was ashamed of myself for knowing so little of so important a body—and that the coming conference would be held in Kyoto, Japan, and that my actual expenses would be allowed. I was tempted to question what motives the gods in the guise of Mr. Embree and Mr. Carter might have in bringing me two such boons simultaneously. The entrance on my fellowship was postponed (the time began when I was in the middle of the Pacific on the homeward voyage).

There was nothing exciting in the trip over. We sailed the latter part of September from Seattle. I made some cordial acquaintances aboard ship; my most constant companion being Mrs. Kuo-Wai Tsu, a Chinese lady, who was returning home after attending the tenth anniversary reunion of her class at Wellesley College. I learned that she was a relative of General Chiang Kai-Shek. She and I talked together a great deal—her English was flawless—we walked the deck together, and danced together. I began by thinking to explore as far as I could the mysteries of the oriental female mind in comparison with those of America, Europe, and South America; I ended by concluding that, essentially, they were all one. But perhaps my friend's years at Wellesley had left her not wholly oriental.

On the morning that we approached the harbor of Yokohama, the sun burst through the mists and struck the summit of Fujiyama with a shaft of light. The snow-capped cone, glittering above the dark sloping sides of the mountain, seemed suspended in air. It was an awful sight as well as one of transcending beauty. I judge there is no experience more fascinating for the American or European traveler than the first landing in Japan. Strange lands are many, but I surmise that in none, other than Japan, is found such perfection of strangeness —strangeness which at once excites the sense of wonder and satisfies the sense of beauty.

I was in a fever to get ashore but, before I could, I was surrounded by a half-dozen reporters. They were as enterprising and insistent as their New York or Chicago brothers could be. They interviewed and photographed me. They asked me many questions about the Negroes in the United States and the National Association for the Advancement of Colored People. They were surprisingly familiar with the aims and work of the organization. What would be the future of the Negroes? Would they turn Communistic? Would they eventually merge with the whites? Would I bring up the question of the Negro in the Institute? Would I write a book on Japan? I had already learned some lessons about giving out spoken interviews on important questions, and my answers were guided by them. I was glad when the reporters left, and I rushed to my stateroom to finish packing and close up my hand luggage. Just as I started at the job, Mrs. Kuo came to the door and said she had decided to make the trip up to Tokyo; would I wait for her? The night before, I had asked her if she had ever visited Tokyo and she had told me "No" and with a definite intimation that she had no desire to see the Japanese capital. And now, as I was preparing to dash ashore, she asked me to wait for her. I did wait until she was ready—fully forty minutes. No occidental woman could have done it better.

Before I finished with my luggage, three reporters came into my stateroom; three of the same who had been interviewing and photographing me. One of them asked, "Mr. Johnson, did you see Fujiyama this morning?" I answered that I had. "Mr. Johnson," he continued, "the people of Japan would be greatly honored to have from you a poem on Fujiyama." With that, he planked a pad down in front of me and offered me a pencil. I was never so taken unawares in my life. I lamely explained that with so inspiring a subject together with the

Japanese language, a fitting poem would come spontaneously, but such a thing was impossible to a poet working in the barbarous English tongue. They went away quite disappointed.

The electric train, swift, clean, efficiently run, landed us in Tokyo. I went at once to the Imperial Hotel, where I had made a reservation before leaving the United States. It was lucky that I had done so; the hotel was crowded; the engineers of the world were holding their convention in Tokyo.

The Imperial, as is of course known, is one of the great cosmopolitan hotels of the world. Everyone who stops there either achieves or has thrust upon him one of two divergent opinions as to its architecture and its plan. Americans, in particular, debate the question, because of the nationality of the architect. I know very little about the æsthetics of architecture, but I could see that the Imperial was not truly oriental or occidental. Nevertheless, I thought it a very skillful combination of Japanese beauty and American convenience. I admired greatly the low roofs, flowering courts, the tiled lobby and corridors; and I was thankful for my private bath and shower with running hot and cold water, the box spring mattress on my bed, and the easy chairs in my room.

Before I went to Japan, a lady, a friend of mine who had just returned from there, advised me that I should by no means stop at the Imperial in Tokyo, but that I should go to a strictly native hotel if I wanted to gain a sense of Japanese life. She warned me, however, that I should have to sleep on a mat and would have no comfortable furniture, and that the Japanese have no ideas about the difference of sex in the use of toilets and baths. She told me of an experience she had had in a bath. She was in the very midst of her ablutions, when a Japanese gentleman who had used the bath just before her re-entered, and without the slightest sign of embarrassment said to her, "Excuse me, Madam, but I think I left my spectacles in here." He had left them, and he got them and went out.

The next morning when I passed through the lobby on my way to breakfast, I stopped at the news-stand and bought a copy of a newspaper published in English. I also bought copies of all the papers printed in Japanese, when the diminutive boy at the counter showed me that my picture was in each one of them. Articles accompanied these pictures, but I never made any attempt to find out what I was quoted as saying. I had long suffered a dread of reading anything in

American newspapers that quoted me on any important question. As I was leaving the stand, the diminutive boy took a postcard out of his pocket and said to me, "Sign? Sign?" I divined that he wanted me to autograph the card for him. When I got my glasses adjusted and looked at it I saw that it was a picture card of Fujiyama. At the side of the mountain was my face which the boy had neatly cut out of one of the newspapers and pasted on the card. I felt highly complimented, and signed it.

I remained in Tokyo three days, then left for Kyoto, where the Conference was to be held. The arrangements for members of the Conference were all that thoughtfulness and courtesy could demand. We found ourselves quasi-guests of the Japanese government. We had been accorded the courtesy of the Port of Yokohama; and been furnished with passes on all railroad and street car lines in Japan, and with franks for telegraph services.

The trip to Kyoto takes about ten hours. On the train which I took I was glad to find Mr. and Mrs. E. C. Carter. Doctor Ignazo Nitobe, the distinguished Japanese statesman and chairman of the Japanese group in the Conference, was also on the same train. Each hour I spent in Japan increased my wonder for Japanese efficiency. There was something absolutely uncanny about all enterprises, all plans, all arrangements moving along without a discernible hitch. There was the railroad, smooth, rapid; the cars in such fine, simple taste; the dining car service excellent and cheap. Soon after leaving Tokyo we partly circled Fujiyama, and had a revolving and swiftly changing view of the mighty mountain. As we skimmed along, I sat on the observation platform, watching the landscape as it unrolled from the train. Nothing met the eye that was sprawling, nothing squalid, nothing ugly. Every patch of land where foothold was possible was cultivated. More and more that perfection of strangeness that is Japan took hold on me.

Kyoto pleased me more than Tokyo. It is a very ancient city and was the capital of Japan for a thousand years before Tokyo became the seat of government. Why the word "Tokyo" is a rearrangement of the letters in the word "Kyoto" some Japanese told me, but, foolishly, I neglected to make either a written or a mental note of it. Kyoto is a city of nearly a million, but it is much more serene than Tokyo, more purely Japanese. It is still the home of the Japanese ancient art handicrafts. During the week I had before the Conference convened I spent some time in the handicraft district watching the curious processes in the making of cloisonné and lacquer and the delicate inlays of gold, silver, and copper. I became interested in Japanese prints, and wanted to purchase some, but thought I had better get some idea about them before I made any purchases. I went into a bookshop and asked for the best book on prints; they sold me a volume by Arthur Davison Ficke, the American poet. I had been with Mr. Ficke in his home a few weeks before I left for Japan, and it vexed me a little to have to pay a double price for the book of a fellow author, which, by the rules of the game, I might have "boned."

The headquarters of the Conference were at the Myako Hotel, and an old and picturesque building located in the outskirts and on a hill that overlooked the whole city. Many wings and additions that had been put on from time to time gave a quaint, rambling effect to the exterior, and made of the interior a labyrinthian puzzle. Attempts at modernizing it had been carried out, but not always successfully. As I remember, to reach certain floors by the elevators, you rode to the floor above and walked down. With many of the other members of the Conference, I stopped at the Kyoto Hotel down in the city. The Kyoto is a ten- or twelve-story brick building, and as modern and up-to-date as any hotel of its size in San Francisco or New York. I felt that the Kyoto carried its ideal of Western efficiency farther than was necessary or even good business. For instance, the waiters were men, dressed in somber tuxedo jackets; while at the Myako, the meals were served by dainty, doll-like Japanese maids in gayly colored kimonos. It appeared that I was doomed to be limited in my observations and study of "native" life.

On the night before the opening of the Conference, the members of the American group, with the Philippine group included, and their relatives and friends, about a hundred in all, dined in a body at the Myako Hotel. I sat at the left of a charming young matron; I knew that she was married because I glanced quickly at her place card and read, "Mrs. Frederick Vanderbilt Field." As we were unfolding our napkins, she turned to me with a smile and asked, "Mr. Johnson, don't you commute in the summers from Hillsdale, New York, down to the city?" I answered, "Why, yes, on Sunday nights I often go to Hillsdale to catch the New York Central, but sometimes I take the New York, New Haven and Hartford out of Great Barrington." Mr. and Mrs. Field lived at Lenox in the summer, and we had more than once ridden down to New York in the same car; but it was in Japan that we came to know each other.

I was tremendously interested in the Conference and learned things about the Far Eastern question that had hitherto rested in that zone of hazy ideas which surrounds everyone's definite knowledge. I contributed as much as I was able to contribute to the round-table discussions. Out of it all, the truth that came home most directly to me was the universality of the race and color problem. Negroes in the United States are prone, and naturally, to believe that their problem is *the* problem. The fact is, there is a race and color problem wherever the white man deals with darker races. The thing unique about the Negro problem in the United States, a uniqueness that has its advantages and disadvantages, is that elsewhere the problem results from the presence of the white man in the midst of a darker civilization, and in the United States, from the presence of the Negro in the midst of a white civilization.

I was curious about the techniques of the Conference. I closely studied the technique of the Japanese and Chinese groups. The discussion of those questions that related specifically to the differences of interests between Japan and China was, generally, a battle of Chinese intellectual agility against Japanese power and might, with the occidental groups acting as interpreters, arbitrators, and pacifiers. The discussion of those questions relating to differences of interest between the oriental and occidental groups was based upon differences in cultures, in philosophies, in religions; at no point were racial differences allowed to come near the surface. It was also the technique of the Japanese and Chinese in the occidental-oriental questions, not only not to mention racial differences but, for the purposes of discussion, to ignore completely their existence. I knew, and I am sure every member of the Japanese and Chinese groups, as well as of the American, British, Canadian, Australian, and New Zealand groups, knew that back of all the economic arguments for the Oriental Exclusion Act passed by the United States were reasons based on differences of race and color. I, of course, realized that this question of race and color was loaded, and, if brought out, might explode and wreck the Conference. Yet, I never became fully satisfied that this ostrich-like behavior, this studied ignoring of a factor so basic to every question being considered, was the wisest policy. It seemed to me to give a slight tinge of insincerity to the atmosphere of a Conference which was earnestly striving to bring about a better understanding and a more cordial relationship between the East and the West.

In questions of differing interests between the Japanese and Chinese groups there was a frankness that was missing when the questions were of differing interests between the occidental and oriental groups. Once, on the part of the Japanese, the frankness was brutal, but, in my opinion, revealed the truth of the situation. Yosuke Matsuoka, of the Japanese group, and former vice-president of the South Manchurian Railway, enraged, like a bull at the hands of the picador, by the lances of international law thrust into him by one of the doctors of philosophy of the Chinese group, burst out, "If Japan in the war with Russia had known of the secret treaty signed by Li Hung Chang and Libanov, there would today be no Manchurian problem; Japan would have taken South Manchuria and held it against Russia. She made her mistake in not taking it when nobody could have stopped her." The words were equivalent to a prediction of what happened this year, 1933, when nobody *could* stop her.

I had difficulty, often embarrassing, but which I shared with a good many others, of not being able always to distinguish Japanese from Chinese by their physical traits. I let that pass, but I constantly strove to get at their distinguishing mental traits. I had boundless admiration for the energy, the enterprise, the genius for organization and execution, and that uncanny efficiency of the Japanese. But all that weighed hardly as much in my balances as the keen intelligence, the poise, the broad and deep philosophy of life of the Chinese. China is, I believe, the only great people that has managed to get along without anthropomorphic Gods as the essence and apex of a national religion. A philosophy of human conduct, more than anything else, seems to fill that place. This is reflected in Chinese character. Intelligent Japanese and Chinese are both stung to the quick by our Exclusion Act, and both resent it, but it appeared to me that, while the Japanese smart under it, the Chinese are able to rise above it. One reason for this, I thought, was the fact that the Chinese are more self-contained and not so solicitous of the approbation of the white world as are the Japanese. I myself reacted differently to these two peoples; the Japanese left me rather cold. Not during the time I was at the Conference did I form cordial relations with any Japanese. Among the Chinese at the Conference, I formed some warm friendships. A difference between the Japanese and Chinese women who were members of the

Conference seemed, to me, notable. The Japanese women, for the most part, sat demure, with little or nothing to say; a number of the Chinese women joined freely in the discussions and even mounted the rostrum at the assemblies and pronounced addresses. This, though, may be partly accounted for by the fact that nearly every one of the Chinese women had an adequate mastery of the English language, an implement that the Japanese women, generally, lacked.

I, however, did enter into friendly relations with a Japanese who had been a student at the Union Theological Seminary; we discovered that we had a mutual friend in Dr. Harry Ward. He invited me to dinner and I went; knowing that for once, anyhow, I should get a glimpse of real Japanese life. The night was rainy and chilly, and I had momentary regrets, when just after we entered his gate, I found that I had to take off my shoes and walk in sandals over a wet stone pavement to the house. At the entrance to the house we were met by his wife and daughter, a girl of about fourteen. They met us on their knees and, bowing low a number of times until their foreheads touched the earth, they kept uttering what I supposed were words of welcome to the lord of the house and his honorable guest. I felt the awkwardness of my position. My Western ideas made me revolt at the sight of these women abasing themselves before me in such a manner. The house was neat, almost bare of furniture, and practically one room; but, by those ingenious translucent partitions, it could be divided into a number of apartments. This gentleman was Western enough to have a dining room table. On it, he himself cooked the national dish, Sukiaki, in a sort of chafing dish of stone. The wife served but did not eat with us. The meal was delicious; and since then I have eaten Sukiaki often in the Japanese restaurants in New York.

At about the middle of the Conference, I received a letter, which is given below. I have never been able to feel sure whether this letter, although it bore every mark of authenticity, was the heart cry of a Japanese schoolboy or whether Wallace Irwin was in Japan and composed it:

Oct. 23.

Mr. Johnson,
Nara City, Nara Hotel.
Venerable Mr. Johnson:
    Please excuse my discourtesy that I have sent this letter to you.
    I am a Japanese boy—fifteen years old. I am a boy who express agreement

against your opinion—for the black race agitation. I have been deeply sym-
pathetise with them in their situation, on hearing. I am glad you came Japan
to attend the meeting. Because, venerable Mr., I hope put myself in your agitation. I think, to do so, is that I will extremely satisfied, reason why, I am a
Japanese. I pray that you make me associate with you, and you lead me to
your agitation. If you admit my entreaty, I will do my best for your agitation.

Mr. May you admit this my entreaty.

Sir, Please admit my entreaty.

Please excuse written very poor English.

Very truly yours,

Masao Kajima,

Shimonoseki City, Nagaskicho, Sasayama.

The Institute had made a point of drawing in a number of young
men, some of whom interested me more than did many of the older
members of the Conference. One of these was Malcolm MacDonald,
son of Ramsay MacDonald. He constantly took part in discussions
of the most involved questions of world politics and economics. He
looked like a boy—he was only twenty-eight—and that made the
grasp he had of world affairs and the masterful manner in which he
was able to evidence it seem the more amazing. Another, and considerably younger, was the Hon. W. W. Astor. We lunched together
and he remarked to me, "I am half American, you know." I knew
that he was a little more than half, but I said to him that the fact
that his mother was one of the Langhorne sisters of Virginia was
generally known to Americans; this seemed to please him a great deal.
He then recounted to me how his mother had helped in forwarding
the fortunes of Roland Hayes in London. But for the most part, he
talked about books, and talked very brilliantly. I began to speculate
upon whether there was something special in English education or
social life that made for early mental maturity.

One day a tall, slender, typically American young man approached
me. He started to introduce himself but I interrupted him, saying,
"How do you do, Mr. Rockefeller?" He invited me to have lunch;
and we were joined by James G. McDonald, of the Foreign Policy
Association. We chatted pleasantly about the Conference and of one
thing and another. A day or two later, I was talking with Édouard
Lavergne, the French observer at the Conference, and he said to me
that Mr. McDonald had asked him how was my French, and that he
had assured him that it was very good. I thanked M. Lavergne for
vouching for me, but we were both puzzled to understand why Mr.

McDonald was interested in knowing whether I spoke French well or ill. The puzzle was solved when Mr. McDonald and Mr. Rockefeller (the third) told me of their plan to have a French table on the voyage back. There would be four at the table, themselves, Adolphe Pervy, a young Frenchman, and me. We should speak only French at table, and there would be a fine of ten cents for each lapse into English. I said how pleased I would be to join the table, but expressed a doubt that, after making some purchases I had my eyes on, I should have enough dimes left to pay for my lapses.

The table was a success. We spoke French at meals for the fifteen days of the voyage, and no one paid a fine. Of course, the rule wasn't actually a hard one, because if you didn't know how to say it, you could remain silent. However, we did talk constantly and on a great many subjects. Several times we discussed the American race question. Mr. Rockefeller interested me much as a person. At first, it seemed not quite congruous that this modest, unassuming, almost shy young man represented such tremendous power. But under his quiet manner, earnestness and a sense of responsibility were steadily revealed.

On every ship there always happens to be one, at least, of those genial busybodies who are never completely happy unless they are carrying out some plan to make everybody else on board happy. There was a man on our ship who, when we were a couple of days out from Honolulu, circulated a petition in the dining salon that requested the captain to wireless the office in Honolulu for permission to put the ship under extra steam so that the passengers might have an additional period of daylight in the Hawaiian capital. He brought the petition to our table and handed it to Mr. Rockefeller, who read it and passed it along. The others of us glanced through it and, without any particular thought, signed our names. The petition man came back in a few minutes with this message, "The captain says that if Mr. Rockefeller will head the petition, he will wireless the Honolulu office." The answer he got was, "Tell the captain I'll speak to him about it." Mr. Rockefeller, following some statements I had made in our table discussions, had evinced more than casual interest in the race question. He confessed that he knew next to nothing about it, and that it was something he wanted to know a great deal about. So a number of times, he and I remained at table after everyone else had left the salon, talking, in English of course, about various phases of the American race problem. The night that the petition was circulated was one of the times that we remained. Before we went on deck, I, out of more than curiosity, asked him if he was going to sign the petition to speed up the ship. "No," he said, "I won't sign it; 'John D. Rockefeller' is more than merely my name."

At the close of the Conference, I realized that I had had a glimpse at only one level of Japanese life, the upper level; and I regretted it. I had stolen a little time off and walked some of the meaner streets of Tokyo and Kyoto, but that had afforded me only a very superficial glance at life on that plane. No opportunity was available to observe Japanese life as a whole; the time which was not taken up by the affairs of the Institute was almost wholly consumed by official entertainments in the grand style. Many luncheons, teas, and dances were given. I do not think I was wrong in feeling that the number and the lavishness of these entertainments went beyond the promptings of mere hospitality, even of that of the Japanese. We were entertained by the Mayor and Chamber of Commerce of Kyoto, and by the Governor of the Osaka Prefecture together with the Mayor and Chamber of Commerce of the city. After the luncheon in Osaka, we witnessed a puppet show. The Japanese puppets are not miniature figures worked on strings; they are large-sized dolls and are carried through the play in the hands of human actors, who, however, do this so skillfully that they lose themselves to the spectators and seem to impart their human qualities to the dolls. The play was a tragedy that held the audience with mounting emotional interest to the end. In Kyoto, Baron and Baroness Fujimura gave a garden party, with geisha dances by three of Japan's most famous cinema stars. I thought that the beauty of the girls and their costumes exceeded that of their style of dancing. In Tokyo, Baron and Baroness Shidehara gave a garden party. Baron and Baroness Mitsui threw open their residence for a garden party and the performance of a "No" play. This example of Japanese ancient classic drama was to me impressive but rather tedious; not at all so absorbing and moving as the puppet show. I could not pretend, even to others, that I derived as much from the drama, interpreted mainly through spoken words that were incomprehensible, as from the puppet show, interpreted through the universal medium of pantomime. On our last night in Japan a ball was given for us at one of the Tokyo clubs; and on the day we sailed we were tendered a luncheon by Viscount Eiichi Shibusawa, the "Grand Old Man" of Japan, who, despite his ninety years, made a speech, and in English.

The culminating social event was a garden party given by the Emperor. The invitations, bearing the Imperial golden, sixteen-petaled chrysanthemum, caused a flutter of excitement. An official informed a group of us that in all the history of Japan less than two hundred foreigners had before this been included among those invited to such a fête. The etiquette of the occasion caused some anxiety and considerable inconvenience: No lady dressed in mourning or wearing a veil would be admitted. Gentlemen were expected to wear frock or cutaway coats and silk hats. The question of silk hats grew serious and developed into something of a panicky scramble; they were borrowed, rented, and reluctantly purchased. On the day of the garden party, the heads of the foreign male guests presented a historical pageant of the top-hat making industry.

I was among the number of those who had not included a silk hat in their wardrobe. I had left one at home that I had not had on my head in more than fifteen years, and I did not want to spend money for another piece of useless headgear. I spoke to one of the clerks at the Imperial about getting me a hat. He assured me that he would do so. On the morning of the party, he told me that the hat was there. I tried it on; it was a brand-new, latest style hat of Japanese make and fitted me becomingly. I asked how much the rental would be. "Five yen." I objected that it was exorbitant; in truth, I fancied the hat, and after some bargaining purchased it for ten yen. And now I own two useless silk hats. The number of guests at the Emperor's garden party was as many as two thousand, I judged. The gardens were as extensive as they were beautiful: after we entered the gates, we walked, it seemed, a mile or more before we reached the place where we were to stand as the Emperor passed by. The crowd lined both sides of the gravel walk. The group I was with stood directly opposite the members of the Japanese Cabinet and the foreign diplomats. We chatted and laughed as we waited, and the wait was long. There were several false signals. Finally, there was the blast of a trumpet. The Japanese guests set the example and became silent. There was no craning of necks, though the Emperor was approaching. I had, I don't know why, expected to hear loud banzais. Instead, there was a hush. As the Emperor and his retinue passed, not a sound could be heard but the crunching of the gravel under their feet. I noted that the Japanese did not look at him, but stood with their eyes cast down. The foreigners did not follow that example. What I saw was a young man, under medium size, dressed in a khaki military uniform, walking by with easy grace; and yet, he was an imperious figure. His retinue consisted of a dozen or so persons; all of the ladies were dressed in native costumes, except the Princess Chichibu, who wore Western dress, and of whom a sight was worth a trip to Japan.

In Honolulu I found that I was scheduled to speak at a luncheon at the superlatively elegant hotel on Waikiki. The luncheon was tendered to the American members of the Institute by the Hawaiian group. I spoke for twenty-odd minutes. I began, according to the thing expected, by paying tribute to the beauty of Honolulu and to its importance as the birthplace of the Institute. Then I spoke of the significance of the Institute and the Kyoto Conference. So far, so good. What I was saying met with unstinted appreciation. Then I brought in the race factor as a vital force that would have to be considered in the plans and purpose of the Institute. The air began to chill, but I had started down a path on which I could not halt and off which I could not turn. I saw what was ahead but I had no choice; I had to keep going. I went steadily on and finished to mild applause. Racial differences were also "ignored" in Hawaii; at least, at that time, and in making such a public speech, I had violated a Hawaiian taboo. Three people—I like to name them, Mrs. E. C. Carter, Miss Elizabeth Green, who lived in Honolulu, and M. Pervy, the young Frenchman—told me that I had made a "great speech and spoken the truth." But such a reception for a speech was a new experience for me, and for a couple of days I felt depressed about it. But I came out of the depression confident that I had never made a less popular or a better speech in my life.

On the day of our arrival in San Francisco Mr. Rockefeller and I were among the speakers (his maiden speech) at a luncheon of the Chamber of Commerce. I sat next to and talked with one of the most interesting men I have ever met, Captain Dollar, founder of the Dollar Steamship Line. On my way to New York I stopped over in Chicago to fill several lecture engagements that had been booked before I went to Japan.

XXXVIII

BACK in New York, I immediately got down to work. I remained in the city during the winter, and in the spring went to Five Acres, where I continued my writing. During the year I wrote and published *Black Manhattan*[1] and *Saint Peter Relates an Incident of the Resurrection Day*.[2] In *Black Manhattan* I attempted to set down the story of the Negro in New York. As a background for present-day Harlem, I began with the "Harlem" of 1626, the year of the establishment of the settlement of New Amsterdam, when the Negro population was eleven, or a little above five per cent of the total non-Indian population. For the sake of the story, I kept down to a small degree the discussion of sociological and economic factors, and eschewed all statistical data. One of my prime purposes in writing the story was to set down a continuous record of the Negro's progress on the New York theatrical stage, from the attempted classical performances of the African Company, at the corner of Bleecker and Mercer Streets in 1821, down to *The Green Pastures* in 1930. I considered that this record alone, done for the first time, was sufficient warrant for the book. In *Saint Peter Relates an Incident of the Resurrection Day*, I attempted an ironic poem about the unknown soldier. The poem was written "While meditating upon Heaven and Hell and Democracy and War and America and the Negro Gold Star Mothers." The book was printed for private distribution only.

Mr. Embree came to New York frequently, and I was in Chicago several times to fill lecture engagements. Once when I was there I found him in the throes of literary composition. He discussed with me the theme of his work: that Negroes in America were evolving into a new race; Brown America, he termed it. On this theme he wrote a truly remarkable book.[3] Before one of his trips to New York he wrote and asked me if it would be possible to arrange for a meeting with some of the principals of the cast of *The Green Pastures*; he was an enthusiastic admirer of the play. The arrangement was made and Mr. Embree gave a dinner at his hotel, with Richard B. Harrison, "The Lawd," as the chief guest. It was one of the happiest parties I

[1] Alfred A. Knopf, New York, 1930.
[2] The Viking Press, New York, 1930.
[3] *Brown America*. New York, The Viking Press, 1931.

ever attended. Mr. Embree had that afternoon been at the meeting of the Spingarn Medal Award Committee, of which he is a member, and he had the pleasure of announcing that Mr. Harrison had been awarded the medal. During the dinner an effort was made to draw from Mr. Harrison what had been the psychological effects upon him of playing the character of the Omnipotent for so long a time. At the direct question, he paused for a moment; we listened, watching him; his fine, beautiful countenance glowed and he said, "If it has had any effect, it has been to deepen my sense of humility." He need not have framed his answer in words; for a man cannot be this or that and hide it; God stamps it in his face.

I saw Mr. Rosenwald again at the funeral of Louis Marshall. I had been asked to serve as an honorary pallbearer—Mr. Marshall had been one of the most valuable and active members of the Legal Committee of the Association. While the honorary pallbearers were waiting in the chapel, I chatted with Mr. Rosenwald and with Judge Benjamin N. Cardozo, the only ones I knew personally. Mr. Rosenwald took the trouble to introduce me to several. He gave me a flattering introduction to Alfred E. Smith. Mr. Smith regarded me for a moment with what appeared like cool curiosity; at least, there was no evidence of any kind of interest. Perhaps he found it difficult to reconcile Mr. Rosenwald's introduction with the incarnate exhibit confronting him.

Toward the end of my fellowship year, Dr. Thomas Elsa Jones, President of Fisk University, came to see me. He talked about the University—and no one can hear President Jones talk about Fisk without feeling the galvanic force of his tremendous energy and enthusiasm—and said that he wanted me on the faculty. The place he wanted me to fill was, in a general way, like that of Robert Frost at Amherst. I was to be guide and mentor of students who had the ambition and gave some evidence of talent to be writers. I was to have entire freedom to organize and carry on this work as I felt was best. The idea and plan were fascinating. The trustees of the University created the Adam K. Spence Chair of Creative Literature, and I was elected as the first occupant.

At the end of the year, I resigned as secretary of the Association, after fourteen years of service with the organization. I was elected to membership on the Board of Directors and made a vice-president. The Rosenwald Fund extended the period of my fellowship through to the time when I should begin my duties at Fisk University. In that period I revised *The Book of American Negro Poetry*, enlarging it to include the younger group of poets, and making the biographical notes critical as well. I also made a beginning on this present volume.

In the spring of 1931, a committee of my friends, headed by staff members of the Association, gave me a farewell dinner at the Hotel Pennsylvania. Three hundred persons attended the dinner, and I experienced the ordeal of hearing one's friends say extremely nice and generous things about one before a large company. In this respect, I was fortunate in the speakers; they were: Walter White, W. E. B. Du Bois, J. E. Spingarn, Miss Mary White Ovington, Robert W. Bagnall, Heywood Broun, M. Dantes Bellegarde, the Haitian Minister to the United States, Mrs. Mary McLeod Bethune, and Carl Van Doren. Arthur B. Spingarn was toastmaster; a letter of tribute from the Hon. Wilbur J. Carr, First Assistant Secretary of State, was read, and Countee Cullen contributed an original poem. Before the speaking began, my brother sat at the piano and played over and sang a number of our old Broadway songs. Many of the guests were old enough to join heartily in the choruses of *The Congo Love Song*, *The Maiden with the Dreamy Eyes*, *Under the Bamboo Tree*, and one or two others. Among those who sang most gleefully was Edward B. Marks, our first publisher, who was seated at the speakers' table. This reminiscent part of the program proved so popular that for a while I wondered if the dinner was being given in my honor or Rosamond's.

In the winter I began my work at Fisk University. It was a grateful relief from the stress and strain that had entered into so considerable a part of my life; and I wondered how I had been able, in such degree as I had, to make of myself a man of action, when I was always dreaming of the contemplative life. Not all of the stress and strain that I experienced while executive head of the Association resulted from efforts to deal with the outside forces antagonistic to the Negro race; much of it came from endeavors to rouse Negroes themselves from apathy, to win over hostile factions and bring about joint action within the race. It would be wrong to think that the Negroes marched as one united and zealous band under the banner of the Association; there were envies, bickerings, rancors, and pure maliciousness to contend with, as well as honest opposition. Negroes among themselves sometimes declare that we are the most disjoined and discordant group in the world, but I judge that we are, after all, merely human. If we could achieve the superhuman state of complete unity on an intelligent plan, not all the forces arrayed against us would be able to block our march forward.

There are moments when I miss the thrill of action. At times when there is a pitched battle between justice and wrong, I have a longing to be back in the thick of the fight. But there are thrills also in the contemplative life; and in it there are also fields on which causes may be won. I am almost amused at the eagerness with which I go to meet my classes. The pleasure of talking to them about the things that I have learned and the things that I have thought out for myself is supreme. And there is no less pleasure in drawing from them the things that they have learned and the things that they have thought out for themselves. I realize that, though I am nominally the teacher, there are many new things that I shall be taught. In touch with the youth of my race in a great university in the midst of the South; I shall be zealous to learn what they are thinking, how the world looks to them, and what goals they are pressing toward. I feel that on this favorable ground I shall be able to help effectively in developing additional racial strength and fitness and in shaping fresh forces against bigotry and racial wrong.

I find that looking backward over three-score years does not lessen my enthusiasm in looking forward. What I have done appears as very little when I consider all that the will to do set me as a task, and what I have written quite dwarfed alongside my aspirations; but life has been a stirring enterprise with me, and still is; for the willingness is not yet over and the dreams are not yet dead.

I am sometimes questioned concerning my glance forward. I am questioned by people who want to know my views about the future of the Negro in the United States:—Will the race continue to advance? Is the national attitude toward the Negro changing; and if so, is it for the better? Will the Negro turn to Communism? My answer always is that the race will continue to advance. In giving that answer, I assume no prophetic attributes; I base it on the fact that the race has given a three-hundred-year demonstration of its ability to survive and advance under conditions and in the face of obstacles that will not, by any discernible probabilities, ever again be so hard. That, I think, gives a definite earnest for the future. His "past performances" give the Negro increasing self-confidence to undertake what is before him. And, today, his self-confidence may be increased by only looking around him and noting what a mess the white race has made of civilization. By looking around, he can only conclude that, while no other race would probably have done any better, no other race could hardly have done any worse. He can at any time negatively increase his own racial self-esteem by taking an objective observation of the brutality, meanness, lawlessness, graft, crowd hysteria and stupidity of which the white race is capable.

Despite the many contrary appearances and all the numerous actual inequalities and wrongs that persist, I feel certain that in the continuous flux of the factors in the race problem the national attitude toward the Negro is steadily changing for the better. When it is borne in mind that the race problem in America is not the problem of twelve million moribund people intent upon sinking into a slough of ignorance, poverty, and decay in the midst of our civilization, in spite of all efforts to save them—*that would indeed be a problem*—but is, instead, the question of opening new doors of opportunity at which these millions are constantly knocking, the crux shifts to a more favorable position, and gives a view that makes it possible to observe that faster and faster the problem is becoming a question of mental attitudes toward the Negro rather than of his actual condition. The new doors of opportunity have been slowly but gradually opening and I believe that changing mental attitudes will cause them to be opened more and more rapidly. I see some signs of these changes in the South; and I think it among the probabilities that a gradual revolution will be worked out there by enlightened white youth, moved consciously by a sense of fair play and decency, and unconsciously by a compulsion to atone for the deeds of their fathers.

I believe that economic factors will work toward the abolishment of many of the inequalities and discriminations in the South. That section, the poorest of the country, must yield to pressure against the policy of maintaining a dual educational system, a dual railroad system, dual public park systems, and draining duplications in many another economic and civic enterprise. The absurdity of a man going into business and at the start barring the patronage of one-third to one-half of the community must eventually counterbalance all the prejudices that bolster up such an unsound practice. This process will be hastened by the growth of the economic strength of Negroes themselves. I here stress the South not under any misapprehension that it is the only section of prejudice and discrimination against Negroes, but because it is *in the South* that the race problem must be solved; because it will not be completely solved in any other section of the country until it is solved there; because essentially the status of the Negro in all other sections will depend upon what it is in the South.

Will the Negro turn to Communism? I do not think so. A restless fringe in the larger cities may go over, but the race shows practically no inclination to do so, either among the intellectuals or the masses. No group is more in need or more desirous of a social change than the Negro, but in his attitude toward Communism he is displaying common sense. There are no indications that the United States will ever adopt Communism, and it is more than probable that in this country it will, in its present form, continue to be an outlawed political and economic creed; then, for the Negro to take on the antagonisms that center against it, in addition to those he already carries, would from any point of view, except that of fanaticism, be sheer idiocy. I feel that the Negro should not hesitate at revolution that would bring in an era which fully included him in the general good, but, despite the enticing gestures being made, I see absolutely no guarantees that Communism, even if it could win, would usher in such an era. Indeed, I do not see that political and economic revolutions ever change the hearts of men; they simply change the bounds within which the same human traits and passions operate. If any such change should tomorrow take place in the United States, the Negro would not find himself miraculously lifted up, but still at the lower end of the social scale, and still called upon to work and fight persistently to rise in that scale. The only kind of revolution that would have an immediately significant effect on the American Negro's status would be a moral revolution—an upward push given to the level of ethical ideas and practices. And that, probably, is the sole revolution that the whole world stands in need of.

Often I am asked if I think the Negro will remain a racial entity or merge; and if I am in favor of amalgamation. I answer that, if I could have my wish, the Negro would retain his racial identity, with unhampered freedom to develop his own qualities—the best of those qualities American civilization is much in need of as a complement to its other qualities—and finally stand upon a plane with other Ameri-can citizens. To convince America and the world that he was capa-ble of doing this would be the greatest triumph he could wish and work for. But what I may wish and what others may not wish can have no effect on the elemental forces at work; and it appears to me that the result of those forces will, in time, be the blending of the Negro into the American race of the future. It seems probable that, instead of developing them independently to the utmost, the Negro will fuse his qualities with those of the other groups in the making of the ultimate American people; and that he will add a tint to America's complexion and put a perceptible permanent wave in Amer-ica's hair. It may be that nature plans to work out on the North Amer-ican continent a geographical color scheme similar to that of Europe, with the Gulf of Mexico as our Mediterranean. My hope is that in the process the Negro will be not merely sucked up but, through his own advancement and development, will go in on a basis of equal partnership.

If I am wrong in these opinions and conclusions, if the Negro is always to be given a heavy handicap back of the common scratch, or if the antagonistic forces are destined to dominate and bar all forward movement, there will be only one way of salvation for the race that I can see, and that will be through the making of its isolation into a religion and the cultivation of a hard, keen, relentless hatred for everything white. Such a hatred would burn up all that is best in the Negro, but it would also offer the sole means that could enable him to maintain a saving degree of self-respect in the midst of his abasement.

But the damage of such a course would not be limited to the Negro. If the Negro is made to fail, America fails with him. If America wishes to make democratic institutions secure, she must deal with this question right and righteously. For it is in the nature of a truism to say that this country can actually have no more democracy than it accords and guarantees to the humblest and weakest citizen.

It is both a necessity and to the advantage of America that she deal with this question right and righteously; for the well-being of the nation as well as that of the Negro depends upon taking that course. And she must bear in mind that it is a question which can be neither avoided nor postponed; it is not distant in position or time; it is im-mediately at hand and imminent; it must be squarely met and answered.

And it cannot be so met and answered by the mere mouthings of the worn platitudes of humanitarianism, of formal religion, or of abstract democracy. For the Negroes directly concerned are not in far-off Africa; they are in and within our midst.

*   *   *

My glance forward reaches no farther than this world. I admit that through my adult life I have lacked religiosity. But I make no boast of it; understanding, as I do, how essential religion is to many, many people. For that reason, I have little patience with the zealot who is forever trying to prove to others that they do not need religion; that they would be better off without it. Such a one is no less a zealot than the religionist who contends that all who "do not believe" will be consigned to eternal hell fires. It is simply that I have not felt the need of religion in the commonplace sense of the term. I have derived spiritual values in life from other sources than worship and prayer. I think that the teachings of Jesus Christ embody the loftiest ethical and spiritual concepts the human mind has yet borne. I do not know if there is a personal God; I do not see how I can know; and I do not see how my knowing can matter. What does matter, I believe, is how I deal with myself and how I deal with my fellows. I feel that I can practice a conduct toward myself and toward my fellows that will constitute the basis for an adequate religion, a religion that may comprehend spirituality and beauty and serene happiness.

As far as I am able to peer into the inscrutable, I do not see that there is any evidence to refute those scientists and philosophers who hold that the universe is purposeless; that man, instead of being the special care of a Divine Providence, is a dependent upon fortuity and his own wits for survival in the midst of blind and insensate forces. But to stop there is to stop short of the vital truth. For mankind and for the individual this state, what though it be accidental and ephemeral, is charged with meaning. Man's sufferings, his joys, his aspirations, his defeats, are just as real and of as great moment to him as they would be if they were part of a mighty and definite cosmic plan.

The human mind racks itself over the never-to-be-known answer to the great riddle, and all that is clearly revealed is the fate that man must continue to hope and struggle on; that each day, if he would not be lost, he must with renewed courage take a fresh hold on life and face with fortitude the turns of circumstance. To do this, he needs to be able at times to touch God; let the idea of God mean to him whatever it may.

THE END

INDEX